Open Innovation through Strategic Alliances

Open Innovation through Strategic Alliances

Approaches for Product, Technology, and Business Model Creation

Edited by
Refik Culpan

First published in 2014 by PALGRAVE MACMILLAN® in the United States—a division of St.Martin's Press LLC, 175 Fifth Avenue, New York, NY 10010.

Where this book is distributed in the UK, Europe and the rest of the world, this is by Palgrave Macmillan, a division of Macmillan Publishers Limited, registered in England, company number 785998, of Houndmills, Basingstoke, Hampshire RG21 6XS.

Palgrave Macmillan is the global academic imprint of the above companies and has companies and representatives throughout the world.

Palgrave® and Macmillan® are registered trademarks in the United States, the United Kingdom, Europe and other countries.

ISBN: 978-1-137-39855-0

Library of Congress Cataloging-in-Publication Data

Open innovation through strategic alliances : approaches for product, technology, and business model creation / edited by Refik Culpan.
    pages cm
    Includes bibliographical references and index.
    ISBN 978-1-137-39855-0 (hardback)
    1. Strategic alliances (Business) 2. Business networks. 3. International business enterprises—Technological innovations. I. Culpan, Refik, editor of compilation.
    HD69.S8O64 2014
    658'.044—dc23

2014011637

A catalogue record of the book is available from the British Library.

Design by Amnet.

First edition: September 2014

10 9 8 7 6 5 4 3 2 1

To my life partner and colleague, Oya, and my children,
Burcu Culpan Scherr and Alpay Culpan.

Contents

Notes on Contributors

Alexander Alexiev is Assistant Professor in Strategic Management and Innovation at VU University Amsterdam. He specializes in service management, exploratory innovation, and top management teams. He obtained his PhD in strategic management from the Rotterdam School of Management, Erasmus University. He has published in the *Journal of Management Studies* (2010) and the edited volume *The Nature of the New Firm* (Edward Elgar, 2011).

Marc Bahlmann is Assistant Professor at the VU University Amsterdam, Faculty of Economics and Business Administration. Dr. Bahlmann received his PhD from the Faculty of Social Sciences (VU University), studying knowledge dynamics among IT-entrepreneurs located in the Amsterdam-based IT and new media cluster. His current research interests include alliance portfolios, open innovation, and regional innovation.

Steve H. Barr is a professor at the Poole College of Management, North Carolina State University. He received his Ph.D. from the University of Iowa. He is a primary faculty member in the creation of graduate student–led new business startups utilizing technologies from the 16 campuses of the University of NC system and the U.S. Navy. This program has provided graduate education to over 420 students, created new high tech business ventures employing over 350 people, and assisted these new business startups in raising over $240 million in capital.

His primary research interests are in the areas of technology commercialization, individual and group decision making, and new business startup. He has published numerous articles in journals such as *Academy of Management Journal, Journal of Applied Psychology, Management Science, Journal of Management, Decision Sciences,* and *Journal of Engineering and Technology Management.* He has served on multiple editorial boards and in leadership roles in Southern Management Association.

John Bell is Head of Strategy and Business Development at Philips Research. As such, he contributes to the strategic direction of research, the research portfolio, and the role of strategic partners (via public funding and open innovation). In addition, he is involved in accelerating end-to-end innovative R&D in Philips. Prior to that, he was VP of corporate strategy and alliances at Royal Philips. In this role, he was responsible for capturing the value potential in the alliances of Philips. In April 2003, John became a professor strategic alliances at the Radboud University of Nijmegen and again in 2013 at University of Tilburg. Before he joined Philips, John was a strategy consultant at PricewaterhouseCoopers. John started his career as Assistant Professor of Strategic and International Management at Tilburg University. Here he wrote his PhD (with honor) on joint ventures and international expansion. John published extensively on strategic alliances in international and national journals and books.

Sushil Bhatia, a globally known award-winning entrepreneur and innovator, has innovated products like Glue Stic, convention/seminar name badges, mailing labels, laser/copier labels, binding systems, decorative labels for shampoo/cosmetic/food containers, and a DeCopier. Dr. Bhatia has founded several companies and is currently the President and CEO of JMD Manufacturing Incorporated. JMD's products are used across many industries such as food, pharmaceuticals, electronics, cosmetic, and toiletry products. For his work he has been featured on television and radio shows like ABC's Good Morning America, CNN, NBC, Canada AM, and NPR, and he has been written up in *The Wall Street Journal, Boston Globe, Economic Times*, and many other publications worldwide. Currently he is also a professor and executive in residence at Sawyer Business School, Suffolk University, Boston, where he teaches innovation and new product development.

Vincent Blok is Assistant Professor at Management Studies, within the Social Sciences Group, at Wageningen University. His research interests include knowledge-intensive entrepreneurship and cross-sector collaborations. He published several scientific articles on entrepreneurship and innovation management in the life sciences.

José C. Casillas is Associate Professor of Management at the University of Seville (Department of Management and Marketing). He received his PhD in international management from University of Seville, and he is the family business chair of the same university. His current research is focused on international businesses, family businesses, entrepreneurship, and growth. He is author of the book *International Entrepreneurship in Family Businesses*, published by Edward-Elgar in 2007. Some of his research has been published in high-impact journals such as *Entrepreneurship, Theory and Practice, Entrepreneurship and Regional Development, International Business Review, Journal of World Business, Family Business Review, International Journal of Technology Management,* and *International Journal of Human Resources Management*. He has participated at different MBA Programs in several iniversities in the Czech Republic, Bolivia, Nicaragua, and El Salvador.

Ravi Chinta is University Research Chair at Center for Management and Entrepreneurship, University of Phoenix. Dr. Chinta has 34 years of experience with 12 in academia and 22 in industry. He brings a unique blend of skills that span across academia and industry; across 14 diverse nations with business and living experience; across small venture-capital startups and very large, multi-billion global firms; and across strategic management and operations management. Dr. Chinta's specific skills include strategy analyses, portfolio level resource allocations, mergers and acquisitions, process improvements, and business partnerships in small, medium, and large organizations. He has 35 publications in such journals as *Academy of Management Executive, Journal of Small Business Management, Long Range Planning, Management Research News, Journal of Technology Management in China, International Journal of Strategic Business Alliances, and International Journal of Business and Globalization.*

Asli M. Colpan is Associate Professor of Corporate Strategy at the Graduate School of Management (where she holds the Mizuho Securities Chair) and The Hakubi Center for Advanced Research, Kyoto University. Her research interests include corporate strategy, corporate governance, business history, and especially the evolution of large enterprises in developed and emerging economies. Her work has been published in such journals as *Industrial and Corporate Change, Journal of Management Studies*, and *Corporate Governance: An International Review*. She is the co-editor of the *Oxford Handbook of Business Groups* (Oxford: Oxford University Press, 2010). In 2010 she was awarded the Tachibana Prize for the most outstanding female scholar at Kyoto University.

Refik Culpan is Professor of Management and International Business at the School of Business Administration, Pennsylvania State University at Harrisburg, United States. He has published numerous books and journal articles nationally and internationally in the areas of strategic management, business strategic alliances, and multinational companies. Additionally, Dr. Culpan has presented papers at national and international conferences. He is a member of the Academy of Management, Academy of International Business, and Strategic Management Society. His book *Global Business Alliances: Theory and Practice* was translated into Chinese, and he edited a volume, *Multinational Strategic Alliances*, dealing with inter-firm collaborations from a global strategic perspective. His articles appeared in *International Journal of Business Strategic Alliances, Management Revue, The International Review of Management Studies; International Journal of Technology, Knowledge, and Society; Management International Review; and Journal of Business Review*, among others.

Prof. Culpan was the founder and editor-in-chief of *International Journal of Strategic Business Alliances* in 2009–2011. He also serves on the editorial boards of several journals. His recent research interests include open innovation, emerging market multinational companies, joint ventures, and inter-firm collaborations.

Robert DeFillippi is Professor of Strategy and International Business and Director of the Center for Innovation and Change Leadership at the Sawyer Business School, Suffolk University. Dr. DeFillippi is an international scholar in innovation and he has held visiting scholar appointments at Cass Business School (London), the Center for Research in Innovation Management at University of

Brighton, and the ARC Centre of Excellence for Creative Industries and Innovation at Queensland University of Technology, Brisbane, Australia. Dr. DeFillippi has also held an Erasmus Mundus visiting professorship at Polytechnico di Milano and a Distinguished Professorship at University of Hull Business School. Dr. DeFillippi received his MA, M.Phil., and Ph.D. from Yale University in Organization Studies. He is the founder and co-editor of the *Business Innovation and Disruption in Creative Industries* book series. He is also consulting editor for the *International Journal of Management Reviews* and he serves on the editorial board of the *Journal of Media Business Studies*. He has published in leading academic journals, including *Academy of Management Review, California Management Review, Research Policy*, and *Organization Studies*.

Ard-Pieter de Man is Professor of Knowledge Networks and Innovation at VU University Amsterdam. His main research area is in alliances and networks. In addition he acts as a consultant to companies in the alliance area via Atos Consulting. He is a member of the Global Board of the Association of Strategic Alliance Professionals. Professor De Man has published in a wide variety of academic outlets.

Eduard de Pinéda holds an MSc in business administration from VU University Amsterdam, with a specialization in strategy and organization. To complete his master's he conducted a study on knowledge intensive business services (KIBS), particularly the relationship between alliance portfolio configuration and innovation. The results of this study constitute the foundation of a chapter published in *Open Innovation through Strategic Alliances*. His interests lie in startups, open innovation, and venture capital. Currently, he is employed as an account manager at Lynx, recognized as the best Dutch online brokerage firm multiple times in row.

Colette Dumas is Professor of Management and Entrepreneurship and Director of the Center for Innovation and Change Leadership at the Sawyer Business School at Suffolk University. Dr. Dumas is an international scholar in change leadership, innovation, and creativity. She has held visiting scholar appointments at McGill University, l'Universidad Autonomo de Guererro, Mexico, and the Warsaw School of Economics. She holds a PhD in human and organization systems and a master's degree in organizational development from The Fielding Graduate Institute, Santa Barbara, California. During her career, Dr. Dumas has been awarded more than $800,000 in research grants. She is the author of over 60 scholarly journal publications, a book, and numerous book chapters and conference papers. Dr. Dumas has served as a consultant and has trained personnel in leading banks and financial institutions, healthcare and pharmaceutical companies, universities, and not-for-profit organization. Dr. Dumas helps organizations to develop and implement effective change leadership programs, build their innovation capabilities and skillsets, and foster creative collaborations. She designs action-learning initiatives that lead to highly effective engagement and sustainable results.

Jaco Fok is General Manager of Open Innovation at Shell Global Solutions International BV. He joined Shell in 2012 to help Shell Innovation make the transition toward a more open innovation management. Next to leading the already successful department entities of GameChanger (radical early stage innovation) and the External Technology Coordination team, Jaco is setting up new innovation network management, an innovation learning program, as well as regional open innovation centers. Before joining Shell, Jaco held several positions with various businesses at DSM during his 23-year career with that company. Most recently Jaco was VP business incubator at DSM as well as director of the innovation center at DSM China, leading global business development teams creating new significant business outside the current DSM business scope. In his previous positions, Jaco was business unit director and innovation director at DSM Dyneema, was an ebusiness programme manager and business manager of savory flavors at DSM Food Specialties, and held various functions in the bakery ingredients and research divisions of Gist-Brocades. Jaco's educational background includes a MSc in chemical engineering at Dutch State University Groningen, a MSc in biochemistry at Dutch state university Utrecht, and an MBA at Rotterdam School of Management, The Netherlands.

Mehmet Gençer is Assistant Professor of Organization Studies at Istanbul Bilgi University, Faculty of Engineering, and chair of the computer engineering department. Dr. Gençer delivers undergraduate courses in the Department of Computer Engineering, in addition to undergraduate and graduate level courses in both the Institute of Natural Sciences and Institute of Social Sciences. His research areas include empirical studies on collaboration in virtual communities, innovation dynamics, and computational socio-economic system models. He has published several journal articles and book chapters nationally and internationally in the areas of strategic management, innovation ecosystems, and software innovation. His articles appeared in *Technology Analysis & Strategic Management Journal, International Journal of IT Standards and Standardization Research, IEEE Computers and Communications*, among others. Additionally, Dr. Gençer has presented research papers and field reviews at national and international conferences. He is a member of European Group of Organization Studies, International Network for Social Network Analysis, and the Association of Computing Machinery. He serves as an organizer in Entrepreneurs Roundtable Istanbul and as a consultant on academy-industry collaboration for Aegean Region Chamber of Commerce.

Takashi Hikino is Associate Professor of Industrial and Business Organization at the Graduate School of Economics and the Graduate School of Management at Kyoto University, Japan. He worked previously at Columbia University as an adjunct professor and also at Harvard Business School and The Center for International Study of MIT as senior research fellow. His research interests are industrial organization, economic growth, business history, economic history, and corporate strategy. His recent publications include *Big Business and Wealth of Nations*, Cambridge University Press, 1997 (co-edited with Alfred D. Chandler and Franco Amatori) and *Oxford Handbook of Business Groups*, Oxford University Press, 2010 (coedited with Asli M. Colpan and James R. Lincoln).

Mariann Jelinek is Richard C. Kraemer Professor of Strategy, Emerita, at the Mason School of Business, College of William and Mary in Williamsburg, VA, where she taught for 22 years. Her prior appointments were at Dartmouth's Tuck School, McGill University, the State University of New York at Albany, and Case Western Reserve University. She also served as visiting research scholar at the Technical University of Eindhoven, the Netherlands, and at the University of Melbourne, Australia. She is author or co-author of more than 50 articles and 5 books. From 1999–2001, she served as director for the Innovation and Organization Change program at the National Science Foundation. She holds a PhD from the University of California, Berkeley, and a DBA from the Harvard Business School.

Benwari L. Kedia, PhD, holds the Robert Wang Chair of Excellence in International Business and is director of the Wang Center for International Business Education and Research (CIBER). Prior to joining the University of Memphis in 1989, Dr. Kedia taught international business and management at Texas Tech University (1975–1978) and at Louisiana State University (1978–1989), where he also served as director of the Division for Business Research and chairman of the Department of Management. Professor Kedia's research has been published in *the Academy of Management Review, Organization Science, Journal of Management Studies, Journal of World Business, Management International Review, Business Horizons, Journal of Teaching in International Business, International Business Review, European Management, Journal, The International Executive, Business and the Contemporary World, International Marketing Review, Journal of High Technology Management Research, Columbia Journal of World Business, California Management Review, Personnel Psychology*, and others. In addition, he has contributed several chapters to leading research and textbooks. He received his Ph.D. from Case-Western Reserve University.

Richard E. Kouri is presently Professor and Executive Director of the MBA-focused BioSciences Management program, Poole College of Management, North Carolina State University. Dr. Kouri is also chief evangelist, Center for Innovation Management Studies. His current interest is focused on creating and linking market and technology maps using big data analytics. He has held academic positions at UNC, Chapel Hill, University of Connecticut, Yale University, Johns Hopkins Medical Center, and University of Maryland. Dr. Kouri has been on the founding teams of twelve startup companies, with three going on to their IPO and three being acquired. Dr. Kouri has helped raise over $221 million in private capital for these companies and has been awarded over $24 million in research funds. The value of the 6 companies that have been acquired or have completed initial public offerings (IPOs) to date totals $775 million.

Scott Mooty is a PhD candidate at the Fogelman College of Business and Economics, University of Memphis. His research interests include the strategic management of innovation practices, strategic and international alliance formation and regulation, alliance portfolios, and organizational learning. Scott currently has papers in review and publication. Scott also holds an MBA from the University of North Alabama with a dual emphasis in management and marketing, where he served as an adjunct professor of management from 2008 to 2011.

Ana M. Moreno-Menéndez is Associate Professor Strategic Management at the University of Seville (Department of Management and Marketing). She received her PhD in entrepreneurship from University of Seville. Her current research focuses on entrepreneurship, growth, international businesses, and family businesses. She is author of the book *International Entrepreneurship in Family Businesses*, published by Edward-Elgar in 2007. Some of her research has been published in high- impact journals such as *Entrepreneurship, Theory and Practice, Entrepreneurship and Regional Development, Journal of World Business, Family Business Review, Management International*, and *Tourism and Hospitality Planning and Development*. She has participated at different MBA programs in several universities in the Czech Republic and Nicaragua.

Paul Mugge is Executive Director CIMS, Poole College of Management, North Carolina State University. Before joining NC State University, he spent 37 years in IBM's R&D community where he held a number of management positions. His key accomplishments include leading the IBM taskforce, which conceived of its ever popular laptop computer, the IBM ThinkPad; leading the team that three years in a row (1990–1992) won the prestigious "Best of Show" Award given to the most innovative product at the COMDEX trade show in Las Vegas. Also, Mr. Mugge is the recipient of the IBM Chairman's Award for leading the reengineering of product development. The goal was to solve what CEO Lou Gerstner termed IBM's "time-to-market crisis." Mr. Mugge picked his team from across IBM—research, software, marketing, etc.—determined IBM's baseline performance and gap to best practice, instituted key performance indicators, and drove the design and implementation of this initiative. The result of this effort was a new business model for faster developing winning products, called integrated product development (IPD).

Hiroyuki Nakazono is a PhD candidate at the Graduate School of Commerce of Doshisha University and chief operating officer of Libarts Inc, Japan. His research interests include corporate strategy, corporate structure, technological innovation, and especially open innovation. He has published in such journals as *Journal of Industrial Management Research* and *Doshisha Business Review of Graduate Studies*.

Beyza Oba is Professor of Organization Studies at the Department of Business Administration, İstanbul Bilgi University, Turkey. She delivers graduate and undergraduate courses in organization theory, strategic management, and innovation management. Her research interests include empirical studies on trust, governance, hegemony, and innovation. She has published in journals like *Business History, Entrepreneurship and Regional Development, Journal of Technology Analysis and Strategic Management and Corporate Governance*. She also has several journal articles in Turkish. Additionally, she has presented research papers in EIASM (European Institute in Advanced Studies in Management), EGOS (European Group of Organization Studies), and British Academy of Management conferences.

Nadine Roijakkers has been an assistant professor of strategy and innovation management at Hasselt University since 2009. Her PhD thesis was on inter-firm collaborative innovation in the pharmaceutical biotechnology industry at the United Nations University/MERIT. During the period 2002–2007, Dr. Roijakkers held a number of positions in research and academia. From 2007 to 2009 she was a senior strategy consultant at KPMG Consulting. Dr. Roijakkers published numerous articles and book chapters on alliance management and innovation management. Her work was published in reputable journals such as *Long Range Planning, Research Policy, Harvard Business History Review, British Journal of Management, European Management Journal, Technological Forecasting and Social Change,* Small Business *Economics,* and *California Management Review.*

Brian Tjemkes is an associate professor at the Faculty of Economics and Business Administration at the VU University Amsterdam, The Netherlands. He has published in the *Journal of Management Studies, Management Decision,* and *Journal of International Management,* among others. His research interests include the management and performance of strategic alliances.

Wim Vanhaverbeke studied philosophy and economics at the Catholic University of Leuven and obtained a DBA at the IESE-business school in Barcelona in 1995. He is currently Professor Strategy and Innovation at the Hasselt University (Belgium) in the Department of Business Studies and is appointed as visiting professor "open innovation" at ESADE (Spain) and the National University of Singapore (Belgium). His research areas are open innovation, alliances, and acquisition of external technological capabilities; alliance management; and new business development and corporate venturing. He teaches strategy, innovation management, corporate venturing and new business development, and international management. He is published in international journals as *Organization Science and Organization Studies, Research Policy,* and *Journal of Business Venturing,* and serves on the editorial board of *Journal of Engineering and Technology Management and Strategic Organization.*

He is co-editor (with Henry Chesbrough and Joel West) of *Open Innovation: Researching a New Paradigm,* a new book about the research challenges related to open innovation (Oxford University Press, 2006; paperback in 2008; Japanese translation 2008). He is extending research about open innovation with different universities and companies around the globe. He established Exnovate, a network of excellence on innovating using technology from external sources. He co-founded the European Innovation Forum with Henry Chesbrough in 2012.

André van Meijeren studied management, economics, and consumer studies at Wageningen University. In 2011 André concluded his BSc with a specialization in strategic management and innovation. In his MSc in management studies, André conducted at Wageningen University and Technological University

Munich, where he specialized in innovation management. In 2013, he finalized his MSc in management with a study on the relational drivers of product innovation in the emerging biochemical industry.

Joel West is Professor of Innovation and Entrepreneurship at the Keck Graduate Institute of Applied Life Sciences, The Clermont Colleges, California. He is one the pioneers of open innovation and contributed tremendously to the understanding of open innovation through his articles, books, and consulting works. As an internationally known researcher on innovation management, Dr. West has been invited to speak at industry and academic events on five continents. He is particularly known for his work on open innovation, as co-editor of *Open Innovation: Researching a New Paradigm* (Oxford, 2006), and as co-founder (with Henry Chesbrough) of the Open Innovation Community. His other research areas include renewable energy, entrepreneurship, intellectual property, open source software, international business, and strategies for IT vendor firms. According to Google Scholar, his research has been cited more than 3,500 times.

He is professor emeritus at San José State University, where he spent nine years as an associate professor and then professor at the College of Business and Lucas Graduate School of Business until retiring in 2011. He has also taught at UC Irvine, Pepperdine, and Temple University Japan. He has a PhD in management from the University of California, Irvine, and a BS in interdisciplinary sciences (meteorology) from the Massachusetts Institute of Technology. Prior to becoming an academic, he had an extensive industry career as an engineer, manager, and entrepreneur in the software industry.

Emiel F.M. Wubben is Associate Professor in Strategic Management at Management Studies, within the Social Sciences Group, at Wageningen University. His fields of expertise are strategic management, especially resource-based view, interorganizational relationships, food valley and synergy parks, academic spin offs, mergers and acquisitions, and their impact on the innovativeness of companies. His predominant field of application interests comprises bio-based businesses.

Richard R. Young, Professor of Supply Chain Management and Director of the MBA Program at Penn State Harrisburg, holds a BS in operations management from Rider University, an MBA from Albany University, and a PhD from the Pennsylvania State University. Prior to academia, he held senior supply chain management positions at American Hoechst Corporation (later Hoechst Celanese), a U.S. subsidiary of Hoechst AG of Germany. Dr. Young has addressed audiences worldwide and consulted with firms in chemicals and plastics, steel and coke, telecommunications, industrial and automotive components, international airlines, railroads, consumer goods, as well as state government and the U.S. military. He is a fellow of the Chartered Institute of Logistics and Transport and was a participant in the Fulbright German Research Seminar.

Foreword

Research on open innovation has grown rapidly since the term was coined over a decade ago. Open innovation came about as organizations realized that it is neither efficient nor effective to innovate by themselves. Now many innovations are produced by working collaboratively with suppliers, customers, and partners of various sorts. External collaboration has many benefits, including faster development of new products and services, decreased cost of product development and process improvement, access to new markets and technologies, and reduced risk in many activities. Open or collaborative innovation began in knowledge-intensive industries, such as biotechnology and computers, but is now being used in traditional industries as well.

Once an organization decides to open up its innovation process, it must consider the various organizational arrangements it can adopt to engage in collaboration. Some organizational processes are fully open, such as the one used by Linux to continually develop its computer operating system. Anyone with computer software expertise can contribute to the development of the Linux kernel. Most open innovation processes, however, are not completely open. Rather, they have been designed so that specific suppliers, customers, or partners can work with the focal organization to accomplish innovation objectives. One popular organizational arrangement is the multifirm network in which the focal organization relies on the expertise of external suppliers to provide it with customized inputs and resources. BMW is a company that uses this approach. Sometimes a network of relationships with external providers occurs naturally, such as the "ecosystem" of application developers that surrounds Apple or the niche product manufacturers that make items that can be added on to products sold by Ikea. A new and very sophisticated means of organizing for collaborative innovation is the collaborative community. Blade.org, a collaborative community of more than two hundred firms in the computer-server marketplace, operated for about five years and developed numerous new solutions via temporary, voluntary networks of firms that were members of the Blade.org community. Running through all of these examples is the common thread of working with external partners to develop innovations of various kinds.

This collection of 14 chapters explores the many different types of strategic alliances that organizations use to engage in open innovation. Examples come from both the public and private sectors, and they represent widely different industries, such as biochemistry, computer software, education, energy, and consumer goods. The types of innovations that are examined also range widely to include product, technology, and business model innovations. As editor, Refik Culpan has assembled an international group of 32 scholars, resulting in a nice blend of cultural perspectives reflective of the global economy. There is much to consider in this volume, and I believe both academics and practitioners can benefit from reading it.

Charles C. Snow
Emeritus Professor of Strategy and Organization
The Pennsylvania State University

CHAPTER 1

Open Innovation: Learning from Alliance Research

Joel West[1]

This volume examines an important area of potential research: the intersection of strategic alliances and open innovation. Although these two streams of research have developed separately, with distinct assumptions and research questions, there is a natural affinity between them in terms of phenomena, theoretical predictions, and managerial implications. As editor Refik Culpan notes in chapter 2, both streams assume that innovation is collaborative (and often complementary) and that such collaborations are crucial for firms to create and capture value from their innovations.

Prior research has defined strategic alliances as cooperation agreements between two organizations. Such alliances allow organizations to pool resources but require (inherently incomplete) contracts, trust-building measures, and ongoing monitoring to limit the potential adverse impacts of imperfectly aligned interests (Gulati, 1995, 1998; Gomes-Casseres, 1996; Das, 2005). Although these alliances are typically created between two firms, companies may also form alliances with universities, nonprofit research organizations, or government laboratories (Baum, Calabrese, and Silverman, 2000).

Larger firms usually engage in multiple alliances with suppliers, customers, and even direct competitors. An important challenge for such firms is managing the portfolio of such alliances in order to assure diversity of technology or market resources, or even to use competition between partners to reduce opportunism. Thus a key challenge for firms is not only managing the activities with a single partner, but also adding, deleting, and coordinating multiple partners in a portfolio (Lavie, 2007). These multiple alliances allow us to consider the role (and success) of any firm as part of a larger network of innovators, using variables such as the number of partners, their status, or their connectedness (Powell and Grodal, 2005).

Much of the interest in strategic alliances comes from their use in spreading the costs and benefits of innovation. While such alliances typically allow learning by both parties, they can create a "learning race" in which each party seeks to gain knowledge from the other party more quickly so that the slower party loses in this collaboration. (Hamel, 1991; Hagedoorn, Link, and Vonortas, 2000; Kale, Singh, and Perlmutter, 2000; Hagedoorn, 2002).

Within this context and based on an interest in interfirm cooperation for innovation, alliances are relevant to open innovation—and vice versa. From the beginning, the focus of open innovation has been on such interfirm cooperation, allowing firms to improve their innovation performance by leveraging innovation creation and commercialization paths outside their firm boundaries (Chesbrough, 2003, 2006; West, Vanhaverbeke, and Chesbrough, 2006).

What is *open innovation*? According to the latest definition by Henry Chesbrough, it is "a distributed innovation process based on purposively managed knowledge flows across organizational boundaries, using pecuniary and nonpecuniary mechanisms in line with each organization's business model" (Chesbrough and Bogers, 2014, forthcoming). Research on open innovation has shown how firms manage both the inflows and outflows of knowledge, how they search for partners and the innovations they provide, and (to a lesser degree) how that knowledge is used after it is sourced.[2]

Researchers have identified three distinct modes of open innovation collaboration: inbound flows of knowledge from external sources, outbound flows that allow firms to monetize their innovation through others, and a coupled mode that combines inbound and outbound. The inbound mode—sourcing external innovations—has thus far been the most common in research and practice, while the coupled mode corresponds to alliances for collaborative R&D between two firms (Gassmann and Enkel, 2004; West and Bogers, forthcoming). The coupled mode subsumes two forms of collaboration. In one, bidirectional knowledge flows link the separate innovation efforts of each organization. In contrast, in the second form, the interactive coupled process involves joint innovation creation beyond the boundaries of a single firm (Piller and West, forthcoming).

Of course, not all alliances are about open innovation, and not all open innovation involves alliances (see Table 1.1). Innovation alliances—those alliances involving the development or commercialization of at least one partner's innovations—would certainly qualify as a purposive, distributed innovation process across organizational boundaries. Because open innovation requires new ideas or practices "that lead to improved outcomes for an organization" (Vanhaverbeke,

Table 1.1 Forms of Interorganizational Cooperation

	Open Innovation	*Noninnovation Cooperation*
Strategic Alliances	Innovation alliances	Other alliances
Interorganizational Transactions	Innovation contests	Procurement of commodities and standardized components

West, and Chesbrough, forthcoming), alliances that do not involve such innovation would not meet the definition of *open innovation*.

Even with the overlap of open innovation and innovation alliances, not all open innovation involves alliances. While alliances by definition involve working with firms (or other organizations), open innovation might also involve cooperation with individuals, communities, or other levels of analysis (West et al., 2006). For example, a considerable literature has developed about how firms can use innovation tournaments to crowdsource innovations from individuals (e.g., Jeppesen and Lakhani, 2010).

But even when the external partner is a firm, there are forms of interorganizational cooperation that can bring open innovation without alliances. By their nature, alliances involve sustained and ongoing cooperation over time (Parkhe, 1993). On the relational-versus-transactional dimension (cf. Robinson, Kraatz, and Rousseau, 1994), alliances are clearly relational (Gulati, 1995; Dyer and Singh, 1998). However, some forms of open innovation involve isolated transactions rather than ongoing relationships. One such example is the innovation contest, as with the X-Prize series of high-stakes innovation competitions that attract recognition far beyond the cash rewards (Ledford, 2006). And, as noted below, many platforms involve sponsors that provide technology to would-be complementors but entail little or no direct interaction.

Thus, only a subset of open innovation involves strategic alliances: an agreement for ongoing innovation collaboration between two organizations—which closely matches the research on innovation alliances. Still, given the strong interest in R&D collaboration by innovation researchers over the past 25 years—and the bias of open innovation research toward firm-to-firm cooperation (West et al., 2006)—there is considerable overlap between these two streams.

The remaining 13 chapters of this book address exactly this overlap (see Table 1.2). Below, I summarize and organize a review of these chapters.

Alliances in Open Innovation

Both in its original conception and in its first decade of publications, open innovation research has focused on the dyadic cooperation between two firms (West et al., 2006; Vanhaverbeke et al., 2014). Thus, studying interfirm alliances for R&D and other innovation-relation collaboration directly corresponds to the goals and precepts of open innovation. Such studies of firm collaboration can be from the perspective of one firm or both firms, and can be at the level of the firm, the project, or the individuals involved.

In chapter 2, Culpan examines this overlap between alliances and the broader process of open innovation. He lists four categories of collaboration: crowdsourcing, third-party apps, university partnerships, and interfirm alliances. The first is usually (not always) associated with working with individuals, while the second (as discussed below) often involves less formal ties than would normally be considered an alliance. University partnerships (discussed below and in chapter 8) are a special form of alliance, while the interfirm collaborations describe the bulk

Table 1.2 Key Questions Posed by Each Chapter

Chapter	Author(s)	Level of Analysis	Key Question
2.	Culpan	all	How do different forms of alliances affect the practice of open innovation?
3.	Roijakkers, Bell, Fok, and Vanhaverberke	alliance	What challenges do MNCs face in implementing external R&D collaborations?
4.	Wubben, Meijeren, and Blok	alliance	What are the relational drivers of successful innovation collaboration between industries?
5.	Moreno-Menéndez and Casillas	alliance	Does openness in innovation lead to increased internationalization?
6.	Young	alliance	How do firms collaboratively innovate with their supply chain to improve performance?
7.	DeFillipi, Dumas, and Bhatia	alliance	How do a customer and supplier create a relational alliance that enables an ongoing process of collaborative innovation?
8.	Chinta and Culpan	alliance	What role do university alliances play in open innovation strategies?
9.	Jelinek, Barr, Mugge, and Kouri	network	How can big data overcome cognitive limits in managing alliance networks?
10.	Tjemkes, de Pinéda, Bahlmann, de Man, and Alexiev	network	How does the approach to building a portfolio of alliances affect the benefits of the portfolio?
11.	Mooty and Kedia	network	How can alliance networks support inbound open innovation for breakthrough innovation?
12.	Nakazono, Hikino, and Colpan	network	How do routines and network embeddedness prevent firms from opening up their innovation processes?
13.	Gencer and Oba	ecosystem	How do ecosystems and other forms of external collaboration enable open innovation in the software industry?
14.	Culpan	all	How do alliances interact with firm decisions about managing open innovation?

of the strategic alliance literature. Within this latter category, Culpan identifies eight different structural forms—three (JV, block equity, and VC) involving equity ties and five (licensing, contractual R&D, networks, community, and consortia) that do not—and explains how they map onto different aspects of the open innovation process.

Antecedents and Consequences

What are the antecedents to the success of innovation alliances and strategic alliances more broadly? This is a question that has long been studied in the alliance literature (e.g., Parkhe, 1993; Doz, 1996).

In chapter 3, Roijakkers, Bell, Fok, and Vanhaverbeke consider the challenges that large multinational corporations (MNCs) face in managing external R&D partnerships, through in-depth case studies of open innovation at two Dutch MNCs (Phillips and Shell). They identify a range of approaches to R&D alliances, ranging from contract R&D intended to produce immediate results, through extended R&D partnerships, to highly selective (and visible) strategic partnerships for joint R&D. For the latter, they highlight the importance of multiproject collaboration agreements—incomplete contracts that make it easy to initiate new collaboration within a well-defined institutional structure.

In chapter 4, Wubben, Meijeren, and Blok examine the alliance challenges faced by nine Dutch firms in the agriculture and chemical industries. Much as Christensen (2006) did for digital amplifiers, they examine how these firms are shifting (or helping shift) chemical feedstocks from fossil fuels to biomass, a shift that spans traditional industry boundaries and thus is facilitated through alliances with partners in complementary industries. Using interviews with a representative of each company, they identified two key measures—strategic alignment and strength of relational ties between parties—that their respondents believe lead to open innovation success.

Beyond predicting the success of an alliance strategy, one can ask the converse question: how do alliances (or successful alliances) affect the other activities of the firm?

In chapter 5, Moreno-Menéndez and Casillas study whether the use of alliances leads to increased internationalization. In a survey of 424 medium and large Spanish manufacturing firms, they note a strong correlation between open innovation activity and measures of internationalization, including export propensity, export intensity, and foreign direct investment. By lagging the regression measures between two successive surveys, they conclude that open innovation in the earlier time period predicts increased internationalization in the later period.

Collaboration with Partners

One of the fundamental questions in alliance research is how do firms manage relationships with their alliance partners (Doz, 1996; Koza and Lewin, 1998). Two chapters in this book examine how firms work with suppliers, long identified as a crucial source of external innovations (von Hippel, 1988; Chesbrough, 2003; Gassmann, Enkel, and Chesbrough 2010).

In chapter 6, Young classifies eight minicases of supplier-customer collaborative innovation into four quadrants based on a two-dimensional matrix of risk and strategic importance. He concludes that product innovations only happen in the highly important dimension, but process innovations (both for production and sourcing more generally) can succeed in all quadrants. As with other research on trust in alliances (e.g., Dyer and Chu, 2003), he shows how trust is essential for collaboration. More generally, he shows that a transactional view of sourcing (by cost-cutting customers) prevents the sort of relational collaboration necessary to foster such innovation.

In chapter 7, DeFillippi, Dumas, and Bhatia examine the unique partnership between two innovative MNCs: Xerox and Procter & Gamble. The collaboration served P&G's goal of reducing costs and increasing integration by outsourcing the management of printing services and built upon Xerox's "Customer-Led Integration"—a form of business-to-business user innovation (cf. Bogers, Afuah, and Bastian 2010). The authors document the institutional structures created to lead and govern this ongoing process of collaborative innovation and the challenges that it overcame in synchronizing the two cultures and incentives. The alliance improved throughput while reducing paper, energy, and overall cost for P&G, while at the same time providing solutions that Xerox could sell to other customers.

While open innovation typically focuses on collaboration between firms, universities can also be important partners for firms. Such efforts allow firms to access scientific breakthroughs, but firms face daunting challenges in aligning the incentives, goals, and cultures between private gain and public science (Perkmann and Walsh, 2007; Perkmann and West, 2012).

In chapter 8, Chinta and Culpan examine the role that business-university R&D collaborations play in a firm's overall open innovation strategy. After identifying the mutual benefits and potential conflicts between businesses and university, they consider such collaborations in the broader context of the "Triple Helix" of business, university, and government (Etzkowitz and Leydesdorff, 2000). They offer an updated technology-commercialization model that points to the central role of university research in creating and developing technological inventions and the concomitant role of the government in funding such early-stage, exploratory work.

Networks and Related Forms

Research on open innovation has considered the role of alliances, networks of alliances, and specialized forms of networks, including consortia, ecosystems, platforms, and communities (West, 2014). Chapters in this book examine how firms manage two of the network forms: alliance portfolios and external ecosystems.

Building and Managing Alliance Portfolios

A given firm's portfolio of alliances defines a network of business relationships (Duysters, De Man, and Wildeman, 1999). From the standpoint of the focal firm, the network is managed as a series of dyadic alliances (although these network partners may have their own alliances). How to most effectively manage such portfolios is a key theoretical and managerial issue for alliance research (cf. Ireland, Hitt, and Vaidyanath, 2002). Two chapters consider factors that predict the success of such portfolio management.

In chapter 9, Jelinek, Barr, Mugge, and Kouri explain how the analysis of "big data" can be used to make more systematic decisions regarding the creation and management of strategic alliances in a firm's portfolio. In particular, they consider how such decisions can overcome the cognitive limits and decision traps that bias managerial decisions. Their chapter describes an industry-funded research center at North Carolina State and how the center has used its data analytical skills to help clients identify potential technologies, partners, markets, materials, and production techniques.

In chapter 10, Tjemkes, de Pinéda, Bahlmann, de Man, and Alexiev examine how start-up firms manage upstream and downstream business relationships. They studied four young Dutch ICT services companies: two were developing new technologies and the other two were developing new markets. They distinguish between the successful portfolio strategies for each of these strategic goals. Overall, they demonstrate how the more successful firms used a more systematic, proactive, and focused approach to build large and diverse portfolios of alliances and other business relationships.

Impacts of Networks upon Success

Within a given industry or region, the pattern of alliances between organizations defines a network. In the United States, such alliances are common among firms embedded in a regional technology cluster (e.g., see Owen-Smith and Powell, 2004). In other countries, firms manage networks of captive suppliers and collaborators, as with the Japanese *zaibatsu* or *keiretsu* (Gerlach, 1992; Dyer, 1996).

In chapter 11, Mooty and Kedia consider the role of alliance networks upon a firm's ability to source radical innovations. Consistent with the Chesbrough (2006) open innovation funnel, they present a framework for classifying and analyzing how a firm harnesses inbound knowledge flows through the process of creating and commercializing a radical innovation. The framework considers three degrees of knowledge flows—transfer, translation, and transformation—across four phases of the commercialization process: conceptualization, incubation, generation, and postgeneration.

In chapter 12, Nakazono, Hikino, and Colpan consider the unique challenges for practicing open innovation by large Japanese MNCs. With high entry barriers faced by potentially innovative start-ups, and institutional and financial constraints that encourage a corporate grouping of related subsidiaries, these MNCs tend to practice open innovation within such groupings. In particular, consistent with open innovation, they form spinoff subsidiary firms to commercialize technologies that don't fit the business model of the parent company. The authors show how these constraints limited open innovation at Panasonic Corporation to new business areas that were not already deeply embedded in the group's technologies and markets.

Ecosystem Management

Finally, in some industries, networks are part of a larger pattern of interdependency among firms; this pattern is referred to as an *innovation ecosystem*[3] (Adner, 2012; Adner and Kapoor, 2010). One particular kind of ecosystem, often found in ICT-producing industries, is the platform, which combines a specific technical product's architecture with a network of firms that make complementary products compatible with that architecture (Gawer and Henderson, 2007; Gawer, 2009).

In chapter 13, Gencer and Oba consider the use of external ecosystems by proprietary software companies. Noting the unique characteristics of the software artifact and the institutional landscape, they contrast closed, open, and hybrid innovation strategies. They consider how firms answer key questions—whether, what, how, and with whom—relating to innovation partnering at different layers within a given software architecture.

Future Opportunities

A major goal of this volume has been to bring together research on strategic alliances and open innovation. In chapter 14, Culpan discusses how alliances are part of a larger, three-part framework of the open innovation strategies employed by firms, linking value architecture to value creation and value capture. The eight forms of alliances identified in chapter 2 thus are a tool in the toolkit of managing open innovation, a management process that leads both to value creation and successful open innovation outcomes. The chapter also identifies ten challenges facing open innovation researchers interested in both the process of open innovation and its overlap with the alliance research.

Building on the insights in the previously mentioned chapters, here I offer my own suggestions as to how research on alliances can inform open innovation—and vice versa—as well as two areas where both can learn from extant research.

How Alliances Can Inform Open Innovation Research

Researchers—both inside and outside of open innovation studies—have expressed concern about the lack of theoretical foundations for open innovation (e.g., Vanhaverbeke et al., 2014). Open innovation is a class of phenomena—and a managerial paradigm (Chesbrough, 2006)—but it borrows causal mechanisms and theoretical predictions from other streams of economics and management research.

Research on strategic alliances has provided repeated and convergent perspectives on how organizations collaborate to pool innovation capabilities and other resources. This research has considered such topics as the choice of alliances versus other mechanisms, the antecedents of alliance success, how success between partners is aligned, and other predictors of success (Koza and Lewin, 1998). By contrasting these two streams of work, the researchers in this volume identify a number of opportunities for open innovation researchers to learn from the older and more established body of alliance research.

The internal view of partnerships
With rare exceptions (e.g., Chiaroni, Chiesa, and Frattini, 2010), open innovation research tells us little about the internal organization of a firm's open innovation activities (West and Bogers, 2014). As chapter 3 reminds us, alliance literature has considered these topics for decades, and thus there is an opportunity to update these insights from alliance management with the twenty-first-century practice of how firms manage open innovation.

Managing partnerships on an ongoing basis
Open innovation literature tends to be transactional or at most focused on one-time collaborations. Missing is the longitudinal perspective on open innovation processes. Chapter 7 shows how the study of long-lived alliances can both provide such a longitudinal perspective and also develop deeper insights as to the incentives, motivations, and challenges of managing alliances within each side of a partnership.

Different collaboration structures
In terms of open innovation collaborations, these multiyear, strategic collaborative R&D efforts are one extreme on a continuum that includes contractual R&D as an intermediate option and a single (nonalliance) transaction at the other extreme. While different researchers have studied differing structures for open innovation collaboration, they would benefit from studying (and extending) chapter 3 by analyzing the variance of contracts, governance, and other institutional structures within a given population.

To partner or not to partner
Open innovation research tends to assume that the adoption of open innovation happens at the firm level rather than at the technology or project level. Alliance research has already considered what factors predict when firms choose alliances and when they don't (e.g., Hennart and Reddy, 1997). We don't assume that a firm that has an alliance portfolio will use alliances for every project, product, or technology, so why would we assume this for open innovation?

Learning from partners
Much of the first decade of alliance research focused on R&D collaborations between large firms, such as within industry consortia or between domestic and foreign manufacturers (e.g., Hamel, 1991). A major concern of these alliances was learning, and developing internal capabilities from such learning. Open innovation has been more about sourcing technology—or transferring the know-how around a specific technology—rather than developing internal capabilities. Open innovation has frequently studied absorptive capacity (West and Bogers, 2014) but not the learning that flows from such capacity. Is this lack of attention a result of corporate practice having changed—away from capability building toward sourcing—or merely because no one has studied it?

Opportunism
Although learning is good for the firm doing the learning, it may not be seen as good by their alliance partner. While innovation alliances typically allow for learning by both parties, they can create a "learning race" in which each party seeks to gain knowledge from the other party more quickly that means one partner loses at the end of such partnership (Hagedoorn, Link, and Vonortas, 2000; Hagedoorn, 2002; Kale, Singh, and Perlmutter, 2000). The pertinent questions here echo those concerning the previous point: are these motivations absent in open innovation or merely unstudied?

Analysis of the network
The importance of the network perspective for understanding external firm collaborations has long been accepted by open innovation scholars (e.g., Vanhaverbeke and Cloodt, 2006; West, 2014). However, the tools and measures used in such studies (e.g., Owen-Smith and Powell, 2004) are not. These measures and analysis techniques (such as embeddedness and social-network analysis) have the potential to inform open innovation research and give it a more systematic view of how firms manage external collaborations. In particular, because open innovation distinguishes between three modes—inbound, outbound, and coupled—using the directionality of knowledge flows to construct a directed graph (cf. Gloor, Laubacher, Dynes, and Zhao 2003) allows that directionality to be utilized in the analysis of open innovation networks.

How Open Innovation Can Inform Alliance Research

While alliance research can inform open innovation, the converse is also true. Here I identify several areas where open innovation can be applied to research on strategic alliances.

Role of the business model
The business model and the importance of aligning innovation to a firm's business model are central to the concept of open innovation (Chesbrough, 2006); however, this precept is largely ignored in open innovation research (Chesbrough and Bogers, 2014; West and Bogers, forthcoming 2014). Chapter 14 shows how value creation and value appropriation are crucial to understanding the benefits of alliances and how such analyses could benefit from incorporating open innovation insights regarding the ways that business model experimentation links to innovation.

Small- and medium-sized firms
Recently, open innovation researchers have been focusing on the differences in how open innovation is practiced in small and medium enterprises (SMEs) (see Vanhaverbeke et al., 2014 for a summary). This research has identified how smaller firms approach open innovation differently, both because of their needs and capabilities and also because of their strategies and decision-making

processes. Alliance research (as in chapter 7) that studies such firms could benefit from this research.

Service innovation

Chapters 7 and 10 examine firms that are seeking to develop and commercialize innovative services, which have different mechanisms for value creation and for creating the scarcity necessary for value capture. In a recent book, Chesbrough (2011) has shown how when open innovation is applied to services, the process of open innovation is transformed to exploit customization and personalization opportunities to meet customer needs in a way that is rarely possible for tangible goods.

Leveraging ecosystems and platforms

For certain industries and classes of goods, the processes of value creation and value capture are embedded in ecosystems or platforms that link the focal firm to its network of complementers (Chesbrough and Appleyard, 2007; Rohrbeck, Hoelzle, and Gemünden, 2009; West, 2014). Such ecosystems and platforms are of critical strategic importance in these industries, but strategic alliance research has largely ignored how incentives and governance are different when compared to other network forms. For example, ecosystems bring added opportunities (and stresses) for aligning the interests of alliance partners, as suggested by chapter 13. At the same time, ecosystems (e.g., the iPhone app store) are increasingly using informal mechanisms for cooperation and generation of complementary parties, suggesting new opportunities for understanding how alliances (or cooperation more generally) is practiced without deep formal contracts.

How Both Can Benefit

In several overlapping areas, both streams of studies in strategic alliances and open innovation are incomplete and would benefit from a deeper understanding of collaboration mechanisms and processes.

Openness strategies

Research on open source software has demonstrated how firms practicing open innovation benefit from a greater degree of openness (e.g., Simcoe, 2006; West and O'Mahony, 2008). A limited amount of alliance research has considered the degree to which openness improves knowledge flows and alliance outcomes (e.g. Dyer and Chu, 2003). However, there are other topics that would benefit from further study, such as the moderators of openness in an alliance context: for example, Chesbrough and Schwartz (2007) concluded that open innovation alliances are more open when they are distant from the firm's core technologies.

The moderating effect of uncertainty
Corporate venture capital is an important mechanism for aligning the relationship between (most often) a smaller innovator and an established firm seeking inbound innovations, and can deepen the alignment of partner interests and thus the strength of alliances. These investments appear to be attractive to firms under conditions of high uncertainty (Van de Vrande, Vanhaverbeke, and Duysters, 2008). Meanwhile, firms can utilize equity alliances as real options to integrate external technologies into the firm (Vanhaverbeke, van de Vrande, and Chesbrough, 2008).

Conclusions

The works in this volume, as referenced in this chapter, are meant to demonstrate the natural alignment of interests between research on open innovation and research on strategic alliances. Both are concerned with interorganizational cooperation, and (often) both are concerned with how these organizations collaborate to create or commercialize innovations. That said, this alignment remains imperfect, and considerable work needs to be done to explore and exploit the opportunities presented by the overlap.

Notes

1. This chapter has been influenced by my open innovation collaborations and conversations with many scholars over the past decade, including Marcel Bogers, Henry Chesbrough, Linus Dahlander, Scott Gallagher, Karim Lakhani, Caroline Simard, Wim Vanhaverbeke, and David Wood. I want to thank editor Refik Culpan for the invitation to participate in this volume, and Wim Vanhaverbeke for his feedback on an earlier version.
2. For recent reviews of open innovation literature, see Dahlander and Gann (2010), West and Bogers (forthcoming 2014), and Chesbrough and Bogers (2014).
3. Some ecosystems include (or are built around) less formal interfirm relationships that don't fit the above definition of an alliance. For example, many third-party developers for personal computing (Apple, Microsoft), open source (Linux), and Software as a Service platforms (Google, Yahoo) develop their complementary goods without a contractual relationship with the platform sponsor, to the degree that the sponsor does not know the full list of its ecosystem members.

References

Adner, Ron. (2012). *The Wide Lens: A New Strategy for Innovation*. New York: Penguin.
Adner, Ron, and Kapoor, Rahul. (2010). "Value Creation in Innovation Ecosystems: How the Structure of Technological Interdependence Affects Firm Performance in New Technology Generations." *Strategic Management Journal* 31 (3): 306–33.
Baum, Joel A. C., Calabrese, Tony, and Silverman, Brian S. (2000). "Don't Go It Alone: Alliance Network Composition and Startups' Performance in Canadian Biotechnology." *Strategic Management Journal* 21 (3): 267–94.

Bogers, Marcel, Afuah, Allan, and Bastian, Bettina. (2010). "Users as Innovators: A Review, Critique, and Future Research Directions." *Journal of Management* 36 (4): 857–75.

Chesbrough, Henry. (2003). *Open Innovation: The New Imperative for Creating and Profiting from Technology.* Boston: Harvard Business School Press.

Chesbrough, Henry (2006) "Open Innovation: A New Paradigm for Understanding Industrial Innovation." In Henry Chesbrough, Wim Vanhaverbeke, and Joel West (eds.), *Open Innovation: Researching a New Paradigm.* Oxford: Oxford University Press, 1–12.

Chesbrough, Henry. (2011). *Open Services Innovation: Rethinking Your Business to Grow and Compete in a New Era.* San Francisco: Jossey-Bass.

Chesbrough, Henry W., and Appleyard, Melissa M. (2007). "Open Innovation and Strategy." *California Management Review* 50 (1): 57–76.

Chesbrough, Henry, and Bogers, Marcel. (Forthcoming 2014). "Explicating Open Innovation: Clarifying an Emerging Paradigm for Understanding Innovation." In Henry Chesbrough, Wim Vanhaverbeke and Joel West (eds.), *New Frontiers in Open Innovation.* Oxford: Oxford University Press, xx–xx.

Chesbrough, Henry, and Schwartz, Kevin. (2007). "Innovating Business Models with Co-development Partnerships." *Research-Technology Management* 50 (1): 55–59.

Chiaroni, Davide, Chiesa, Vittorio, and Frattini, Federico. (2010). "Unraveling the Process from Closed to Open Innovation: Evidence from Mature, Asset-Intensive Industries." *R&D Management* 40 (3): 222–45.

Christensen, Jens Frøslev. (2006). "Wither Core Competency for the Large Corporation in an Open Innovation World?" In Henry Chesbrough, Wim Vanhaverbeke, and Joel West (eds.), *Open Innovation: Researching a New Paradigm.* Oxford: Oxford University Press, 35–61.

Dahlander, Linus, and Gann, David M. (2010). "How Open Is Innovation?" *Research Policy* 39 (6): 699–709.

Das, T. K. (2005). "Deceitful Behaviors of Alliance Partners: Potential and Prevention." *Management Decision* 43 (5): 706–19.

Doz, Yves L. (1996). "The Evolution of Cooperation in Strategic Alliances: Initial Conditions or Learning Processes?" *Strategic Management Journal* 17 (S1): 55–83.

Duysters, Geert, De Man, Ard-Pieter, and Wildeman, Leo. (1999). "A Network Approach to Alliance Management." *European Management Journal* 17 (2): 182–87.

Dyer, Jeffrey H. (1996). "Does Governance Matter? Keiretsu Alliances and Asset Specificity as Sources of Japanese Competitive Advantage." *Organization Science* 7 (6): 649–66.

Dyer, Jeffrey H., and Chu, Wujin (2003). "The Role of Trustworthiness in Reducing Transaction Costs and Improving Performance: Empirical Evidence from the United States, Japan, and Korea." *Organization Science* 14 (1): 57–68.

Dyer, Jeffrey H., and Singh, Harbir. (1998). "The Relational View: Cooperative Strategy and Sources of Interorganizational Competitive Advantage." *Academy of Management Review* 23 (4): 660–79.

Etzkowitz, Henry, and Leydesdorff, Loet. (2000). "The Dynamics of Innovation: From National Systems and 'Mode 2' to a Triple Helix of University–Industry–Government Relations." *Research Policy* 29 (2): 109–23.

Gassmann, Oliver, and Enkel, Ellen. (2004). "Towards a Theory of Open Innovation: Three Core Process Archetypes." R&D Management Conference, Lisbon, July 6–9.

Gassmann, Oliver, Enkel, Ellen, and Chesbrough, Henry. (2010). "The Future of Open Innovation." *R & D Management* 40 (3): 213–221.

Gawer, Annabelle (2009). "Platform Dynamics and Strategies: From Products to Services." In Annabelle Gawer (ed.), *Platforms, Markets and Innovation.* Cheltenham, UK: Edward Elgar, 45–76.

Gawer, Annabelle, and Henderson, Rebecca. (2007). "Platform Owner Entry and Innovation in Complementary Markets: Evidence from Intel." *Journal of Economics and Management Strategy* 16 (1): 1–34.

Gerlach, Michael L. (1992). "The Japanese Corporate Network: A Blockmodel Analysis. *Administrative Science Quarterly* 37 (1): 105–39.

Gloor, Peter A., Laubacher, Rob, Dynes, Scott B. C., and Zhao, Yan. (2003). "Visualization of Communication Patterns in Collaborative Innovation Networks-Analysis of Some W3C Working Groups." In *Proceedings of the Twelfth International Conference on Information and Knowledge Management,* ACM, 56–60.

Gomes-Casseres, Benjamin. (1996). *The Alliance Revolution: The New Shape of Business Rivalry.* Boston: Harvard Business School Publishing.

Gulati, Ranjay. (1995). "Does Familiarity Breed Trust? The Implications of Repeated Ties for Contractual Choice in Alliances." *Academy of Management Journal* 38 (1): 85–112.

Gulati, Ranjay. (1998). "Alliances and Networks." *Strategic Management Journal* 19 (4): 293–317.

Hagedoorn, John. (2002). "Inter-firm R&D Partnerships: An Overview of Major Trends and Patterns Since 1960." *Research Policy* 31 (4): 477–492.

Hagedoorn, John, Link, Albert N., and Vonortas, Nicholas S. (2000). "Research Partnerships." *Research Policy* 29 (4): 567–86.

Hamel, Gary. (1991). "Competition for Competence and Interpartner Learning within International Strategic Alliances." *Strategic Management Journal* 12 (S1): 83–103.

Hennart, Jean-Francois, and Reddy, Sabine. (1997). "The Choice between Mergers/Acquisitions and Joint Ventures: The Case of Japanese Investors in the United States." *Strategic Management Journal* 18 (1): 1–12.

Ireland, R. Duane, Hitt, Michael A., and Vaidyanath, Deepa. (2002). "Alliance Management as a Source of Competitive Advantage." *Journal of Management* 28 (3): 413–46.

Jeppesen, Lars Bo, and Lakhani, Karim R. (2010). "Marginality and Problem-Solving Effectiveness in Broadcast Search." *Organization Science* 21 (5): 1016–33.

Kale, Prashant, Singh, Harbir, and Perlmutter, Howard. (2000). "Learning and Protection of Proprietary Assets in Strategic Alliances: Building Relational Capital." *Strategic Management Journal* 21 (3): 217–37.

Koza, Mitchell P., and Lewin, Arie Y. (1998). "The Co-evolution of Strategic Alliances." *Organization Science* 9 (3): 255–64.

Lavie, Dovev. (2007). "Alliance Portfolios and Firm Performance: A Study of Value Creation and Appropriation in the US Software Industry." *Strategic Management Journal* 28 (12): 1187–212.

Ledford, Heidi. (2006). "Kudos, Not Cash, Is the Real X-Factor." *Nature* 443 (7113): 733.

Owen-Smith, Jason, and Powell, Walter W. (2004). "Knowledge Networks as Channels and Conduits: The Effects of Spillovers in the Boston Biotechnology Community." *Organization Science* 15 (1): 5–21.

Parkhe, Arvind. (1993). "Strategic Alliance Structuring: A Game Theoretic and Transaction Cost Examination of Interfirm Cooperation." *Academy of Management Journal* 36 (4): 794–829.

Perkmann, Markus, and Walsh, Kathryn. (2007). "University-Industry Relationships and Open Innovation: Towards a Research Agenda." *International Journal of Management Reviews* 9 (4): 259–80.

Perkmann, Markus, and West, Joel. (2012). "Open Science and Open Innovation: Sourcing Knowledge from Universities." Available at Social Science Research Network: http://ssrn.com/abstract=2133397. Last Revision: April 10, 2014. Accessed on April 12, 2014.

Piller, Frank, and West, Joel. (2014). "Firms, Users, and Innovation: An Interactive Model of Coupled Open Innovation." In Henry Chesbrough, Wim Vanhaverbeke, and Joel West (eds.), *New Frontiers in Open Innovation*. Oxford: Oxford University Press, 29–49.

Powell, Walter W., and Grodal, Stine. (2005). "Networks of innovators." In Jan Fagerberg, David C. Mowery and Richard R. Nelson (eds.), *The Oxford Handbook of Innovation*. Oxford: Oxford University Press, 56–85.

Robinson, Sandra L., Kraatz, Matthew S., and Rousseau, Denise M. (1994). "Changing Obligations and the Psychological Contract: A Longitudinal Study." *Academy of Management Journal* 37 (1): 137–52.

Rohrbeck, René, Hoelzle, Katharina, and Gemünden, Hans Georg. (2009). "Opening Up for Competitive Advantage—How Deutsche Telekom Creates an Open Innovation Ecosystem." *R&D Management* 39 (4): 420–30.

Simcoe, Tim. (2006). "Open Standards and Intellectual Property Rights." In Henry Chesbrough, Wim Vanhaverbeke, and Joel West (eds.), *Open Innovation: Researching a New Paradigm*. Oxford: Oxford University Press, 161–183.

van de Vrande, Vareska, Vanhaverbeke, Wim, and Duysters, Geert. (2009). "External Technology Sourcing: The Effect of Uncertainty on Governance Mode Choice." *Journal of Business Venturing* 24 (1): 62–80.

Vanhaverbeke, Wim, and Cloodt, Myriam. (2006). "Open Innovation in Value Networks." In Henry Chesbrough, Wim Vanhaverbeke, and Joel West (eds.), *Open Innovation: Researching a New Paradigm*. Oxford: Oxford University Press, 258–281.

Vanhaverbeke, Wim, van de Vrande, Vareska, and Chesbrough, Henry (2008). "Understanding the Advantages of Open Innovation Practices in Corporate Venturing in Terms of Real Options." *Creativity and Innovation Management* 17 (4): 251–58.

Vanhaverbeke, Wim, West, Joel, and Chesbrough, Henry. (2014). "Surfing the New Wave of Open Innovation Research." In Henry Chesbrough, Wim Vanhaverbeke, and Joel West (eds.), *Open Innovation: New Frontiers and Applications*. Oxford: Oxford University Press.

von Hippel, Eric. (1988). *The Sources of Innovation*. New York: Oxford University Press.

West, Joel. (Forthcoming 2014). "Challenges of Funding Open Innovation Platforms: Lessons from Symbian Ltd." In Henry Chesbrough, Wim Vanhaverbeke, and Joel West (eds.), *New Frontiers in Open Innovation*. Oxford: Oxford University Press.

West, Joel, and Bogers, Marcel. (Forthcoming 2014). "Profiting from External Innovation: A Review of Research on Open Innovation." *Journal of Product Innovation Management*.

West, Joel, and O'Mahony, Siobhán. (2008). "The Role of Participation Architecture in Growing Sponsored Open Source Communities." *Industry and Innovation* 15 (2): 145–68.

West, Joel, Vanhaverbeke, Wim, and Chesbrough, Henry. (2006). "Open Innovation: A Research Agenda." In Henry Chesbrough, Wim Vanhaverbeke, and Joel West (eds.), *Open Innovation: Researching a New Paradigm*. Oxford: Oxford University Press, 285–307.

CHAPTER 2

Open Innovation Business Models and the Role of Interfirm Partnerships

Refik Culpan[1]

Open innovation has become a popular topic in management literature since Chesbrough published his book with the same title in 2003 (Chesbrough, 2003). Consequently, no longer does it only exist in the realm of conceptualization; at numerous companies it has been applied. Chesbrough (2003) suggests that companies using the closed innovation paradigm are fundamentally inwardly focused when it comes to the development of new ideas, knowledge, and creativity; the notion of the closed innovation paradigm is not unlike that of a castle or silo. The underlying logic of this approach implies a need for vertical integration with the aim of centralized, internal research and development. But the logic underlying the closed innovation paradigm has been challenged in the transformative era of e-business and social media, due to the interdependence of various firms on other firms for critical technologies and other resources. In an information economy, firms are operating in a more open, fast-paced global environment, where firms can create ideas for external or internal use and can access ideas from outside as well as from within. The availability and quality of these external ideas have changed the logic that once led to the formation of internal, centralized R&D silos and that have now evolved with the open innovation paradigm that enables a firm to leverage and share distributed knowledge. Now firms must manage innovation in an uncertain world, and they must adopt an open innovation paradigm and become strategically agile and aligned by leveraging multiple paths to market their in-house technologies, by sharing ideas and intellectual property (IP), and by accessing and integrating external knowledge through strategic alliances and collaborative partnerships.

The basic idea of open innovation is that firms seek out new knowledge and applications that lie outside their boundaries by collaborating with external sources, including suppliers, customers, independent organizations, and even competitors at times. New ideas from external sources may become the seed for an internal innovation process (outside-in process) or innovations developed internally may be exploited for new applications or uses in the external environment (inside-out process). The principal notion of open innovation reflects a paradigm shift in the generation of innovative ideas and practices from "closed innovation" to "open innovation." The former suggests that companies rely on internal knowledge generation for the purpose of controlling the innovation process, but the latter assumes firms can and should use external ideas in addition to internally generated ones, and pursue internal and external paths in advancing their products, technologies, or business models.

The open innovation paradigm creates an environment where firms welcome the external activities of other firms in exploring sources of innovation and opportunities. With rapid advances in network technology, virtualization, and cloud computing, more and more enterprises are pursuing strategic alliances and collaborative partnerships with other firms around the world to complement their strategic initiatives and strengthen their competitiveness by bypassing the comparatively slower and more costly process of building internal competencies, capabilities, and resource strengths to endeavor new innovations and market opportunities. Collaborative arrangements can help a firm to lower its costs or gain access to needed expertise and capabilities in idea generation, while strategic allies with distinctive competencies and technological know-how enable a firm to manage innovation in an uncertain world and pursue opportunities in unfamiliar international markets.

Indeed, strategic alliances have become so essential to exploring disruptive or radical innovations in many industries that they have become a core element of the open innovation paradigm, dynamic value propositions, and business strategy. Increasingly, firms are involved with more than one cooperative strategy. In addition to forming their own alliances with individual companies, a growing number of firms are joining forces in multiple cooperative strategies in a dynamic, collaborative alliance network to stimulate rapid value-creating innovations. Now almost all innovations require some form of collaborative arrangements for development or commercialization (within a complementary ecosystem), though the failure rate of such collaboration remains high. But, not surprisingly, many competitors have often collaborated in such areas as new-product and technology developments to build their innovative competencies.

Many authors have noted that we need to understand the underlying antecedents, applications, and consequences of open innovation (Allarakhia, Kilgour, and Fuller, 2010; Chesbrough, 2006, 2010; Chiaroni, Chiesa, and Frattini, 2009; Dahlander and Gann, 2010; West and Wood, 2013). In this chapter, I will begin a discussion of the main theoretical arguments for collaboration and inter-firm partnerships; and in the subsequent chapters, I will review some of the more practical benefits of open innovation paradigms in the different areas of business operations. I will link the rationale for collaboration with different forms and structures of strategic alliances, focusing on the specific cases of supplier relations and subcontracting, crowdsourcing, interfirm partnerships, innovation networks, and business-university R&D collaborations.

This chapter starts with the presentation of various open innovation business modes to enhance our understanding of their meanings and applications. More specifically, it discusses the utilization of interfirm partnerships between firms to achieve the goals of open innovation. Although there is no shortage of writings on open innovation from the last decade (Antikainen, Mäkipää, and Ahonen, 2010; Chesbrough, 2003; Grönlund, Sjödin, and Frishammar, 2010; Ili, Albers, and Miller, 2010; Ili, Albers, and Miller, 2010; Snow and Culpan, 2011), analyses of specific business approaches to open innovation are scare (Hoegl, Lichtenthaler, and Muethel, 2011; Kutvonen, 2011). Toward this end, the chapter makes a contribution to the current literature on OI by introducing and comparing some interfirm partnerships through which open innovation can be achieved successfully. It lays the groundwork for the rest of the book, which presents various descriptions, analyses, and case studies of open innovation in a strategic alliance context.

This chapter is structured as follows. First, it defines open innovation and its variety of forms and modes. Second, it explains and compares different business modes of open innovation in a systematic way by considering its sources, phases, governance, and impacts. And last, it highlights the significance of interfirm partnership in realizing open innovation and concludes with suggestions for future research and applications.

Innovation and Strategy

Innovation has long been a central consideration of business strategies within firms since it is considered a powerful instrument for gaining competitive advantages. To gain or sustain competitive advantage and assure above-average returns, companies are historically eager to allocate generous resources to their R&D endeavors; this is truer of some industries (e.g., medicine, pharmaceuticals, defense, electronics, and information systems) than it is of others (e.g., real estate, travel, and tool manufacturing). Nonetheless, there has been a common belief among business scholars and managers that business strategy should somehow incorporate product, technology, or business process innovations. Afuah (2009) claims that strategic innovation should incorporate new game strategies for competitive advantage. Moreover, Quinn and his colleagues claim that "knowledge building, innovation, and scientific-technological advances are critical ingredients for economic growth and competitive advantage" (1997, 19). Likewise, based on many years of research and company case studies, Christensen and Raynor (2003) argue that innovation can be a predictable process that delivers sustainable, profitable growth. A company business strategy often focuses on growth and always on competitive advantage as a fundamental element of long-term success. Booz & Company's research showed that nearly every company follows one of three fundamental innovation strategy models—Need Seekers, Market Readers, and Technology Drivers—where each model has its own distinct approach to the innovation process and to the customers and markets the companies serve (Jaruzelski and Holman, 2011).

With the coming of the era of open innovation, closed innovation endeavors have been determined to be costly and often unfruitful in delivering desired strategic outcomes; therefore, firms should seriously undertake alternative approaches in building or sharing their knowledge and technologies beyond their boundaries. Along these lines, Chesbrough and Appleyard (2007) offer the following argument: "Traditional business strategy has guided firms to develop defensible positions against the forces of competition and power in the value chain, implying the importance of constructing barriers to competition, rather than promoting openness. Recently, however, firms and even whole industries, such as the software industry, are experimenting with novel business models based on harnessing collective creativity through open innovation. The apparent success of some of these experiments challenges prevailing views of strategy" (57).

Basically open innovation has been the cornerstone of new strategic thinking, and an increasing number of firms have experimented and benefitted from incorporating open innovation in their business strategies, which have gone on to create archetypes for others. The use of open innovation in a strategic fashion has gone beyond the usual industries, like software, to almost all kinds of businesses. This point will be elaborated upon more in the next section.

Changing Notions of Competition and Innovation

Historically, the development of innovation has suffered from the separation—in location and time—of knowledge development, invention, and the commercialization process. As a result, innovation cycle times have often been measured in years for major technological developments. In modern business environments, however, innovation has become a major source of competitive advantage and rapid technological change and sophisticated customer expectations have placed a premium on rapid innovation development. In high-velocity global industries, a single organization is often not self-sufficient in developing and applying new knowledge to create new products, services, and technologies (Chesbrough, 2010; Dodgson, Gann, and Salter, 2006). OI is a fundamental change in the method of organizational idea generation and the way those ideas are introduced to market. In the traditional model of closed innovation, companies generated their ideas by working alone, managing the development of innovation internally. In the new OI model, the boundaries of the firm are permeable, and companies like Nokia, Qualcomm, and Oracle have found ways to harness external ideas while leveraging their in-house R&D. For example, Nokia adopted Microsoft's operating system for its mobile phones to keep up with the competition from Samsung and Apple in the smartphone market. By seeking out new knowledge and creative ideas wherever they may be found in the technological and business environment, firms adopting open innovation models can compress innovation cycle times and increase the frequency of innovation, as elements of enhanced strategic advantage. This is not to say that all companies or industries are conducive to open innovation. However, open innovation offers a viable alternative platform for knowledge creation and implementation in product, technology, or business-model development.

Companies must still perform the difficult and arduous work necessary to convert promising research results into products and services that satisfy customers' needs (Chesbrough, 2003). In this age of rapid technological advances—ranging from stem-cell discoveries, to information and communication revolutions, to alternative energy sources—the need for collaboration is unequivocal and imperative in order for firms to combine their knowledge bases and innovation-related competencies in the race to develop and commercialize products and technologies. In this sense, OI practices can be explained by a number of theories such as the resource-based view (Barney, 2001; Peteraf, 1993; Wernerfelt, 1984), dynamic capabilities of firms (Teece, 2007, 2009; Winter, 2003; Zollo and Winter, 2002), and knowledge management (Bhatt, 2001; Hedlund, 1994; Sanchez and Heene, 1997; Teece, 1998) for competitive advantage.

Munsch (2009) has defined three major benefits of open systems: "(1) New ideas can be contributed from a much larger range of parties and from different perspectives than what might be contributed internally. (2) Business and financial risk can be mitigated by the participation of one or more third parties and greater market scale can be achieved by joining forces. (3) Speed to market may be accelerated by particular contributions made by other partners or contributors in the ecosystem" (49). A fourth can be added to these three benefits: the wide acceptance and use of a company product and/or technology by customers as a result of the collaboration of large parties provides a competitive edge for a firm in relation to its competitors (e.g., the availability of over 750,000 apps for Apple iPads and iPhones).

Nonetheless, in order to attain and sustain the benefits of open innovation, a change in managerial mentality and corporate strategic orientation is essential, and a firm must be willing to open its doors to new ideas in order to fuel the development of original products, processes, or business systems. Creativity cannot or should not be confined within the firm's boundaries. New ideas leading to innovation may come from different external collaborators, including suppliers, customers, firms in related industries, and even perhaps competitors. In fact, corporate innovation strategy is forever morphing, and firms need to constantly adapt to changing environments. Consequently, firms need to deploy different OI models to accommodate the changing needs of a fast-paced, uncertain world as elaborated in this and following chapters.

Principal Models and Modes of Open Innovation

Principal Models of Open Innovation

As the benefits of open innovation have been recognized, several models and modes of this new strategic approach have emerged. Some firms have invited creative ideas from the external environment (selected professionals or the public at large), while others have formed a network or consortium of collaborators. Still others have released their proprietary knowledge (i.e., patents) to others to commercialize new drugs, goods, or technologies. In essence, open innovation can be materialized either as an inbound innovation process utilizing new ideas from the external environment or an outbound innovation process offering the firms' proprietary knowledge to others or a combination of both types, as depicted in Table 2.1.

Enkel and her colleagues (2009) define three core models that can be differentiated in OI: an outside-in process, an inside-out process, and a coupled process (a combination of the first two).

An *outside-in process* refers to the enriching of a company's own knowledge base through the integration of suppliers, customers, and external knowledge sourcing (Enkel et al., 2009). A number of scholars (Laursen and Salter, 2006; Lettl, Herstatt, and Gemuenden, 2006) claim this process can increase a company's innovativeness. Engel and her colleagues (2009) argue that "the outside-in process reflects companies' experience that the locus of knowledge creation does not necessarily equal the locus of innovation" (313). In fact, in their study of 144 companies, Enkel and Gassmann (2008) found that knowledge sources are mostly clients (78 percent), suppliers (61 percent), and competitors (49 percent), as well as public and commercial research institutions (21 percent). Furthermore, they noted the following: "A surprisingly large body of other sources was used (65%), namely non-customers, non-suppliers, and partners from other industries. Within this process, we can see an increasing awareness of the importance of innovation networks, new forms of customer integration, such as crowdsourcing, mass customization, and customer community integration, as well as the use of innovation intermediaries, such as Innocentive, NineSigma, or yet2.com" (Enkel et al., 2009, 313).

And *inside-out process*, however, refers to making gains by bringing ideas to market, selling IP, and multiplying technology by transferring ideas to other users. With this process, firms try to externalize their knowledge and innovation to bring ideas to market faster than they could through internal development. Moreover, there would be occasions where unused IP of the firm could be utilized with partnering with another firm. By using licensing, joint ventures, spin-offs, and so forth, firms can expand their markets beyond their traditional sectors so that they are able to generate more revenues. A number of large multinational

Table 2.1 Open Innovation Models and Specific Modes

Open Innovation Models	Open Innovation Modes in Ecosystems			
	Third-party apps	Crowdsourcing	Interfirm partnerships	Business-university R&D collaborations
Outside-in process	o	o	o	o
Inside-out process			o	o
Coupled process			o	o

companies, for example, use such an out-licensing strategy. Out of this orientation, newer business patterns—like corporate venturing (Vanhaverbeke et al., 2008), new ventures and spin-offs (Chesbrough, 2007), and cross-industry innovation (the commercialization of one's own technologies in new markets) (Gassmann and Enkel, 2010)—have been developed.

A *coupled process* refers to a combination of the previous two processes; basically it points to cocreation among (mainly) complementary partners through interfirm collaborations where each party commits some resources and assets for the success of the venture. Enkel and her colleagues (2009) argue that companies that establish the coupled process combine the outside-in process (to gain external knowledge) with the inside-out process (to bring ideas to market) and, in doing so, jointly develop and commercialize innovation. They point out that examples of this kind of model usually involve open source project development (Von Hippel and Von Krogh, 2006); peer production through communities (Lakhani et al., 2008), consumers (Hienerth, 2006; Lettl et al., 2006), end users (Franke and Shah, 2003), universities, or research organizations (Perkmann and Walsh, 2007); and partners from other industries (Gassmann and Enkel, 2010). Furthermore, Enkel and her coauthors (2009) report in their study that the companies integrated external knowledge on 35 percent of all R&D projects and used possible external partners in different ways. For example, 83 percent mainly linked with noncompeting market and technology leaders, 79 percent with world-class universities, and 61 percent with local firms (Enkel et al., 2009).

In a close examination of the use of the three models described above, one can observe various modes of application—including third-party apps, crowdsourcing, interfirm partnership, and business-university partnerships—in the context of open ecosystems as shown in Table 2.1. A clarification of the concept of innovation modes in ecosystems in relation to the three OI models mentioned above illustrates a wide range of OI applications in practice.

Matching Innovation Strategy to Innovation Ecosystem

As Adner (2006) claims, most breakthrough innovations do not succeed in isolation. They need complementary innovations to attract customers. With this premise, Adner (2006) defines *innovation ecosystems* as "the collaborative arrangements through which firms combine their individual offerings into a coherent, customer facing solution" (98). Furthermore, Adner and Kapoor (2010) argue that the success of an innovating firm often depends on the efforts of other innovators in its environment; they add that challenges faced by external innovators affect the focal firm's performance. To address this, they first characterize the external environment according to the structure of interdependence by following the flow of inputs and outputs in the ecosystem to distinguish between upstream components that are bundled by the focal firm and downstream complements that are bundled by the firm's customers. The authors hypothesize that the effects of external innovation challenges depend not only on the magnitude of innovations, but also on their location in the ecosystem relative to the focal firm. They identify a key asymmetry that results from the location of challenges relative to a focal firm—greater upstream innovation challenges in components enhance the benefits that accrue to technology leaders, while greater downstream innovation challenges in complements erode these benefits. They further contend that the effectiveness of vertical integration as a strategy to manage ecosystem interdependence increases over the course of a technology's life cycle. After exploring their arguments in the context of the global semiconductor lithography equipment industry from its emergence in 1962 to 2005 across nine distinct technology generations, they find strong empirical support for their arguments.

Modes of Open Innovation

Based on this concept of innovation ecosystems, a variety of innovation approaches can be pursued. As more companies adopt of open innovation paradigms, we need to distinguish and analyze different modes of innovation ecosystems to better understand and more effectively apply this popular development. For this purpose, we can identify four major modes of open innovation: (1) leveraging innovation ecosystems through the involvement of interested parties (excluding interfirm partnerships) for the development and use of third-party apps, (2) crowdsourcing, in the form of inviting the public at large to contribute new ideas, (3) building interfirm partnerships between firms to collaborate in launching new products or technologies, and (4) business-university R&D collaborations. We must state, however, that these different modes can overlap conceptually. Nonetheless, for the sake of simplicity, we will treat them separately with distinct examples and cases. A quick review of each mode is discussed below.

Leveraging Innovation through Ecosystems for the Development and Use of Third-Party Apps

Innovation ecosystems refer to the interdependence of focal or sponsoring firms with its complementors (e.g., suppliers, subcontractors, customers). Adner and Kapor (2010) aptly underline the value creation in innovation ecosystems by examining the structure of technological interdependence that affects firm performance in the new technology generation. In addition, West and Wood (2013) point out evolving innovation ecosystems with a reference to the Symbian platform. The two key factors they identified "in the success of general-purpose computing platforms are the creation of technical standards architecture and managing an ecosystem of third party suppliers of complementary products." These innovation ecosystems are more a reality in the information and computer technology (ICT) industry today than in any other industries, but creating platforms is the common theme beyond the ICT industry. In fact, as Gawer claims (2011), "Industry platforms are technological building blocks (that can be technologies, products, or services) that act as a foundation on top of which an array of firms, organized in a set of interdependent firms (sometimes called an industry 'ecosystem'), develop a set of inter-related products, technologies and services"(287).

Third-party applications are particularly ubiquitous in the ICT sector, where numerous programs are written to work within operating systems developed by companies other than the provider of the application. For example, Microsoft systems come with several software applications not originally developed by Microsoft. Apple products and Linux systems provide additional examples of the ubiquitous use of third-party applications in the information systems.

Third-party applications can be stand-alone programs, or they can be small plug-ins that add functionality to an existing parent program. The former category is endless, while the latter is limited in scope. On a typical system, stand-alone third-party applications include dozens of programs. Web browsers like Opera, Safari, and Firefox and email clients like Thunderbird, The Bat!, and Pegasus are some examples of popular stand-alone third-party applications. Third-party apps are especially prevalent in information and communication devices, such as smartphones, media players, tablets, and game players. These apps include a great variety of tools, including maps, navigation systems, film and music players, social network programming, weather, and financial information, to name a few. Apple Incorporated is the champion for third-party apps, having more than 750,000 apps for its iPhones, iPads, and iPods. Just the sheer size of availability of that many apps gives the company a competitive advantage over its competitors and points out a strategic advantage of open innovation. The use of third parties to develop additional apps increases the convenience of the core, or original, software at no cost to the originating firm. Customers are given a wide choice of functional uses, which increases demand for the core product and builds in switching costs for competitive products. As a result, it is no surprise that technology firms encourage app developers to come up with new apps that appeal to consumers. In fact, it is a win-win situation for the company and its app developers.

This innovation ecosystem mode reflects a special version of open innovation benefitting the firm without imposing extra burden on its own resources. Think of the amount of resources and time a smartphone builder would have to spend in developing thousands of such apps by itself. Without such an open innovation mechanism in place, no company could effectively handle such voluminous app developments. Nonetheless, more than cost savings, it is the creativity gains that underline open ecosystems. Although this is a special form of open innovation more relevant to ICT companies, it illustrates value creation and capture through numerous industry platforms. It demonstrates a successful OI application where there is a clearly synergistic relationship between technology sponsors and third-party app developers. That is why latecomers to the market, such as Microsoft in the area of smartphones, have been encouraging app developers to create more apps for their products: more apps translate into greater acceptance of their products by consumers. In these open ecosystems, the sponsor is able to work with its third-party developers as its complementors, which can generate mutual benefits for both. For example, in the US video game industry, those firms that are able to produce games in-house (ensuring the availability of a wide range of games at the console's launch) and that encourage third-party development of games (to ensure the number of game titles grows quickly) have been quite successful.

Crowdsourcing: Inviting the Public at Large to Contribute New Ideas

Creative new ideas are the essence of innovation, and they may come from many different sources. In this crowdsourcing mode of open innovation, firms invite virtually anyone to make suggestions for the development of a new product or service and promise to reward those idea champions once their suggestions are selected. To illustrate this particular model, Proctor & Gamble's experience teaches us a valuable lesson. P&G has launched an online site called "Connect + Develop" through which anyone can make a suggestion for a new product on the company's website. P&G's website describes this innovation strategy as follows: "P&G's 'Connect + Development' open innovation has established more than 1000 action agreements with innovative partners. Connect + Development enables us to share our R&D and brand strength with partners' worldwide, bringing great ideas to market—and into the lives of consumers—faster" (www .pg.com, 2010). In chapter 7, DePhilippi, Dumas, and Bhatia use the case of Xerox-P&G's cocreation of innovation to explicate this point further.

P&G claims that more than 50 percent of product initiatives involve significant collaboration with outside innovators. It solicits promising products, technologies, business models, methods, trademarks, or designs that can help improve the lives of the world's consumers from any venue. P&G also seeks new ideas for the further development of existing brands. If there is a promising idea, the Connect + Develop team at P&G works with the idea creator. As a result, by this open innovation platform, P&G has developed such famous brands as Swiffer Duster and Olay Derma-Pad among others.

This business mode is similar to the first one described above, but it differs in two ways. First, it can be used by all kinds of firms, not just technology-based firms in the ICT industries (like Apple, Google, Samsung, and Microsoft). Second, there is no definite platform to start with; thus any idea about a new product or service is welcome as long as it is feasible. As a result, many idea creators can make suggestions for creative products that could be passed onto the company's R&D process for assessment and possible commercialization. Of course, out of the many suggestions made, probably only a few of them will be deemed feasible for commercialization or application. Afuah and Tucci (2012) argue that under certain circumstances crowdsourcing transforms distant searches into local searches, improving the efficiency and effectiveness of problem solving. "Under such circumstances a firm may choose to crowdsource problem solving rather than solve the problem internally or contract it to a designated supplier. These circumstances depend on the characteristics of the problem, the knowledge required for the solution, the crowd, and the solutions to be evaluated"(Afuah and Tucci, 2012, 335).

Nonetheless, the crowdsourcing mode for open innovation generates a large pool of ideas for the company without any or with only a nominal cost. It can generate new ideas from practically anyone around the world, which translates into a vast knowledge source for innovation for the company to exploit. Although it is an important source for open innovation, in this book we will primarily focus on the two modes that we will explore next.

Building Interfirm Partnerships to Generate New Ideas and Knowledge

As Chesbrough (2006) suggests, the "open business model" in general calls for companies to make greater use of external ideas and technologies in their own businesses, while letting their unused knowledge be used by other companies. "This requires each company to open up its business model to let more external ideas and technology flow in from outside and let more internal knowledge flow to the outside. With a more open business model, open innovation offers the prospect of lower costs for innovation, faster times to market, and the chance to share risks with others" (Chesbrough, 2006, xiii). According to Chesbrough (2006), an open business model uses this unique division of innovation labor between the firm and its collaborator by both creating value and capturing a portion of that value.

This type of open business mode may involve all three OI models—outside-in, inside-out, or coupled processes. A company can collaborate with other firms in the same industry or in a different industry to acquire new knowledge. In such a collaborative mode, the firm seeks out and uses the knowledge resources of others for innovation in collaboration with the creators. Alternatively, it can also share its idle knowledge resources, such as registered but unused patents, and other unemployed research outcomes with other firms that have the potential to utilize them for successful applications. Also, the firm wishing to collaborate with others can use a coupled process by combining both outside-in and inside-out exchanges. In this fashion, firms will be able to exploit the competencies of others. Such a business mode creates a win-win situation for the participants as they enjoy lower costs of innovation, faster time to market, and risk sharing as well. In fact, companies like Qualcomm (in cellular phone technology), Genzyme (in biotechnology), and Chicago (in musical stage productions and a movie) have already benefitted from using such open business modes.

This mode of open innovation through interfirm partnership is more common and comprehensive than the others and requires a firm to build interfirm connections for innovation into its more general business strategy. It goes beyond just the establishment of a website or a collaborative product-development team to fundamental changes in the firm's structure and culture in order to accommodate open innovation as an ongoing activity of the organization.

Such innovation collaboration sometimes involves establishing a network of firms to collaborate to develop or enhance the applicability of a specific product or technology. Snow and his colleagues (2009, 2011) call this pattern a "collaborative community of firms." In this mode, a leading firm invites and organizes a number of firms to participate and collaborate on an innovative project. Through a community of firms, numerous firms work together to generate an open innovation model. Snow and his colleagues argue that "in cases where knowledge is widely distributed, the locus of innovation is a community of firms, not individual firms. Technological advances and complexities trigger founding firms(s) to initiate, and member firms to participate in, a community-based organization by engaging in innovative collaboration and expecting to benefit various ways" (Snow, Strauss, and Culpan, 2009:59). To illustrate this particular model, IBM's Blade.org initiative is worthy of mention.

> Blade.org is a collaborative community of firms focused on the development and adoption of open blade server platforms, an innovative computer server technology developed in late 1990s. Blade.org was established in early 2006 by IBM and seven other founding firms to increase the number of blade platform "solutions" available for customers and to accelerate the process of bringing them to market. From the original eight founding companies, Blad.org has grown to a community of more than 100 member firms including leading blade hardware and software providers, developers, distribution partners and end users from around the world. (Snow, Strauss, and Culpan, 2009, 62)

As described above, building a community of firms helps to launch innovation, accelerate commercialization of a product or service, and encourages a wider usage among its member firms. Snow and Culpan (2011) claim a collaborative community of firms is an organizational form to be used increasingly in knowledge-intensive industries where continuous innovation is strategic imperative.

Business-University R&D Collaborations

Business firms have been collaborating with public and private research institutions for many years to develop new products and technologies; however, the emergence of the open innovation paradigm has been changing these relationships, as elaborated upon by Chinta and Culpan in chapter 9, where the expansion of portfolio partners is discussed. Businesses and universities share a common interest in developing new knowledge that can be used in creation of new technologies and products through collaborations. (For that matter, we could include other government and private research institutions, but in this book we will focus only on business-university collaborations.) By participating in all phases of knowledge management (creation, transfer, and utilization) through collaborations, businesses and universities complement and benefit each other.

Nonetheless, significant challenges arise when business-university collaborations are viewed through an OI lens. Chapter 9 advances our thinking about open innovation in the context of business-university collaborations by exploring policy and practices in the United States and several other countries. Furthermore, Perkmann and Walsh (2007) note that although differences exist in university-industry collaborations across industries and scientific disciplines, how such collaborative relationships are organized and managed has a direct and important impact on the benefits that are incurred from them.

Interfirm Partnerships for Open Innovation

As stated above, interfirm partnerships happen to be the most common form of open innovation. Hence, I will elucidate the nature and various forms of interfirm partnerships that can be used for open innovation. Interfirm partnerships can be classified in two general categories—namely, equity-based alliances, which include equity joint ventures (hereafter I will refer to them as *joint ventures*), equity block ownership (one company buying a portion of equities of another company), and venture capital (VC) investments, and nonequity type alliances, including licensing, bilateral R&D agreements, network organizations, collaborative communities of firms, and consortia. See Figure 2.1. Although these interfirm partnerships may be formed for a variety of reasons (e.g., market penetration and growth, to compete against a powerful rival, to develop a supplier or production partnership), here I will be addressing those interfirm partnerships created only for innovation purposes, encompassing both product and technology innovations. Obviously, equity investments provide investors with some power and control over their invested organization; consequently, more investments mean more control. In a joint venture (JV), a parent company with higher equity investment can exercise greater control over the venture. In the case of a JV, a new legal entity is created by the parent companies, whereas in block ownership and VC investments, the investing firms wield their controls proportionately with their equity investments.

When the number of partners is considered in addition to the equity involvement by the partners, interfirm partnerships can be viewed as *dyadic partnerships* or *multiple partnerships*, as displayed in Table 2.2. In this study, both dyadic and multiple partnerships will be considered with respect to the equity positions of

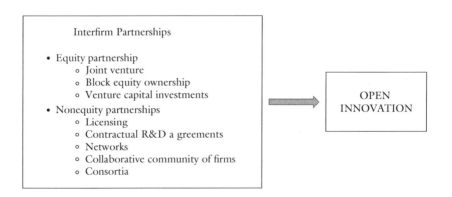

Figure 2.1   Various Forms of Interfirm Partnerships for Open Innovation

Table 2.2 Interfirm Partnerships and Partner Involvements

	Equity Investments	Nonequity Involvements
Dyadic Partners	JV with two partners Block equity ownership Venture capital investment	Licensing R&D Agreements
Multiple Partners	JV with multiple partners	Networks Collaborative community of firms Consortia

the partners. Consequently under equity-based partnerships there may be joint ventures with only two partners or multiple partners; some venture capital (VC) firms invest in start-up firms to promote a new technology (e.g., Intel's Intel Capital investing in complementary start-up companies), and another type of partnerships is called block equity ownerships whereone company acquires some shares of another (e.g., Renault's purchase of 44 percent of Nissan's equity shares). Under nonequity partnerships, there may also be bilateral R&D agreements, networks, communities of firms, and consortia. All these collaborative arrangements can be used to develop or share new ideas or knowledge so that the engaging firms can build new competencies to innovate new products and technologies.

Furthermore, as presented in Table 2.3, I consider the modes of interfirm partnerships for open innovations in terms of four dimensions: (1) source, (2) phase, (3) governance form, and (4) impact. These dimensions for each strategic alliance mode for open innovation present special characteristics that will be briefly discussed below. To fully understand the dynamics, relationships, and outcomes of such interfirm collaborations and appreciate open innovation, these characteristics need to be defined. In our analysis, we treat alliance types according to OI processes—the directions of knowledge flows, whether they are an inside-out or outside-in process. Firms can use either process, but outside-in processes are used most often to acquire new ideas and knowledge assets.

The Source of Open Innovation

In interfirm partnerships, the knowledge that yields the creative ideas for open innovation can be developed or acquired from partnering firm(s). This means the focal firm has several choices for initiating open innovation through strategic partnership through one of the equity-based or nonequity-based partnerships, as shown in Table 2.2. It must be noted, however, that there are some difficulties that companies encounter when they seek out external knowledge and technologies to combine with their own knowledge assets. Chesbrough (2006) identifies the following issues in accessing external information: managing and protecting identity, managing contamination of risk, identifying useful and nonobvious sources, fostering a two-sided market (linking plentiful sources of ideas to a plentiful group of potential buyers), and scaling efficiently with volume. Being

Table 2.3 Interfirm Partnerships for Open Innovation and Their Properties

Interfirm Partnerships	Source of OI	Phase of OI	Governance of OI	Impact of OI
Joint Ventures	Partner firms' knowledge repertoires and assets	Development and application (inside out)	Joint venture's CEO and BOD as appointed and controlled by parent firms	Generation of new products or technologies as shared by parent companies
Equity Block Ownership	Target or investing firm's knowledge assets	Exchange and co-develop knowledge (outside in; inside out)	Equity ownership by a firm gives voice in its management	Capitalization on joint knowledge in development of new products or technologies
Bilateral R&D Agreements (outside in)	Reaching out to new ideas and knowledge of another firm	Development and application in primary value chain activities	The parties agree on a protocol in sharing the knowledge and its outcome; semistructured	Leverage another firm's idea and knowledge; benefit mutually
Licensing	Licensor's knowledge repertoire and assets	Application of knowledge sharing	Licensing protocol setting norms for both licensor and licensee	Leverage another firm's idea and knowledge; benefit mutually
Bilateral R&D Agreements (inside out)	Collaborate with a capable organization with relevant new idea and knowledge	Commercialization of donor firm's proprietary knowledge	The parties agree on a protocol in sharing the knowledge and its outcome; semistructured	Leverage company knowledge otherwise remains unused; benefit mutually
Networks	Member firms' knowledge assets	Development and application (outside in; inside out)	Network center coordinating relationships; semistructured	Share jointly produced knowledge and benefit from the innovation
Collaborative Community of Firms	Network of firms with complementary technologies	Development and application (outside in; inside out)	A focal firm initiates and controls the structure with a protocol; fully structured	Resource and benefit sharing among member firms; reduced costs and risk
Consortia	Knowledge assets of numerous member firms	Development and applications (inside out; outside in)	Agreed protocol dictating relationships	Knowledge sharing among members; competency building

mindful of these issues, companies can choose a particular source or a combination of sources for their open innovation enterprises. Of course, industry characteristics can also influence the type of sources to be employed. For example, a start-up firm in information and computer technologies may find financial support from a VC firm while firms in new material sciences and stem-cell research may seek collaboration with universities to achieve tangible results.

The Phase of Innovation

As stated above, open innovation theory suggests that the process of generating new ideas should not be restricted to internal capabilities and resources. The generation of new ideas often pertains to an early stage in the development of innovation. However, experience teaches us that not all new ideas produce innovation; therefore, during the initial phase of development the company needs to develop mechanisms or systems to rigorously examine new ideas and determine which projects warrant pursuing further or modifying the original projects.

Open innovation can also be initiated at a later stage of the development process, a more common practice at many technology and pharmaceutical companies. This relates to a firm's ability to transfer intellectual property (IP) from another firm and then to transform that IP into a new product or service for commercialization. In this mode, firms can benefit from sharing their IPs with other companies that have the motivation and capabilities to turn IPs into marketable products or technologies. In this case, open innovation can help the company convert prototypes or newly developed technologies into commercial products. As Chesbrough (2006) reports, there are many unused patents at major companies that can be commercialized in collaboration with entrepreneurial firms. Thus, the innovation process can occur at two stages—namely, idea development and idea application.

The Governance of Open Innovation

Depending on the equity involvement by and the number of participants, which may range from two collaborating firms to a large number of parties in an OI process, the governance form of the open business model can vary considerably. In the case of OI models with equity investments, the investing parties want to have control over the target enterprise. For example, a joint venture, as an independent legal entity established by parent companies, is controlled by its parent companies; likewise, a newly established enterprise by an inventor and a VC firm is managed jointly by its originators, with clarifications on the relationships between the parties and the rights and responsibilities of each party. In chapter 3, Rijakker and her colleagues point out implementation issues and routes to success for open innovation through R&D partnership, while Tjemkes et al., in chapter 10, elaborate on the role of alliance portfolios in relation to venture start-ups and radical innovation.

In the cases of nonequity arrangements, partner relationships are defined by a contract that usually spells out the specific rights and obligations of each party concerning its contributions, expectations, and responsibilities, as well as the benefits from the outcome. Depending on the type of nonequity alliance arrangement, parties are expected to define in their contracts in concrete terms the ways that sharing in the expected innovation will affect their resource commitments, roles, responsibilities, and benefits. For example, in the case of a collaborative community of firms, it is necessary to articulate the purpose of creating the community and the requirements for participation; additionally, the administrative structure and procedures must be defined. In the creation of a collaborative community of firms, the leading and founding firms play key roles in laying the groundwork and developing the rules of the game for the total group. Snow and his colleagues (2009) elaborate on the creation and development of a community of firms as follows:

> With respect to community creation, a carefully crafted mission and vision that contains both shared technical and economic interests facilitate the attraction of firms which are willing and able to contribute the creative commons of community . . . With respect to community development, important design elements of the governance structure are bylaws and represent the legal organization of the community and the provide clarity and comfort that the community is safe environment for commercial activities, administrative services and volunteer committees that perform both technical and marketing work and that maintain the community's intellectual commons (repository of shared knowledge) (61)

The above explanations show that a community of firms reflects a fully structured design specifying the roles and expectations of each member and the committees running the technical and marketing activities of the community.

In an agreement that creates a dualistic collaboration for sharing IP knowledge, the parties will sign a protocol defining each one's rights and responsibilities and the way in which the parties share both the costs and benefits of the anticipated innovation. Although designing comprehensive agreements will minimize potential conflicts later, there will always be room for potential conflicts or clashes between the parties. Hence, as a number of scholars note (Cullen, Johnson, and Sakano, 2000; Culpan, 2008; Das and Teng, 1998; Gulati, 1995; Reuer and Ariño, 2007), trust between the parties plays a significant role in ensuring smooth partner relationships and the realization of the objectives of the collaborative venture. This particular aspect is examined in detail in chapter 14.

The Impacts of Open Innovation

OI models provide alternative platforms by which companies can stimulate creative ideas without straining their own resources, in the case of outside-in open innovation, or by benefitting from their unused knowledge repertoires, in the case of inside-out open innovation. In either case, parties that depend on a strategic alliance mode can enjoy the benefits generated by new products or technologies by leveraging their partner's (or partners') new ideas and knowledge. Through such collaborations, firms can harnes and leveragetheir knowledge and experiences more systematically to attain above-average returns and competitive advantages over rivals. De Jong and his colleagues (2008) assert that "enterprises draw on alternative pathways to bring new ideas to market and to benefit from external knowledge to discover and realize innovative opportunities" (4). In addition, by building collaborative ties for innovation, firms reduce the cost of acquiring the knowledge necessary to drive the innovation process while sharing the risks of development. Firms that employ outside-in innovation also gain by leveraging the costs of unused intellectual property.

For firms that intend to use interfirm partnerships for open innovation, it is important for them to know how successful each mode may be and in which contexts each mode would be most effective. Identifying some common open innovation strategic partnerships and their properties, as presented in Table 2.3, helps both researchers and managers to evaluate their utility in the business ecosystems.

Discussion

As explained above, open innovation through interfirm partnerships provides the firm an unconventional but effective platform to launch original products, technologies, or business models. There are, however, two important points that deserve attention. First, open innovation will not or should not replace conventional in-house R&D efforts, but rather it should be considered as complementary to internally developed new ideas and knowledge. When a firm stops its in-house innovation and outsources creative production and marketing entirely, it will not be able to sustain its competitive advantage for a long time. However, firms supplementing their in-house innovation with open innovation through interfirm partnerships will be in a better position than those firms using only closed innovation models and modes.

Second, there are certain challenges and risks involved in engaging in open innovation. For example, the effective implementation of OI models requires a change in managerial mind-set so as to welcome collaborative knowledge sharing with other firms. I will elaborate further on these challenges in chapter 14. There are also difficulties when working in a collaborative venture with partners (especially multiple parties) that might have different managerial attitudes, aspirations, and expectations, as well as different organizational cultures. As Chesbrough (2006) aptly notes, one major obstacle to OI applications is the "not invented here" syndrome among managers, resulting in a resistance to the ideas from the external sources. If employees see open innovation, particularly outside-in open innovation, as a threat, they will resist it. After testing open innovation forms—both outside-in (inbound) and inside-out (outbound)—versus closed innovation, Hoegl and his colleagues (Hoegl et al., 2011) conclude that employee attitudes that favor internal innovation often impede the successful implementation of open innovation strategies. They also found that a group of companies that pursued both inbound and outbound open innovation achieved the highest average return on sales. However, the companies that pursued traditional closed innovation strategies had a higher average return on sales, as compared to the group of companies that transferred their own technology to others without acquiring much technology from external sources. These findings suggest that a focus only on outbound innovation may be disadvantageous, as the firm risks transferring its crown jewels. But, it should be noted that the study by Hoegl and his colleagues (2011) was conducted with some German companies whose managers may have more a conservative mentality when it comes to the generation of innovation since many German companies are privately owned firms and cautious about interfirm collaborations. Nonetheless, their study underscores the need to change employee attitudes when managers aim to employ open innovation strategies. Managers, they note, need to communicate their open innovation strategies to employees. Firms should have executives who champion innovation and devise suitable incentives and organizational structures to encourage open innovation. Also, it must be noted that the culture of an organization must support open innovation endeavors. To ensure the success of an OI process, a firm must have in place certain values and norms in an environment that supports open-minded thinking, that is accepting of new ideas from external sources, and that embraces a willingness to exchange information with the external world.

There are some additional challenges and risks involved in employing OI models. First of all, there is a partnership risk, meaning that the firm depends upon its collaborator's goodwill and commitment to the joint project. However, there might be difficulties in working together, especially with multiple parties that have different aspirations and expectations and different organizational cultures and managerial attitudes when it comes to collaborative ventures and the risks of losing proprietary knowledge or the possibility of creating a potential competitor. In addition, Adler (2012) aptly points out two other types of risk in innovation ventures: co-innovation risk and adoption risk. "Co-innovation risk refers to the extent to which the success of the firm depends upon the successful commercialization of other innovations while adoption risk means the extent to which partners need to adopt the firm innovation before end consumers have a chance to assess the full value proposition" (Adler, 2012, 6). In chapter 14, I will examine further the issues of open innovation applications and their effective management.

Today, the costly, complex, and risky process of developing new products and technologies requires companies to consider alternative models and approaches. Building interfirm partnerships for open innovation offers a sound alternative approach to conventional ways of developing and researching new products and services, bringing them to market, or improving existing ones. For example, a recent accidental fire in Boeing's popular Dreamliner 787 jets has forced Boeing to seek help outside the aerospace industry to determine the precise cause of the two malfunctioning lithium-ion batteries. Consequently, Boeing CEO, Jim McNerney, discretely persuaded the CEOs of General Motors and General Electric to lend Boeing their best electrical experts to work on this problem.

In this current chapter, by examining different interfirm partnerships for open innovation, we provide useful insights into the use of such modes and their properties. Although OI business models have been the subject of many studies, this study specifically deals with the modes and subtleties involved in employing interfirm partnerships as the dominant modes for open innovation. The implications of this study for researchers and managers can be outlined as follows.

For researchers, it may stimulate further studies to consider industry-specific models and the number of participants in a particular model (e.g., collaborations between two parties, few parties, or numerous parties). Learning about different governance forms for interfirm partnerships (e.g., joint ventures, diversified business groups) will provide additional insights into open innovation as a competitive tool. Furthermore, in studying the potentials and challenges of the transfer of knowledge and experience from one firm to another, the following chapters in this book will be helpful in drawing some general conclusions for OI success.

For managers, the current study provides an opportunity to appreciate various interfirm alliance arrangements (e.g., forming a joint venture, buying the equity of another firm, establishing an inventor-VC partnership, licensing, building a community of firms, developing a network organization, and consortia) as a tool for open innovation. Thereby, they might ponder the appropriateness of a particular interfirm partnership by better understanding the properties of these alliances, including the sources of knowledge, phases of knowledge generation, governance forms of the alliance, and ultimate benefits from the partnership. Consequently, managers will be able to make more informed decisions for open innovation through interfirm partnerships as a viable strategic option for competitive advantage and rent generation.

In conclusion, chapter 2 provides a systematic comparison of different interfirm partnerships for open innovation by considering the different modes and the sources, phases, governance forms, and implications of such business arrangements. In addition, it lays the ground for the following chapters to examine in more detail open innovation through interfirm partnerships and university-business collaborations. For example, interfirm partnerships will be examined in specific industries (see chapters 4, 5, and 14) and countries (see chapters 5 and 14) to understand them fully and to realize their potential benefits and their results. It would still be interesting to learn, for example, the various issues relating to collaborations between firms in the same versus different industries and between firms and other research organizations (e.g., universities) in creating new ideas and knowledge (see chapter 8). Also, it would be interesting to know the success rates of different OI applications through interfirm partnerships (see chapters 3 and 11).

In the closing chapter (chapter 14), I will elaborate further on major challenges and prospects of strategic alliances for open innovation where business strategies and managerial issues and future trends in open innovation will be discussed.

Note

1. The author thanks Joel West and Jeff Tsai for their insightful comments on earlier drafts of this chapter.

References

Adler, R. (2012). *The Wide Lens: A New Strategy for Innovation*. New York: Portfolio/Penguin.

Adner, R. (2006). "Match Your Innovation Strategy to Your Innovation Ecosystem." *Harvard Business Review* 84 (4): 98.

Adner, Ron. (2012). *The Wide Lens: A New Strategy for Innovation*. Penguin.

Adner, Ron, and Kapoor, R. (2010). "Value Creation in Innovation Ecosystems: How the Structure of Technological Interdependence Affects Firm Performance in New Technology Generations." *Strategic Management Journal* 31 (3): 306–33. doi:10.1002/smj.821.

Afuah, A. (2009). *Strategic Innovation*. New York: Routledge.

Afuah, A., and Tucci, C. L. (2012). "Crowdsourcing as a Solution to Distant Search." *Academy of Management Review* 37 (3): 355–75. doi:10.5465/amr.2010.0146.

Allarakhia, M., Kilgour, D. M., and Fuller, J. D. (2010). "Modelling the Incentive to Participate in Open Source Biopharmaceutical Innovation." *R&D Management* 40 (1): 50–66. doi:10.1111/j.1467-9310.2009.00577.x.

Antikainen, M., Mäkipää, M., and Ahonen, M. (2010). "Motivating and Supporting Collaboration in Open Innovation." *European Journal of Innovation Management* 13 (1): 100–119. doi:http://dx.doi.org.ezaccess.libraries.psu.edu/10.1108/14601061011013258.

Barney, J. B. (2001). "Resource-Based Theories of Competitive Advantage: A Ten-Year Retrospective on the Resource-Based View." *Journal of Management* 27 (6): 643–50. doi:10.1177/014920630102700602.

Bhatt, G. D. (2001). "Knowledge Management in Organizations: Examining the Interaction between Technologies, Techniques, and People." *Journal of Knowledge Management* 5 (1): 68–75. doi:10.1108/13673270110384419.

Chesbrough, H. (2010). *Open Services Innovation: Rethinking Your Business to Grow and Compete in a New Era*, 1st ed. Hoboken, NJ: Jossey-Bass.

Chesbrough, H. W. (2003). *Open Innovation: The New Imperative for Creating and Profiting from Technology*. Harvard Business School Press.

Chesbrough, H. W. (2006). *Open Business Models: How to Thrive in the New Innovation Landscape*. Harvard Business School Press.

Chesbrough, H. W., and Appleyard, M. M. (2007). "Open Innovation and Strategy." *California Management Review* 50 (1): 57–76.

Chiaroni, D., Chiesa, V., and Frattini, F. (2009). "Investigating the Adoption of Open Innovation in the Bio-pharmaceutical Industry: A Framework and an Empirical Analysis." *European Journal of Innovation Management* 12 (3): 285–305. doi:http://dx.doi.org.ezaccess.libraries.psu.edu/10.1108/14601060910974192.

Christensen, C. M., and Raynor, M. E. (2003). *The Innovator's Solution: Creating and Sustaining Sucessful Growth*. Boston, MA: Harvard Business School Press.

Cullen, J. B., Johnson, J. L., and Sakano, T. (2000). "Success through Commitment and Trust: The Soft Side of Strategic Alliance Management." *Journal of World Business* 35 (3): 223–40. doi:10.1016/S1090-9516(00)00036-5.

Culpan, R. (2008). "The Role of Strategic Alliances in Gaining Sustainable Competitive Advantage for Firms." *Management Revue-The International Review of Management Studies* 19 (1–2): 94–105.

Dahlander, L., and Gann, D. M. (2010). "How Open Is Innovation?" *Research Policy* 39 (6): 699–709. doi:10.1016/j.respol.2010.01.013.

Das, T. K., and Teng, B.-S. (1998). "Between Trust and Control: Developing Confidence in Partner Cooperation in Alliances." *The Academy of Management Review* 23 (3): 491. doi:10.2307/259291.

De Jong, J. P. J., Vanhaverbeke, W., Kalvet, T., and Chesbrough, H. (2008). *Policies for Open Innovation: Theory, Framework and Cases.* Vision Era.Net.

Dodgson, M., Gann, D., and Salter, A. (2006). "The Role of Technology in the Shift towards Open Innovation: The Case of Procter & Gamble." *R&D Management* 36 (3): 333–46. doi:10.1111/j.1467-9310.2006.00429.x.

Enkel, E., Gassmann, O., and Chesbrough, H. (2009). "Open R&D and Open Innovation: Exploring the Phenomenon." *R&D Management* 39 (4): 311–16. doi:10.1111/j.1467-9310.2009.00570.x.

Franke, N., and Shah, S. (2003). "How Communities Support Innovative Activities: An Exploration of Assistance and Sharing among End-Users." *Research Policy* 32:157–78.

Gassmann, O., and Enkel, E. (2010). "Creative Innovation: Exploring the Case of Cross-Industry Innovation." *R&D Management* 40 (3): 256–70.

Gawer, A. (2011). *Platforms, Markets and Innovation.* Edward Elgar Publishing.

Grönlund, J., Sjödin, D. R., and Frishammar, J. (2010). "Open Innovation and the Stage-Gate Process: A Revised Model for New Product Development." *California Management Review* 52 (3): 106–31.

Gulati, R. (1995). "Does Familiarity Breed Trust? The Implications of Repeated Ties for Contractual Choice in Alliances." *Academy of Management Journal* 38 (1): 85–112. doi:10.2307/256729.

Hedlund, G. (1994). "A Model of Knowledge Management and the N-form Corporation." *Strategic Management Journal* 15 (S2): 73–90. doi:10.1002/smj.4250151006.

Hoegl, M., Lichtenthaler, U., and Muethel, M. (2011). "Is Your Company Ready for Open Innovation?" *MIT Sloan Management Review* 53 (1): 45–48.

Ili, S., Albers, A., and Miller, S. (2010). "Open Innovation in the Automotive Industry." *R&D Management* 40 (3): 246–55. doi:10.1111/j.1467-9310.2010.00595.x.

Jaruzelski, B., and Holman, R. (2011). "The Three Paths to Open Innovation." *strategy+business*, May 23. http://www.strategy-business.com/article/00075?gko=e1727 (accessed October 22, 2013).

Kutvonen, A. (2011). "Strategic Application of Outbound Open Innovation." *European Journal of Innovation Management* 14 (4): 460–74. doi:http://dx.doi.org.ezaccess.libraries.psu.edu/10.1108/14601061111174916.

Laursen, K., and Salter, A. (2006). "Open for Innovation: The Role of Openness in Explaining Innovation Performance among U.K. Manufacturing Firms." *Strategic Management Journal* 27 (2): 131–50.

Lettl, C., Herstatt, C., and Gemuenden, H. G. (2006). "Users' Contributions to Radical Innovation: Evidence from Four Cases in the Field of Medical Equipment Technology." *R&D Management* 36 (3): 251–72. doi:10.1111/j.1467-9310.2006.00431.x.

Munsch, K. (2009). "Open Model Innovation." *Research Technology Management* 52 (3): 48–52.

Perkmann, M., and Walsh, K. (2007). "University-Industry Relationships and Open Innovation: Towards a Research Agenda." *International Journal of Management Reviews* 9 (4): 259–80.

Peteraf, M. A. (1993). "The Cornerstones of Competitive Advantage: A Resource-Based View." *Strategic Management Journal* 14 (3): 179–91. doi:10.1002/smj.4250140303.

Quinn, J. B., Baruch, J. J., and Zien, K. A. (1997). *Innovation Explosion: Using Intellect and Software to Revolutionize Growth Strategies*. Simon & Schuster.

Reuer, J. J., and Ariño, A. (2007). "Strategic Alliance Contracts: Dimensions and Determinants of Contractual Complexity." *Strategic Management Journal* 28 (3): 313–30. doi:10.1002/smj.581.

Sanchez, R., and Heene, A. (1997). *Strategic Learning and Knowledge Management*, 1st ed. New York: John Wiley & Sons, Inc.

Snow, C. C., and Culpan, R. (2011). "Open Innovation through a Collaborative Community of Firms: An Emerging Organizational Design." In T. K. Das (ed.), *Strategic Alliances for Value Creation* (pp. 279–300). Charlotte, NC: Information Age Publishing.

Snow, C. C., Strauss, D. R., and Culpan, R. (2009). "Community of Firms: A New Collaborative Paradigm for Open Innovation and an Analysis of Blade.org." *International Journal of Strategic Business Alliances* 1 (1): 53–72.

Teece, D. J. (1998). "Research Directions for Knowledge Management." *California Management Review* 4 (3): 289–92.

Teece, D. J. (2007). "Explicating Dynamic Capabilities: The Nature and Microfoundations of (Sustainable) Enterprise Performance." *Strategic Management Journal* 28 (13): 1319–50. doi:10.1002/smj.640.

Teece, D. J. (2009). *Dynamic Capabilities and Strategic Management:Organizing for Innovation and Growth: Organizing for Innovation and Growth*. Oxford University Press.

Von Hippel, E., and Von Krogh, G. (2006). "Free Revealing and the Private-Collective Model for Innovation Incentives." *R&D Management* 36 (3): 295–306. doi:10.1111/j.1467-9310.2006.00435.x.

Wernerfelt, B. (1984). "A Resource-Based View of the Firm." *Strategic Management Journal* 5 (2): 171–80. doi:10.1002/smj.4250050207.

West, J., and Wood, D. (2013). "Evolving an Open Ecosystem: The Rise and Fall of the Symbian Platform." In R. Adler, J.E. Oakley, and B.S. Silverman (eds) *Advances in Strategic Management* (vol. 30 Collaboration and Competition in Business Ecosystems) (pp. 27-67). Emerald Group Publishing, Bingley, the U.K.

Winter, S. G. (2003). "Understanding Dynamic Capabilities." *Strategic Management Journal* 24 (10): 991–95. doi:10.1002/smj.318.

Zollo, M., and Winter, S. G. (2002). "Deliberate Learning and the Evolution of Dynamic Capabilities." *Organization Science* 13 (3): 339–351. doi:10.1287/orsc.13.3.339.2780.

CHAPTER 3

Open Innovation through R&D Partnerships: Implementation Challenges and Routes to Success

Nadine Roijakkers[1], John Bell, Jaco Fok, and Wim Vanhaverbeke[2]

Introduction

The purpose of this chapter is to describe some of the implementation challenges related to practicing open innovation (OI) through R&D partnerships
with different types of partners and ways for companies to successfully deal
with these challenges internally. OI has been a hot item in both academic publications and the popular literature in the past decade. Several authors have
described the open innovation activities of firms and have delineated various OI
options, such as R&D partnerships, technology licensing, corporate venturing,
and so forth, and the effects these actions have on the innovative performance of
mainly large companies (Chesbrough, 2003; Chesbrough, Vanhaverbeke, and
West, 2006; Dahlander and Gann, 2010). Despite this wealth of attention, several research topics have remained largely un(der)explored in OI research until
recently: the relation between OI activities and corporate strategy; the relation
between open innovation and internal firm functions, such as the legal department and IP management; and the relation between open innovation and the
internal changes necessary to successfully implement these initiatives, to name
but a few (Chesbrough, Vanhaverbeke, and West, forthcoming). In short, OI
literature has remained relatively thin on issues that are related to the management and internal organization of OI. Notwithstanding these shortcomings in
OI research, the well-developed body of literature on strategic alliances has put
forward many interesting insights as to what companies can do internally to
improve the likelihood of their alliance success (see for example the important

work of Draulans, De Man, and Volberda, 2003; Dyer, Kale, and Singh, 2001; Kale, Dyer, and Singh, 2001, 2002; Kale and Singh, 2009). Most of these contributions point out that it is crucial for companies to learn from their experiences with alliances, to centralize the alliance knowledge management function within a dedicated organizational unit, and to leverage best practices across their alliance portfolios (Anand and Khanna, 2000; Dyer and Singh, 2001; Kale, Singh, and Bell, 2009).

In this chapter we will draw on these important insights from the strategic alliance literature to study open innovation through R&D partnerships and what companies can do internally to deal with some of the management challenges related to different kinds of research and technology partners. Particularly, we have conducted research at two large multinationals practicing open innovation through research relations with several types of technology partners—that is, Royal Philips (headquartered in the Netherlands and active in health care, lighting, and consumer lifestyle) and Royal Dutch Shell (a Dutch-British global group of energy and petrochemicals companies). OI managers at both companies were interviewed using semistructured interview sheets. Examples of questions asked include the following:

- What is the role of open innovation through R&D partnerships in your company?
- What types of research partners do you discern?
- What are some of the implementation challenges associated with working with these different types of technology partners, and how do you deal with these issues internally?

Subsequently, the interviews were transcribed and sent to the interviewees for approval. The transcripts were then thoroughly analyzed, and the results provided us with rich insights regarding the types of OI partners these companies typically collaborate with, their way of classifying partners in terms of their significance for the corporate OI strategy, the problems they face in working with different types of partners, and how they deal with these problems internally in order to raise the odds of successful collaborative innovation. Figure 3.1 and Table 3.1 for the most part summarize our main findings and form the basis for the remainder of this chapter.

The chapter is structured as follows: In the next section, we first describe different types of R&D partners and classification schemes companies typically use to denote the significance of research partners for their corporate OI strategy. Next, we discern a series of implementation challenges related to working with specific types of OI partners, such as small- and medium-sized enterprises (SMEs) or universities. In light of important insights drawn from the strategic alliance literature, we then describe how companies deal with these challenges internally, for example, by distilling and leveraging best practices across their R&D partnerships, and thus raise the chances for the success of their OI activities. In more detail, we then zoom in on one of these best practices used by large multinationals to increase the efficiency and effectiveness of their OI relations with strategic suppliers through multiple project collaboration agreements (MPCAs).

Types of OI Partners and Partner Classification Schemes

Both Philips and Shell have a longstanding history in collaborating with different kinds of partners for innovation as well as for other purposes. Being active in the oil and gas industry on a global basis, for example, Shell has traditionally cooperated with local parties to conduct exploration and production activities in different countries. As far as open innovation is concerned, both Philips and Shell have actively searched for external technical knowledge through scouting and scanning, technology in-licensing, bilateral research contracts with universities, acquiring high-tech companies, strategic R&D alliances, collaborating with suppliers on innovation, making use of the mediating services of technology innomediaries (open innovation intermediaries offering and organizing open innovation capabilities for other firms) such as Ninesigma both have also externalized unused internal technological knowledge through out-licensing and spin-offs. More recently, we have witnessed a change in OI focus at both companies. While Philips has been known for its inside-out OI activities for many years, selling off many of its patents, the company's current OI strategy is more focused on outside-in OI, where interesting ideas, concepts, business models, and services for its businesses are searched for beyond the company's boundaries. These ideas, technologies, technical components, and so forth are internalized—that is, integrated with Philips's internal competencies—and further developed into technological solutions that fit with customer needs. In a recent press release, for example, Philips announced its partnership with Utrecht University on MRHIFU, or the heating up of tumors/tumor cells by making use of ultrasound technology, which is a nice example of its outside-in OI strategy to strengthen its activities in the health-care sector.

At Shell, the OI focus has shifted from collaborating predominantly with partners operating in the energy sector to searching for (radically) innovative ideas in both related and unrelated industries, such as aerospace, gaming, and the medical sector. One of the ways they have supported this strategic shift is by setting up a unit called "Shell Gamechanger," which acts as an angel investor searching for radically new technological ideas both inside the company and beyond and helping individual inventors to develop a proof of concept that signals the value of a new idea or technology to interested parties. In the gaming industry, for example, Shell is approaching producers of graphics cards, such as Intel and Nvidia, to search for new ways to graphically represent the huge amounts (i.e., petabytes) of geophysical data retrieved from scanning reservoirs in such a way that it enables Shell to create an accurate view of the subsurface of the earth. While collaborating with companies in the aerospace industry, Shell gains experience in further improving the reliability and safety of its operations and critical equipment.

When we examine the OI activities of both Philips and Shell, we can distinguish several categories of potential research partners: individual scientists at universities or research institutes (such as MIT or Fraunhofer), individual scientists that have already formed a start-up company (SME) or are willing to found one, large companies, and suppliers. For each type of technology partner, large companies typically set up classification schemes that enable them to classify research partners according to their significance for the corporate OI strategy (see De Man, Van der Zee, and Geurts, 2000, for examples of such classification schemes used at other companies). Figure 3.1 represents such a classification scheme for R&D relations according to strategic significance. The figure is set up as a continuum where relations can vary from arm's-length contractual OI arrangements at the left-hand side of the figure to well-embedded strategic research partnerships at the right-hand side of the figure. In what follows, we will describe some of the characteristics associated with both extremes of Figure 3.1.

Companies practicing OI through research contracts typically have many of these arrangements with a multitude of technology partners (e.g., universities, SMEs, large companies, or suppliers), where they conduct one or two isolated projects with each partner at a time. These OI partners can be top-notch players in their research fields, and companies may work with them on projects in these fields, but the relation does not have to be recurring nor does it have to be extended to other fields. These short-term contractual relations resemble relatively loose buyer-supplier relationships where companies clearly specify their technological needs regarding the subcontracted research, and research partners deliver in accordance with the contractual terms. As contractual R&D relations are not crucial for the company's corporate OI strategy, these contracts receive a fairly low level of management attention and may sometimes be handled by operational units, such as purchasing (De Man, Van der Zee, and Geurts, 2000).

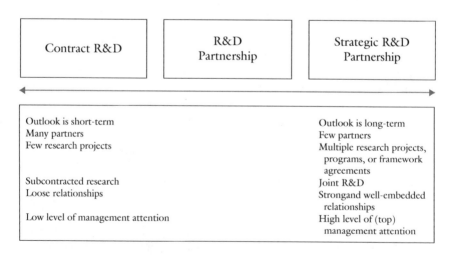

Figure 3.1 Classification Scheme of R&D Relations according to Strategic Significance

At the other end of the spectrum, we find strategic R&D partnerships. For the most part, companies have only a handful of strategic partners. Often a vice president is assigned to handle a partner account, where this top manager is in charge of managing and cultivating the relationship with a particular technology partner. Companies typically integrate their strategic technology partners in their organizational and communication structures, where key employees at all management levels are tightly linked to their counterparts in partner firms. Strategic partners are highly significant for the corporate OI strategy, and relations with these partners are managed in light of long-term strategic technology goals and mutually beneficial future collaborative research scenarios. With strategic partners, companies conduct joint research through a series of research projects or long-term R&D programs running for several years (De Man et al., 2000).

In this section we have identified various types of R&D partners as well as the manner in which companies practicing OI tend to classify these technology partners in terms of their strategic significance. Large multinationals usually have an extensive portfolio of technology partners and OI relations, where there is a mix of partners with varying effects on the corporate OI strategy (including many contractual partners and only a few strategic partners) (see also De Man et al., 2000). In the following section, we will describe our research results in terms of the management challenges related to R&D partnering with different kinds of OI partners.

Implementation Challenges Associated with R&D Partnering

Several empirical studies in OI have shown that companies increasingly strengthen their internal innovation activities by engaging in large numbers of research partnerships with different kinds of technology partners (Chesbrough, 2003; Deeds and Rothaermel, 2003; Hagedoorn, 2002). As such, companies gain access to external innovative ideas, technologies, and knowledge bases that are typically widespread and that they would not be able to access otherwise. While some studies have pointed out that companies engaging in R&D partnerships generally outperform those that do not in terms of innovativeness and financial performance, others have even shown that it is mostly a large diversity in the partnership portfolio in terms of different types of technology partners (e.g., universities, suppliers, competitors, customers, etc.) that has a particularly strong positive effect on innovative and financial performance (Baum, Calabrese, and Silverman, 2000; De Man and Duysters, 2005; Faems, Van Looy, and Debackere, 2005). Despite these important positive effects related to OI through R&D partnering, other academics have increasingly brought the less positive side effects of collaborating with large numbers of partners to the forefront (see for example Das and Teng, 2000; Dyer et al., 2001; Faems, De Visser, Andries, and Van Looy, 2010; Kale et al., 2001; Kelly, Schaan, and Joncas, 2002; Kogut, 1989). These authors have pointed out that collaborating with a large number of different types of partners introduces a high level of management complexity within the firm, where different OI partners require a different management approach. Each type of technology partner comes with a different set of implementation challenges that need to be managed well if the firm wants to reap some of the aforementioned benefits of engaging in OI through R&D partnering (Kelly et al., 2002). Based on our interview results, we will describe some of the implementation challenges related to R&D partnering with universities/research institutes, SMEs, large firms, and suppliers in the following (see Table 3.1).

Researchers have already addressed some of the management issues in relation to public-private research collaboration and have pointed at the cultural differences between companies and universities/research institutes, as well as

Table 3.1   Open Innovation through R&D Partnerships: Partner Types and Implementation Challenges

University or Research Institute	SME	Large Company	Supplier
Have specialties or research areas where IP is protected and not made available for sublicensing to the partner firm; have licensing officers that focus on protecting IP, thus slowing down projects	Different way of doing business; different business language; different expectations regarding the value of innovation	Have technology road maps where collaborative research projects have to fit within these road maps	Buyer-supplier model is still very much prevalent but difficult to work in collaborative mode (suppliers deliver what is asked but do not make commitments beyond that to create goodwill in partnership)
Have sets of rules and procedures that can be rigid	Lack of trust, fear of being mistreated, (over) protective of knowledge and ideas	Do not want their core technology being made available to competitors	
Process-oriented rather than results-oriented	Lack of knowledge regarding commercialization process and requirements	Want both cheap and fast technology solutions as well as exclusivity; the two do not match	
Have different views on making knowledge publicly available	Lack of resources in general	Have other priorities	
Top-notch institutions may impose burdened requests			
Different expectations regarding (financial) returns			

bureaucratic inflexibility, as some of the main reasons why these relationships can be somewhat challenging (see for instance Siegel, Waldman, Atwater, and Link, 2003). Our research brings forward a number of implementation challenges in relation to collaborating with universities/research institutes that are somewhat similar to the ones found in the existing literature (see Table 3.1). First, we find that some universities/research institutes can be somewhat process-oriented rather than results-oriented. While companies expect to receive clearly specified and agreed-upon research results in relation to their payments, universities/research institutes sometimes see high value in the search process itself even if this process does not generate the intended innovative idea or technology. Second, universities/research institutes typically aim for publicizing their research results and sharing these results with the wider scientific community while the company they have been doing research for wants to use the new ideas or techniques to achieve competitive advantage and thus sees more merit in protecting the knowledge. These different viewpoints on publicizing technical knowledge and different ways of working are behavioral outcomes of academic and company cultures that sometimes do not match and make collaboration quite challenging. Third, when it comes to bureaucracy and the inflexibility associated with rigid rules and procedures, we find similar results to existing research (Siegel et al., 2003). Some top-notch universities/research institutes have a set of stringent rules and procedures that can make collaboration difficult at times. One of these rules mentioned in the interviews, for example, relates to some universities/research institutes practice of claiming ownership to all knowledge/ideas generated on their premises, where the partner company can at best receive a technology licensing deal to access this knowledge that it contributed to. Fourth, a number of universities/research institutes have licensing officers in place that focus on strongly protecting IP in specialty areas such that partners cannot get any access to IP that relates to the core research area of the university/research institute they are collaborating with. This makes collaboration difficult and can slow down research projects tremendously (Siegel et al., 2003). Fifth, universities/research institutes sometimes expect to receive additional financial reimbursements for their research efforts while the company is already paying in-kind by granting access to different kinds of resources, such as its technical employees and researchers. As a final challenge to making R&D partnerships with universities/research institutes work, interviewees mention that it can be difficult to draw the attention of top-notch institutions, which are mostly overloaded with project proposals and research requests.

With respect to the management problems relating to OI relations between large companies and SMEs, several researchers have identified certain characteristics of SMEs that can sometimes be difficult to deal with for a large multinational (see for example Doz, 1988; Slowinski, Seelig, and Hull, 1996; Van de Vrande, De Jong, Vanhaverbeke, and De Rochemont, 2009) (see also Table 3.1). In general, SMEs are far less endowed in terms of financial and human resources compared to their large counterparts, which may result in friction and delays where the smaller firm, for example, cannot spend as much management effort on a research project as its larger research partner (Van de Vrande et al., 2009). In a similar manner, SMEs typically have a different way of conducting their business and speak a different business language than large multinationals, which can lead to frustrations on both sides (Botkin and Mathews, 1992; Child and Faulkner, 1998; Kelly et al., 2002; Mohr and Spekman, 1994). While large firms usually have many processes, rules, and procedures in place for most of their business activities, SMEs are for the most part led by the manager-entrepreneur, who has a much more informal, intuitive style of leadership (Slowinski et al., 1996). Another challenging aspect of working with SMEs, as worded by our interviewees, is the fact that SMEs often have high expectations with respect to the financial value of their innovative idea, patent, or technology. With a less-developed knowledge base regarding the requirements of the commercialization process and the huge sums of money associated with turning a novel idea into a commercially viable product, SMEs tend to have unrealistic expectations in relation to their financial reimbursements, thus complicating contract negotiations between large and small firms. A final challenge that was mentioned in the interviews and which can also be found in the literature on technology alliances (Gulati, 1995; Hagedoorn, Roijakkers, and Van Kranenburg, 2008; Kelly et al., 2002; Parkhe, 1998) is the lack of trust in SMEs toward their larger counterparts, leading them to be (over)protective of their technical knowledge assets and also slowing down research projects to a large extent.

The third type of partner for which we have identified a set of management challenges is "large firms" (see Table 3.1). While many authors have written about the challenges of collaboration among large companies and SMEs, the literature that considers issues in relation to R&D partnerships between large firms is largely nonexistent. Our interviewees point out a number of management challenges when it comes to their research relations with other large multinationals. First, large multinationals have their own technology road maps and their own sets of research (and other) priorities that they are typically not willing to stray from. In practice, this means that joint, collaborative research projects have to fit within these technology road maps for large partners to have any interest in them at all. Second, many large technology partners claim exclusivity where they do not want their core technologies and research outcomes to be accessible by third parties. If the goal of a research partnership, however, is to develop a new technology in a relatively cheap and fast manner, it can be difficult to collaborate on an exclusive basis, as other partners may need to be involved to share their knowledge and thus speed up the process (see Table 3.1).

With respect to OI relations with suppliers, the literature has pointed out that companies increasingly try to involve suppliers in their research and product-development processes to gain access to their specific technological capabilities and expertise and thus improve the efficiency and effectiveness of innovative component design and engineering (Burt and Soukup, 1985; Kamath and Liker, 1994; Ragatz, Handfield and Scannell, 1997). Some authors have pointed out that this increased involvement of suppliers in R&D activities has not brought all positive effects and that it, in many cases, does not even lead to decreased costs or development lead times nor higher final product quality (McCutcheon, Grant, and Hartley, 1997). Wynstra, Van Weele, and Weggeman (2001) imply that suppliers' involvement in R&D can be beneficial if companies manage this involvement well and deal with the most important issues related to this form of cooperation. In particular, they mention that a source of problems can lie within supplier organizations, where they are not always well equipped for working in a collaborative innovation mode (Wynstra et al., 2001). In line with this, our interviewees mention that their suppliers sometimes have difficulties in moving beyond the buyer-supplier relation (i.e., delivering according to predefined specs and contracts) toward a mutually beneficial collaborative research partnership where technology partners are equals and proactive when it comes to investing time, resources, and know-how into the relationship and fulfilling each other's technological needs (see Table 3.1).

In this section, on the basis of our interview results, we have identified a number of important management challenges related to setting up and implementing research partnerships with different kinds of OI partners. In the previous section, we pointed out that technology partners have varying degrees of significance when it comes to their importance for reaching strategic OI goals at a corporate level. Implementation challenges typically become more problematic the higher the strategic significance level of a particular technology partner is. However, while implementation problems can be more challenging with strategic partners, the maneuvering room for solving issues involving strategic technology partners is also bigger. These types of partners are typically linked to VPs and are well embedded in organizational structures, where the amount of management attention to spend on these problems and the level of resources made available for solving issues is fairly high. In the next section, we will examine ways of dealing with implementation challenges in an effective manner, leading to a higher likelihood of partnership success.

How to Deal with OI Implementation Challenges Internally: The R&D Partnering Process and the OI Management Department

In the previous sections, we have described how different types of OI partners can bring different implementation and management challenges to the forefront. Furthermore, the intensity of the research relationship (i.e., contract, partner, or strategic partner) can have an influence on the magnitude of implementation challenges and their potential of being dealt with in a successful manner. While the literature on open innovation has not put forward many insights into how to manage and organize OI internally, the strategic alliance literature has extensively studied many of the critical success factors behind the effective implementation of an alliance strategy (Draulans et al., 2003; Duysters, Kok, and Vaandrager, 1999; Dyer et al., 2001; Kale et al., 2001; Kale and Singh, 2009; Kelly et al., 2002). Specifically, these alliance researchers have pointed out that allying companies need to learn from their prior experiences with alliances, centralize alliance knowledge management within a dedicated and separate alliance department, and develop/leverage best alliance practices across the alliance port-folio to increase the likelihood of success of new alliances. Based on the interviews we conducted and in line with the strategic alliance literature, in this section we identify a number of ways to effectively deal with OI implementation challenges where companies can set up internal tool kits, processes, and functions that will help them initiate and manage their OI partnerships with different types of tech-nology partners in a successful manner.

The strategic alliance literature has identified a number of ways in which ally-ing companies can prepare their internal organization for entering into strategic alliances, where these internal processes and functions add to the success of these collaborative relations. Kale and Singh (2009) describe the alliance-formation and management process, where different stages in the relationship can be dis-tinguished: selection, formation, management, and evaluation. For each of these stages, companies can develop a set of tools that supports the alliance process and increases its effectiveness. In the first alliance stage, for example, partner-selection tools that help companies to select alliance partners that fit with their company's strategy, organization, culture, knowledge base, and ways of work-ing can lead to more compatibility among partners and thus more commit-ment to joint efforts (see Beamish, 1987; Dacin, Hitt, and Levitas, 1997; Kelly et al., 2002; Shah and Swaminathan, 2008). These tools can be lists of criteria/checklists that enable companies to evaluate their potential partners on strate-gic, operational, technological, and cultural grounds. Our interviewee at Philips stressed the importance of such self-developed tools to help managers decide which technology party to approach and engage with. In our section on OI implementation challenges, we have described how particular types of research partners, such as universities and SMEs, can sometimes be challenging to work with, considering their different cultures, attitudes, and ways of working. Phil-ips's partner-selection tools help them overcome these challenges by enabling them to search for and find OI partners with similar attitudes (e.g., open mind-sets, flexible procedures, open attitudes toward knowledge sharing, etc.) that are compatible with their organization. High compatibility at the very start of a research relationship can significantly improve the chances for success (Beamish, 1987; Draulans et al., 2003).

In the alliance-formation and management stages, continuously evolving alli-ance tool kits, including contract templates and guidelines for setting up effective alliance-management/communication structures, can also be of crucial impor-tance in supporting the effective set-up and management of strategic alliances (Hakansson, 1993; Kale and Singh, 2009; Kelly et al., 2002). In the interviews, OI managers described their strategic supplier programs, where these important OI relations are intensely managed by the appropriate management levels within the organization, thus increasing the success chances of these research relation-ships. In setting up and managing technology partnerships with suppliers, com-panies make use of specific sets of guidelines associated with establishing effective coordination and communication structures with strategic suppliers where they, for example, make sure that different hierarchical levels within the partnering organizations are well connected (i.e., from CTO-CTO level all the way down to operations). As such, strategic goals for the R&D partnership are discussed and decided upon at the CTO level, after which these goals are translated into middle-management objectives and operational focus and subsequently implemented at lower levels within the partnering organizations (Gulati, Lawrence, and Puranam, 2005; Gulati and Singh, 1998). In managing OI implementation challenges in relation to university/research institute relations, companies make use of standardized framework contracts, where individual research projects can easily be added to the original R&D agreement in a flexible manner, thus speeding up the OI partnering process with universities/research institutes, which can be slow sometimes.

Companies that distinguish an alliance-evaluation stage in their alliance process, where they weigh their set of relations with different kinds of partners at regular intervals and as such learn from these alliance experiences, have a higher chance of engaging in successful new strategic alliances (for specific alliance-evaluation techniques, see Draulans et al., 2003; Kale and Singh, 2009). Our interviewees mentioned that evaluating their R&D partnerships and deducing best OI practices from these experiences that can be spread throughout their organizations are highly valuable processes in open innovation. Both Philips and Shell are highly experienced in technology partnering and have emphasized the importance of the learning and knowledge-management processes associated with this experience (see also Anand and Khanna, 2000). In dealing with SMEs or universities/research institutes, both companies have gained a lot of experience, where specialized employees are highly practiced in dealing with these types of technology partners on a daily basis, speaking their language, and developing knowledge and capabilities in relation to these types of OI partners. These employees are, for instance, knowledgeable on the specific research topics covered by different universities/research institutes, their way of working, their set of rules and procedures, and they can help researchers within their organization find the right research partners on projects. As all contacts with universities/research institutes go through these employees, they can also put internal researchers into contact with their colleagues who have already dealt with a particular university/ research institute before, thus making sure that existing knowledge and best OI practices within the organization are made available to all employees engaging in OI activities.

Typically the knowledge-management processes and best practices concerning strategic alliances are organized within a centralized alliance management or best practice department, where this separate organizational unit gathers and spreads alliance knowledge as well as ensures a coordinated approach to all collaborative activities within the firm. Several authors have emphasized that companies with a separate alliance-management function are more successful in strategic alliances than their counterparts where alliance knowledge and best practices are scattered throughout the organization (see for example the work of Dyer et al., 2001, on Eli Lilly and Hewlett-Packard; Kale et al., 2009, on Philips; Hoang and Rothaermel, 2005, on the effect of alliance departments on innovative performance in general). Both Philips and Shell have separate OI management departments, where all OI experience and knowledge (general as well as specific to a particular kind of technology partner) is located, captured, and transformed into processes, best practices, and tool kits that are constantly under development and where these standardized processes are made available through coaching and guidance to all employees engaging in OI activities. These departments that are involved in all open innovation activities of the firm are also crucial in creating awareness and commitment toward OI throughout the organization (see also Kale and Singh, 2009).

While the strategic alliance literature is fairly rich on accounts of successful alliance departments within large organizations and the particular roles played by these departments in driving forward alliance activities (Dyer et al., 2001), our research identifies another important role for OI management departments. The open innovation management literature offers relatively few insights on how to manage and organize OI internally: How can, for example, the human resources department support open innovation activities? What kinds of selection and training processes can they develop to increase the organization's skill base in OI? These questions have remained largely unanswered, but our research indicates that OI management departments can play a crucial role in involving these departments in open innovation and jointly develop OI supporting tools and processes for each function. In this respect, our interviews show that OI management departments are collaborating with legal departments to come up with new, more flexible IP strategies, contracts, and business models to better accommodate OI endeavors. This internal collaboration has resulted in the development of a limited number of standard commercial models for collaborating with SMEs; a few simple checklists can be worked through, resulting in a standard contract within just a few weeks' time. It would be rather difficult for companies to align their different functions in terms of their open innovation strategy if OI knowledge and expertise were scattered across the organization rather than centralized within a separate department. This important role goes beyond the internal coordination role identified in Dyer et al., 2001, where alliance departments mobilize internal resources to make individual alliances work, in that current OI departments are driving factors in stimulating and coordinating internal collaboration between organizational functions on developing innovative tools/processes for improving OI activities throughout the organization.

In this section, we have pointed out that large multinationals can deal with some of the implementation issues in relation to their technology partners by developing and implementing adequate OI processes for the selection, formation, management, and evaluation stages of R&D partnering and instigating an OI management department to leverage best practices across OI activities and stimulate the joint development of supporting tool kits with other internal functions. In the next part of this chapter, we will describe one of these best practices—that is, strategic supplier programs—in more detail to illustrate its workings.

Best Practice Highlighted: Strategic Supplier Programs/MPCAs

In the previous sections, we have already touched upon the subject of strategic supplier programs, where large companies maintain long-term strategic R&D partnerships with a small set of important suppliers in order to repeatedly involve these crucial sources of technical expertise early on in their product development efforts through multiple OI projects. (These types of technology relations can be located at the right-hand side of Figure 3.1.) By contrast, with many other suppliers, large companies typically set up isolated one-off joint development agreements covering only a specific research project at hand. Many large multinationals structure recurrent OI relationships with their strategic suppliers through so-called umbrella agreements or multiple project collaboration agreements (MPCAs). In doing so, these companies ensure that their supplier relations are highly flexible, where each new joint development project can be easily integrated under the umbrella agreement, thus speeding up the collaborative process. By making use of such best practices, companies can significantly add to the chances of success of their strategic supplier partnerships. In this section, we will explain the workings of MPCAs in more detail. (The example of MPCAs does not come from either Philips or Shell but from another large multinational that wishes to remain anonymous.)

An MPCA is an umbrella agreement for all OI projects conducted with one particular strategic supplier by multiple business units. An MPCA can be defined according to the main phases that can be distinguished for most large-scale research projects:

- Definition: During this phase, the input of market research teams link consumer needs to R&D project specifications.
- Invention: This phase is the main R&D process where all inventions in a certain business area are linked to a specific technology/supplier.
- Integration and Demonstration: In the last phase, pilots and tests are run in order to upscale viable technical solutions to meet consumer needs on a commercial scale.

All three phases are closely linked to different sets of OI agreements. For instance, in the first phase, the company has to define consumer needs, where marketing/sales departments and R&D departments determine consumer needs and potential technologies to address these needs. The company then sends out a nonconfidential brief to multiple suppliers through multiple avenues (e.g., through technology innomediaries, such as Ninesigma); suppliers can express their interests in solving the technical problem at hand in a nonconfidential way. If the company wants to know more about the ideas or potential technological solutions offered by a particular supplier, it can start interacting with this supplier by negotiating a one-way confidential disclosure agreement (CDA). As such, the company commits itself not to analyze, for example, the chemical substance it received from the supplier but to use it only for testing in its applications. The company subsequently requests a proof of concept and evaluates whether the two firms can agree upon the terms and conditions. Once the supplier is selected, the collaboration can start. At that point in time (i.e., the second and third phases), the R&D partners write up a two-way CDA where technical knowledge is shared within a technical discussion subagreement (TDS). The companies then typically set up a long-term joint development program involving multiple R&D projects and define technical and commercial success factors; if the OI relation turns out to be successful, marketing departments take over by exploring potential markets for the new technology.

The entire process normally takes between one and three years and is typically subject to a set of key success factors that determine which are the cut-off points for further collaboration or, in the worst case scenario, for exiting the R&D partnership. This is an important point since MPCAs cover a long-term OI relation between large companies and their strategic suppliers with a lot of unknowns at the start. If the company is no longer interested in the R&D partnership at a particular point in time (e.g., if a different technology is discovered or a competitor is already on the market with similar products), the company has to reimburse some of the investments undertaken by its strategic technology partner. If this is not included in the MCPA, most suppliers will be very reluctant to even start substantial investments in a particular technology. Similarly, once the supplier agrees to be a strategic OI partner under an umbrella agreement or MPCA, the supplier has to stick to the details of the agreement, which implies, for example, that the supplier can no longer "play the market." The strategic supplier has to move from a relatively loose buyer-supplier relationship to a well-embedded collaborative mode of interaction with its partner. It is therefore of crucial importance to create up-front transparency on financial expectations (margins, profits) and put measures in place to drive beneficial and collaborative behavior on the part of both parties. Prices tend to be fixed in advance and are generally maintained as long as the MPCA contract stipulates. This may become a painful experience for the supplier when prices of raw materials increase; therefore, in most cases, clauses are included in the MPCA, which delineate that the strategic supplier can adjust (after mutual agreement) prices in case the costs of raw materials surpass critical levels. When it comes to IP ownership in strategic OI relations between large multinationals and their strategic suppliers, it is usually the case that strategic suppliers own the IP rights and that the companies get exclusive rights to use technologies in applications they are interested in. In other words, multinationals allow their strategic suppliers to license technologies to other firms as long as the same technologies are not used in their preferred applications.

Conclusions and Implications

Based on interviews conducted at two large multinationals (i.e., Shell and Philips), this chapter has described a number of important management problems related to engaging in OI through R&D partnerships with different types of technology partners and put forward some ways for companies to internally prepare their organizations for implementing effective OI relationships. Large multinationals typically set up OI relationships with universities/research institutes, SMEs, other large companies, and their suppliers. These technology relationships can vary in strategic significance from loosely organized R&D contracts (low strategic importance) to strong, long-term strategic OI partnerships (high in strategic significance). Many companies use partner classification schemes to denote the importance of their technology partners for achieving corporate OI goals. In this chapter we have illustrated one example of such a scheme, but there are many others (De Man et al., 2000). Large multinationals usually have OI partnership portfolios, where they have a small number of strategic partners (these can be universities/research institutes, SMEs, large companies, or suppliers) and a multitude of contractual partners. Each type of partner comes with a different set of implementation challenges that need to be overcome if the multinational wants to reap the benefits of open innovation (Kelly et al., 2002). While implementation problems with contractual partners are usually not at the heart of top management concerns, issues with strategic technology partners are comparatively high on the corporate agenda. Our interview results are well in line with existing research on the implementation problems in relation to R&D partnerships with universities/research institutes, SMEs, and suppliers. When it comes to technology partnering between large multinationals and other large OI partners, the existing literature does not offer many insights. We find that the challenges faced by large partners typically require that these companies stick to their own technology road maps and R&D programs, where collaborative projects with large counterparts simply have to fit within these plans for the initiatives to be undertaken at all.

The current OI literature does not offer an integrated view of how to overcome implementation challenges associated with OI relationships or how to organize internally to optimally prepare for OI activities. As such, we heavily draw on the strategic alliance literature (Dyer et al., 2001; Kale et al., 2002; Kale and Singh, 2009) to point out that companies have a higher likelihood of successfully dealing with implementation challenges if they set up an internal OI management process with a continuously evolving tool kit tied to each of the phases this process covers (i.e., selection, formation, management, and evaluation). Furthermore, the establishment of an internal OI management department that captures and leverages OI best practices (such as MPCAs for strategic suppliers) across the company is generally related to higher success rates of OI strategies. Besides the important roles of such a separate department as identified by the strategic alliance literature (e.g., creating OI awareness and commitment throughout the company), our research identifies an additional function for this department that may be particularly interesting for OI scholars studying OI implementation and management: an OI department can play a crucial role in stimulating and coordinating the collaborative efforts of different internal departments, such as the legal department, to come up with much needed OI supporting tools and processes.

While this research offers some interesting new insights, it also suffers from limitations, the most important one being the fact that the interviews were conducted at only two large multinationals. The chapter does signal the need to conduct more in-depth case studies into OI best practices deduced and leveraged at large multinationals. Such case studies can shed light on the processes and tools companies develop internally to improve the effectiveness of their OI relations and thus significantly advance our current knowledge of how to effectively manage and organize open innovation through R&D partnerships.

Notes

1. Corresponding author: Nadine.Roijakkers@UHasselt.be
2. The authors would like to acknowledge the contributions of Shell and Philips to this chapter.

References

Anand, B., and Khanna, T. (2000). "Do Firms Learn to Create Value? The Case of Alliances." *Strategic Management Journal* 21 (3): 295–315.

Baum, J., Calabrese, T., and Silverman, B. (2000). "Don't Go It Alone: Alliance Network Composition and Startups' Performance in Canadian Biotechnology." *Strategic Management Journal* 21 (3): 267–94.

Beamish, P. (1987). "Joint Ventures in LDCs: Partner Selection and Performance." *Management International Review* 27 (1): 23–27.

Botkin, J., and Mathews, J. (1992). *Winning Combinations: The Coming Wave of Entrepreneurial Partnerships between Large and Small Companies.* New York: Wiley.

Burt, D., and Soukup, W. (1985). "Purchasing's Role in New Product Development." *Harvard Business Review* 63 (5): 90–97.

Chesbrough, H. W. (2003). *Open Innovation: The New Imperative for Creating and Profiting from Technology.* Boston: Harvard Business School Press.

Chesbrough, H. W., Vanhaverbeke, W., and West, J. (2006). *Open Innovation: Researching a New Paradigm.* Oxford: Oxford University Press.

Chesbrough, H. W., Vanhaverbeke, W., and West, J. (forthcoming). *Exploring the Next Wave of Open Innovation Research,* Oxford: Oxford University Press.

Child, J., and Faulkner, D. (1998). *Strategies of Cooperation: Managing Alliances, Networks, and Joint Ventures.* Oxford: Oxford University Press.

Dacin, M., Hitt, M., and Levitas, E. (1997). "Selecting Partners for Successful International Alliances: Examination of US and Korean Firms." *Journal of World Business* 32 (1): 3–16.

Dahlander, L., and Gann, D. M. (2010). "How Open Is Innovation?" *Research Policy* 39 (6): 699–709.

Das, T., and Teng, B. (2000). "Instabilities of Strategic Alliances: An Internal Tension Perspective." *Organization Science* 11 (1): 77–101.

De Man, A.-P., and Duysters, G. (2005). "Collaboration and Innovation: A Review of the Effects of Mergers, Acquisitions and Alliances on Innovation." *Technovation* 25 (12): 1377–87.

De Man, A.-P., Van der Zee, H., and Geurts, D. (2000). *Competing for Partners.* Amsterdam: Prentice-Hall.

Deeds, D., and Rothaermel, F. (2003). "Honeymoons and Liabilities: The Relationship between Age and Performance in Research and Development Alliances." *Journal of Product Innovation Management* 20 (6): 468–84.

Doz, Y. (1988). "Technology Partnerships between Larger and Smaller Firms: Some Critical Issues." *International Studies of Management and Organization* 17 (4): 31–57.

Draulans, J., De Man, A-P., and Volberda, H. (2003). "Building Alliance Capability: Management Techniques for Superior Alliance Performance." *Long Range Planning* 36 (2): 151–66.

Duysters, G., Kok, G., and Vaandrager, M. (1999). "Crafting Successful Strategic Technology Partnerships." *R&D Management* 29 (4): 343–51.

Dyer, J., Kale, P., and Singh, H. (2001). "How to Make Strategic Alliances Work." *MIT Sloan Management Review* 42 (4): 37–43.

Faems, D., Van Looy, B., and Debackere, K. (2005). "Inter-organizational Collaboration and Innovation: Toward a Portfolio Approach." *Journal of Product Innovation Management* 22 (3): 238–50.

Faems, D., De Visser, M., Andries, P., and Van Looy, B. (2010). "Technology Alliance Portfolios and Financial Performance: Value-Enhancing and Cost-Increasing Effects of Open Innovation." *Journal of Product Innovation Management* 27 (6): 785–96.

Gulati, R. (1995). "Does Familiarity Breed Trust? The Implications of Repeated Ties for Contractual Choice in Alliances." *Academy of Management Journal* 38 (1): 85–112.

Gulati, R., Lawrence, P., and Puranam, P. (2005). "Adaptation in Vertical Relationships: Beyond Incentive Conflict." *Strategic Management Journal* 26 (5): 415–40.

Gulati, R., and Singh, H. (1998). "The Architecture of Cooperation: Managing Coordination Costs and Appropriation Concerns in Strategic Alliances." *Administrative Science Quarterly* 43 (4): 781–814.

Hagedoorn, J. (2002). "Inter-firm R&D Partnerships: An Overview of Major Trends and Patterns since 1960." *Research Policy* 31 (4): 477–92.

Hagedoorn, J., Roijakkers, N., and Van Kranenburg, H. (2008). "The Formation of Subsequent Inter-firm R&D Partnerships between Large Pharmaceutical Companies and Small, Entrepreneurial Firms: How Important Is Inter-organizational Trust?" *International Journal of Technology Management* 44 (1–2): 81–92.

Hakansson, L. (1993). "Managing Cooperative Research and Development: Partner Selection and Contract Design." *R&D Management* 23 (4): 273–85.

Hoang, H., and Rothaermel, F. (2005). "The Effects of General and Partner-Specific Experience on Joint R&D Project Performance." *Academy of Management Journal* 48 (2): 332–45.

Kale, P., Dyer, J., and Singh, H. (2001). "Value Creation and Success in Strategic Alliances: Alliancing Skills and the Role of Alliance Structure and Systems." *European Management Journal* 19 (5): 463–71.

Kale, P., Dyer, J., and Singh, H. (2002). "Alliance Capability, Stock Market Response and Long-Term Alliance Success: The Role of the Alliance Function." *Strategic Management Journal* 23 (8): 747–67.

Kale, P., and Singh, H. (2009). "Managing Strategic Alliances: What Do We Know Now, and Where Do We Go from Here?" *Academy of Management Perspectives* 23 (3): 45–62.

Kale, P., Singh, H., and Bell, J. (2009). "The Network Challenge: Strategies for Managing the New Interlinked Enterprise." In P. Kleindorfer and Y. Wind (eds.), *Relating Well: Building Capabilities for Sustaining Alliance Networks*, pp. 353–363. London: Pearson Press.

Kamath, R., and Liker, J. (1994). "A Second Look at Japanese Product Development." *Harvard Business Review* 72 (6): 154–70.

Kelly, M., Schaan, J.-L., and Joncas, H. (2001). "Managing Alliance Relationships: Key Challenges in the Early Stages of Collaboration." *R&D Management* 32 (1): 11–22.

Kogut, B. (1989). "The Stability of Joint Ventures: Reciprocity and Competitive Rivalry." *Journal of Industrial Economics* 38 (2): 183–98.

McCutcheon, D., Grant, R., and Hartley, J. (1997). "Determinants of New Product Designers' Satisfaction with Suppliers' Contributions." *Journal of Engineering and Technology Management* 14 (3): 273–90.

Mohr, J., and Spekman, R. (1994). "Characteristics of Partnership Success: Partnership Attributes, Communication Behaviour, and Conflict Resolution Techniques." *Strategic Management Journal* 15 (2): 135–52.

Parkhe, A. (1998). "Understanding Trust in International Alliances." *Journal of World Business* 33 (3): 219–40.

Ragatz, G., Handfield, R., and Scannell, T. (1997). "Success Factors for Integrating Suppliers into New Product Development." *Journal of Product Innovation Management* 14 (3): 190–202.

Shah, R., and Swaminathan, V. (2008). "Factors Influencing Partner Selection in Strategic Alliances: The Moderating Role of Alliance Context." *Strategic Management Journal* 29 (5): 471–94.

Siegel, D., Waldman, D., Atwater, L., and Link, A. (2003). "Commercial Knowledge Transfers from Universities to Firms: Improving the Effectiveness of University-Industry Collaboration." *Journal of High Technology Management Research* 14 (1): 111–33.

Slowinski, G., Seelig, G., and Hull, F. (1996). "Managing Technology-Based Strategic Alliances between Large and Small Firms." *SAM Advanced Management Journal* 61 (2): 42–47.

Van de Vrande, V., De Jong, J., Vanhaverbeke, W., and De Rochemont, M. (2009). "Open Innovation in SMEs: Trends, Motives, and Management Challenges." *Technovation* 29 (6–7): 423–37.

Wynstra, F., Van Weele, A., and Weggeman, M. (2001). "Managing Supplier Involvement in Product Development: Three Critical Issues." *European Management Journal* 19 (2): 157–67.

CHAPTER 4

Relational Drivers of Open Innovation Alliances in Biochemistry

Emiel F. M. Wubben, Andre van Meijeren, and Vincent Blok

Introduction

This chapter focuses on relational drivers of open innovation regarding biomass-related strategic alliances in the emerging field of biochemistry. Around the world, significant steps are being taken to move from today's fossil-based economies to more sustainable economies based on biomass (De Jong and Jorgensen, 2012), driven by a growing need to address major societal challenges, such as climate change, energy security, and resource scarcity, and the desire to profit from economic growth opportunities (Odegard, Croezen, and Bergsma, 2012; Sanders, Langeveld, and Meeusen, 2010). This process is called *biomass valorization* (Wubben, Runge, and Blok, 2012), which means creating value from biomass by making it available for economic purposes via innovative products and/or processes. Biomass includes materials from crops growing on land or sea and residues from forestry, agriculture, the food industry, and other industrial sectors (Koppejan et al., 2009). Bio-based products are already used in construction and insulation, packaging, and automotive and consumer goods. An analysis of the European market for wholly or partly biomass-based products in 2005 indicates 780 bio-based product categories, representing a joint production value of 450 billion euros (Nowicki et al., 2008). Biomass may be used for nonfood applications, such as materials, chemicals, transport fuels, and energy (Annevelink and Harmsen, 2010). Europe's potential market size of bio-based (parts of) products is already calculated to rise up to roughly 315 billion euros per annum (Nowicki et al., 2008). Brasil's rise as a newly industrialized country indicates the importance of its growing bio-based economy, which is based on its systematic substitution of petroleum with bioethanol extracted from sugarcane. The availability of biomass is expected to continue in meeting the increasing demand of the bio-based economy (Dornburg et al., 2008). Today more than ever before, biomass is converted into a variety of bio-based products and applications (Harmsen and Bos, 2011).

Biochemistry is an emerging business at the intersection of agriculture and chemistry (Janssens, Aramyan, and Van Gallan, 2011; Enzing et al., 2008; Nowicki et al., 2008), also referred to as "green chemistry" or "bio-based chemistry" (Harmsen and Hackmann, 2012). It is described as a process-industrial sector that uses biomass for the production of chemicals and materials (WTC, 2011). The rise of biochemistry is driven by ongoing technological inventions, by the growing interest in the high valorization of biomass (Annevelink and Harmsen, 2010; WTC, 2011), and by capitalizing on the success of biofuels for the production of bio-based products. In Europe, the energy balance of most types of biofuels turns out to be neutral at best, resulting in a shift in R&D into more value-added businesses, such as biochemistry. The prospects for biochemistry are such that there are claims that it will be able to replace most of today's petrochemistry (WTC, 2010, 2011). Firms forge cross-industry alliances to materialize the required industry convergence for business development in biochemistry.

Turning biomass into marketable products requires cooperation between different sectors (e.g., agriculture and chemistry) and different actors (e.g., biomass suppliers, technology developers, and commercial partners) (Wubben et al., 2012). Since biochemistry is a relatively new industry and particular alliances in this sector are rather underresearched, this chapter explores open innovation activities aimed at biochemistry development from an interfirm relational perspective. Literature has shown that the development of new industries, like biochemistry, benefits from cross-industry open innovation alliances. But supporting evidence of this claim is rather scarce. Conventionally, agrifood and chemistry were completely separate industries (Boehlje and Bröring, 2011), with their own players, regional strongholds, and research agendas. Given the importance of collaboration among agricultural and chemical firms (Blaauw, Haveren, Scott, and Bos, 2008) and the lack of academic literature examining such relationships, the objective of this chapter is to answer the following key research question: what are the cross-industry drivers for open innovation performance from an inter-firm relational perspective?

To this end, we conducted nine case studies in biochemistry in the Netherlands, where agrifood and petrochemistry are the two largest economic (export) industries, and companies in both industries recognize that opportunities in this emerging segment, called *biochemistry*, are particularly promising (VNCI, 2011; WTC, 2011; SER, 2010; Communicatie EnergieTransitie, 2009; Nowicki et al., 2008).

This chapter is structured as follows. Section one comprises an extensive literature review on open innovation and strategic alliances, followed by three research propositions; while section two presents a theoretical framework for our study. Section three explains our research methodology, and section four presents the results of our findings. Finally, section five summarizes our conclusions and recommendations.

Literature Review

Following on what we have stated in the introduction, elucidating the concept of cross-industry alliances may help to understand the expected convergence of established industries into biochemistry, catalyzed by innovations and new business developments. It is important to make clear that cross-industry drivers for open innovation and strategic alliances together seem to promote the innovation performance of firms. We therefore present a concise review of the concepts of *open innovation, strategic alliances,* and *strategic networks* respectively.

Open Innovation

Since the late 1970s, product life-cycle models have been used to explain the emergence and decline of various products in traditional industries (Gort and Klepper, 1982; Utterback and Suarez, 1993; Utterback, 1994). Such models are, however, unable to explain the emergence of new industries creating a new crossing of traditionally distinct industries (Klepper, 1997), where established and new firms compete to claim shares in a new industry. One example is the Internet-based "new economy," which is at the crossroads of established industries.

In management literature, various forms of the industry-convergence model have explained the emergence of industries by illustrating the merging, demerging, and eventual demise of existing industries (e.g., Curran, Broring, and Leker, 2010; Hacklin, 2008; Lei, 2000). A convergence of industries could eventually lead to the emergence of new industry segments, either replacing or complementing former industries at their intersection (Hacklin, 2008). Firms subject to complementary convergence have the choice of pursuing an active role in the new segment or concentrating on the traditional business. In contrast, firms in former industries eventually being replaced by the emerging industry segment, so-called substitutive convergence, have to engage in innovation aimed at the new field to survive. The key factor for firms to survive in times of substitutive industry convergence is innovation.

The need for innovation has been widely addressed for a number of reasons, including economic development, competitive advantage, and corporate success (Lee, Oson, and Trimi, 2010; Smith, 2010; Cooper, 2001; Freeman and Soete, 1997; Utterback, 1994; Drucker, 1986; Schumpeter, 1934). The innovation process, however, might be conducted with a varying degree of openness, ranging from closed to open innovation. Firms with the philosophy of closed innovation manage innovation within their internal boundaries, investing in R&D to attain and develop unique ideas on their own, and then manufacture, market, distribute, and service products from those ideas by themselves (Chesbrough, 2003). Since the close of the twentieth century, through an open innovation approach, firms have been able to improve the innovation process for launching new products and reducing time to market (Chesbrough, 2003; Chesbrough, 2005; Christensen, Olesen, and Kjaer, 2005). Firms engaged in open innovation "use purposive inflows and outflows of knowledge to accelerate internal innovation and to expand the markets for external use of innovation respectively" (Chesbrough, 2006, 1).

During times when industries are converging, however, firms often lack the necessary knowledge and competences to engage in innovation in the new emerging segment in a successful way (Bröring and Leker, 2007; Bröring, Cloutier, and Leker, 2006; Stieglitz, 2003), as these resources are located in different industries (Bierly and Chakrabarti, 1999). Firms need to open the innovation process to source essential resources beyond their own boundaries (Bröring, 2010). At the interfirm level, open innovation management requires cooperation between partnering firms in order to develop, organize, and structure joint innovation activities (Bossink, 2002). In this process, firms may establish either an outside-in process (inbound innovation), an inside-out process (outbound innovation), or a coupled process in the development of their relationships (Enkel, Gassmann, and Chesbrough, 2009; Smith, 2010). For the joint development and commercialization of innovations in an alliance, partnering firms have to establish a coupled innovation process (so-called cocreation), combining the outside-in and inside-out processes (Enkel et al., 2009). The related reciprocal resource exchanges are crucial to success in this coupled innovation process.

According to some scholars (Cockburn and Henderson, 1998; Granstrand, Bohlin, Oskarsson, and Sjoberg, 1992; Arora and Gambardella, 1990) firms no longer rely exclusively on internal or external (closed or open) innovation sourcing strategies but seek a balanced strategy. The reasons for a balanced strategy are that too much openness might negatively affect a firm's long-term innovation success, on the one hand, as it may lead to a loss of control, knowledge, intellectual property, and core competences (Enkel et al., 2009), while, on the other hand, too much closedness disserves increasing demands for shorter innovation cycles and reduced time to market. Therefore, open innovation should be in balance with internal innovation strategies to succeed in innovation.

In sum, for the joint development and commercialization of innovation, partnering firms have to adopt an open innovation strategy through an alliance, characterized by reciprocal exchange of resources, balanced with the internal R&D strategies of the individual firms. Firms have to forge strategic alliances that bridge value chains from disparate industries for innovation in emerging, new interindustry segments. Therefore, we posit that firms in joint innovation projects in biochemistry benefit from cross-industry alliances and offer the following proposition:

> Proposition 1: Cross-industry coupled and balanced innovation processes are positively related to the innovation performance of firms in joint innovation projects in biochemistry.

Strategic Alliances

Along with the open innovation perspective, strategic management scholars recognize the importance of strategic alliances to bridge resource, technological, and commercial gaps for the development of innovation (Batterink, 2009; Eisenhardt and Schoonhoven, 1996). Alliances can be defined as "any volunteering and enduring arrangements between two or more firms involving the exchange, sharing, or co-development of products, technologies, or services" (Gulati, 2007, 1). Studies confirm that both direct alliance relationships (e.g., Stuart, 2000; Deeds and Hill, 1996) and indirect interfirm relationships in an alliance network (e.g., Owen-Smith and Powell, 2004; Ahuja, 2000) enhance the innovation performance of firms.

Researchers in alliance literature consider complementary resources and partner alignments as relational drivers of competitive advantage. Dyer and Singh (1998), for example, argued firms can achieve competitive advantages over other firms by creating interfirm relationships, called *relational rents*. Wubben and his colleagues (2012) recognized these relational rents to be a characteristic of the alliance or network, and investigated and confirmed the stated relational drivers for bio-based innovations. Partnering firms should be complementary on technological and knowledge resources for creating relational rents to advance bio-based innovation. Complementary resources are the distinctive resources and capabilities of alliance partners "that collectively generate greater advantages than the sum of those obtained from the individual endowments of each partner" (Dyer and Singh, 1998, 666–67). Partnering firms should have complementary or even overlapping technological and market knowledge, expertise, and resources (Emden, Calantone, and Droge, 2006). Complementary expertise was found to be a key factor in partner selection for successful alliances (Barnes, Pashby, and Gibbons, 2002). Moreover, complementarities in technological resources and expertise between the partnering firms were found to be a key aspect in interfirm relationships to advance bio-based innovation (Wubben et al., 2012).

Regarding partner alignment, firms in an alliance should reach alignment at both strategic and relational levels, enabling the creation of relational rents, to advance bio-based innovation. *Strategic alignment* should focus on the motivations of partners for entering the alliance, and their goals, which should not conflict (Emden et al., 2006). It was found that successful partners in advancing bio-based innovations have nonconflicting motives and goals at the strategic level (Wubben et al., 2012). *Motives* refer to the reasons for joining an alliance, while goals refer to the more explicit expectations. The importance of complementary, nonconflicting, or even congruent (Bremmers and Sabidussi, 2009) *goals* has been recognized empirically in the selection of partners (Barnes, Pashby, and Gibbons, 2002; Baily, Masson, and Raeside, 1998).

Regarding *relational alignment*, we distinguish between compatible cultures, openness to change, and long-term relational orientation (Emden et al., 2006). First, partner firms should have compatible cultures (Emden et al., 2006; Baily et al., 1998). Second, in line with the open innovation perspective

(Chesbrough, 2003), partners should have a flexible attitude toward their role and task in the network. Cultures should be open toward change to succeed in innovation (Lee, Olson, and Trimi, 2010; Odenthal, Tovstiga, Tambe, and Van Oene, 2004). In other words, *expectational alignment* is assumed to be an important factor in creating and maintaining partner alignment. Third, both partners should aim at a long-term relationship (Emden et al., 2006). Underlying the importance of alignment in the long-term relational orientation, several studies address the presence of commitment in open innovation projects as important to success (Bremmers and Sabidussi, 2009; Bonney, Clark, Collins, and Fearne, 2007).

In sum, partner alignment within an alliance affects open innovation performance positively. It should be reached at strategic and relational levels. Therefore, we posit the following:

> Proposition 2: Both the strategic and relational alignments of the partnering firms in the alliance are positively related to the innovation performance of firms in joint innovation projects in biochemistry.

Strategic Networks

From a network perspective, firms involve a network of direct and indirect interfirm relationships when forming and maintaining alliances (Schilling and Phelps, 2007), although there are at least three different views on optimal network configurations. A first perspective on optimal network configurations, classified as the *bonding view* (Coleman, 1988, 1990), claims social capital investments to be most valuable when partners have strong relationship ties. The main argument for this is that network closure makes partners more willing to share tacit knowledge (Coleman, 1988, 1990). Consequently, the benefits of strong ties are reflected in innovation trajectories that allow for the exchange of more complex and proprietary information (Hansen, 1999; Tsai and Ghoshal, 1998).

A second perspective on the optimal network configuration, developed by Granovetter (1973, 1985), introduced the distinction between *strong and weak* ties, associating strong ties with a dense network structure. Strong ties indicate intensive and frequent contact, relating to overlapping informational resources and ease of mutual understanding. Strong ties between firms facilitate information flows, but firms are likely to possess highly redundant information. Firms with weak ties are likely to possess more diverse knowledge and information, increasing the chance of finding novel ideas, but the weakness of the tie increases the difficulty of information flow among them.

As a third perspective, classified as the *bridging view* (Adler and Kwon, 2002), the structural configuration of relationships, especially the element of the structural hole, plays a major role in the value of social capital to promote innovations (Burt, 1992, 1997). The bridging tie is "a tie that spans a structural hole" (Reagans, Zuckerman, and McEvily, 2004:103). Bridging ties connect firms separated by a structural hole, enabling access to new and novel information to serve as bridge to new opportunities. Strong ties bind, and bridging ties span structural holes. Sparse networks with diverse structural holes are expected to provide access to a wide range of nonredundant information sources (Adler and Kwon, 2002). Interestingly, Burt (2000) does endorse the benefit of network closure, stating that "network closure can be essential to realizing the value buried in the holes" (410). The three views on optimal network configurations are not deemed mutually exclusive.

Recent studies on optimal network structure incorporate elements of both strong and bridging ties in a tie portfolio (Levin and Cross, 2004; Obstfeld, 2005), together advancing innovation (Tiwana, 2008). Bridging ties allow for diversity in accessible (structural-hole spanning) knowledge, capabilities, and perspectives but lack the characteristics to integrate them. In contrast, strong ties ease knowledge integration for realizing innovation but lower the chance of innovation due to redundant knowledge, perspectives, and capabilities. Strong ties (e.g., trust, reciprocity, close interaction) support the integration of diverse knowledge, but capabilities are made accessible by bridging ties. An alliance simultaneously possessing strong and bridging ties has access to a diverse array of knowledge, perspectives, and skills and has the mechanisms for knowledge integration to realize innovation (Tiwana, 2008). Drawing on the network literature, we derive that a combination of strong and bridging ties is expected to influence innovation performance positively. Thus, we propose the following proposition:

> Proposition 3: Relationship ties, specified by the combination of strong ties and bridging ties, are positively related to the innovation performance of firms in joint innovation projects in biochemistry.

After deriving three propositions, we can now offer our conceptual framework for our study.

Conceptual Framework

Since this chapter aims to disclose key cross-industry drivers for innovation performance in biochemistry from an interfirm relational perspective, this study drew its conceptual bases from innovation management, strategic alliance literature, and network literature to specify the following three variables: innovation strategy, partner alignment, and relationship ties. See Figure 4.1.

First, based on the literature on innovation management, partnering firms aiming at the joint development and commercialization of innovation should establish an open innovation strategy, within which the innovation process is composed of inbound and outbound innovation (a coupled process). The concept of open innovation strategy is characterized by the actual exchange of resources (Chesbrough, 2003). More specifically, the open innovation strategy is operationalized by the reciprocal exchange of resources (Enkel et al., 2009), balanced with internal innovation practices of the partnering firms (Enkel et al., 2009; Odenthal et al., 2004).

Second, drawing from the strategic alliance literature we focused on strategic alignment and relational alignment (Emden et al., 2006). Strategic alignment needs to be reached in the motives and goals of the partners (Barnes et al., 2002; Baily et al., 1998). The motives for entering the alliance and the goals of the partnering firms are supposed to be complementary, nonconflicting, or even congruent (Bremmers and Sabidussi, 2009; Emden et al., 2006). Relational alignment is operationalized by alignment in innovation culture, commitment, and expectations. Partner firms should have compatible cultures (Emden et al., 2006; Baily et al., 1998). Cultures should be open to change to succeed in innovation (Lee et al., 2010; Odenthal et al., 2004). Underlying the alignment in the long-term relational orientation, the presence of commitment in open innovation projects is very important (Bremmers and Sabidussi, 2009; Bonney et al., 2007). Finally, firms should also have a flexible attitude toward their own role and task in the network and that of their partner. This describes expectational alignment. Thus, as displayed in Figure 4.1, the five operational variables specify the exogenous variables for partner alignment.

Third, regarding the optimal network structure most conducive to innovation, strong relationship ties between partnering firms are assumed to enhance the realization of innovation when the relationship simultaneously bridges structural holes between the firms. Based on Granovetter's (1973) view, the following items operationalize the concept of strong ties: amount of time, emotional intensity, intimacy, and reciprocal services associated with the tie. A defining characteristic of bridging ties is nonredundancy (Burt, 1992), for example, the connected actors are heterogeneous in their backgrounds, experiences, knowledge, and skills. Figure 4.1 presents the theoretical framework with the key relational drivers and their relationships. This theoretical framework will be applied in our field research as discussed in the following section.

Methodology

In our study, explorative research was necessary because of the novelty of research on innovation alliances in biochemistry, scarcity of good data, and confidentiality issues. Therefore, we have chosen a case study method for collecting and analyzing empirical data. As Yin (2003) points out, a case study methodology is suitable when seeking to understand phenomena in unique real-life settings, which are too complex for more strict research methods like surveys and experiments.

Our empirical research examines multiple case studies to investigate the proposed propositions on the relational drivers, as presented in the theoretical framework above. Multiple case studies can be highly valuable and representative when every case serves a specific purpose within the overall scope of the study (Eisenhardt, 1989). Furthermore, for this chapter, explanatory case research (McCutcheon and Meredith, 1993) turned out to be most suitable, since neither pure case reporting nor theory development was done on the basis of the empirical data. We use cases predicting contrasting results (Yin, 2003) by selecting

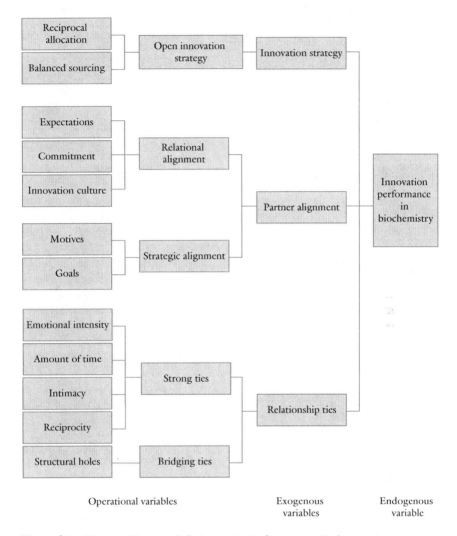

Figure 4.1 Theoretical Framework for Innovation Performance in Biochemistry

comparable yet quite different cases. The following case selection criteria were used:

1. Involvement of a commercial firm, located in the Netherlands
2. Involvement in biomass valorization for chemicals/materials
3. Active in joint innovation projects for bio-based chemicals/materials
4. Engagement in cross-industry interfirm alliance(s)
5. Involvement in cross-industry alliance with other focal firms (or another focal firm)
6. Industry background of focal firm in either agriculture or chemistry

Sufficient homogeneity of cases is secured by the first four criteria, whereas the fifth criterion is included to enable the cross-industry bilateral study of relationships. Nevertheless, the focal firms were not obliged to provide access to potentially sensitive data on individual particular innovation projects and/or relationships. Criterion six allows for variety among the cases included in the data set. We expect an outsider interview to increase the external validity of the case study research by assessing the cases from a broader perspective. Two specific criteria are used to select the outsider—namely, firm-level involvement in cross-industry alliances in biochemistry and familiarity with the firms. Initial interviews were used to find sufficient, suitable cases. The sensitive search for research objects resulted in nine innovative firms involved in biomass valorization for chemicals/materials that have cross-industry relationships with other firms in joint innovation projects. We note that the fulfillment of the criteria has been examined both prior to the case study interview and afterward. The only divergence was from the fifth criterion; the preferred focus of the majority of interviews was not on a cross-industry alliance with another focal firm. The commercial sensitivity of the relationships did not allow us to interview key partners. As a result, none of the cases included interviews with both firms in the key cross-industry alliance, although this is quite common in alliance research.

The characteristics of the most valuable cross-industry interfirm relationship in realizing innovation performance are investigated by means of interviews and a content analysis of related documents. At each focal firm, a face-to-face semi-structured interview was conducted with the person who is responsible for and actively involved in the joint project. This person was often the general manager, R&D manager, or new business development director of the focal firm. We also used related literature and documents to substantiate our interview results. We employed the snowball principle to find the suitable information in this relatively unexplored research area. The case study results are compared within and across the selected cases for internal research validity and assessed from a broader perspective by deploying an outsider for external validity. Due to the scattered expertise in the biochemical domain, we are reluctant to call the outsider "an expert."

The interviews focused at the cross-industry alliance of the focal firm with the most valuable partner firm in realizing innovation in the joint project. Each interview started with an introduction of the focal firm and innovation project. Following the project introduction, the questionnaire started off with a set of three questions to map the innovation network. Of this set of questions, a first question aimed to map the categories of parties in the innovation network, followed by a second question that mapped the most important individual partners among the parties. A third question was geared to bring about industry background and the project role of the commercial firms among the most valuable project partners. For practical reasons, the remainder of the interview was limited to exploring one critical commercial relationship within the innovation network. The three key relational variables—consisting of innovation strategy, partner alignment, and relationship ties—were measured by a combination of open and multiple-choice questions. The questionnaire concluded with a set of three questions aimed at mapping the innovation performance of the alliance.

In order to measure the operational variables of the theoretical framework, 21 validated interview questions were taken directly or derived from previous studies in the field of strategic alliances and innovation management. The questionnaire was semistructured, meaning that 9 open questions were alternated with 12 more structured multiple-choice or scaled questions. The combination of open and closed questions enabled us to combine the time-saving advantages of multiple-choice or scaled questions with the flexibility and content validity of open questions. Per interview, data on the 12 operational variables were measured by 21 questions, bringing about both open answers and 37 individual Likert-scale scores. Interviewees were explicitly asked to complement or discuss important relational aspects in addition to the aspects covered by the questionnaire.

As displayed in Table 4.1, the case studies comprise a total of nine focal commercial firms in the Netherlands in either agriculture or chemistry industries. We had to list all of the participating firms anonymously for confidentiality reasons. Each focal firm is considered in a broad innovation network comprising a variety of external parties, such as suppliers, customers, and R&D institutions. Sometimes even competitive partners were involved in the process, as in the cases of Bioingredient-firm and Biopolymers-firm. The focal Protein-firm is separated into two cases, as denoted Protein-firm (T) and Protein-firm (P), because this case study involved two different cross-industry relationships with innovations

Table 4.1 Focal Firms and Key Alliance Partners

Focal Firms	Alliance Partners	Nature of Collaborations
Sugar-firm	Biochemical-firm	Basic research, sugar beet to PLA
Potato-firm	Lysine-firm	Process development, potato skins to lysine
Bio-ingredient-firm	Detergent-firm	Commercialization, inulin to anti–lime scale product
Protein-firm (T)	Biotechnology-firm	Process development, potato to protein ingredients
Protein-firm (P)	Application-firm	Product and market development, proteins to food and nonfood applications
Biochemical-firm	Paper-firm	Process development, paper waste to PLA
Biotech-firm	Sewage-firm	Basic research, paper waste from sewage to chemicals/materials
Biocomposites-firm	Flax-firm	Process and product development, flax to composite
Biopolymers-firm	Plant-firm	Commercialization, starch to biodegradable plant pot
Furanics-firm	Papermill-firm	Basic research, paper waste to furanics

in technology or product development. Thus, the nine focal firms bring about ten relationships. The alliances were found to span quite different positions in the bio-based production chain process. In seven case studies, the alliances span two or three successive stages in the bio-based chain while in the cases of Bioingredient-firm and Biocomposites-firm the alliances encompass the entire supply chain.

Let us explain in detail the nine different innovation projects. To extract value out of (residual) beet components, the Sugar-firm entered a joint project investigating the possibilities of a production process of sugar beet to bio-based plastics. The Potato-firm entered a joint project to develop a production process of lysine from potato skins. Bioingredient-firm entered a joint project to develop a bio-based antilime product from a technological and market perspective. The subsidiary of the Protein-firm was founded on the basis of a joint project. Its internal bio-refinery process is optimized through cooperation with a Biotechnology-firm (T), while the ingredient-based applications are developed through cooperation with a product development–oriented Application-firm (P). The Biochemical-firm entered a joint project to explore the use of cellulosic residues from paper mills for the production of its chemical building blocks for application in bio-plastics. Biotech-firm is involved in a joint project that investigates the valorization opportunities of cellulose from toilet paper removed from sewage at communal water treatment plants. The Bio-composites-firm entered into a joint project to develop a flax-based special textile for the composites industry. Biopolymers-firm entered into a joint project focused on the development and commercialization of a biodegradable bio-based plant pot. Furanics-firm leads a joint project focused on the use of residual flows from paper industries and other nonfood crops for the production of its chemical building block Furanics. Having presented both the methodology of the empirical research and findings, we will next turn to the analysis of the results of our research.

Results

Due to the sheer volume of data derived from secondary documents, coded statements, and 37 individual scores per respondent, we need to be selective with data representation. Here, representative qualitative information will be presented in different formats. We start with information on the key assumption lingering behind this research—namely, that cross-industry strategic alliances are positively related with open innovation performance in the emerging biochemistry industry. In viewing the cases along the four different phases of the innovation model (i.e., knowledge development, technology development, product development, and market development/commercialization), a fine distribution of cases can be traced. Three cases (Sugar-firm, Biotech-firm, Furanics-firm) are currently situated in the first phase (knowledge development), focusing on researching (technical) feasibility with the goal of commercialization. Two cases (Potato-firm, Biochemical-firm) are currently situated in the technology-development phase, having developed successful technologies allowing the derivation of components from biomass. However, the application of these components is not yet economically viable. Only the case of Biocomposites-firm is situated in the product-development phase, as it has already created prototypes and has begun product development. Finally, three cases (Bioingredient-firm, Protein-firm, Biopolymers-firm) are in the market-development phase, which involves a pilot plant, scaling up, market launch, and commercialization of, for example, bio-based plant pots or dishwashing tablets. All nine focal firms forged strategic alliances with firms originating from either the agricultural or chemical sectors in order to realize biochemical/biomaterial innovations: "Collaboration among agricultural and chemical firms is required for the emergence of biochemistry" (outsider). All interviewees perceive commercial firms from disparate industries to be among the most valuable partners in the innovation network. Eight focal firms explicitly participate in projects aiming at market entry. Innovation performance is even expected in the recently initiated alliances, building as they do upon performance in the recent past. One can conclude that the results confirm the key assumption of this chapter that the open innovation performance of firms in joint innovation projects in biochemistry benefits from cross-industry strategic alliances.

The degree of recognition of the three relational variables—namely, innovation strategy, partner alignment, and relationship ties—was investigated by the interviews with three open questions. Interviewees were invited to (1) elaborate on the collaboration with the partner in the innovation process, (2) describe what relational aspects they sense/perceive the same as their partner, and (3) specify the practical/operational collaboration. A categorical relationship has been found between innovation strategy and open innovation performance and between partner alignment and open innovation performance, for all nine case studies. However, the results show a wide variety of relational aspects, only broadly confirming the relatedness between relationship ties and open innovation performance in the case studies.

Innovation Strategy

In terms of innovation strategy, as the first of the three proposed relational drivers for innovation performance, the related questions measured the existence of open, reciprocal, and balanced innovation strategies in the alliances. Therefore, we investigated the level of resource allocation to the joint project by the partners on the following six categories: knowledge, expertise, information, staff/support, technical equipment, and funds/money. Overall, the interviewees scored particularly high on the allocation of knowledge (avg: 6.4) and expertise (avg: 6.0): "Because of the collaboration we did not have to invent the wheel again" (an interviewee at Biopolymers-firm). Three interviewees (Bioingredient-firm, Biocomposites-firm, Furanics-firm) indicated that R&D-related resources are mainly exchanged in the early phases, whereas later on only resources needed for market development and commercialization are exchanged. Three interviewees

(Potato-firm, Biochemical-firm, Furanics-firm) stressed the importance of an intermediary in gathering the required level of materials for the chemical partner. In sum, interviewees on average indicate a high allocation of all six resource categories to the joint project by one or both firms (avg: 5.7). Interviewees pointed to various factors, like innovation phase and firm size, which may affect the level of resource allocation to a joint project.

Reciprocal allocation was measured by investigating which of the alliance firms allocated the particular resources to the project. Six interviewees on average perceived reciprocal allocation of resources in their relationships (avg: ≥5.5; 1.0 is one-sided contribution only; 7.0 stands for two-sided resources). Four of these interviewees (Sugar-firm, Bioingredient-firm, Biocomposites-firm, Biopolymers-firm) on average perceived highly reciprocal allocation between the partners (avg: ≥6.5), while three interviewees (Biotech-firm, Biochemical-firm, Protein-firm) on average perceived relatively low reciprocity in resource allocation (avg: ≤4.5). Three interviewees (Biochemical-firm, Sugar-firm, and Potato-firm) indicated that the contribution in resource allocations is affected by the partner in the alliance where the technology/process development is situated: "Investments in money and staff were in the preliminary phases mainly done by the biomass-supplying firm to develop a technology to convert biomass" (an interviewee at Potato-firm). Evidently, the project role and interest influenced the level of resource allocation (i.e., available funds/money, staff, expertise, and knowledge) (interviewees at Furanics-firm and Biotech-firm). In sum, resource allocation was on average scored as moderately reciprocal.

In researching the presence of *balanced innovation sourcing*, interviewees were asked whether the focal firm invested in internal R&D activities apart from the joint innovation project. Seven interviewees confirmed that their firm invested in parallel internal R&D activities: "Internal R&D aimed at knowledge development creates the seeds for future innovation projects" (an interviewee at Protein-firm). Generally, interviewees remarked that internal R&D activities are oriented toward a wider context than the joint project. The other focal firms indicated they innovate entirely openly, without conducting internal R&D activities parallel to the joint innovation activities.

Partner Alignment

Partner alignment is the second relational driver for open innovation performance according to our conceptual model. Partner alignment is operationalized by relational and strategic alignment. *Relational alignment* was measured by investigating alignment in expectations, commitment, and innovation culture. The results show that seven interviewees on average perceived to be aligned on project *expectations* (avg: ≥4.7 on a scale of 1 to 7 being very high alignment), referring to several aspects of expectational alignment, like cost price, market size, sales, project duration, and time horizons. The focal firms indicated they were roughly aware of the project expectations of the partner (8 out of 9), and most stated the expectations became more specific over the course of the project (6 out of 9). Investigating the level of *commitment* from the focal firm toward its partner, interviewees on average perceived moderate commitment of their firm toward the alliance partner (avg: 4.4): "Achieving results in alliances is a prerequisite for building commitment" (an interviewee at Potato-firm). Four interviewees (at Biochemical-firm, Furanics-firm, Potato-firm, and Protein-firm) referred to the availability of comparable alternatives, the network of the partner, and the level of project success as affecting the level of commitment. Interviewees on average scored higher on partner alignment in commitment than scoring on commitment itself (avg: 5.4 versus 4.4 interviewees). Regarding *innovation culture*, eight interviewees on average perceived they were aligned in innovation culture with the partner, determined by open innovation and learning (avg: ≥5.0), characterized by discussing project experiences and sharing failure tolerance. However, five focal firms (Sugar-firm, Potato-firm, Bioingredient-firm, Protein-firm, and Biotech-firm) indicate that tolerance for and learning from failures is restricted in commercialization-focused projects.

Research on *strategic alignment* is meant to investigate alignment in motives and goals. Seven interviewees perceived a rather high partner alignment in partnership *motives*, often referred to as "partnership objectives" (Score: ≥5.0). Three interviewees (Sugar-firm, Potato-firm, Biotech-firm) explicitly indicated they have compatible and similar *joint* partnership motives, whereas four (interviewees at Sugar-firm, Potato-firm, Biochemical-firm, Bioingredient-firm) perceived *individual* partnership motives and related interests to be more or less dissimilar: "It is not possible to have completely similar partnership motives as the partner. Nevertheless, the partnership motives need to be compatible and be shared" (an interviewee at Bioingredient-firm). Based on averages, five focal firms perceived high partner alignment in project *goals* (avg: ≥5.3). Four focal firms (Sugar-firm, Potato-firm, Biotech-firm, Biocomposites-firm) on average scored moderate on alignment in project goals (avg: 4.0), as the interviewees perceived little to no partner alignment in individual project goals.

In sum, the results on partner alignment, relational alignment in expectations, innovation culture, and commitment, on average scored (reasonably) high in eight cases (avg: ≥4.7). However, strategic alignment in motives and goals is on average found to be (reasonably) high in six case studies (Av: ≥4.7) and rather low in three cases (Av: ≤4.3).

Relationship Ties

Finally, relationship ties were posited to be the third relational driver for open innovation performance. Relationship ties were operationalized by investigating a combination of strong and bridging ties. Strong ties were researched by measuring the emotional intensity, contact frequency, intimacy, and reciprocity between the firms. Eight interviewees perceived *emotional intensity* to be (often) present in the relationship with their partner (avg: ≥5.5), stating that trust with essential project details and reliability in keeping promises are important aspects. The Protein-firm underlined the importance of trust, as it affects failure tolerance in innovation alliances positively. An interviewee argued that time to build trust, which generally takes long, strongly depends on whether the firm already belongs to the focal firm's network. Furthermore, it was stated that project details are more easily shared at lower organizational levels. Regarding *contact frequency*, all nine interviewees indicated they have contact at the managerial level with the partner firm monthly or less than once a month. Bio-ingredient-firm, which cooperated in both R&D and commercialization activities simultaneously, distinguished contact frequency in ad hoc contact between sales departments and more structured contact between R&D departments. Four focal firms (Sugar-firm, Bioingredient-firm, Biotech-firm, and Biopolymers-firm) stated that contacts were made via multiple channels, like interalliance project meetings, videoconferences, phone, and mail. In sum, contacts at the management level seem to take place monthly or less frequently, but various factors were mentioned that affect contact frequency, such as the project phase, intermediary involvement, communication channels, and the type of department.

Intimacy between the partnering firms was measured by investigating the range of topics discussed in the relationship. Four focal firms discussed only work or business topics with the partner firm. Intimacy was perceived to be really personal by three representatives (Potato-firm, Biocomposites-firm, and Biotech-firm): "Intimacy was strongly dependent on personality. Firm size does not impact intimacy" (an interviewee at Biocomposites-firm). In sum, intimacy was perceived as important in the relationship by only three interviewees. Personality, firm background, and partnership duration were factors that may affect intimacy in alliances. In contrast, on average, *reciprocity* in the relationship was perceived as (very) high by six interviewees, indicating fair share of gains and joint efforts to be important aspects of the alliance (avg: ≥6.0). In sum, among the four aspects of strong ties investigated, emotional intensity and reciprocity were perceived to be important aspects in the relationships.

Bridging ties were investigated by measuring the extent to which structural holes between the partners exist. Six representatives indicated their firm was (very) different from the partner firm in terms of skills and abilities, background and experiences, and expertise and competences (avg: ≥5.3). Interviewees characterized the alliance as bridging major structural holes, materialized by relationship ties between the cooperating firms. Firms in the alliances were very different, and there were complementary resources.

Analysis

This section analyses and draws conclusions from the three propositions that were posited in the literature section above. Proposition 1 is confirmed by the numerical data on the case studies. Proposition 1 holds that cross-industry coupled and balanced innovation processes are positively related to the innovation performance of firms in joint innovation projects in biochemistry. Coupled innovation processes relate to both substantial and reciprocal contributions to innovation projects. Strategic balance refers to work on innovations both within the alliance and internal to the company. See Figure 4.2.

Open innovation strategies within the alliances have been confirmed to be important in all nine case studies (ten paired relationships), being materialized in the resource allocation of one or both alliance firms to the joint innovation project. Reciprocity in resource allocation (six out of ten) and strategic balance in innovation sourcing (seven out of ten), within and outside the alliance, are confirmed to be important aspects of the open innovation strategy. "Resource allocation in an open innovation alliance is like a balance, which reciprocates during the project" (an interviewee at Furanics-firm). Nevertheless, reciprocity was moderate at best in three joint innovation projects. The derived overall averages on the three variables resource allocation, reciprocal allocation, and balanced sourcing are found to be high for all three variables (avg: 5.7, 5.1, and 5.8, respectively). Figure 4.2 presents the average resource allocation for each of the six investigated resource categories. It is evident that knowledge, expertise, information, staff/support, technical equipment, and funds/money are allocated substantially to the joint project by one or both firms (avg: ≥5.0). Most interviewees spontaneously added the allocation of biomass materials to the project, not covered by one of the stated resource categories. Interestingly, Figure 4.2 shows that the contribution of resource knowledge, expertise, and staff/support is quite often one-sided.

Proposition 2 is partly confirmed by the data gathered through the case studies. This proposition holds that the relational alignment and strategic alignment of partnering firms in the alliance are positively related to the innovation performance of firms in joint innovation projects in biochemistry. Regarding strategic alignment, six focal firms are highly aligned with their partners (avg: ≥4.7), more often on motives than on goals. Individual project goals have

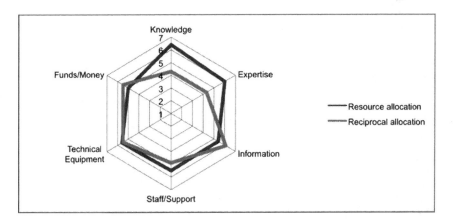

Figure 4.2 Average Resource Allocation and Reciprocal Allocation (N = 10)

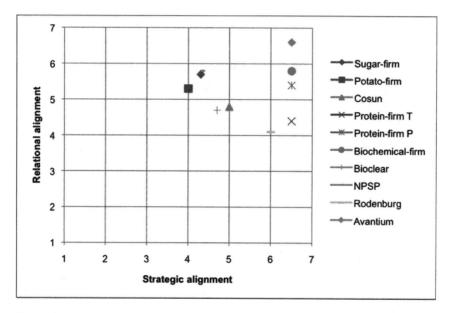

Figure 4.3 Strategic and Relational Alignment Perceived in Cases (N = 10)

to be compatible, although they are often dissimilar due to the different chain positions of the alliance partners. From a relational perspective, eight focal firms on average were well aligned with their partners with respect to expectations, innovation culture, and commitment (avg: ≥4.7). (See Figure 4.3.) Nevertheless, some of the scores on expectations and commitment were (very) low, bringing for example the average score for commitment down to 4.4 across the total set of alliances. In contrast, none of the alliances scored very low on innovation culture.

All alliances are placed in the upper-right quadrant of Figure 4.3, impying that, in general, the focal firms are aligned with their partner from both a strategic and relational perspective. The contrary example of a lack of partner alignment at both the strategic and relational level in combination with negative publicity around the partner resulted in a breakdown of one of the cases involving the Bio-ingredient-firm. Four interviewees underlined the importance of a starting phase prior to the joint project in order to reach partner alignment at both the relational and strategic level. Some interviewees signaled the importance of partner alignment in vision, regarding, for instance, product/process innovation (Protein-firm), product value (Protein-firm, Biocomposites-firm), intellectual property (Biocomposites-firm), and/or residual flows as a product (Biochemical-firm, Biotech-firm).

Proposition 3 is partly confirmed by the data on individual alliances. This proposition holds that relationship ties, specified by the combination of strong ties and bridging ties, are positively related to the innovation performance of firms in joint innovation projects in biochemistry. Figure 4.4 presents an overview of the results on the four aspects that operationalize the strength of ties. Interviewees considered emotional intensity and reciprocity as important aspects of their relationship (overall avg: 5.5 and 5.6, respectively). In contrast, they did not perceive the amount of time and intimacy to be important aspects in their relationship (overall avg: 3.5 and 3.3, respectively).

Interviewees indicated that relationship ties bridging structural holes between partnering firms are an important relational aspect. Especially resource complementarities were underlined as a prerequisite for every innovation project with two or more contributing partners (avg: ≥5.3): "After quitting the partnership, we experienced how complementary the partner was in missing its resources" (an interviewee at Bio-ingredient-firm). Consequently, this part of the proposition can be confirmed. Counter to the proposition, the proposed combination of strong and bridging relationship ties was not confirmed by the results. Interviewees on average perceived their relationship ties to be more bridging than strong (overall avg: 5.4 versus 4.8, respectively). A detailed analysis of the data shows that strong ties did not complement weak ties in low-scoring cases, and vice versa. To conclude on relationship ties, it can be stated that bridging relationship ties and/or strong relationship ties (emotional intensity, reciprocity) can be a driver for open innovation performance in biochemistry.

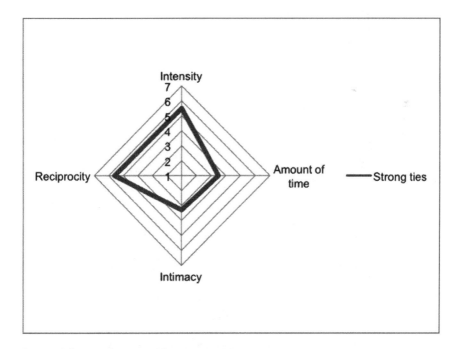

Figure 4.4   Average Aspects of the Strength of Ties (N = 11)

Conclusions

The objective of this chapter was to find the key cross-industry drivers for open innovation performance from a relational perspective. The literature study allowed us to posit three propositions on plausible drivers for cross-industry open innovation performance and to develop the conceptual framework that was assessed empirically. Nine cases were selected, on which we held interviews with interviewees of the focal firms, extensively gathered secondary documents, and evaluated matters with an outsider with expertise in the innovation alliances in the field of biochemistry. Interviews consisting of open and closed questions brought about rich data on nine cross-industry alliances at agricultural and chemical firms, derived from both secondary documents, coded statements, and over 30 individual scores per respondent. On the basis of within-case and cross-case analysis, we could first of all conclude that innovation performance in joint innovation projects in biochemistry benefits from cross-industry strategic alliances. All nine cases included commercial firms from different industries as vital partners for realizing innovation in the joint project.

We focused on three relational drivers—namely, innovation strategy, partner alignment, and relational ties—of cross-industry innovation performance. Regarding the first driver of innovation strategy, it was found that resource allocation, reciprocal allocation, and a strategic balance with internal innovation sourcing strategies are important operational variables of the innovation strategy. Interestingly, reciprocity in resource allocations was identified as less prevalent than the contribution of resources by partnering firms and (external-internal) balanced innovation activities. The second driver of partner alignment was also recognized in the case studies. Motives turned out to be a stronger operational variable than goals for strategic alignment. Expectations, commitment, and innovation culture seemed to be important operational variables of relational alignment, topped by innovation culture. Regarding the third relational driver, relationship ties bridging structural holes reflect an accurate operationalization of the driver relationship ties. But in contrast to bridging ties, the interviewees pointed out negative impacts that strong ties might have on firm performance. As a consequence, only emotional intensity and reciprocity in an alliance were recognized as appropriate variables reflecting strong relationship ties. Therefore, the variable of strong ties is represented with dotted lines in the revised framework (see Figure 4.5). Overall, our research shows that key cross-industry drivers for the innovation performance of firms in joint innovation projects in biochemistry are innovation strategy, partner alignment, and relationship ties between the partnering firms.

In a series of research projects on the drivers for innovation in biomass valorization (e.g., Wubben et al., 2012), our work is the first study aimed at disclosing cross-industry drivers for innovation in the context of biochemistry from an interfirm perspective. Although data gathering is very difficult in such competition-sensitive and transitory settings, further research is recommended, preferably encompassing the complete innovation network of the focal

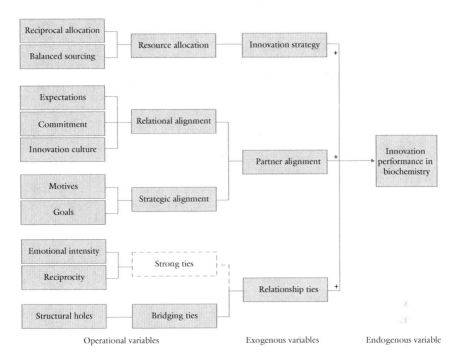

Figure 4.5 Revised Theoretical Framework

firms—including bilateral research of key alliance partners and the less important network partners—reducing common method bias, and surfacing network-
level effects. Certainly, future research on the topic could be extended to a larger
sample, broadened to other cross-industry bio-based cases (e.g., pharmacy, water,
and paper industries) or replicated in other countries to reduce country-specific
biases.

   Firms considering engaging in biochemistry are recommended to work on
drivers—including innovation strategy, partner alignment, and relationship
ties—in the selection of partners and the realization of cross-industry innovation.
Regarding the selection of partners, this chapter suggests that firms should focus
on partners from disparate industries with different backgrounds and experiences, skills and abilities, and different expertise and competences. Successful
partnering for biochemistry innovations should target bridging structural holes.
In the partner selection procedure, firms may use indicators for alignment such
as the compatibility of project goals, partnership objectives, project expectations,
commitment, and innovation and learning culture. After the selection of possible
partners, firms are recommended to invest in emotional intensity and reciprocity in the relationship with their partner. Furthermore, firms are recommended
to focus on both strategic and relational alignment within the cross-industry
alliance. Firms should exclude partners with conflicting individual project goals

and/or partnership motives. Furthermore, firms are recommended to invest in the alignment of expectations, commitment, and innovation culture. Following the selection of actual partners, an effective open innovation strategy implies that resources should be integrated from partners and balanced with internal innovation activities. By this research, we hope that we have contributed to both researchers and businesses interested in open innovation by exploring relational drivers of cross-industry innovation alliances.

Acknowledgments

Financial support from the ERDF-grant, via the EU-Interreg IV-B NWE project ARBOR (www.nweurope.eu and www.arbornwe.eu) is gratefully acknowledged. The statements made in this chapter are the sole responsibility of the authors.

References

Adler, P. S., and Kwon, S.-W. (2002). "Social Capital: Prospects for a New Concept." *Academy of Management Review* 27 (1): 17–40.

Ahuja, G. (2000). "Collaboration Networks, Structural Holes, and Innovation: A Longitudinal Study." *Administrative Science Quarterly* 45 (3): 425–55.

Annevelink, E., and Harmsen, P. (2010). *Bioraffinage: naar een optimale verwaarding van biomassa.* Wageningen, The Netherland:Wageningen UR Food & Biobased Research.

Arora, A., and Gambardella, A. (1990). "Complementarity and External Linkages: The Strategies of the Large Firms in Biotechnology." *The Journal of Industrial Economics* 38 (4): 361–79.

Bailey, W. J., Masson, R., and Raeside, R. (1998). "Choosing Successful Technology Development Partners: A Best-Practice Model." *International Journal of Technology Management* 15 (1): 124–38.

Barnes, T., Pashby, I., and Gibbons, A. (2002). "Effective University-Industry Interaction: A Multi-case Evaluation of Collaborative R&D Projects." *European Management Journal* 20 (3): 272–85.

Batterink, M. (2009). *Profiting from External Knowledge: How Firms Use Different Knowledge Acquisition Strategies to Improve Their Innovation Performance* (Vol. 3): Wageningen, The Netherland: Wageningen Academic Publishers.

Bierly, P., and Chakrabarti, A. K. (1999). "Managing through Industry Fusion." In Brockhoff, K., Chakrabarti, A. K., and Hauschildt, J. (eds.), *The Dynamics of Innovation: Strategic and Managerial Implications*, 3–26. New York: Springer.

Blaauw, R., Haveren, J. v., Scott, E. L., and Bos, H. L. (2008). "Biomass for the Dutch Chemical Industry." *Wageningen: Agrotechnology and Food Sciences Group (Report Agrotechnology and Food Sciences Group)*, 907.

Boehlje, M., and Bröring, S. (2011). "The Increasing Multifunctionality of Agricultural Raw Materials: Three Dilemmas for Innovation and Adoption." *International Food and Agribusiness Management Review* 14 (2): 1–16.

Bonney, L., Clark, R., Collins, R., and Fearne, A. (2007). "From Serendipity to Sustainable Competitive Advantage: Insights from Houston's Farm and Their Journey of Co-innovation." *Supply Chain Management: An International Journal* 12 (6): 395–99.

Bossink, B. A. (2002). "The Development of Co-innovation Strategies: Stages and Interaction Patterns in Interfirm Innovation." *R&D Management* 32 (4), 311–20.

Bremmers, H. J., and Sabidussi, A. (2009). "Co-innovation: What Are the Success Factors?" *APSTRACT: Applied Studies in Agribusiness and Commerce* 3 (1–2): 29–35.

Bröring, S. (2010). "Developing Innovation Strategies for Convergence: Is Open Innovation Imperative?" *International Journal of Technology Management* 49 (1): 272–94.

Bröring, S., Cloutier, M. L., and Leker, J. (2006). "The Front End of Innovation in an Era of Industry Convergence: Evidence from Nutraceuticals and Functional Foods." *R&D Management* 36 (5): 487–98.

Bröring, S., and Leker, J. (2007). "Industry Convergence and Its Implications for the Front End of Innovation: A Problem of Absorptive Capacity." *Creativity and Innovation Management* 16 (2): 165–75.

Burt, R. (1992). *Structural Holes: The Social Structure of Competition.* Boston: Harvard Business School Press.

Burt, R. S. (1997). "The Contingent Value of Social Capital." *Administrative Science Quarterly* 339–365.

Burt, R. S. (2000). "The Network Structure of Social Capital." *Research in Organizational Behavior* 22:345–423.

Chesbrough, H. W. (2003). *Open Innovation: The New Imperative for Creating and Profiting from Technology:* Harvard Business Press.

Chesbrough, H. W. (2005). Open Innovation: A New Paradigm for Understanding Industrial Innovation, *Open Innovation: Researching a new paradigm*: Oxford University Press.

Chesbrough, H. W. (2006). *Open Innovation: Researching a New Paradigm*: Oxford University Press.

Christensen, J. F., Olesen, M. H., and Kjaer, J. S. (2005). "The Industrial Dynamics of Open Innovation: Evidence from the Transformation of Consumer Electronics." *Research Policy* 34 (10): 1533–49.

Cockburn, I. M., and Henderson, R. M. (1998). "Absorptive Capacity, Coauthoring Behavior, and the Organization of Research in Drug Discovery." *The Journal of Industrial Economics* 46 (2): 157–82.

Coleman, J. S. (1988). "Social Capital in the Creation of Human Capital." *American Journal of Sociology* 94: S95–S120.

Coleman, J. S. (1990). *Foundations of Social Theory.* Cambridge, MA: Belknap Press of Harvard University Press.

Communicatie EnergieTransitie (2009). *Bio-based economy in Nederland; macro-economische verkenning van grootschalige introductie van groene grondstoffen in de Nederlandse energievoorziening.* Sittard: Platform Groene Grondstoffen van EnergieTransitie.

Cooper, R. (2001). *Winning at New Products: Accelerating the Process from Idea* to Launch, 3rd ed. Perseus Cambridge.

Curran, C.-S., Broring, S., and Leker, J. (2010). "Anticipating Converging Industries Using Publicly Available Data." *Technological Forecasting and Social Change* 77 (3): 385–95.

De Jong, E., and Jorgensen, H. (2012). "Bio-based Chemicals Value Added Products from Biorefineries." *IEA-Bioenergy Task* 42. http://www.biorefinery.nl/ieabioenergytask42/(Accessed on April, 8, 2014).

Deeds, D. L., and Hill, C. W. (1996). "Strategic Alliances and the Rate of New Product Development: An Empirical Study of Entrepreneurial Biotechnology Firms." *Journal of Business Venturing* 11 (1): 41–55.

Dornburg, V., Faaij, A., Verweij, P., Langeveld, H., van de Ven, G., Wester, F., et al. (2008). *Biomass Assessment: Assessment of Global Biomass Potentials and Their Links to Food, Water, Biodiversity, Energy Demand and Economy: Main Report.* For the

Netherlands Research Programme on Scientific Assessment and Policy Analysis for Climate Change, Netherlands Environmental Assessment Agency MNP, WAB report 500102 012.

Drucker, P. F. (1986). *Managing for Results: Economic Tasks and Risk-Taking Decisions.* New York: Perennial Library.

Dyer, J. H., and Singh, H. (1998). "The Relational View: Cooperative Strategy and Sources of Interorganizational Competitive Advantage." *Academy of Management Review* 23 (4): 660–79.

Eisenhardt, K. M. (1989). "Building Theories from Case Study Research." *Academy of Management Review* 14 (4): 532–50.

Eisenhardt, K. M., and Schoonhoven, C. B. (1996). "Resource-Based View of Strategic Alliance Formation: Strategic and Social Effects in Entrepreneurial Firms." *Organization Science* 7 (2): 136–50.

Emden, Z., Calantone, R. J., and Droge, C. (2006). "Collaborating for New Product Development: Selecting the Partner with Maximum Potential to Create Value." *Journal of Product Innovation Management* 23 (4): 330–41.

Enkel, E., Gassmann, O., and Chesbrough, H. (2009). "Open R&D and Open Innovation: Exploring the Phenomenon." *R&D Management* 39 (4): 311–16.

Enzing, C., van der Giessen, A., van Groenestijn, J., and van Dongen, M. (2008). *Biobased Economy: Exploring the Opportunities for The Netherlands.* Delft: TNO/ InnoTact.

Freeman, C., and Soete, L. L. (1997). *The Economics of Industrial Innovation*: Psychology Press.

Gort, M., and Klepper, S. (1982). "Time Paths in the Diffusion of Product Innovations." *The Economic Journal* 92 (367): 630–53.

Granovetter, M. (1985). "Economic Action and Social Structure: The Problem of Embeddedness." *American Journal of Sociology* 481–510.

Granovetter, M. S. (1973). "The Strength of Weak Ties." *American Journal of Sociology* 1360–80.

Granstrand, O., Bohlin, E., Oskarsson, C., and Sjoberg, N. (1992). "External Technology Acquisition in Large Multi-technology Corporations." *R&D Management* 22 (2): 111–34.

Gulati, R. (2007). *Managing Network Resources: Alliances, Affiliations and Other Relational Assets*: Oxford University Press Oxford.

Hacklin, F. (2008). *Management of Convergence in Innovation: Strategies and Capabilities for Value Creation beyond Blurring Industry Boundaries: Contributions to Management Science*: Springer.

Hansen, M. T. (1999). "The Search-Transfer Problem: The Role of Weak Ties in Sharing Knowledge across Organization Subunits." *Administrative Science Quarterly* 44 (1): 82–111.

Harmsen, P. F. H., and Bos, H. L. (2011). "Communicatie biobased economy." Wageningen UR Food & Biobased Research. Report 1108.

Harmsen, P., and Hackmann, M. (2012). *Groene bouwstenen voor biobased plastics: biobased routes en marktontwikkeling*: Wageningen UR Food & Biobased Research.

Janssens, B., Aramyan, L., and Van Galen, M. (2011). *Verbinding zoeken: verkenning innovatie en kennis op de raakvlakken van topsectoren*: LEI.

Klepper, S. (1997). "Industry Life Cycles." *Industrial and Corporate Change* 6 (1): 145–82.

Koppejan, J., Elbersen, W., Meeuwsen, M., and Bindraban, P. (2009). *Beschikbaarheid van Nederlandse biomassa voor elektriciteit en warmte in 2020*: Procede Biomass.

Kwon, I. K. W. G., and Suh, T. (2004). "Factors Affecting the Level of Trust and Commitment in Supply Chain Relationships." *Journal of Supply Chain Management* 40 (2): 4–14.

Lee, S. M., Olson, D. L., and Trimi, S. (2010). "The Impact of Convergence on Organizational Innovation." *Organizational Dynamics* 39 (3): 218–25.

Lei, D. T. (2000). "Industry Evolution and Competence Development: The Imperatives of Technological Convergence." *International Journal of Technology Management* 19 (7): 699–738.

Levin, D. Z., and Cross, R. (2004). "The Strength of Weak Ties You Can Trust: The Mediating Role of Trust in Effective Knowledge Transfer." *Management Science* 50 (11): 1477–90.

McCutcheon, D. M., and Meredith, J. R. (1993). "Conducting Case Study Research in Operations Management." *Journal of Operations Management* 11 (3): 239–56.

Nowicki, P., Banse, M., Bolck, C., Bos, H., and Scott, E. (2008). *Biobased Economy: State-of-the-Art Assessment*. The Hague: LEI.

Obstfeld, D. (2005). "Social Networks, the Tertius Iungens Orientation, and Involvement in Innovation." *Administrative Science Quarterly* 50 (1): 100–130.

Odegard, I., Croezen, H., and Bergsma, G. (2012). *Cascading of Biomass. 13 Solutions for a Sustainable Bio-based Economy*. Delft: CE Delft.

Odenthal, S., Tovstiga, G., Tambe, H., and Van Oene, F. (2004). "Co-innovation: Capturing the Innovation Premium for Growth." *Prism* 1:41–55.

Owen-Smith, J., and Powell, W. W. (2004). "Knowledge Networks as Channels and Conduits: The Effects of Spillovers in the Boston Biotechnology Community." *Organization Science* 15 (1): 5–21.

Reagans, R., Zuckerman, E., and McEvily, B. (2004). "How to Make the Team: Social Networks vs. Demography as Criteria for Designing Effective Teams." *Administrative Science Quarterly* 49 (1): 101–33.

Sanders, J., Langeveld, H., and Meeusen, M. (2010). *The Biobased Economy: Biofuels, Materials and Chemicals in the Post-Oil Era*: Taylor and Francis.

Schilling, M. A., and Phelps, C. C. (2007). "Interfirm Collaboration Networks: The Impact of Large-Scale Network Structure on Firm Innovation." *Management Science* 53 (7): 1113–26.

Schumpeter, J. A. (1934). *The Theory of Economic Development: An Inquiry into Profits, Capital, Credit, Interest, and the Business Cycle*. London: Transaction Publishers.

SER (2010). *Meer chemie tussen groen en groei: de kansen en dilemma's van een biobased economy*: Social Economic Council.

Smith, D. (2010). *Exploring Innovation*: McGraw-Hill Higher Education.

Stieglitz, N. (2003). "Digital Dynamics and Types of Industry Convergence: The Evolution of the Handheld Computer Market." In J.F. Christensen and P. Maskell (eds) *The Industrial Dynamics of the New Digital Economy*, (pp.179–208). Northampton, MA: Edward Elgar Publishing.

Stuart, T. E. (2000). "Interorganizational Alliances and the Performance of Firms: A Study of Growth and Innovation Rates in a High-Technology Industry." *Strategic Management Journal* 21 (8): 791–811.

Tiwana, A. (2008). "Do Bridging Ties Complement Strong Ties? An Empirical Examination of Alliance Ambidexterity." *Strategic Management Journal* 29 (3): 251–72.

Tsai, W., and Ghoshal, S. (1998). "Social Capital and Value Creation: The Role of Intrafirm Networks." *Academy of Management Journal* 41 (4): 464–76.

Utterback, J. M. (1994). *Mastering the Dynamics of Innovation*. Boston: Harvard Business School Press.

Utterback, J. M., and Suarez, F. F. (1993). "Innovation, Competition, and Industry Structure." Research Policy 22 (1): 1–21.

VNCI (2011). "Biobased Economy: Benut complexiteit biomoleculen." *Chemie Magazine*, June 2011.

WTC (2010). *Groene Chemie: Essay 2010*: Wetenschappelijke en Technologische Commissie voor de Biobased Economy.

WTC (2011). *Naar groene chemie en groene materialen: kennis- en innovatieagenda voor de biobased economy*: Wetenschappelijke en Technologische Commissie voor de Biobased Economy.

Wubben, E. F., Runge, N. A., and Blok, V. (2012). "From Waste to Profit: An Interorganisational Perspective on Drivers for Biomass Valorisation." *Journal on Chain and Network Science* 12 (3): 261–72.

Yin, R. K. (2003). *Case Study Research: Design and Methods*, Thousand Oaks, CA: SAGE Publications.

CHAPTER 5

Open Innovation and Internationalization Behavior: The Case of Spanish Firms

Ana M. Moreno-Menéndez and Jose C. Casillas

Introduction

Internationalization and innovation have previously been considered as related concepts. One of the main streams of the stage-model (innovation-model) literature assumes that internationalization can be described as an innovative behavior, in which firms take decisions and try to minimize risk by following a step-by-step process (Bilkey and Tesar, 1977; Reid, 1981; Czinkota, 1982; Cavusgil, 1980). More recently, a new line of research has been undertaken to establish whether innovation and internationalization strategies are complementary or substitutive. Investigations by Elena Golovko and Giovanni Valentini (2011) and Bruno Cassiman and Elena Golovko (2011) show that product innovation encourages small- and medium-sized enterprises' (SMEs) export activity, whereas Kumar (2009) finds a negative relationship between product and market diversification.

However, there has been no investigation into how different types of innovative behavior influence a firm's decisions on internationalization. The objective of our chapter is to show how innovative firms that adopt an open strategy are more likely to engage in the internationalization process than closed innovators do. In the open innovation mode, a firm participates in innovation networks that may involve international partners. The effect of these international connections is (1) to develop the firm's internal capabilities for managing international relationships, (2) to develop international relational capital, and (3) to allow the firm to identify and exploit international opportunities. Consequently, open innovation can be instrumental in a firm's internationalization.

Basically, we argue that open innovation encourages more internationalization than closed innovation. Open innovation can be accomplished through either "inbound open innovation," which is considered to be a way for a firm to acquire new knowledge by creating networks with others in order to generate and develop new products or technologies, or "outbound open innovation," where a firm passes on its knowledge to other firms (Chesbrough, 2003). In general, open innovation strategies assume that the relevant knowledge may be located anywhere in the world and that any new product, process, or service can potentially be employed in any geographical context. Furthermore, firms with an open innovation orientation are likely to generate better networking capabilities, which are useful for international expansion (Bianchi et al., 2011; Bishop, 2008).

Internationalization is increasingly becoming a networking process. Recent international business literature clearly indicates that the most important determinant of internationalization is how well the firm is connected to foreign partners, customers, suppliers, and so on (Chetty and Stangl, 2010; Johanson and Vahlne, 2009, 2013). We propose that firms whose internal and external R&D expenditure is combined with a broad network of alliances with different innovation partners demonstrate greater internationalization behavior through exports and foreign direct investments (FDIs). Open innovation and internationalization are strategies that mutually influence each other; open innovators pursue more intensive international expansion than closed innovators. We believe that as a result of this orientation open innovation provides these firms with the additional benefits of internationalization: geographic and economic diversification and penetration into new markets.

Our chapter is structured as follows. In the next section, we will discuss internationalization and innovation activities. Then we explore the relationship between open innovation and international expansion from the network viewpoint, defining the determinants of this relationship. We also put forward arguments for the advantages of open innovation for a firm's international expansion, compared to closed innovation. In the following section, we set out the empirical evidence for the relationship between open innovation and firm internationalization, with the descriptive analysis of a sample of 424 Spanish innovative firms, in order to evaluate the influence of open innovation activities on international growth over a five-year period (2005–09). The final section is a discussion of the results attained and our conclusions.

Internationalization and Innovation

Internationalization and innovation have traditionally been viewed as broadly similar strategies. Parallel to the development of the Uppsala school of the internationalization process (the U-Model), another trend emerged (the I-Model), whose fundamental thesis views internationalization as a process of business innovation (Lim, Sharkey, and Kim, 1991). These initial models were based on Rogers's (1962) sequential model of adopting innovations. Both phenomena share many common characteristics: they develop in an uncertain environment where there is a lack of information; in order to control and minimize risk, both internationalization and innovation are stage processes, developed in cumulative steps; consequently, both are long-run strategies.

According to this classical perspective of the internationalization process, a lack of information and resources creates uncertainty, forcing firms to reduce the risk they are willing to tolerate for each decision. Consequently, for their first foreign venture, firms tend to choose geographical markets that are less uncertain, or, put another way, markets about which they have more information. There is a general consensus on the establishment of a sequential model, taking steps in which, as the firm passes from one phase to the next, its international commitment is strengthened. The main differences in defining the phases in the incremental internationalization models stem from the number of phases identified by each author and their understanding of the beginning of the process. Bilkey and Tesar (1977) and Czinkota (1982) argue that businesses do not show any interest in exporting during their initial stages until they receive demands from foreign partners, while Cavusgil (1980) and Reid (1981) claim that the internationalization idea originates within the firm and then is carried out with foreign partners. Bilkey and Tesar (1977) and Czinkota (1982) think that the process begins from outside the firm, moving to the inside, as opposed to Cavusgil (1980) and Reid (1981), who describe the process as progressing from within the firm to the outside (Andersen, 1993).

From the "international new venture" perspective (Oviatt and McDougall, 1994), innovation has also been considered as key to rapid internationalization. Several investigations have stressed that "born-global " firms (Knight and Cavusgil, 2004; Weerawardena et al., 2007) tend to be concentrated in the technological industries. Likewise, Oviatt and McDougall (1999) argue that technology-intensive sectors are more open to changes and are more likely to offer new opportunities. Firms use information, knowledge, and technologies that lead to rapid internationalization and that are generally associated with strategies oriented to serving specific niche markets where the firms can exploit their own innovation capabilities (Madsen and Servais, 1997; Ramos, Acedo, and González, 2011; Weerawardena et al., 2007).

To summarize, until recently internationalization and innovation have been not viewed as interdependent concepts. However, a new line of research has been looking at whether innovation and internationalization are complementary or substitutive strategies and how they might be interrelated. In this sense, the literature assumes that the relationship between internationalization and innovation is bidirectional (see Figure 5.1).

On the one hand, there are many ways in which innovation activities enhance internationalization. First, innovative activities improve a firm's productivity (Salomon and Shaver, 2005). Previous research shows that exporting

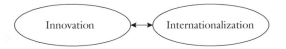

Figure 5.1   Reciprocal Influence of Innovation and Internationalization

firms have a higher productivity before undertaking exporting than nonexporters (Cassiman and Golovko, 2011). A second impact of innovation on internationalization is the application of R&D expenditure to a wider range of markets. As Autio, Sapienza, and Almeida (2000) state, high-technology firms may proactively choose to internationalize in order to recover significant R&D costs (e.g., Preece, Miles, and Baetz, 1998). Similarly, Vernon (1966) links internationalization to product life cycle. According to this study, young and innovative firms with a new product will initiate export activities to exploit their market power. Consequently, product innovation prompts internationalization in the search for increased markets for these newly developed products and services (Hitt, Hoskisson, and Kim, 1997). Third, innovation activity improves firms' international competitive advantage, according to the resource-based view of the firm (Barney, 1991). Innovation therefore leads to results that help firms to leverage their resources when competing in international markets. Finally, innovation generates new knowledge that is useful for internationalization activities. As Autio, Sapienza, and Almeida. (2000) state, knowledge-intensive firms can exploit international growth opportunities and are less constrained by distance or national boundaries (see also Eriksson et al., 1997, 2000).

On the other hand, innovation activities do not only exert a positive influence on internationalization behavior; the reverse is also possible. Internationalization activities provide an important source of knowledge and learning; for example, Zahra, Ireland, and Hitt (2000) point out that international expansion (into a diversity of countries and using various entry modes) promotes breadth, depth, and skills in technological learning. This effect has been extensively studied within multinational corporations (MNCs). Ghoshal (1987) suggests that differences between countries hide different stocks of "soft" resources, such as interorganizational relationships or cultural-based knowledge. MNCs have access to a wider and more diverse stock of knowledge that is based on a greater exposure to different innovation systems. There has been extensive research into learning through international joint ventures (Hamel, 1991; Lyles and Salk, 1996) and the flow of knowledge between the subsidiaries of an MNC (Bartlett and Ghoshal, 1989; Gupta and Govindarajan, 1991).

Networks and the Openness of Internationalization and Innovation

Since the turn of the century, there has been a change in the way firms progress through internationalization and innovation processes: from an internal and closed perspective to an external and open approach. Today, networks are the most important resources for internationalization and innovation. As a result, firms that develop their networking capabilities through alliances, joint ventures, consortia, and informal relationships with a large and diverse range of partners are able to improve simultaneously the performance of their internationalization and innovation processes (Figure 5.2).

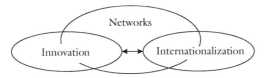

Figure 5.2   Innovation and Internationalization through Networks

Open Internationalization through Networks

Networks have become a central feature of the international business literature, both from the stage-model perspective (Johanson and Vahlne, 2009; 2013) and the international new venture approach (Jones and Coviello, 2005). The title of one of the most influential papers by Johanson and Vahlne (2009) neatly summarizes this change in the focus of international business theories: "The Uppsala Internationalization Process Model Revisited: From Liability of Foreignness to Liability of Outsidership." For these authors, "(1) markets are networks of relationships in which firms are linked to each other in various, complex and, to a considerable extent, invisible patterns, and (2) these relationships offer potential for learning and for building trust and commitment, both of which are preconditions for internationalization" (Johanson and Vahlne, 2009, 1411–12).

But the "international entrepreneurship" perspective also highlights the role of networks in explaining international new ventures (INVs) and born-global firms (Jones and Coviello, 2005). One of the distinguishing features of INVs is their participation in networks as a way of facilitating rapid internationalization (Oviatt and McDougall, 1994; Coviello and Munro, 1995). Larson and Starr (1993) point out that an INV will consciously manage its network from the earliest stage of its life cycle. Ellis (2000) concludes that the network relationships of an internationalizing firm are dominated by strong social or personal elements. Many INVs are founded on the basis of a network developed by their founders prior to start-up. A combination of congenital and vicarious learning interacts to develop useful knowledge for international expansion (De Clerq et al., 2012). Bruneel, Yli-Renko, and Clarysse (2010) underline the impact of the management team's pre-start-up international experience (congenital learning) and the interorganizational learning from key exchange partners (customers, suppliers, investors, etc.) on the speed of the firm's internationalization.

Networks therefore play a central role in firms' internationalization processes. Networks provide learning opportunities through contacts with customers, suppliers, institutions, governments, distributors, competitors from different countries, and cultural and institutional bases.

Open Innovation through Networks

Innovation is no longer an isolated process. Firms adopt the ideas and knowledge of their external partners in their innovation activities to develop new products, services, and business models. Open innovation assumes that external and internal sources of knowledge can be combined to develop more valuable innovations (Chesbrough, 2003b). Ahuja (2000) argues that both direct and indirect links can influence the ability of a firm to innovate. Shan, Walker, and Kogut (1994) demonstrate a positive relationship between cooperation and innovative output in biotechnology firms, while Laursen and Salter (2006) find a curvilinear (inverted-U) relationship between performance and a broad, in-depth search for external sources of innovation.

Chesbrough (2003b) suggests that firms that are "too focused internally" are "prone to miss a number of opportunities because many will fall outside the organization's current business or will need to be combined with external technologies to unlock their potential" (Laursen and Salter, 2006, 132). This assumption has been applied to many different types of firms: in mature sectors (Chiaroni, Chiesa, and Frattini, 2011) and knowledge-intensive industries (Hughes and Wareham, 2010; Prugl and Schreider, 2006) and including those with different types of partners, customers, (Chesbrough and Crowther, 2006; Hienerth, 2006) competitors, and so on.

As we mentioned above, two different processes used to be considered in relation to open innovation: inbound open innovation, referring to the internal use of external knowledge, and outbound open innovation, which refers to the external exploitation of internal knowledge (Huizingth, 2011). Bianchi and his colleagues (2011) identify three types of inbound and outbound activities: (a) licensing agreements, (b) nonequity alliances, and (c) technical and scientific services (purchase and supply). All of these involve relational activities with different types of partners in order to explore and/or exploit potential innovation (Lichtenthaler and Lichtenthaler, 2009).

Interaction between Internationalization and Innovation through Networks

Networks are a source of competitive advantage for firms, and relational capital can be seen as a core asset for innovation and internationalization. Gassman (2006) suggests that open innovation is more appropriate in contexts characterized by globalization, technology intensity, technology fusion, new business models, and knowledge leveraging. At the same time, the global presence of MNCs in a wide range of foreign countries provides a valuable source of knowledge for innovation (Barkema et al., 1997; Rosenkopf and Nerkar, 2001). The potential for a company to develop open innovation in an international context depends on four key factors (OECD, 2008): (1) how easy it is to innovate (the opportunity conditions), (2) how easy it is to protect innovation (the appropriability conditions), (3) the degree to which innovations of today are the basis for the innovations of tomorrow (cumulativeness), and (4) the degree of multidisciplinarity and the cross-functional complexity of knowledge.

Additionally, Chetty and Stangl (2010), using ten case studies, conduct an interesting analysis regarding which type of partner is more relevant for incremental and radical processes of internationalization and innovation. We summarize their results in Figure 5.3. They identify ten partner categories— suppliers, customers, distributors, competitors, governments, financial, industry, universities, institutes, and social—and evaluate the importance of each one for the development of internationalization and innovation activities.

Regarding internationalization and innovation activities, Chetty and Stangl (2010) identify four clusters or groups with different network configurations. Group 1 (radical internationalization and radical innovation) creates several network relationships, but the most influential of these are customers and competitors. For this group, universities are useful for innovation activities, while distributors are relevant only for international expansion. Group 2 (radical internationalization and incremental innovation) creates many important relationships for internationalization and innovation activities, but customers and financial networks emerge as the most influential for both types of activity. Group 3 (incremental internationalization and radical innovations) only uses the customer for both internationalization and innovation activities. And finally, Group 4 (incremental internationalization and incremental innovations) regards both customer and social relationships very highly. As the research shows, customer relationships are also the most influential for internationalization and innovation.

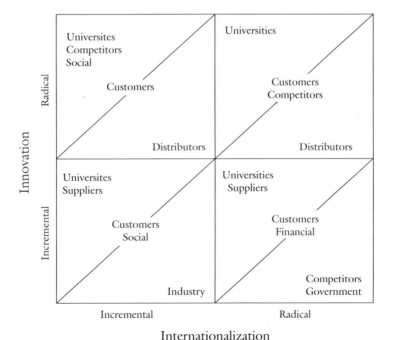

Figure 5.3   Relevant Partners for Internationalization and Innovation
Source: Adapted from Chetty and Stangl (2010).

A study carried out by the Organization for Economic Cooperation and Development (OECD) in 2008 reached a similar conclusion. This research suggests that for international innovation, companies collaborate most frequently with customers and suppliers. Surprisingly, while universities and government research institutes are generally considered to be an important source of knowledge for company innovation, collaboration with these institutions is less frequent, perhaps because public research is more focused on upstream research activities (exploration), with only a modest impact on innovation (OECD, 2008).

International Innovation Networks

Firms are becoming increasingly involved in interorganizational networks with a variety of structures (Ahuja, Soda, and Zaheer, 2012; Castro, Casanueva, and Galán, 2013). Several types of network architecture have been investigated in the field of firm internationalization, such as constellations, or alliances between multiple firms within the same sector (Gomes-Casseres, 1994; Das and Teng, 2002), and the global providers' network, with its vertically structured hierarchical relations (Dyer and Nobeoka, 2000), which give rise to the phenomenon of the "global factory." This type of structure is intensively used in certain sectors, such as automobiles and aeronautics (Dyer and Nobeoka, 2000; Garcia-Pont and Nohria, 2002). Other models include adaptive business (eco)systems (Miguel-Dávila, Lopez, and De Pablos, 2012), which consist of several actors who interact in a semistructured way to achieve common objectives, such as production systems orchestrated by a central player (Apple, Google), collaborative production communities (Wikipedia or Linux), innovation networks (Procter & Gamble's extended ecosystem), and market platforms (eBay).

International innovation networks consist of the R&D centers that a firm operates in different countries, together with its collaborations with various international partners in the field of innovation (providers, competitors, clients, etc.). These new modes of operating have given rise to the concept of the "global factory," a term coined by Peter Buckley at the end of the last decade. The global factory is the structure in which multinational enterprises integrate their global strategies through a combination of innovation, distribution, and production of both goods and services (Bartels, Buckley, and Mariano, 2009). In the introduction to their work, they state that "the global factory encompasses the activities of a global firm, or a global network of firms, that organizes servicing production, distribution, marketing, design, branding and innovation of a set of products and services. As will be seen, these products and services and their subcomponents, inputs and intellectual property may not be owned by a single firm at any one time but their component activities are controlled by a system described here as the global factory" (Bartels, Buckley, and Mariano, 2009, 1).

The key idea is that multinational enterprises (MNEs) are becoming much more like distinct networks. Global factories used to be divided into three components: (1) original equipment manufacturers (controlling the brand, design, R&D, and engineering), (2) contract manufacturers, who provide manufacturing and logistics services, and (3) warehousing, distribution, and adaptation providers. A fundamental aim for this type of network organization is to have an international reach so that differences in the localization of each unit create comparative, competitive, and technological advantages. Host-country policies designed to improve dynamic comparative advantage can encourage economic activity, and international innovation networks can influence a country's innovation systems. The innovation networks of MNEs represent nodes between national systems of innovation across borders, connecting various actors in the science, technology, and industry systems across countries and regions. International innovation networks promote the dynamics of knowledge transfer across countries and in different directions (inwards and outwards). International R&D activities are also likely to have a positive effect on the competitiveness of MNC activities in their own countries.

These international innovation networks can be headed by a large company, with a constellation of SMEs, private R&D facilities, universities, suppliers, and so on. One example of this kind of network is the global open innovation model used by Novartis. The basis of this Swiss company's innovation strategy is to have strong internal R&D centers in different countries (Switzerland, the United Kingdom, France, the United States, Japan, and India), complemented by inward-outward licensing, targeted mergers and acquisitions, and external collaborations. Novartis has more than eight thousand associate R&D personnel in 59 countries worldwide; it has set up external collaborations with more than 120 companies and 280 academic institutions and has financed more than 150 entrepreneurial ventures (OECD, 2008).

However, global open innovation networks can also be developed between SMEs, without a large MNC firm taking the lead role. Small entrepreneurial firms are able to create small- to medium-sized networks with other SMEs in different locations. This process is sometimes combined with radical transformations that take place in local clusters, where small, district-level firms evolve toward more complex network configurations by leveraging a mix of short- and long-range (local and foreign, respectively) ties. The focus on small entrepreneurial firms and the related deep transformation in local clusters and districts is very important from the policy-making perspective. In global factories, different activities in the value chain are sliced up and distributed across a wide number of developing and industrialized countries.

Open Innovation and Internationalization in Spanish Manufacturing Firms

Methodology

Sample

We used a sample of innovative firms in order to analyze the relationship between open innovation and internationalization activities. The sample was obtained from the Spanish Survey of Business Strategies (SBS). The reference population of the SBS consists of Spanish firms with ten or more employees in the manufacturing industry, to enable the study of their export activity. This survey is carried out periodically on a representative sample of Spanish manufacturing firms and includes aspects such as size, geographical distribution, sectoral activity, and so forth. For our investigation, we chose firms with data available in two years, 2005 and 2009, to allow us to analyze the innovation and internationalization processes from a dynamic perspective. (The database included a total of 1,473 firms with information from both years.) For the purpose of our study, we selected firms that had undertaken R&D activities in one of the two years identified.

Our sample consisted of 424 firms. In 2005 the average size of firms in the sample was 610 employees, although the median was 258 employees, and our sample therefore was dominated by medium and large firms, according to European parameters. The average age of firms in the sample was 35 years (median 31 years). A broad range of manufacturing sectors was represented in the sample, with sector 9 (chemical industry and pharmaceutical products) being the most common. Table 5.1 summarizes the sample characteristics.

Variables

Internationalization variables. International behavior was measured through two dimensions, representing different methods of operating abroad. The first refers to export behavior. We have identified two variables for this dimension: (1) export propensity (Calof, 1994), a dichotomous variable that takes the value 1 if the firm exports and 0 if there were no exports in the years in question; and (2) exporting intensity (Bonaccorsi, 1992), which is measured as the quotient between the value of the exports and the firm's sales. The second dimension reflects the existence of foreign subsidiaries (FDIs). As before, we used a dichotomous variable to indicate whether the firm has subsidiaries abroad (value 1) or not (value 0) and a second variable to measure the number of foreign subsidiaries. All of these variables were measured for the years 2005 and 2009, which then provided information on the firms' temporal evolution.

Innovation variables. To measure the use of open innovation, we used two separate indicators. The degree of openness of innovation is related to the combination of internal and external resources, and we have identified three options for the use of resources for innovation. The first of these involves internal R&D activities with no external contracting in; in the second option the firm exclusively contracts in external R&D activities; and the third option is a mixture of both internal and contracted-in external R&D activities. Consequently, firms that adopt this last option will have the greatest degree of openness in their innovations (Knudsen and Mortensen, 2011).

Similarly, the openness of a firm's innovation activities can be measured by the balance of internal and external R&D expenditure. To measure the balance between both types of expenditure, we used a concentration index: the Herfindahl index, which shows that firms whose R&D costs are spread equally across

Table 5.1 Sample Characteristics

Size	Number	Percentage
Fewer than 50	56	13.2%
50 to 99	39	9.2%
100 to 249	106	25.0%
250 to 499	118	27.8%
500 or more	105	24.8%

Age		
Less than 10	49	11.6%
10 to 24	126	29.7%
25 to 49	161	38.0%
50 to 99	78	18.4%
100 or more	10	2.4%

Industry		
Meat industry	8	1.9%
Food and tobacco products	31	7.3%
Drinks	12	2.8%
Textiles and clothing	16	3.8%
Leather and footwear	5	1.2%
Wood product manufacturing	6	1.4%
Paper manufacturing	10	2.4%
Graphic arts	3	0.7%
Chemical industry and pharmaceutical products	61	14.4%
Rubber and plastics	28	6.6%
Nonmetallic mineral products	22	5.2%
Iron and non-iron metals	27	6.4%
Metal products	31	7.3%
Agricultural and industrial machinery	41	9.7%
Computing, electronic, and optical appliances	25	5.9%
Machinery and electrical equipment	27	6.4%
Motor vehicles	41	9.7%
Other transportation equipment	15	3.5%
Furniture manufacturing	14	3.3%
Other manufacturing industries	1	0.2%

internal and external resources have a low concentration (minimum value 0.5), compared to those whose R&D expenditure is exclusively external or internal (maximum value 1). Table 5.2 sets out the open innovation activities of the firms in our sample. Just over half (53 percent) of the firms state that they have

Table 5.2 Firm Characteristics and Open Innovation Activities

	Internal R&D	External R&D	Internal and external R&D	Balanced R&D	Total
Up to 9 employees	24	11	21	0.89	56
10 to 49 employees	49	28	68	0.85	145
50 to 250 employees	32	16	70	0.82	118
250 or more employees	29	9	67	0.79	105
Total	134	64	226	0.83	424
Up to 9 years	20	7	22	0.84	49
10 to 24 years	36	18	72	0.82	126
25 to 49 years	48	34	79	0.85	161
50 to 99 years	25	3	50	0.80	78
100 or more years	5	2	3	0.86	10
Total	134	64	226	0.83	424
Meat industry	3	1	4	0.77	8
Food and tobacco products	10	6	15	0.83	31
Drinks	5	2	5	0.84	12
Textiles and clothing	6	2	8	0.84	16
Leather and footwear	0	3	2	0.96	5
Wood product manufacturing	2	2	2	0.91	6
Paper manufacturing	4	1	5	0.84	10
Graphic arts	1	1	1	0.84	3
Chemical industry and pharmaceutical products	25	3	33	0.83	61
Rubber and plastics	9	6	13	0.86	28
Nonmetallic mineral products	10	3	9	0.83	22
Iron and non-iron metals	9	2	16	0.83	27
Metal products	7	8	16	0.85	31
Agricultural and industrial machinery	16	4	21	0.86	41
Computing, electronic, and optical appliances	6	1	18	0.80	25
Machinery and electrical equipment	11	1	15	0.81	27
Motor vehicles	3	12	26	0.80	41

(Continued)

Table 5.2 Firm Characteristics and Open Innovation Activities (*Continued*)

	Internal R&D	External R&D	Internal and external R&D	Balanced R&D	Total
Other transportation equipment	2	1	12	0.70	15
Furniture manufacturing	5	5	4	0.91	14
Other manufacturing industries	0	0	1	0.73	1
Total	**134**	**64**	**226**	**0.83**	**424**

Table 5.3 Difference between Firms in Relation to Open Innovation

	Chi-square	p-value	ANOVA	Ad hoc test
Size	16.078	<0.01	0.008	1–4
Age	20.064	<0.01	0.506	
Industry	59.883	0.013	0.531	

simultaneously developed internal and external R&D activities. The biggest firms (by size) were proportionately more inclined (63.8 percent) to carry out open innovations, while the smaller firms tended to concentrate their R&D activities either internally or externally. (Only 37 percent of firms with fewer than ten employees were involved in open innovation.) Regarding firm age, the oldest firms were more involved in this type of innovation (64.1 percent), excluding firms over one hundred years old. Finally, by sector, the following stand out as representing over 60 percent of firms: (1) other transport materials (80 percent), (2) computing and electronics (72 percent), and (3) motor vehicles (63.4 percent). The first two columns of Table 5.3 show the results of the chi-square test, which show significant differences in the extent of open innovation according to size, age, and sector.

The second indicative variable for the use of open innovation is the degree to which R&D costs are divided between internal and external resources (balanced R&D). The average for this indicator in each sector is shown in Table 5.2.

The overall average for this indicator is 0.836. Some correspondence can be observed between the value of this variable and the percentage of firms that combine their internal and external R&D sources. To verify whether there are any differences between firms in different sectors, we carried out a variance analysis (ANOVA), the results of which can be seen in Table 5.3. This analysis only identifies differences according to size: specifically, between firms with fewer than 10 employees (less balanced internal and external R&D costs) and firms with more than 250 employees (more balanced internal and external R&D costs).

Investigation Results

Having described the characteristics of the firms in the sample, with particular emphasis on their innovation activities (internal, external, and both), we will now analyze the relationship between these activities and international behavior, including both exports and foreign subsidiaries. The rows in Table 5.4 represent the innovation source (internal, external, or both), and the columns show the different dimensions of international behavior in 2005 and 2009.

Regarding export propensity (the percentage of exporting firms), we observe, primarily, that in both years the firms with an open innovation orientation have a much higher export propensity than the other firms. Of the 394 firms that were exporting in 2005 (92.9 percent of the total), over half (54.5 percent) were engaged in open innovation activities. This figure increased in 2009 to 55.3 percent. We note that both of these percentages are above the 53.3 percent of firms with an open innovation focus.

Regarding export intensity (the percentage of exports as part of total sales), the data again demonstrate that firms that simultaneously develop internal and external R&D activities have a greater export intensity; 35 percent in 2005, rising to 38 percent in 2009. With respect to direct foreign investments, in 2005

Table 5.4 Open Innovation Activities and International Activities (Static)

	Export (1/0)	Export intensity	MNC (1/0)	No. of foreign subsidiaries
Year	2005	2005	2005	2005
Internal R&D activities	118	0.33	37	1.63
External R&D activities	61	0.31	18	0.72
Internal and external R&D activities	215	0.38	82	2.85
Total	394	0.35	137	2.14
Chi-square	0,029	0.192	0.174	0.209
Year	2009	2009	2009	2009
Internal R&D activities	118	0.35	40	2.01
External R&D activities	60	0.29	17	0.66
Internal and external R&D activities	221	0.42	95	2.10
Total	399	0.38	152	1.85
Chi-square	0.001	0.006	0.016	0.261

only 137 firms from the sample and 152 in 2009 (32.3 percent) stated that they had foreign subsidiaries. Of these, approximately 60 percent (59.8 percent in 2005 and 62.5 percent in 2009) were involved in open innovation. Again, this percentage is above the average. Finally, if we observe the number of foreign subsidiaries, where there is an average of two subsidiaries per firm, the data indicate that firms that combine internal and external sources of R&D have more subsidiaries (2.85 in 2005 and 2.10 in 2009).

An analysis of the chi-square shows that in both years there were significant differences in the export propensity of firms that adopted open innovations and those that did not. In the case of export intensity (exports/sales), the differences are only significant in 2009, which seems to indicate that there is a certain time delay between the introduction of open innovation practices and their effect on export intensity. A somewhat similar result is seen in firms that have FDIs, or not, when the differences are significant in the second year. Finally, the chi-square shows no significance concerning the number of foreign subsidiaries.

These data refer separately to the two years that were analyzed. However, both innovation and internationalization should be considered as processes that develop over time, and it is therefore important to analyze how the development of open innovation activities affects the evolution of the international behavior of the firms in the sample. The columns in Table 5.5 show the growth in export intensity and the number of subsidiaries according to the type of innovation the firm adopts. We can therefore see that the highest growth rates are seen in firms with a more open approach to their innovation activities. However, the difference is not that significant (chi-square).

A second variable that indicates the adoption of open innovation methods is the balance between internal and external R&D activities (balanced R&D expenditures). As explained in the methodology, we have used an entropy index to measure this balance. The lowest value for this index (0.5) is registered when R&D expenditure is distributed equally between internal and external sources, and its highest value (1) is given when the firm only adopts a single type of R&D (internal or external).

Table 5.5 Open Innovation Activities and International Activities (Dynamic)

	Inc. export intensity	Inc. no. of foreign subsidiaries
Year	2005–09	2005–09
Internal R&D activities	6.08	0.13
External R&D activities	2.60	0.01
Internal and external R&D activities	11.41	0.16
Total	8.45	0.13
Chi-square	0.749	0.883

Table 5.6 Balance between Internal and External R&D by Firm Size and Age

Size	N	Average	Age	N	Average
Up to 9 employees	56	0.895	Up to 9 years	49	0.844
10–49 employees	145	0.855	10–24 years	126	0.827
50–250 employees	118	0.822	25–49 years	161	0.852
250+ employees	105	0.794	50–99 years	78	0.807
Total	**424**	**0.836**	100+ years	10	0.862
F statistic		4.023	**Total**	**424**	**0.836**
Chi-square		0.008	F statistic		0.831
Bonferroni (differences between the following groups)		2-4, 3-4	Chi-square		0.506

Table 5.7　Correlation between Open Innovation and International Activities

	Balanced R&D
Export (1/0) 2005	–0.053
Export (1/0) 2009	–0.113*
MNC 2005	–0.102*
MNC 2009	–0.100*
Export intensity 2005	–0.006
Export intensity 2009	–0.026
No. foreign subsidiaries 2005	–0.05
No. foreign subsidiaries 2009	–0.049
Inc. export intensity (2005–09)	–0.082
Inc. no. foreign subsidiaries (2005–09)	–0.035

Table 5.6 sets out the average values of this variable according to firm size and age. It can be observed that, while there are no significant differences according to age, there are significant differences according to firm size. The largest firms (over 250 employees) have the lowest score, indicating a greater balance between internal and external R&D expenditure. Similarly, although the differences are not significant, the data indicate that the adoption of open innovation practices tends to increase in line with a growth in firm size (the entropy index value decreases).

Table 5.7 shows the correlation between the entropy index that measures the internal and external R&D balance and the different variables related to the international activity of the firms in our sample.

We observe that all of the correlations are negative, which demonstrates the existence of a positive relationship between internationalization and the balance of the internal and external output for innovation activities. It is particularly significant that the correlation is stronger for export propensity in 2009 than in 2005; that is to say, firms that were developing open innovation activities in 2005 were more likely to be exporting four years later (delay effect). A similar effect (albeit the correlations are not significant) can be seen for export intensity. Finally, looking at the growth in firms' international involvement (growth in export intensity and the number of foreign subsidiaries), the results again show that this growth is greater when internal and external R&D expenditures are more balanced.

Discussion and Conclusions

Globalization and the development of information and communication technologies are two phenomena that characterize recent decades. These two phenomena are not independent but rather are linked to each other in such a way that a firm's internationalization and its innovation activities are closely related. Moreover, an increasing number of firms in information and communication technologies capitalize on open innovation (West and Gallagher, 2006); however, this trend goes beyond this particular sector, having become popular across many sectors (Gassmann, Enkels, and Chesbrough, 2010). One consequence of this popular trend is that the degree of openness that firms demonstrate in relating to their environments in the development of their knowledge bases affects their global competitiveness.

In the past, the dominant organizational model was hierarchical, in which organizational boundaries were clear and where the development of activities was predominantly endogenous. Firms evolved through a gradual process, in which the key resources and capacities required to compete were either generated internally or acquired externally, in a path-dependent process. Nowadays, firms are opening up their organizational models so that competitive advantages arise as a result of their ability to access internal and external resources and capabilities in the development of new products and in the commercialization of existing ones. This new scenario underlies the role of firm networks, the adoption of open innovation, and the rapid internationalization that results from the ability to access geographically dispersed resources.

Knowledge (of technologies and markets) is the key factor in competition. This knowledge is increasingly specialized, dispersed, and uncertain, and firms are unable by themselves to master all of the resources that they need at any one time. Therefore, the more links a firm has with other companies, institutions, providers, clients, and so forth in a variety of national contexts, the greater its ability and flexibility to compete in a global environment.

In this study, we have analyzed the relationship between the development of open innovations and a firm's internationalization process. Our premise is that firms that adopt a model of open innovation, through a balanced combination of internal and external innovation, are more likely to develop greater international activity. We have looked at the theories of the relationship between innovation and internationalization and have analyzed a sample of 424 Spanish innovating companies over the period 2005 to 2009. This analysis demonstrates that, as we proposed, firms that are more open in the field of innovation also tend to display a more intensive international behavior. Similarly, this relationship is observed to strengthen as time passes.

The study of this subject is important for both academics and practitioners. Our chapter helps to close the gap between innovation and internationalization processes (Wynarczyk, Piperopoulos, and McAdam, 2013) by explicitly considering the role of openness in innovative activities. We propose a new way of developing innovation activities that will help to achieve firm internationalization, compared to traditional ways of internationalization. For practitioners, we suggest that the degree of openness in innovation provides strategic benefits for achieving international expansion.

The development of international firm networks is useful for both innovation and foreign expansion. The knowledge required for innovation is spread around the world, while the profitable exploitation of these innovations demands the ability to commercialize them over a widespread geographical area. The appearance of highly specialized, but global, market niches favors the growth of born-global firms and micro-multinationals that are well connected to a network of sophisticated, but geographically dispersed, clients. Firm constellations, vertical and horizontal networks, the global factory, and international innovation networks have created new, open organizational models that engender new value-generation ecosystems. This work highlights the reciprocal relationships and complementarity of innovation and internationalization through alliances and networks with other firms, providers, clients, and competitors, as well as with other institutions and organizations across the globe.

References

Ahuja, G. (2000). "Collaboration Networks, Structural Holes and Innovation: A Longitudinal Study." *Administrative Science Quarterly* 45:425–55.

Ahuja, G., Soda, G., and Zaheer, A. (2012). "Introduction to the Special Issue: The Genesis and Dynamics of Organizational Networks." *Organization Science* 23 (2):434–48.

Andersen, O. (1993). "On the Internationalization Process of Firms: A Critical Analysis." *Journal of International Business Studies* 24 (2): 209–31.

Autio, E., Sapienza, H. J., and Almeida, J. G. (2000). "Effects of Age at Entry, Knowledge Intensity, and Imitability on International Growth." *Academy of Management Journal* 43 (5): 909–24.

Barkema, H. G., Shenkar, O., Vermeulen, F., and Bell, J. H. J. (1997). "Working Abroad, Working with Others: How Firms Learn to Operate International Joint Ventures." *Academy of Management Journal* 40:426–42.

Barney, J. B. (1991). "Firm Resources and Sustained Competitive Advantage." *Journal of Management* 17:99–120.

Bartels, F. L., Buckley, P., and Mariano, G. (2009). "Multinational Enterprises' Foreign Direct Investment Location Decisions within the Global Factory." *United Nations Industrial Development Organization*, Vienna, 2009.

Bartlett, C. A., and Ghoshal, S. (1989). *Managing Across Borders: The Transnational Solution*. Boston: Harvard Business School Press.

Bianchi, M., Cavaliere, A., Chiaroni, D. Frattini, F., and Chiesa, V. (2011). "Organisational Modes for Open Innovation in the Bio-pharmaceutical Industry: An Exploratory Analysis." *Technovation* 31:22–33.

Bilkey, W. J., and Tesar, G. (1977). "The Export Behavior of Smaller Wisconsin Manufacturing Firms." *Journal of International Business Studies* 9:93–98.

Bishop, K. (2008). "Internationalisation and Cooperation Strategies in Knowledge-Based Ventures." *International Journal of Entrepreneurship and Innovation, 9* (3):199–207.

Bonaccorsi, A. (1992). "On the Relationship between Firm Size and Export Intensity." *Journal of International Business Studies* 23 (4): 605–35.

Bruneel, J., Yli-Renko, H., and Clarysse, B. (2010). "Learning from Experience and Learning From Others: How Congenital and Inter-organizational Learning Substitute for Experiential Learning in Young Firm Internationalization." *Strategic Entrepreneurship Journal* 4:164–82.

Calof, J. L. (1994). "The Relationship between Firm Size and Export Behavior Revisited." *Journal of International Business Studies* 25:367–87.

Cassiman, B., and Golovko, E. (2011). "Innovation and Internationalization through Exports." *Journal of International Business Studies* 42:56–75.

Castro, I., Casanueva, C., and Galán, J. L. (2013, forthcoming). "Dynamic Evolution of Alliance Portfolios." *European Management Journal.*

Cavusgil, S. T. (1980). "On the Internationalization Process of Firms." *European Research* 8:273–81.

Chesbrough, H. (2003). *Open Innovation: The New Imperative for Creating and Profiting from Technology*. Cambridge, MA: Harvard Business School Publishing.

Chesbrough, H. (2003b). "The Era of Open Innovation." *MIT Sloan Management Review* 44 (3): 35–41.

Chesbrough, H., and Crowther, A. K. (2006). "Beyond High Tech: Early Adopters of Open Innovation in Other Industries." *R&D Management* 36 (3): 229–36.

Chetty, S. K., and Stangl, L. M. (2010). "Internationalization and Innovation in a Network Relationship Context." *European Journal of Marketing* 44 (11/12): 1725–43.

Chiaroni, D., Chiesa, V., and Frattini, F. (2011). "The Open Innovation Journey: How Firms Dynamically Implement the Emerging Innovation Management Paradigm." *Technovation* 31: 34–43.

Coviello, N. (2006). "The Network Dynamics of International New Ventures." *Journal of International Business Studies* 37:713–31.

Coviello, N. E., and Munro, H. J. (1995). "Network Relationships and the Internationalization Process of Small Software Firms." *International Business Review* 6 (4): 361–86.

Czinkota, M. R. (1982). *Export Development Strategies: U.S. Promotion Policy*. New York: Praeger Publishers.

Das, T. K., and Teng, B. (2002). "Alliance Constellations: A Social Exchange Perspective." *Academy of Management Review* 27: 445–56.

De Clercq, D., Sapienza, H. J., Yavuz, R. I., and Zhou, L. (2012). "Learning and Knowledge in Early Internationalization Research: Past Accomplishments and Future Directions." *Journal of Business Venturing* 27: 143–65.

Dyer, J. H., and Nobeoka, K. (2000). "Creating and Managing a High-Performance Knowledge-Sharing Network: The Toyota Case." *Strategic Management Journal* 21:345–67.

Ellis, P. (2000). "Social Ties and Foreign Market Entry." *Journal of International Business Studies* 31 (3): 443–69.

Eriksson, K., Johanson, J., Majkgard, A., and Sharma D. D. (2000). "Effect of Variation on Knowledge Accumulation in the Internationalization Process." *International Studies of Management and Organization* 30 (1): 26–45.

Eriksson, K., Johanson, J., Majkgard, A., and Sharma, D. D. (1997). "Experiential Knowledge and Cost in the Internationalization Process." *Journal of International Business Studies* 28 (2): 337–60.

Garcia-Pont, C., and Nohria, N. (2002). "Local versus Global Mimetism: The Dynamics of Alliance Formation in the Automobile Industry." *Strategic Management Journal* 23: 307–21.

Gassman, O. (2006). "Opening Up the Innovation Process: Towards an Agenda." *R&D Management* 36 (3): 223–28.

Gassmann, O., Enkels, E., and Chesbrough, H. (2010). "The Future of Open Innovation." *R&D Management* 40 (3): 213–21.

Ghoshal, S. (1987). "Global Strategy: An Organizing Framework." *Strategic Management Journal* 8 (5): 425–40.

Golovko, E., and Valentini, G. (2011). "Exploring the Complementarity between Innovation and Export for SMEs' Growth." *Journal of International Business Studies* 42:362–80.

Gomes-Casseres, B. (1994). "Group versus Group: How Alliance Networks Compete." *Harvard Business Review* 72 (4): 62–74.

Gupta, A. K., and Govindarajan, V. (1991). "Converting Global Presence into Global Competitive Advantage." *Academy of Management Review* 16 (4): 768–92.

Hamel, G. (1991). "Competition for Competence and Inter-partner Learning within International Strategic Alliances." *Strategic Management Journal* 12 (summer): 83–103.

Hienerth, C. (2006). "The Commercialization of User Innovations: The Development of the Rodeo Kayak Industry." *R&D Management* 36 (3): 273–94.

Hitt M. A., Hoskisson, R. E., and Kim, H. (1997). "International Diversification: Effects on Innovation and Firm Performance in Product-Diversified Firms." *Academy of Management Journal* 39:1084–119.

Hughes, B., and Wareham, J. (2010). "Knowledge Arbitrage in Global Pharma: A Synthetic View of Absorptive Capacity and Open Innovation." *R&D Management* 40 (3): 324–43.

Huizingth, H. (2011). "The Commercialization of User Innovations: The Development of the Rodeo Kayak Industry." *R&D Management* 36 (3): 273–94.

Johanson, J., and Vahlne J. E. (2009). "The Uppsala Internationalization Process Model Revisited: From Liability of Foreignness to Liability of Outsidership." *Journal of International Business Studies* 40:1411–31.

Johanson, J. E., and Vahlne, J. (2013). "The Uppsala Model on Evolution of the Multinational Business Enterprise: From Internalization to Coordination of Networks." *International Marketing Review* 30 (3): 189–210.

Jones, M. V., and Coviello, N. E. (2005). "Internationalization: Conceptualising an Entrepreneurial Process of Behavior in Time." *Journal of International Business Studies* 36 (3): 284–303.

Knight, G. A., and Cavusgil, S. T. (2004). "Innovation, Organizational Capabilities and the Born-Global Firm." *Journal of International Business Studies* 35 (2): 124–41.

Knudsen, M. P., and Mortensen, T. B. (2011). "Some Immediate—but Negative—Effects of Openness on Product Development Performance." *Technovation* 31:54–64.

Kumar, M. V. S. (2009). "The Relationship between Product and International Diversification: the Effects of Short-Run Constraints and Endogeneity." *Strategic Management Journal* 30:99–116.

Larson, A., and Starr, J. A. (1993). "A Network Model of Organization Formation." *Entrepreneurship Theory and Practice* 17 (2): 5–15.

Laursen, K., and Salter, A. (2006). "Open for Innovation: The Role of Openness in Explaining Innovation Performance among U.K. Manufacturing Firms." *Strategic Management Journal* 27:131–50.

Lichtenthaler, U., and Lichtenthaler, E. (2009). "A Capability-Based Framework for Open Innovation: Complementing Absorptive Capacity." *Journal of Management Studies* 46 (8): 1315–38.

Lim, J., Sharkey, T., and Kim, K. (1991). "An Empirical Test of an Export Adoption Model." *Management International Review* 31(1): 51–62.

Lyles, M. A., and Salk, J. E., (1996). "Knowledge Acquisition from Foreign Parents in International Joint Ventures: An Empirical Examination in Hungarian Context." *Journal of International Business Studies* 27 (5): 877–903.

Madsen, T. K., and Servais, P. (1997). "The Internationalization of Born Globals: An Evolutionary Process?" *International Business Review* 6 (6): 561–83.

Miguel-Dávila, J. A., López, D., and de Pablos, C. (2012). "El sector de la telefonía móvil como modelo de negocio abierto en un contexto de innovación sistémica." *Universia Business Review* 36: 48–63.

OECD. (2008). "Open Innovation in Global Networks." *Policy Brief*, November, 1–8.

Oviatt, B. M., and McDougall, P. P. (1994). "Toward a Theory of International New Ventures." *Journal of International Business Studies* 25 (1): 45–64.

Oviatt, B. M., and McDougall, P. P. (1999). "A Framework for Understanding Accelerated International Entrepreneurship." In Rugman, A. M., and Wright, R. W. (eds.), *Research in Global Strategic Management: International Entrepreneurship*, 23–40. Stamford, CT: JAI Press.

Preece, S. B., Miles, G., and Baetz, M. C. (1998). "Explaining the International Intensity and Global Diversity of Early-Stage Technology-Based Firms." *Journal of Business Venturing* 14 (3): 259–81.

Prugl, R., and Schreider, M. (2006). "Learning from Leading-Edge Customers at The Sims: Opening Up the Innovation Process Using Toolkits." *R&D Management* 36(3): 237–50.

Ramos, E., Acedo, F. J., and González, M. R. (2011). "Internationalisation Speed and Technological Patterns: A Panel Data Study on Spanish SMEs." *Technovation* 31:560–72.

Reid, S. D. (1981). "The Decision–Maker and Export Entry and Expansion." *Journal of International Business Studies* 12:110–12.

Rogers, E. M. (1962). *Diffusion of Innovations*. New York: Free Press.

Rosenkopf, L., and Nerkar, A. (2001). "Beyond Local Research: Boundary-Spanning, Exploration, and Impact in the Optical Disk Industry." *Strategic Management Journal* 22 (4): 287–306.

Salomon, R., and Shaver, J.M. (2005). "Export and Domestic Sales: Their Interrelationship and Determinants." *Strategic Management Journal* 26 (9): 855–71.

Shan, W., Walker, G., and Kogut, B. (1994). "Interfirm Cooperation and Startup Innovation in the Biotechnology Industry." *Strategic Management Journal* 15 (5): 387–94.

Vernon, R. (1966). "International Investment and International Trade in the Product Cycle." *Quarterly Journal of Economics* 80:190–207.

Weerawardena, J., Sullivan Mort, G., Liesch, P., and Knight, G. (2007). "Conceptualizing Accelerated Internationalization in the Born Global Firm: A Dynamic Capabilities Perspective." *Journal of World Business* 42:294–306.

West, J., and Gallagher, S. (2006). "Challenges of Open Innovation: The Paradox of Firm Investment in Open-Source Software." *R&D Management* 36 (3): 319–31.

Wynarczyk, P., Piperopoulos, P., and McAdam, M. (2013). "Open Innovation in Small and Medium-Sized Enterprises: An Overview." *International Small Business Journal* 31 (3): 240–55.

Zahra, S. A., Ireland, R., and Hitt, M. A. (2000). "International Expansion by New Venture Firms: International Diversity, Mode of Market Entry, Technological Learning, and Performance." *Academy of Management Journal* 43:925–50.

CHAPTER 6

Accessing Innovation in Supply Chains

Richard R. Young

Introduction

Firms obviously intentionally purchase innovation when they source equipment, raw materials, and components for assembly. There are also myriad instances where innovation is acquired serendipitously but is nonetheless an important part of the value proposition. The supply chain is, hence, a key conduit for the flow of innovation between firms. Indeed, innovation can be considered a highly specialized form of information that may have long- or short-term implications and may be shared using formal or informal means; however, it is often ad hoc, meaning that while the knowledge flows and sharing are real, many firms do not account for such when engaging customers and suppliers. Firms need to embrace the concept of open innovation flow into their supplier selection criteria and in their relationships with their customers.

A leading contemporary view of the supply chain, the "supply chain operations reference model," [I will argue that this model, which is copyrighted, needs to be capitalized] calls for repeatable plan, source, make, deliver, and return activities across participating firms. Supply chains are traditionally considered to consist of three flows: physical, information, and financial. Of the three, information flow is considered to have the most impact because of the influence it has on successful physical flows, and, therefore, it largely consists of transactional information or, as in the case of forecasts, future transactional information.

The concept of open innovation is not a new one, although the terminology could be attributed to Henry Chesbrough (2003), who has encouraged firms to seek sources of innovation from others in order to improve products and processes more quickly—specifically by moving *outside* of their four walls (Chesbrough, 2007). Furthermore, he has emphasized that innovation must become the responsibility of others in addition to those on the technical side of the organization (Chesbrough, 2012). Moreover, he has been clear about the need to identify sources that are external to the firm, and for this there are some ready-made opportunities that in many respects are both already substantially vetted and could be be readily leveraged. These ready-made sources—specifically its customers and suppliers—are to be found in each firm's supply chain.

Thomas Kuhn (1970) popularized the use of the word "paradigm" when he posited that many great discoveries result when persons from outside of a field look at a problem and arrive at a solution because they did not know what questions to not ask (1970). Partners in the supply chain may well be a great source for knowledge acquisition [ok] because they may be sufficiently outside of one's paradigm but know enough of their specific operational dynamics so that a firm need not make major investments in time and effort in order to engage the appropriate experts. That said, it may be instructive to explain the supply chain and illustrate how supply chain relationships drive innovation. [ok]

This chapter first reviews the traditional supply chain model with physical, information, and financial flows and then notes the importance of knowledge flows and sharing as a fourth flow. In doing so, it provides eight company cases that demonstrate knowledge flows and sharing between a firm and its customers and between the firm and its suppliers in a supply chain context. Further, it breaks down [I like my word choice better, but won't press the issue] the eight case studies into a matrix that can further illustrate how leveraging the supply chain may be a most opportunistic approach to engaging in open innovation. Finally, the chapter emphasizes the importance of accessing innovation through relationships up and down the supply chain.

Supply Chain Management

The term "supply chain" has been attributed to various sources, including Thomas Stahlkamp, the former vice president of Chrysler, who used the term in the early to mid-1980s when Chrysler was struggling to stay in business. Historically, Chrysler was always the least vertically integrated of the Big Three US automakers and as such was the most heavily dependent on its supply base. Stahlkamp realized that Chrysler was vulnerable to the performance of its suppliers, but even more importantly each of those immediate, or tier-one, suppliers were vulnerable to the performance of their suppliers, which the literature would now term tier two (tier^2) and beyond (tier^n).

In the mid-1990s several leading firms and at least one research university came together to establish the Supply Chain Council and with it, perhaps being the most significant endeavor, the supply chain operation reference (or SCOR) model note that this model has a copyright and our permission to use it requires the° symbol], as shown in Figure 6.1 (Supply Chain Council, 2013). The council initially posited that all firms engage in four basic activities: source, make, deliver, and return. In traditional terms, it meant that they purchased materials, transformed them, and sold them to customers. Moreover, there was an overarching *plan* function that coordinated their respective efforts. The council, however, went further and recognized that both suppliers and customers also have *source-make-deliver* activities and that successful firms actually also have their *plan* activities helping coordination with other organizations that transcend their corporate boundaries While the *return* function is included within the model, it deals with reverse flows within the supply chain, an opportunity for innovation but a topic that is considered outside of the scope of this chapter.

Supply chains, therefore, only end when, from a supply standpoint, we determine those firms that extract raw materials from the earth or harvest it. Similarly, from a customer perspective, the chain only ends when a product or service is consumed.

The second major contribution that the SCOR model [see previous note] provides is the recognition of three parallel flows: physical, information, and financial. While *physical flows* are perhaps the most obvious and the ones that have historically been the focus of much of the effort of purchasing and distribution activities, the other two-information and financial flowsmay be particularly useful [ok] in achieving smooth business operations [ok]. Physical flows cannot function properly without *information flows*, which refer most often to transactional information; however, information flow [ok] should also consist of technical data and forecasts from a strategic standpoint. *Financial flows* are a part of the supply chain because funds are required as payment for goods as well as investments. Financial flows normally work best when physical flows are operating properly, but it has already been established that these require proper and timely information. Figure 6.2 shows these flows as elements of the SCOR model.

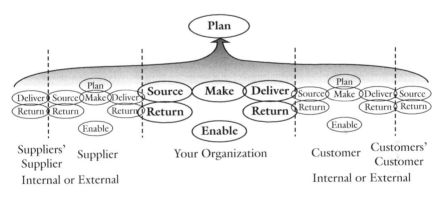

Figure 6.1 Supply Chain Operational Reference Model: Repeating Activities

Source: Supply Chain Council (2010). Supply Chain Operational Reference Model. Permission granted. Cypress, TX.

Figure 6.2 SCOR Model Flows

Source: Supply Chain Council (2013). (Permission Granted).

Firms make considerable investments in processes that enable them to conduct business with one another. Online ordering, electronic data interchange, and integrated applications—such as continuous planning, forecasting, and replenishment (CPFR)—have streamlined the information exchanges with the result being more responsive physical flows. Electronic funds transfer (EFT) has done the same for financial flows.

The obvious question is whether there is, in fact, a *knowledge flow and sharing* that parallels the three other flows of the SCOR model [see previous note on copyrighted model]. While there is ample room for arguing that there can be no supply chain without the physical, information, and financial flows, there is no such compelling reason to suggest that there must be a *knowledge flow and sharing*; however, if one defines the value proposition with one's partners properly, then the *knowledge flow and sharing* must be active.

Looking for Innovation in the Supply Chain

While much of the literature focuses on product innovation, the adoption and adaptation of best practices also suggests that there is ample reason to pursue process innovations. Many advancements in both product and process innovation are serendipitous or ad hoc, rather than planned or the outcome of some established process. Booth (2010) states that "contrary to popular belief research and development happens all over the place and not just in R&D departments. It can pop up all over your supply chains and your organization (which is a good thing if it is recognized and controlled)" (69).

One method for identifying opportunities can be found in the "supply market segmentation" proposed by Kraljic (1983), where the risks in the supply market for a given item or service are juxtaposed with the importance of that item or its profit potential for the buying firm. [ok] Bonoma and Shapiro (1983) advanced the concept of segmentation and included supplier capabilities in the schema. More recently there are several academic researchers who have been proponents of strategic sourcing. Particularly, Cavinato (2006) and Carter (2006), two prolific writers who emphasize that supply chain management needs to be strategic rather than transactional. Their rationale is that there are scarce resources devoted to managing those suppliers and that they need to be applied to those activities providing the most value to the firm.

Supply segmentation is a key method for identifying where specific types of innovations may be found within the supply chain. Table 6.1 sorts out these various possibilities relative to the importance of the item or service versus the risk in the respective supply market.

Even before the advent of the term *supply chain*, there were institutionalized efforts to extend problem solving beyond the boundaries of the firm to other immediately adjacent members of the supply chain. The cornerstone for collaborative innovation between supply chain partners is trust, specifically trust that has been nurtured over time. The nature of trust is not well understood; it can oftentimes be inadvertently, but easily, lost (Fawcett, S., Jones, S., and Fawcett, A., 2012).

Table 6.1 Sorting Innovation Opportunity Types

	Relatively Low Importance or Profit Potential	Relatively High Importance or Profit Potential
High Risk/Unique Items	Bottleneck: spare parts often available only from an OEM source; price is seldom an issue, and buyers seek innovative methods to avoid the presence of bottleneck items and services	Critical: high-technology, often low-volume and difficult-to-obtain materials and items; continuous development and improvement also assures unique properties
Low Risk/ Commonly Available Items	Routine: ubiquitous, commonly found, little to no brand preference; differentiation often found through convenience of purchase or order placement	Leverage: many sources with differentiation occurring on price and lead time; specifications often determined by industry practice or published standard

Customer service efforts may not normally embrace innovation, but with a focus on problem solving many, in fact, do just that. Heading backward up the supply chain, many firms engaged in supplier-development activities have similar characteristics. They may not have intended to spawn innovation, per se, but may nevertheless have done so.

To demonstrate how innovation flow can be realized, eight case studies were developed from a range of industries and spanning multiple decades. The independent variables were later derived and summarized into some generalized theories that appear to underscore the use of supply chain theory with regard to innovation. Specific names and other forms of identity have been omitted.

Case A: Medium-Sized Injection Molder

Firm A was an injection molder using a range of various polymers to satisfy the needs of smaller-volume customers in Southern California. Among its customers was a specialty manufacturer of diagnostics products that required precision-molded plastic partigen [you are not likely going to find this in an ordinary dictionary, but these are plates that hold a specific reagent media and the term as used here is correct] plates that were filled with reagent media used for testing various environments, a major one being the presence of mold spores. The customer was not easy to satisfy, and Firm A had been encountering major quality problems with parts not meeting the physical dimensions specified. The customer had become backlogged and began missing order promises to its customers. Firm A was not going to lose the business immediately because of switching costs related to the steep learning curve. Firm A needed a solution, which turned out to be technical assistance from one of its customer's other divisions. Ultimately, this resulted in a technical service representative from that division visiting and ultimately solving the problem.

Problem solving may or may not be considered innovation, yet Firm A's customer was back in business, and Firm A later became known for high-precision products of consistent quality. Its business more than doubled, with partigen plates being a key product offering. Moreover, the relationship between Firm A and its customer was strengthened.

In the above matrix, the partigen plates were an important source of profit for both customer and supplier; additionally, there were no other sources readily available—the item was classified as *critical*. Supplier development was a source of innovation in this case even if it did occur somewhat accidently.

Case B: The Pharmaceutical Firm

The situation with case B closely parallels the circumstances of case A. Firm B had elected to make a change to the plastic bottles that it used for prescription medications. The bottles were made of high-density polyethylene (HDPE) and after filling had a tamper-proof seal added as required under federal law. With an incompatibility between the bottle and the seal, none of the packaged product met quality standards. Like in case A, Firm B began missing customer delivery dates and had a large quantity of product in inventory that could not be shipped.

While the outcome in case B was similar to that of case A, the circumstances for arriving at a solution were different. Firm B was a business unit of a large, multidivision chemical company that also produced several types of plastic molding resins. Firm B's management connected with the technical services function of a sister division that produced polymers. The resulting change to the resin specification yielded a three-fold win: 1) the pharmaceutical division got bottles that met federal requirements and was thus able to ship product, 2) the bottle manufacturer got a solution to a problem that was plaguing several of its key customers, and 3) the plastics division was able to increase sales by adding a new customer. Problem solving can lead to innovation and in this case that innovation was not necessarily a product one, but a process for sharing information across the supply chain.

The nature of the supply market showed that an abundance of firms were capable of producing molded plastic bottles. The item was important to Firm B because it could not ship without them; however, the item was classified as a *leverage* item.

Case C: The Automotive OEM Parts Producer

A producer of body panels for the automotive industry engaged in a joint effort to reduce waste and hence costs with its principal customer. An important element of this effort was for the automotive firm to embed ten engineers at Firm C's plant and to task them with identifying and eliminating waste no matter where they found it. One significant effort was the reengineering of the purchase–sales transaction system. Originally, each shipment from Firm C represented a separate transaction with the requisite paperwork flowing between the two firms. Given that operations were on a 24-7 basis, this resulted in hundreds of orders, invoices, and payment remittances. Initially, Firm C employed over a dozen persons to handle transactions.

Firm C and its customer had been doing business for several years, and the intent was for that to continue into the future. Reengineering the purchasing process resulted in the elimination of purchase orders, replacing them with a long-term forecast broken down into weekly units. At an agreed upon time, the forecast became the commitment. Instead of invoicing each shipment, Firm C would submit only one invoice to its customer each month, and payment to Firm C was no longer made by paper checks but with a single electronic funds transfer within 48 hours of receipt of the invoice. Each firm reduced transactional personnel by 70 percent, and the process worked so well that Firm C then took the process to its major supplier, a producer of galvanized steel coils, and got even further cost savings. Years later, these enhancements have resulted in closer relationships that have continued to endure and also abet further process innovation.

There are many metal stampers supplying the US automotive industry. While switching costs are considered substantial, the automotive industry does do so on a frequent basis. This would suggest that there is less risk in the marketplace for a family of items that are of high importance. The matrix quadrant could, therefore, be considered *leverage*.

Case D: The Plastics Fabricator

Not all knowledge flows from customer to supplier as in the first three cases. Firm D, a fabricator of plastic foam parts, had a reputation for being an artisan in foam. For some time, Firm D had produced generic parts used by a manufacturer of custom architectural windows and doors for commercial buildings; Firm D was then approached by this manufacturer to develop a spacer that would prevent windows from rubbing against one another in shipment. This was important to the window manufacturer because damaged windows could not be installed, putting the building project behind schedule and requiring product return and expensive rework. A reputation for poor quality would be devastating as reputations were no secret in the building trades.

Firm D was able to design a unique yet inexpensive foam spacer that solved the problem with the result being improved profitability as well as an enhanced reputation for on-time, quality performance for the window manufacturer. However, to illustrate how knowledge flows can be easily lost, the customer sought a lower price for the plastic spacers and switched its purchases away from Firm D. They ultimately found a lower-cost supplier but managed to also give away a source of innovation that might have yielded other types of useful solutions. The savings from purchasing the parts for a lower price was infinitesimal compared to the value obtained through innovation.

The item was readily available from other sources, there was little risk in the supply market, and the immediate profit potential appeared to be very small. The customer viewed the item as *routine*, where in fact it was more likely to be *leverage* or even *critical*. A key finding from this case is that miscategorization can lead to underappreciation for the related innovation.

Case E: The Aerospace Components Manufacturer

Many firms have vertically integrated operations but rely on outside suppliers to supplement their requirements. Firm E, a producer of specialized engine components used in jet aircraft engines, typifies this situation. Having many small suppliers of machined parts, the issue was on-time delivery and price; however, strategically the former would always trump the latter. A major bottleneck for the small suppliers was the cost of consumable tooling, specifically the cutting tools used on lathes, milling machines, and screw machines. Firm E's purchasing group saw an opportunity to name these small firms as approved buyers off of Firm E's tool contracts, an advantageous arrangement because pricing was usually a function of volume.

The small suppliers saw an immediate value and began reducing the prices of parts sold to Firm E. The next step was Firm E telling the suppliers that they could use the contracts to purchase tooling for any work that they had, not just that pertaining to Firm E's needs. The buyer-seller relationship was substantially strengthened with the result being a willingness by the small suppliers to be flexible in solving problems for Firm E, especially when it came to reducing lead time and producing parts for unforeseen and emergency needs. Firm E, much like Firm C, was able to significantly improve its on-time performance, and its customers rewarded it with an increase in order volume.

Much like the situation with Firm C, however, after a change in management, the arrangement was viewed as low volume, and all future purchases were dictated to be strictly on price. As last seen, Firm E, was incurring many late deliveries because of the lost collaborative relationships, and it was seeing a reduction in order volume as a result.

The tooling was actually a *bottleneck* item for Firm E's suppliers. The influence that Firm E was able assert was more a matter of process innovation rather than product.

Case F: The Commercial Printer
There are situations when apparent innovations are not the advancements that were originally intended. Firm F was a large commercial printer that used a substantial volume of paper that would come in jumbo rolls by multiple railcars each week. Historically, the outer wrapper for a jumbo roll was more of the same paper, meaning that there was some loss as this was where any dirt, moisture, or tears would occur. The paper mill, recognizing this potential for loss, sought to solve the problem by wrapping each jumbo roll with asphalt-coated paper. Case F considered the impact, both savings and additional costs that the change would incur, with the result that the innovation was quashed. The asphalt-coated paper, as it turned out, would not have been able to be recycled but rather disposed of as a hazardous waste, meaning that the cost would have exceeded the intended benefits.

Printing paper, although available from myriad sources, was extremely important to Firm F; hence, as an end item, it could be deemed a *leverage* item. The roll wrapper, while not part of the product that Firm F needed, could have become a *bottleneck* item if Firm F had revised its purchasing specification to require asphalt-coated rolls, but a plain wrapper was likely to remain a *routine* item.

Firm F and its supplier continue to have a good relationship, but the lesson learned from the [feel that this still adds context to the case] situation was that true innovation was more likely to occur between the buyer and seller working in partnership rather than by unilateral action by just one party.

Case G: A Major Importer

A chemical producer was heavily dependent on its ability to import both finished products and raw materials from Europe, while another chemical producer, ostensibly a competitor in some markets, was heavily dependent on its ability to export. The risk exposure that both firms had was the potential for the International Longshoremen's Association (ILA) to call for a work stoppage whenever its contract expired. The stoppage would affect all ports from Miami to Portland, Maine. Many firms were thinking of removing westbound containers at Halifax before they reached the United States, but the volume was calculated to be some 20 to 50 times the capacity of that port.

Looking for a solution, Firm G realized that it was not the only one confronting the problem and reached out to an executive of one of the affected lines. He provided the genesis of an innovative idea: establish a container line that used small vessels and called at ports not operated by the ILA. The problem would be having enough freight to make the operation economically viable in both directions. Firm G reached out to some of its competitors and found one with sufficient volume. Jointly they approached interested parties and launched a new container line, assuring that its ships would be sufficiently full to be profitable between Europe and North America.

Analyzing this instance with the above matrix, shipping as a service also fits the description of a process required for the delivery of products as well as for the receipt of raw materials. Under normal circumstances, the shipping industry has many participants in the market, meaning that as a service it would be categorized as *routine*. However, when capacity becomes constrained, such as with the anticipated work stoppage, the category appears to shift to *bottleneck*.

Case H: An Electronic Components Producer

This firm used a particular nonferrous metal in the production of miniature electronic components that were increasingly in demand by computer and telecommunications equipment manufacturers. As industrial requirements began to outstrip worldwide capacity for this rare element, engineers and metallurgists from both Firm H and its key supplier began to increasingly collaborate on research that would lead to higher performance from lesser quantities of the metal.

As collaboration continued, key supply management representatives were added to the discussions as both the customer and the supplier recognized that the continuing streams of innovation were dependent upon maintaining a long-term relationship. Moreover, short-term gains in the form of lower prices from other suppliers could have a potential deleterious effect.

The elemental metal was only available from five suppliers worldwide: three in the United States and one each in Japan and Germany. The risk posed by the limited number of participants in the supply market plus the high profit potential that the metal represented easily positioned it in the *critical* quadrant.

Findings

Product Innovation

The key forms of product innovation appear to be found in the critical and leverage quadrants of the segmented supply matrix. For critical items, this is likely because of the long-term buyer-seller relationships that need to be in place when buyers have few alternative sources in the supply market. Leverage items may enjoy those same benefits when buyer firms elect to engage in longer-term relationships. A corollary to this finding is that a short-term or transaction-based approach to buyer-seller relationships tends to curtail the flow of innovation.

Process Innovation

Process innovation appears to be potentially available for any of the quadrants, no matter whether they are critical, leverage, bottleneck, or routine. Whereas product innovation is not normally sought in the routine and bottleneck quadrants, there remains opportunities for process innovation provided there is sufficient trust that has evolved from longer-term relationships. Table 6.2 summarizes the cases discussed earlier in this chapter vis-à-vis product (labeled "T") versus process (labeled "S") innovation.

Suppliers and Customers

Innovation can be driven in either of two directions, from customers to suppliers or from suppliers to customers. There may be instances where, due to sequential relationships in the supply chain, a supplier's supplier or a customer's customer may be the source of innovation. Without the appropriate relationships in place, however, these potential opportunities are never to be realized.

Table 6.2 Product versus Process Innovation

	Relatively Low Importance or Profit Potential	Relatively High Importance or Profit Potential
High Risk/Unique Items	Case E (S) Case G (S) Constrained	Case A (T) Case D (T) Actual Case H (T)
Low Risk/Commonly Available Items	Case G (S) Normal Case D (T) Perceived Case F (T)	Case B (T) Case C (C)

*Transportation is labeled a process rather than a product.

Relationship-driven means more than just the buyer-seller relationship, where the key metrics are typically price, delivery, and quality. While these are important for successful operations in the short term, considering only [ok] this set of metrics engenders [ok] an inability to quantify innovation over the longer term. This inability suggests that innovation may stem from the buyer-seller relationship, often as process types. Product innovation appears to flow from not only those with buying and selling responsibilities, but also between engineering and technical personnel, which raises the question of how these relationships occur. From the cases considered, the relationships appeared to first be the product of the commercial interests, but only after some period of stability and growth in trust did the knowledge flows and sharing occur. Moreover, innovation when dependent upon commercial interests can be fragile and therefore easily lost, as happened in case D.

Innovation Is a Supply Chain Flow

This chapter began with a brief discussion of the SCOR model [see earlier comments as a means for describing the various flows in the supply chain. In each of the cases considered, there was some form of open innovation, whether product or process, that flowed between customers and suppliers. See Figure 6.3. Such being the case, the SCOR model [ditto] might be modified to recognize that innovations can exist. Hence, it is recommended that managers be cognizant of the value of knowledge flows and sharing as depicted in Figure 7.3 to capitalize on the capabilities of customers and suppliers collaborating in the creation of new products and processes.

Summary and Conclusion

While Chesbrough (2003) advanced the idea of open innovation and the need for firms to access the intellectual capital of others, this chapter has suggested that there is a readily accessible group of organizations available within one's respective supply chains for making innovative changes in the process, most notably those suppliers and customers that are already a part of a firm's supply

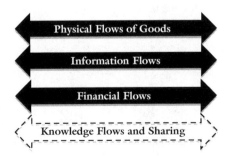

Figure 6.3   SCOR Model Modified with Knowledge Flows and Sharing

chain. Along these lines, Thomke and von Hippel (2002) point to customers as innovators in creating new value. Additionally, Paton and McLaughlin (2008) argue that sustainable growth is based upon identifying, supporting, and nurturing meaningful service exchanges that exploit, develop, and embody value-added knowledge transfer within and across industries. Not all of those supply chain members, however, are created equally; as the segmented supply matrix illustrates; some may be better innovation candidates than others.

As explained in the previous chapters, open innovation can be instrumental in achieving either product or process innovation, or both. The key to accessing innovation is through relationships up and down the supply chain, but with the caveat that those relationships will usually hinge on commercial activity and a modicum of trust. Decisions to change suppliers or the loss of customers will often result in the loss of any innovation connection; hence there is an ongoing need to include recognition of the knowledge flow in any procurement or sales decisions. This is a difficult assessment because innovation has a future payoff and is therefore not easily quantified for management decision making.

Finally, while Chesbrough (2012) stated that firms should not attempt to confine the realm of innovation to the technical experts, leveraging supply chain partners for innovation becomes an endeavor that goes beyond those charged with only commercial responsibilities. Innovation can be an additional flow to be found across the supply chain for better strategic outcomes. In other words, its absence can mean that a firm will not likely be reaping the full value from its partners.

While most open innovation literature focuses on interfirm innovation alliances in horizontal relationships, this chapter, as demonstrated with eight case studies, emphasizes the importance of knowledge flows and sharing that can occur in products or processes in supply chains involving the customers and suppliers of the firm.

References

Bonoma, T., and Shapiro, B. (1983). *Segmenting the Industrial Market.* Lexington, MA: Lexington.

Booth, C. (2010). *Strategic Procurement.* London: Kogan Page.

Carter, J. (2006). "Developing and Implementing Supply Chain Strategies." In Cavinato, J., Kauffmann, R, and Flynn, A. (eds). *Supply Management Handbook*, 81–98. New York: McGraw-Hill.

Cavinato, J. (2006). "Supply Management: ISM's Leadership View." In xxxxxx Cavinato, J., Kauffmann, R, and Flynn, A. (eds) *Supply Management Handbook*, 1–15. New York: McGraw-Hill.

Chesbrough, H. (2003). *Open Innovation: The New Imperative for Creating and Profiting from Technology.* Boston, MA: Harvard Business Review Press.

Chesbrough, H. (2007). "Why Bad Things Happen to Good Technology." *The Wall Street Journal*, April 28. http://online.wsj.com/article/SB117735510033679362.html (accessed October 6, 2013).

Chesbrough, H. (2012). "Henry Chesbrough on Open Innovation." *CIO Journal*, September 24. http://deloitte.wsj.com/cio/2012/09/24/henry-chesbrough-on-open-innovation (accessed October 6, 2013).

Fawcett, S., Jones, S., and Fawcett, A. (2012). "Supply Chain Trust: The Catalyst for Collaborative Innovation." *Business Horizons* 55:163–78.

Kraljic, P. (1983). "Purchasing Must Become Supply Management." *Harvard Business Review* (Sep.–Oct.):109–17

Kuhn, T. (1970). *The Structure of Scientific Revolutions*, 2nd ed. Chicago: University of Chicago.

Paton, R. A., and McLaughin. (2008). "Service Innovation: Knowledge Transfer and Supply Chain." *European Management Journal* 26 (2): 77–83.

Supply Chain Council. (2012). *Supply Chain Operations Reference Model, v. 11.* http://supply-chain.org/f/SCOR-Overview-Web.pdf (accessed February 26, 2014).

Thomke, S. H., and von Hippel, E. (2012). "Customers as Innovators: A New Way to Create Value." *Harvard Business Review 80* (4): 76–81.

CHAPTER 7

Genesis and Evolution of the Xerox-P&G Co-innovation Partnership: Lessons Learned[1]

Robert DeFillippi, Colette Dumas, and Sushil Bhatia

Case Study Methods Summary

The following case study of the Xerox-P&G co-innovation partnership is based on the analysis of documentary data and interviews conducted between September 2010 and December 2010 with the key leadership responsible for the design and implementation of the co-innovation partnership. Interviews were conducted with four senior Xerox executives and two senior P&G executives associated with the co-innovation partnership. Each interviewee received an interview protocol covering the themes and questions in advance. Each interview (averaging 60 minutes in length) was transcribed verbatim and reviewed by the research team to identify key themes and insightful quotes, which are used throughout the case study. A longer version of this case study was reviewed and approved for factual accuracy by the Xerox and P&G executive team that provided us access to the interviewees participating in this study and to in-house company documents.

Xerox's Customer-Led Innovation

Innovation is not something you do alone. You have to collaborate with people across the value chain as well as with the customers throughout the whole innovation process . . . You have to be willing to take risks in innovation and of course research and exploration. It's pushing the boundaries of the unknown. That's a pretty scary proposition because you don't know whether or not it's going to be successful.[2]

Xerox has been recognized since the early 1960s as an innovative company whose commercial success was the result of its impressive record of innovative products. Xerox investments in innovation included the following:

- A $1.6 billion research and development (R&D) investment annually by 2009 (including the R&D investments of its joint venture Fuji Xerox)
- Major research centers in the United States, Canada, Europe, and Asia
- 55,000 worldwide patents, ten issued each week
- More than five hundred awards received for its contributions to innovation in the three years 2006–09

Some historical facts about Xerox Company are presented in Table 7.1 below. Illustrative of Xerox's recognition for its world-class innovation was its receipt of numerous innovation awards. For example, Xerox was named the Product Development and Management Association's Outstanding Corporate Innovator in 2006. One year later, Xerox Corporation received the US National Medal of Technology, "recognizing over fifty years of innovation in marking, materials, electronics, communications and software that created the modern reprographics, electronic printing, and print on demand industries."[3] The National Medal of Technology was the highest honor awarded by the president of the United States to America's leading innovative companies. Past recipients of the award had included IBM, Bell Labs, DuPont, and Dow Chemical.

Despite Xerox's history of innovation achievement, there have been criticisms of Xerox's tradition of engineering- and science-led innovation. In the past, Xerox would gather customer feedback after having created the product. Most typically, customer requests for upgrades and/or new features would be contemplated in subsequent product releases. Xerox had so dominated the global market for copiers and printers that it could put a product out with little to no customer input

Table 7.1 Xerox: Fast Facts 2009

Founded	1906, Rochester, NY, as the Haloid Photographic Co.
Headquarters	Norwalk, Connecticut
CEO	Ursula M. Burns (joined the company in 1980 as a summer engineering intern)
Employees	53,600
Patents	9,400+
2009 revenue	$15.2 billion
Highlights	1959, first plain-paper copier; 1963, first desktop plain-paper copier; 1970, Xerox PARC research center founded; 1977, first laser printer; 1981, Xerox 8010 Star PC, with mouse and window-based GUI released; 2009, Ursula M. Burns becomes CEO, the first African-American woman to head that large of a company

Source: http://www.xerox.com/about-xerox/company-facts/enus.html

and still get sales. However, increasing competition within its markets led to an emphasis within Xerox on customer-led innovation, in which customer inputs were proactively solicited much earlier in the innovation process. At the same time, the company realized that customers were not always technologically savvy enough to tell them what they wanted. The company therefore began involving customers in its R&D labs, to show them what was possible and therefore make the development process itself customer focused. In the words of one Xerox technology executive: "We have technology showcase centers where we show people technology and not products."[4]

Sophie Vandebroek (Xerox's chief technology officer and president of the Xerox Innovation Group) stated the new goal of customer-led innovation quite succinctly: "Customer-led innovation is all about bringing together researchers with deep expertise in the technologies and the future trends with customers who know their pain points and their wishes."[5]

Customer-led innovation (CLI) was focused on sharing customer knowledge with the goal of accelerating the pace of bringing new technologies to the marketplace. The CLI team established contacts between researchers, engineers, and customers. Researchers frequently sought opportunities to work directly with customers and deployed ethnographic methods to learn about customer needs and pain points. The customer was also viewed as a partner in innovation, and CLI encouraged "dreaming with customers" about what the future could be like.

Xerox often initiated customer-led innovation by showing its technology rather than its finished products to the customers. These initial introductions to Xerox's technology capabilities were then followed by dreaming sessions in which clients were invited to dream up how Xerox technology might help them in alleviating points of pain in their work environment and that of their customers. Xerox technologists (engineers and scientists involved in innovation) were thus encouraged to meet face-to-face with some of the 1,500 to 2,000 customers who visited these showrooms at the company's four global research facilities each year. Others worked on-site for a week or two with customers, observing how they utilized current technologies and how Xerox might assist them in providing innovation as a service solution to their needs. See Figure 7.1 and Table 7.2 for the financial performance of Xerox.

Sophie Vandebroek described three approaches for engaging customers in co-innovation with Xerox:

> Each of our research centers around the globe has an innovation showroom. And what we do is we bring customers in; often it's individual customers or a couple of people from the company. And we ask them to share their pain points. We ask them to share their wishes about how they do business today and then we have researchers share some of the technology trends, some of the really cool projects that we are working on in the labs, whether it's a new solution or a service or a new technology. Then together, the customers and the researchers, we start "dreaming" about how this technology can truly address the business issues and create a better future for the customer. So that's our first approach: bring the customer into one of our research centers and have dreaming sessions.

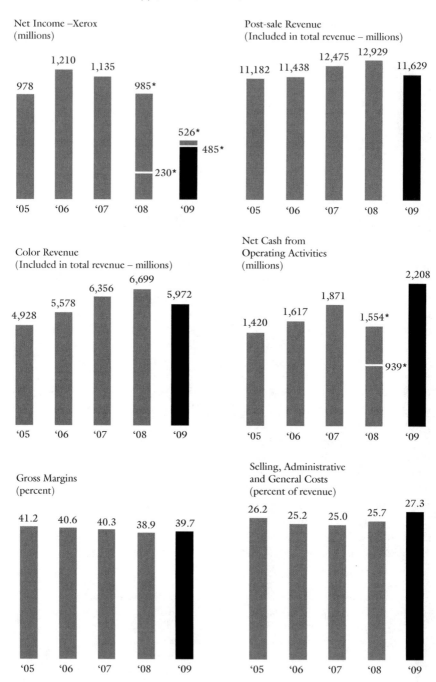

Figure 7.1   Financial Data of Xerox

Source: http://www.xerox.com/annual-report-2009/pdfs/2009_Annual_Report.pdf

Table 7.2 Financial Performance of Xerox—Five Years in Review

	(In millions, except per-share data)				
	2009	2008	2007[2]	2006	2005
Per-Share Data					
Income from continuing operations					
Basic	$0.56	$0.26	$1.21	$ 1.25	$0.91
Diluted	0.55	0.26	$1.19	1.22	0.90
Earnings					
Basic	$0.56	$0.26	$1.21	$ 1.25	$0.96
Diluted	0.55	0.26	1.19	$ 1.22	0.94
Common stock dividends declared	$0.17	$0.17	$0.0425	$—	$—
Operations					
Revenues	$15,179	$17,608	$17,228	$ 15,895	$15,701
Sales	6,646	8,325	8,192	7,464	7,400
Service, outsourcing, and rentals	7,820	8,485	8,214	7,591	7,426
Finance income	713	798	822	840	875
Income from continuing operations	516	265	1,165	1,232	948
Income from continuing operations—Xerox	485	230	1,135	1,210	933
Net income	516	265	1,165	1,232	993
Net income—Xerox	485	230	1,135	1,210	978
Financial Position					
Working capital	$5,270	$2,700	$4,463	$ 4,056	4,390
Total assets	24,032	22,447	23,543	21,709	21,953
Consolidated Capitalization					
Short-term debt and current portion of long-term debt	$988	$1,610	$525	$ 1,485	1,139
Long-term debt	8,276	6,774	6,939	5,660	6,139
Total Debt	9,264	8,384	7,464	7,145	7,278
Liabilities to subsidiary trusts issuing preferred securities[(1)]	649	648	632	624	724
Series C mandatory convertible preferred stock	—	—	—	—	889
Xerox shareholders' equity	7,050	6,238	8,588	7,080	6,319
Noncontrolling interests	141	120	103	108	90
Total Consolidated Capitalization	$17,104	15,390	$16,787	$14,957	$15,300

(Continued)

Table 7.2 Financial Performance of Xerox—Five Years in Review (*Continued*)

	(In millions, except per-share data)				
	2009	*2008*	*2007*[2]	*2006*	*2005*
Selected Data and Ratios					
Common shareholders of record at year-end	44,792	46,541	48,261	40,372	53,017
Book value per common share	$8.11	$7.21	$9.36	$7.48	$6.79
Year-end common stock market price	$8.46	$7.97	$16.19	$16.95	$14.65
Employees at year-end	53,600	57,100	57,400	53,700	55,220
Gross margin	39.7%	38.9%	40.3%	40.6%	41.2%
Sales gross margin	33.9%	33.7%	35.9%	35.7%	36.6%
Service, outsourcing, and rentals gross margin	42.6 %	41.9%	42.7%	43.0%	43.3%
Finance gross margin	62.0%	61.8%	61.6%	63.7%	62.7%

[1]For 2005, the amount includes $98 reported in other current liabilities.
[2]2007 results include the acquisition of GIS.

Source: http://www.xerox.com/annual-report-2009/financial-performance/five-years-results.html

The second approach includes anthropologists on our staffs in our Palo Alto Research Center as well as in Grenoble, France, and Bangalore, India. These are experts in work practices who go "live" at our customer's businesses for extended periods of time to not only hear and listen about how the customer really does his or her work but to really observe. Recently, our anthropologists have done some studies in China and India. They have spent time with some of our customers that work from home, from their car or from the airport. This way we really understand what their struggles are such that we can innovate solutions for their unspoken problems.

The third approach, which is more of a traditional approach in industry, is to have focus groups where you bring a set of customers together and discuss some of the new ideas that are in product development or solutions development, and you share it and you get the customer's reaction and feedback on the actual concepts you are working on.[6]

Patrick Mazeau, a manager within customer-led innovation at Xerox, described the dreaming sessions utilized at Xerox's research center in Grenoble, France:

During dreaming sessions, we discuss the potential scenarios of an innovation. We speak 20 percent of the time and the customer speaks 80 percent of the time. We listen to the customer. We briefly explain the technology we want to test for the customer. The role of the facilitator is to stimulate dialogue, make sure questions that have been raised are answered. We accept different directions. We accept that the customer sees things differently than us. We ask customers for prioritization. If they have $100 to spend, what is priority? During the best dreaming sessions, there are usually 6–8 active members; half the customer and half Xerox. The facilitator is from Xerox. The Xerox representative is different each time—it depends upon the technology. The facilitator manages the conversation during the session but has important pre-work to do beforehand. The researchers are looking for feedback (from the customer). They come from different technical groups. They present the core technology they are working on, looking for scenarios and applications. The more scenarios you have, the better it is to convince the business group of the real value of your technology and ideas. We really listen to the customer's ideas and feedback.[7]

Patrick Mazeau next described the role of the dreaming sessions in which P&G began their co-innovation partnership:

During the first dreaming session in December 2008 with P&G, before we signed an agreement with them, we learned about their vision. They wanted us to learn from them how people were using machines—machine learning. They wanted a better understanding of the patterns of usage of office equipment. They wanted to know who the head users of office equipment were, why they weren't optimizing the usage of equipment. It took us time to understand. P&G agreed to pilot the technology in their headquarters. In dreaming sessions, many ideas are expressed. You can't implement them in two months. You form ideas into pilots/real products.[8]

Sophie Vandebroek summarized the challenge facing the engineers and technologists under her charge:

The big thing we have to teach the researchers and engineers is not to go in with the problem already solved. There is a temptation to quickly get to the answer, but you have to leave possibilities open and be able to constructively listen to what the customer is saying, or else you might filter out the real issues. As we get our researchers to do that, we'll come up with more creative solutions.[9]

The New Xerox Focus on Services[10]

For decades, Xerox and other printer-and-copier companies built their businesses by pushing customers to buy more office machines and selling them significant volumes of ink, toner, and related consumables. However, starting in the mid-1990s, Xerox and its rivals began advising big customers to reduce their number of machines and find ways to cut printing costs. The services push came as office copiers, fax machines, and printers merged into multifunction devices that were linked to corporate computer networks. Although these devices often cost $10,000 to $20,000, vendors installed them when they managed a company's printing because, compared with desktop devices, they were more efficient, broke down less, and could use cheaper supplies. In many organizations, copiers were purchased by facilities managers; printers, by the IT department; and fax machines, by office managers. That resulted in multiple service contracts and a wide variety of brands and supplies—especially ink and toner cartridges, which were usually the biggest expense. Most organizations didn't know how many devices they had and how many pages they printed, according to Gartner's analyses of the printing markets. As a result, new business opportunities in providing printing and document management as a service became increasingly apparent.[11]

Several potential strategic advantages could follow from Xerox's focus on services. First, a service business offered the promise of steadier sources of revenue and profit than product businesses, which were more susceptible to peaks and valleys of economic cycles. Second, service businesses fostered closer relations with corporate customers and often yielded higher profit margins.[12]

To drive this strategy forward, in late 2001 the company launched Xerox Global Services to help customers improve efficiencies in their document-intensive business processes. A key component of Xerox Global Services was its focus on the office. To help improve the productivity of the office environment, Xerox introduced the office document assessment (ODA) tool, which analyzed the total costs associated with alternative document-making processes. A typical ODA report offered a range of suggestions for increasing office efficiency, improving worker productivity, and reducing costs. Often central to such suggestions was reducing the number of devices through consolidation, which would lead to reductions in the use of toner, paper, and other consumables, all of which Xerox sold. The reduction in total devices could be substantial, moving from a ratio of more than one device per employee to a ratio of one device per ten or more employees. Xerox sold this set of services primarily as a way to increase its clients' productivity and lower its costs. But environmentally aware customers recognized and valued the benefits that accompanied reductions in material use. As one Xerox customer commented, "Not only is our printing system a massive expense, but it also impacts our rubbish disposal. We can save a small forest each year!" Xerox concluded that framing its services as a means to help both the environmental and financial bottom lines made an attractive value proposition for many customers.[13]

For Xerox, this strategy moved the company from focusing on products that were becoming commoditized to a mix of products and services that increased revenue. In 2005, approximately 22 percent of Xerox's revenue was driven by Xerox Global Services. As a result of its service strategy, Xerox was able to build closer customer relations, which had three main advantages. First, the customer was less likely to change suppliers. Second, through these closer relationships, Xerox could expand the range of products they sold to their services client. Third, Xerox could use this business model to attract new customers impressed by the company's social consciousness, manifested in its array of environmentally friendly services and product offerings.

Managed Print Services at Xerox

In a Managed Print Service (MPS) contract, a service provider, such as Xerox, takes primary responsibility for meeting the customer's office printing needs. This can include the printing equipment (plus existing third-party equipment if this was required by the customer), the supplies, and the service and overall management of the customer's fleet of printer and multifunctional peripheral (MFP) assets. MFPs are multifunction printers that act as a printer, scanner, fax machine, and photocopier. The primary services offered by MPS vendors, such as Xerox, includes assessments of the clients' print service needs, selective or general replacement of hardware (optimization), and the service, parts, and supplies needed to operate the new and/or existing hardware. The provider also tracks the use of the printer, fax, copier, and related print services assets, identifies print service problems, and monitors user satisfaction. The MPS provider analyzes the information gathered in the course of tracking and makes (or recommends to the customer) the changes needed to ensure overall efficiency and the means to satisfy changing user needs.

Xerox's MPS services are available to clients ranging from small to medium to global enterprises. Their value proposition is to help their clients reduce costs, enhance employee productivity, provide data and document security, and achieve environmental sustainability goals (reductions in carbon footprint, energy consumption, and solid waste). The MPS service invests in such counterintuitive activities as assisting their clients in reducing the purchasing of printing hardware equipment and consumable supply purchases (paper, ink), which could be perceived as directly opposing the sales objectives of Xerox's print division. However, the service contract revenues associated with these MPS relationships are viewed as more sustainable long-term customer relationships that could assure a longer and more stable source of revenue in the future.

Xerox describes its MPS value proposition thus:

> By offering services grounded in rigorous, data-driven Lean Six Sigma–based methodologies, Xerox's suite of MPS offerings helps clients better manage the volume of documents flowing through the organization and the costs associated with printing, sharing and updating them. From small businesses to global enterprises, Xerox optimizes the use of multi-vendor output devices, like printers, fax machines and copiers, and delivers change management support so employees can successfully adapt to new technology and work processes. Xerox also helps clients meet environmental goals by reducing paper use, decreasing power use and eliminating landfill.[14]

By the end of 2008, Xerox was internally preparing for the introduction of its Enterprise Print Services (EPS), its first offering to help companies better manage documents across their global print infrastructure—from the office to the in-house print center to the virtual workplace. Enterprise Print Services expanded the scope of Xerox's offerings beyond the traditional MPS focus and offered enterprise-wide print and document process management services. "By expanding MPS beyond the office walls, organizations have total control over company-wide print spend," said Ken Weilerstein, vice president, in research at Gartner, Inc. "This is significant because internal and external print shop costs can often exceed office printing spending, so optimizing across all print environments will uncover even more sources of cost savings."[15] Xerox's growth into EPS would help the company transition its business portfolio from a mature, low-margin hardware business (copiers and print hardware and consumables) to a portfolio that included a growing portion of business from the service sector, which offered long-term customer relationships and recurring revenue opportunities. Most MPS and EPS contracts were five years in length. The EPS strategy's broad scope in servicing the complete print environment of their customers provided additional opportunities for Xerox to develop both deeper and broader sets of relationships across the businesses and functional areas of their clients, making possible follow-on services from within Xerox's full portfolio of service offerings. Although the value propositions of cost reduction and access to external skills were compelling drivers, larger enterprises with global reach were increasingly looking for innovation as well in their outsourced service contracts and tended to view these relationships as strategic partnerships.

The Managed Print Services Market in 2009

Worldwide managed print services comprised a $20.3 billion market in 2009, up 47 percent from 2008, according to Photizo Group, a market researcher out of Lexington, Kentucky.[16] The segment looked increasingly attractive to printer, copier, and multifunction device manufacturers in a year when shipments of hardware were down 7 percent to $49.8 billion. While experiencing double-digit growth in 2008, the MPS market saw growth slow in 2009 primarily because of deteriorating global economic conditions. The MPS market was still not fully developed, and offerings were at different levels of maturity. In many emerging countries, much of the consolidation that MPS usually entailed was already present because organizations never bought much equipment due to its cost. And the improved service that MPS would deliver in Western economies was irrelevant in many emerging countries where labor was relatively low cost. However, there were new business opportunities in the dynamic and rapidly advancing developing countries, such as Brazil, Mexico and China, where the growth was coming from signing up local organizations[17]

The MPS market in 2009 had three distinct tiers of providers:

- Tier 1—Canon, HP, Lexmark, Ricoh, Xerox: worldwide MPS providers that accounted for approximately 84 percent of market share
- Tier 2—Dell, Fuji Xerox, HCL, Kyocera Mita, Konica Minolta, Oce, Oki Printing Solutions, Pitney Bowes, Samsung Electronics, Sharp, Toshiba: providers with primarily a regional presence in either the Americas, Europe, the Middle East and Africa (EMEA), or Asia/Pacific that accounted for approximately 15 percent of market share
- Tier 3—Regional and national providers that accounted for approximately 1 percent of market share: ComputerCenter, Lanxum, LowCost, Office-Max, Pulsar Tec, SCC, Sindoh, Technoset, WeP Peripherals

By 2009 the top-tier office-machine makers participating in this segment (Xerox, HP , Canon, Ricoh, Lexmark) were competing with each other with value propositions that offered cost savings to their clients brought about by reducing the numbers of printers and copiers installed on office floors and desktops, replacing them with multifunction printer/copier/scanner/fax machines. By 2009, Xerox was leading all tier-one MPS providers with worldwide market share of 40 percent, followed by HP at 19 percent, Ricoh (including Ikon) at 13 percent, Lexmark at 7 percent, and Cannon at 5 percent. Xerox's 2009 global revenues were $1.958 billion. In North America, Xerox's revenues were $1.252 billion, and they held 45 percent of the North American market.[18]

Procter and Gamble (P&G)

William Procter, a candlemaker, and James Gamble, a soap maker, formed Procter and Gamble (P&G) in 1837; it was headquartered in Cincinnati, Ohio, and would go on to become as global Fortune 500 Corporation. , According to CNNMoney.com, 2007) "In the early parts of 2007, P&G was the 25th largest US company by revenue, 18th largest by profit, with 138,000 employees and more than 300 brands sold in 180 countries.

Ranked 10th in Fortune Most Admired Companies list. P&G's corporate motto was 'Touching Lives, Improving Life.'"

For most of its history, P&G had been America's preeminent consumer-products company, with brands such as Tide (a pioneer in laundry detergents) and Pampers (the first disposable diapers). P&G built its brands through innovative marketing techniques, including advertising nationally. It was the first firm to develop the idea of brand management. But by the 1990s, it appeared that P&G was in danger of losing its prominent position to its major competitors, including Kimberley Clark and Colgate Palmolive. One option for P&G to maintain its profit growth was through cost cutting. However, the essential challenge facing

Table 7.3   Financial Performance of P&G—Five Years in Review

	Financial Summary (Unaudited)				
Amounts in millions, except per share amounts	*2009*	*2008*	*2007*	*2006*	*2005*
Net Sales	$79,029	$81,748	$74,832	$66,724	$55,292
Operating Income	16,123	16,637	15,003	12,916	10,026
Net Earnings	13,436	12,075	10,340	8,684	6,923
Net Earnings Margin from Continuing Operations	14.30%	14.40%	13.40%	12.70%	12.00%
Diluted Net Earnings per Common Share from Continuing Operations	$ 3.58	$ 3.56	$ 2.96	$ 2.58	$ 2.43
Diluted Net Earnings per Common Share	4.26	3.64	3.04	2.64	2.53
Dividends per Common Share	1.64	1.45	1.28	1.15	1.03

Source: http://www.pg.com/fr_FR/downloads/annual_reports/PG_2009_AnnualReport.pdf

P&G was how to grow its business. During the 1990s, as market power shifted from manufacturers like P&G to retailers such as Wal-Mart, the resulting squeeze on P&G's margins and profits called for new and different strategies.

In response to these economic and competitive challenges, in 1999 P&G appointed new CEO Durk Jaeger, who during his 17-month stint at the top could not reverse this slide, resulting in his departure. In June 2000, Alan Lafley was appointed as the new CEO. To better focus on serving the needs of P&G's consumers, Lafley put a tremendous emphasis on the firm's brands. In describing the P&G of the future, he said, "We're in the business of creating and building brands." Lafley also pushed everyone at P&G to approach its brands more creatively. "People remember experiences," Lafley explained. "They don't remember attributes or benefits."[19] P&G enjoyed a longstanding track record of producing high-quality products. Consumers wanted high-quality products at reasonable and affordable prices, and this was the main reason why P&G drove the consumer-products industry worldwide. Lafley, as CEO, also challenged the supremacy of P&G's R&D operations. Confronting head-on the stubbornly held notion that everything must be invented within P&G, he instead asserted that half of the firm's new products should come from the outside. The percentage of new product ideas coming from outside the firm increased from 10 percent when he took over to almost 50 percent by 2009.

Lafley and his team preserved the essential part of P&G's R&D capability— world class technologists who were masters of the core technologies critical to the household and personal care businesses—while also bringing more P&G employees outside R&D into the innovation game. They sought to create an enterprise-wide social system that would harness the skills and the insights of the people throughout the company and give them a focus on the consumer. The focus on innovation also had a direct effect on P&G's portfolio of businesses. It sold off many of its businesses in the food-and-beverage area, so it could concentrate on products that were driven by the kind of innovations it knew best. The result was that with a narrow mix of businesses P&G was able to devote the resources and attention needed to build an organization-wide innovation culture.

P&G also focused on creating a practice of open innovation, taking advantage of the skills and interests of people throughout the company and looking for partnerships outside P&G. It started the practice of accessing externally developed intellectual property for its business and allowing externally developed assets and know-how to be used by P&G.

Historically, P&G had relied on internal capabilities and those of a network of trusted suppliers to invent, develop, and deliver new products and services to the market. It did not actively seek to connect with potential external partners. Similarly, the P&G products, technologies, and know-how that were developed were used almost solely for the manufacturing and selling of P&G's core products. Beyond this, it seldom licensed them to other companies. By 2000, the world had become much more connected. In the areas in which P&G did business, there were millions of scientists, engineers, and other companies globally. P&G changed its approach and decided to collaborate with this external world of expertise by embracing open innovation and in 2001 launched its "Connect and Develop" initiative.

Connect and Develop included a global team that searched for solutions to business needs via external networks of contacts from varying industries and scientific and business disciplines. The team also ran an innovation portal (pgconnectdevelop.com) in five languages to solicit innovative ideas for challenges that they would post on the site. This practice became the forerunner to the use of crowdsourcing information technology (and related innovation services) to disseminate innovation challenges online for the collection, screening, and selection of the most promising solutions provided from its online suppliers, whether from sources inside or outside the company. Additionally P&G encouraged the cross-pollination of ideas via several other innovation practices. One practice was to share employees with noncompeting companies. In 2008 Google and P&G swapped two dozen employees to provide P&G greater exposure to online models and to allow Google to learn more about how to build brands (Brown and Scott, 2011).

Open innovation at P&G worked both ways—inbound and outbound—and encompassed everything from trademarks to packaging, marketing models to engineering, and business services to design. P&G committed itself to the goal of becoming the partner of choice for innovation collaborations. This goal extended not only to partners for its consumer-products offerings but also for partners to help it innovatively manage its internal business processes (Brown and Scott, 2011). It was in this context of increasing commitments to innovation collaboration that P&G began its search for an MPS partner.

P&G's Search for a Partner

With 135,000 employees in 80 countries, P&G printed and copied millions of documents annually, and in early 2008, those documents came from 45,000 individual devices—copiers, printers, scanners, and fax machines—that were shared by just four employees each on average. Each P&G facility was free to buy its own devices and supplies, a practice that "was absolutely not efficient," said Caroline Basyn, the director of P&G's Global Business Services. She proposed outsourcing printing at all two hundred P&G sites to an MPS provider. At the time, she said "I want to manage this whole print fleet as if it was one printer." Basyn described how P&G went about its search for a partner:

Procter & Gamble began in early 2008 to investigate the efficiency of its document and print systems. We inventoried 45,000 individual devices—including copiers, printers, scanners and fax machines—and found that, on average, each device supported only four people. In addition, each work site managed its own fleet, and P&G did not have a consistent method to purchase supplies or provide maintenance. So we began looking for ways to optimize our document and print processes. We knew that managed print services (MPS) could simplify and digitize our global printing infrastructure by consolidating devices and by helping to control how and when documents are printed. It would also identify ways to drive costs out and deliver substantial sustainability benefits. We also wanted a print strategy that would deliver innovative ways for P&G employees to be more productive and more mobile.

In September 2008, we began working with Xerox, which helped us set goals for an MPS implementation. The goals included:

- Supporting P&G's "Give Back 500 Million Minutes" program by reducing the time employees spend on print- and output-related issues;
- Implementing strategies to move paper-based processes to the digital realm for ease of movement and use, security improvement, retention and access;
- Reducing operational costs by an estimated 20 to 25 percent; and
- Cutting print-related power usage by 30 percent and paper consumption by 20 to 30 percent annually.[20]

At the time Xerox was one of a half dozen vendors who had worked with P&G on outsourced printing and document services (see Table 7.4). Indeed Xerox was a relatively minor vendor in terms of its share of the outsourced printing contracts awarded by P&G. However, P&G was embarking upon a strategy of becoming a fully digitized service provider that would require its work not only on routine outsourcing of its print service but would also require P&G to work in creating innovative printing solutions that did not currently exist within the company, nor within the industry at large. P&G's CEO Bob MacDonald had

Table 7.4 Timeline of P&G-Xerox Partnership

2007	Caroline Basyn went to United States for new assignment
June 2008	RFP created by P&G for print-service strategic partnership
June 2008	Sophie Vandebroek and Caroline Basyn met for the first time
September 15	Xerox CEO in office of P&G CIO explaining how committed Xerox would be to this partnership if awarded the contract
September 2008	Awarded contract to Xerox
December 2008	Signed contract
Between September 2008 and January 2009	Set up partnership
January 2009	Started the project/deployment
January 2009	First Innovation Council review/kickoff of process
February 2009	Dreaming Session in Grenoble, France, at Xerox R&D Center
April 2009	First run-through of what should be in the pipeline
May 2009	Dreaming Session
July 2009	Dreaming Session

Source: Personal interview with Sophie Vandebroek at Suffolk University, November 15, 2010.

announced a goal for his company: "I think we can be the first company in the world to digitize our work from end to end."[21] MacDonald identified five digital capabilities that it sought to optimize through the use of improved managed print hardware and software services:[22]

- Scanning documents to email
- Printing documents from anywhere to anywhere in the P&G world
- Leverage secure printing
- Avoid banner ads
- Print two sides

This goal of digitization required a substantial investment in digital printing innovative technology and services. It thus complemented the second goal of the vendor contract. Fillipo Passerni, the CIO and president of Global Business Services at P&G, described the second goal of the vendor contract: "Simplifying our global printing structure helps increase reliability and efficiency, transforming the way we work."[23] Specific objectives related to this goal included reducing the number of devices in use at P&G, standardizing the types of devices in use, and selecting one go-to vendor for support.

These twin goals of efficiency and innovation to transform the way P&G did business required them to search for a partner who could both contribute to the high-quality rationalization of current print and document services as well as offer innovative technologies and tools for transforming P&G's digital management of information and documents. Xerox was ultimately selected from an array of possible vendors (including Hewlett-Packard, Canon, and others) due to Xerox's impressive record of industry leadership in creating innovative products and service solutions. It was regularly ranked as the top MPS provider by Gartner in its review of MPS vendors (see section on managed print services). Moreover it appeared that the two companies had compatible innovation cultures for working together and complementary technical and business capabilities. Caroline Basyn also acknowledged several potential obstacles to the partnership with Xerox:

> I was looking for a partner that had a global footprint. Xerox didn't have a global footprint on their own but Xerox had a partnership with Fuji Xerox. We had to know—how close was the relationship between Fuji and Xerox so that they could act as one and not two. Fuji Xerox was owned 75 percent by Fuji / 25 percent by Xerox. We ultimately learned that services provided in Asia by Fuji Xerox—by Xerox and Fuji Xerox—functioned as one company.
>
> Another challenge was that P&G had a huge contract with HP. They owned all their help desks, people supporting all my PC's and printers on all my sites. Would they be able to give integrated and seamless support to all my users?
>
> The third question or challenge—P&G has big sites such as Geneva's, Singapore's, big plants and big deadlines and tiny sites—Nigeria, for example. Would it be financially viable and cost effective for those tiny sites to follow the business plan we put in place for document management innovations and process improvements?

We wanted to create a transformational platform: different types of printers and devices all connected so that all are available to end-users wherever they are. Anything you want from the standpoint of productivity, sustainability, mobility.[24]

The P&G Strategic Partnership

On April 7, 2009, Xerox announced that it would manage P&G's global print operations with the aim to cut costs by 20 to 25 percent. Xerox indicated it won a five-year deal to manage P&G's "print shops, offices and home-based work settings" (Dignan, 2009). Xerox claimed it was aiming to cut P&G's print power usage by 30 percent and P&G's paper consumption by 20 to 30 percent. Xerox's Global Services would be required to develop and deliver an enterprise-wide strategy expected to free up hundreds of minutes of time annually for each of P&G's 170,000 employees worldwide. Xerox would also be expected to provide onsite training to help P&G's employees manage the new print environment, including tips on how to reduce the time spent on print-related activities. The change-management program would focus on how best to support the staff during the transition in order to minimize disruptions. Xerox would also create a web portal for online learning and easy procurement of equipment, consumables, and support for P&G's employees. "We believe this agreement with P&G will be a benchmark for all companies to get more out of the print infrastructure they've invested in—from the print shop to remote locations," said Stephen Cronin, president of Xerox Global Services.[25]

This partnership provided an important opportunity for Xerox's move to widen the scope of its MPS offerings across the enterprise and thus manage and control printing in several parts of the organization—at the desktop, in the home or from other remote locations, or in internal print rooms. This wider set of Enterprise Print Services (EPS) represented a new stage in broadening and deepening the scope of Xerox's print service offerings to its customers. Moreover, the opportunity to co-develop innovative print solutions with P&G was aligned with Xerox's research investments in partnership projects that directly supported their business partners through a co-development model. However, Xerox had not yet fully implemented this co-innovation model with a global client as preeminent in its own right for innovation as P&G. Therefore, the stakes were especially high for Xerox to create value for its customer through a successful program of cocreated innovation projects.

Sophie Vandebroek described this partnership and what was required for it to succeed: "It's a truly strategic commitment between both companies. From us what is required is that we flawlessly implement the base service that we are providing to the customer. That is the ticket to the game. Once you have a flawless execution you can then start thinking about how we innovate together."[26]

Caroline Basyn recognized some innovative aspects of this partnership with Xerox:

Part of winning the deal was not only having MPS around the globe for P&G but also continuously innovating with them [Xerox] during and beyond the contract.

Most contracts are between 3–10 years. Within the Request For Proposal (RFP)— we insisted on ongoing innovation. I thought it [the Xerox-P&G partnership] was so innovative and extraordinary. We're used to working with partners but this was the first time we created an Innovation Council. Once we signed the RFP we were going to do continuous innovation. How do you do that? It's co-managed, hence you need quarterly reviews. Things have to be disciplined or it won't get done. We're all busy. Good project and program management. During the quarterly reviews we have a Business Review in the am and the Innovation council meeting in the pm. We also have an annual review at the top level where we go over execution and financial savings. We discuss: here are our projects, here's how they moved through the pipeline.[27]

Caroline Basyn shared her perspective on how P&G's vision for its co-innovation partnership with Xerox evolved: "We anticipated the partnership would extend above and beyond the P&G office facilities but not services business. It was a surprise to everyone. We like to work with partners we trust and have longstanding relationships. We really want to make it work so that both are successful and we can build on those successes. With success comes other success."[28]

Formation of Innovation Council

Caroline Basyn identified three guiding goals for the partnership that were an initial mandate for the Innovation Council:

Both Sophie and I decided to build our partnership upon three overarching themes:

> 1. *Sustainability how to reduce print physical resource consumption and environmental burden*
> 2. *Productivity —how to improve end user productivity*
> 3. *Mobility —how to improve mobility of end users*

We created the charter. We created it together. I brought business knowledge. Sophie knew innovation and technical capability. Sophie and I managed our business on a very rigorous basis. At the time we signed the agreement, I was managing five key vendors on a daily basis; overall health of the relationship, business plan, operation excellence and project progress, innovation. Xerox quickly became a "best in crowd" partnership.[29]

Tom Kavassalis, vice president of strategy and alliances for the Xerox Innovation Group (XIG), described the organization of the Innovation Council:

About a half of dozen representatives were appointed from each company. It was important to ensure you had representatives from the value chain that would cover developing, implementing, and deployment. The Innovation Council had representatives from across the value chain—technology, engineering, and business leaders from across the value chain. The business leaders were from the customer facing side that would be responsible for the deployment.

Sophie and Caroline were the co-chairs. There is a practice in Xerox to have a Focus Executive. That is a senior manager in the company whose principal role is to ensure strong partnerships, that the right conversations are taking place, and that the doors to the executive suite are opened. Sophie Vandebroek was our focus executive for the P&G partnership.

A Process Person was designated by both sides to make sure we focused on the right things, make sure meetings happened, and make sure homework was done. She dialogued with everyone, tracked progress of projects through stages and greased the wheels that need greasing.

It's important to have the right people involved. People initially from Global Business Services including Print Services were involved. They put ideas on the table: How to get new value for product and print division. How to put Xerox know-how into P&G products. As the partnership goes broader and deeper we will need to formulate who else needs to be involved,

Xerox's current and previous CEO planned to have a session with P&G's CEO once a year. There were also quarterly reviews with Senior Executives in both companies.[30]

The Rhythm of Partnership

Whereas P&G was a consumer-products company accustomed to market-led innovation at a breathtaking speed, Xerox was a technology company whose technology had historically followed a more leisurely pace of science-led innovation. Could the two rhythms of these companies be reconciled so that P&G did not grow impatient for innovation solutions from its partner? How could the Innovation Council keep the pace of innovation progress on track with P&G's own timetable for realizing its digital vision for itself?

Sophie Vandebroek shared a concern with aligning Xerox's way of innovating with the demands of its fast-moving innovation partner. She acknowledged that there existed both a "new" Xerox innovation culture that was engaging with its partner in customer-led innovation and an "old" Xerox innovation culture that had deep roots in its legacy of technology-led innovation. Such technology-led innovation had helped transform the document industry. But could these two operating cultures (customer-led and technology-led) somehow align and integrate into this partnership and in future Xerox innovation partnerships? In order for Xerox to fully achieve its vision for the P&G co-innovation partnership, it would need to integrate the service delivery capabilities it had developed for its MPS offerings with the customer-led innovation capabilities it had developed in its approach to innovation.[31]

The Innovation Council was responsible for setting the policies that governed the co-innovation partnership. The Innovation Council faced an ambitious agenda. It needed to address how this partnership would work: whether the two companies possessed compatible operating cultures, mutual trust, and credible commitments to this partnership. The partnership further required compatible operating systems and management processes for meeting the mutual needs of Xerox and P&G. A way to evaluate the progress toward achieving each company's respective goals for the partnership was also part of its working agenda.

Results and Recognition for the Xerox-P&G Co-innovation Partnership

Within one year of the formation of the partnership, Xerox announced the first innovation solution that it had cocreated with P&G—the mobile print solution. The solution (based on Xerox's mobile technology research) allowed P&G employees to use a smartphone to easily transmit documents to a secure server or cloud. Documents were held in the cloud until the employee walked up to any printer in the network and entered a code to release the prints. The mobile print solution was the first contribution in support of P&G's "Give Back 500 Million Minutes" program by reducing time employees spend on print- and output-related issues.[32]

The Xerox-P&G co-innovation partnership also garnered professional recognition. At the end of 2010, Xerox and P&G received the "Dynamic Duo" award for best partnership from the Outsourcing Institute and Vantage Partners as part of the third annual Outsourcing Relationship Management Awards— the RMMYs. According to one Xerox blogger, the RMMY panel judges chose the Xerox-P&G co-innovation partnership because of its "clear communication, their mutual investment in success that goes beyond what's in the contract, their defined metrics and joint dedication to enhancing and modifying the way they reach their measurable objectives. (*Dziedzic, 2010)* " The writer goes on to note that the following features of the partnership best practices were cited by the judges in their award recognition:

- Problem solving as a team: Xerox is known for the "dreaming sessions" it conducts with customers—building a spirit of co-inventing and continuous improvement from the very beginning of the relationship. P&G representatives visited Xerox's Research Centre Europe in Grenoble, France to "dream" together with Xerox researchers and scientists about how to make P&G employees more productive, more sustainable and more mobile. The result was a matrix of innovative projects that both companies are working to implement.

- Putting plans into practice: To quickly attack the problems that are real and important for P&G, Xerox created an "Innovation Council"—a group made up of representatives from both companies that meets and prioritizes innovation opportunities that make sense for P&G. P&G brings stakeholders to the forum who can weigh in on the IT infrastructure and business units, while Xerox offers representatives from across the value chain that can conceive and implement these innovations.

- Commitment at all levels: P&G made the MPS project a priority and assigned the appropriate resources—including offering Xerox their "A team" and requiring Xerox to provide its A team. They demand that Xerox measure targets so that everyone is aligned and knows what expected. They pick their priorities—what's important, where they need help, what they foresee as challenges. They encourage and expect that their partners will work with one another.[33]

Epilogue: Xerox Co-innovation Partnerships and Print Services Management in 2013

Since the conclusion of our case study, several trends are evident in 2013. First, in its most recent in-house reference (accessed July 27, 2013) to the P&G co-innovation partnership, Xerox reports the following results from its partnership.

P&G has slimmed its print and copy fleet from 45,000 devices to 10,000. And there are now, on average, 14.3 employees using each device. The typical end user saves more than 200 minutes per year (a company-wide time savings of 138 business days annually). The benefits for device administrators are even more impressive: an average of 650 minutes saved per year. Beyond employee productivity, P&G has realized cost savings and sustainability benefits. Xerox now manages the company's global print operations, from print shops to offices. With 139 sites transitioned thus far, P&G has reduced printing costs by 21 percent, paper consumption by 30 percent, and energy costs by 30 percent. Moreover, P&G printed eight million fewer pages. "The equipment is much more reliable, and our employees can use it anytime, anyplace," says Caroline Basyn.[34]

In 2011 Cisco and Xerox announced they were forming a strategic alliance that would help client organizations by delivering Xerox's managed print and cloud IT outsourcing (ITO) services over Cisco Borderless Networks. The alliance made clients' IT applications more accessible for their workforce and improved efficiency with mobile printing—the ability to print from any device, anytime, anywhere. The combined solution monitors print technology, reduces operating costs, protects confidential data from any location, and improves employee productivity with advanced mobile and cloud printing applications.[35] This co-innovation partnership created a complementary capability to the mobile print solution previously developed by Xerox in its co-innovation partnership with P&G, thus broadening Xerox's overall MPS capabilities for all its clients.

In the most recently available ratings of print services firm capabilities and market positioning, the three leading industry reporting services (IDC, Forrester, and Quocirca) placed Xerox in the top tier of MPS vendors worldwide.[36] IDC positioned Xerox in its 2011 survey as the leading print services firm in terms of print services strategy and capabilities. Quocirca rated Xerox as the leading Managed Print Service (MPS) firm in terms of market presence and completeness of their offerings (print service solutions).

Lastly, in its 2012 vendor ratings, Forrester gave Xerox the highest possible scores in global delivery, mobile printing, technology and solution ownership, integration of IT outsourcing support, enterprise print support, MPS market experience, MPS strategy, organizational commitment, MPS revenue, and enterprise engagement.[37]

The preceding epilogue suggests that Xerox has leveraged its co-innovation partnership with P&G to broaden its print service capabilities made available to other clients. The subsequent Cisco strategic alliance provided an opportunity to complement the mobile print solutions cocreated with P&G with the new cloud computing capabilities cocreated with Cisco. Lastly, the most recent vendor assessments of Xerox all strongly suggest that it is an industry leader in providing Managed Print Services. Several of its distinctive capabilities (e.g., mobile printing and enterprise engagement) can be directly linked to the Xerox-P&G co-innovation partnership, and these capabilities have apparently been continued in subsequent Xerox engagements with other clients.

Lessons Learned

The Xerox-P&G co-innovation partnership offers valuable lessons for both theory and practice. From a practice perspective, the partnership reinforces the importance of sustained commitment and trust between partners. It also shows the need for developing effective governance mechanisms and metrics that guide both organizations in managing and evaluating the progress of the partnership. This management and evaluation occurs on both an overall relationship level and at the level of specific project commitments. This case study further demonstrates the necessity for selecting technically capable and interpersonally compatible leaders to guide the relationship during the challenging and uncertain twists and turns of a partnership. Sophie Vandebroek and Caroline Basyn, as co-leaders, shared remarkably similar cultural and academic backgrounds. Both were women who had risen through the science and technology ranks in an often male-dominated world. Moreover, they shared a cultural connection to Belgium. Sophie had been born and raised in Belgium, and Caroline pursued a master's degree there. From a theory perspective, the Xerox-P&G co-innovation partnership represents an example of B2B cocreation (Roser, DeFillippi, and Samson, 2012). The B2B literature tends to focus on cocreation as co-innovation. This perspective on cocreation has historically drawn from two distinct literature streams: supply chain innovation and strategic alliance innovation. The supply chain cocreation stream focuses on vertical partnerships between co-innovating vendors and their customers as a more interdependent and reciprocal value-creation alternative to strategic outsourcing (Hoecht and Trott, 2006). Similarly, the strategic alliance literature considers cocreation in the context of fostering more collaborative and trust-based modes of co-innovation between two or more autonomous firms that are working together in either a contractually based or equity-based relationship (Doz and Hamel, 1998). The Xerox-P&G partnership suggests a hybrid between supply chain and strategic alliance in that, like supply chain partnerships, there is a vertical supplier-customer relationship between the two parties, but, like the strategic alliance, there is also a more collaborative and trust-based mode of co-innovation. The Xerox-P&G relationship is more than a supply chain contract because both firms cocreated their innovation projects, and thus value was cocreated by both parties (Prahalad and Ramaswamy, 2004).

Notes

1. We wish to thank Xerox's chief technology officer, Sophie Vandebroek, for championing this case study, as well as the Xerox Corporation for their support of our case study activities and the dissemination of our findings. We also acknowledge Elizabeth McGovern, the Strategy and International Business Department office coordinator, for editing our chapter to ensure its conformity with the requirements of our publisher and for identifying some rough spots in our writing and offering helpful improvements.
2. S. Vandebroek, personal communication, November 15, 2010.
3. Xerox Corporation. (June 14, 2007). "Xerox Receives the National Medal of Technology." Xerox Business Wire News Release. Xerox Company History and Xerox Milestones.mhthttp://finance.boston.com/boston/news/read/2338851/xerox_receives_the_national_medal_of_technology (accessed April 25, 2011).
4. Kelley, B. (October 26, 2009). "Optimizing Innovation—Francois Ragnet of Xerox." Business-strategy-innovation.com. http://www.business-strategy-innovation.com/2009/10/optimizing-innovation-francois-ragnet.html accessed July 5, 2010).
5. S. Vandebroek, personal communication, November 15, 2010.
6. S. Vandebroek, personal communication, November 15, 2010.
7. P. Mazeau, personal communication, September 28, 2010.
8. P. Mazeau, personal communication, September 28, 2010.
9. S. Vandebroek, personal communication, November 15, 2010.
10. Rothenberg, S. (January 1, 2007). "Sustainability through Servicizing." Sloanreview.mit.edu. http://sloanreview.mit.edu/the-magazine/2007-winter/48216/sustainability-through-servicizing/2/ (accessed April 25 2011).
11. Weilerstein, Ken, Drew, Cecile, and Li, Yulan. (2010). "Magic Quadrant for Managed Print Services, Worldwide." Gartner Research ID Number: G00206095.
12. Lohr, S. (September 29, 2009). "Xerox buys Affiliated, Fueling Shift to Services." *The New York Times.* Technology Section, page B1.
13. Rothenberg, S. Sustainability through Servicizing.
14. Xerox Print Services overview brochure. "Xerox Print Services Control Costs and Increase Your Office Productivity." http://www.xerox.com/downloads/usa/en/gdo/brochures/XPS_CostControlBrochure-USEng.pdf (Feb 3, 2011).
15. Xerox Newsroom. (October 29, 2009). "Xerox Launches Enterprise Print Services." http://news.xerox.com/news/NR_2009Oct29_Xerox_Enterprise_Print_Services (please include an access date accessed Feb 3, 2011).
16. ZD Net. (June 28, 2010). "Managed Print Services Now Worth over $20 Billion." http://www.zdnet.com/blog/doc/managed-print-services-now-worth-over-20-billion/1478 (accessed Feb 3, 2011).
17. Dummy
18. Xerox 2009 Annual Report. http://www.xerox.com/annual-report-2009/pdfs/2009_Annual_Report.pdf (accessed April 25, 2011).
19. Lafley, A.G. January 2005. "Lafley on P&Gs's Gadget 'Evolution.'" Bloomberg Business Week. http://www.businessweek.com/stories/2005-01-27/lafley-on-p-and-gs-gadget-evolution (accessed February 4, 2011).
20. Basyn, C. (October 15, 2010). "Optimizing a Global Print Environment. Baselinemag.co. http://www.baselinemag.com/c/a/Printers/Optimizing-a-Global-Print-Environment-434200/ (accessed February 3, 2011).

21. Caroline Basyn, Global Business Services, P&G Presentation on Managed Print Services: "Beyond Cost-Out . . . To Break Through Top and Bottom-Line Growth."
22. Caroline Basyn, Global Business Services, P&G Presentation on Managed Print Services: "Beyond Cost-Out . . . To Break Through Top and Bottom-Line Growth."
23. BizCommunity.com. (2009). "P&G Awards Global Print Contract to Xerox," May 6, 2009. http://marketing.bizcommunity.com/Article/196/188/35649.html (accessed February 3, 2011).
24. Basyn, C. (October 15, 2010). "Optimizing a Global Print Environment." Baselinemag.co. http://www.baselinemag.com/c/a/Printers/Optimizing-a-Global-Print-Environment-434200/ (February 3, 2011).
25. BizCommunity.com. (2009) "P&G Awards Global Print Contract to Xerox," May 6, 2009. http://marketing.bizcommunity.com/Article/196/188/35649.html (accessed February 3, 2011).
26. S. Vandebroek, personal communication, November 15, 2010.
27. C. Basyn, personal communication, September 28, 2010.
28. C. Basyn, personal communication, September 28, 2010.
29. C, Basyn, personal communication, September 28, 2010.
30. T. Kavassalis, personal communication, September 28, 2010.
31. S. Vandebroek, personal communication, November 15, 2010.
32. Xerox News. (2010). "New Xerox Mobile Print Solution to Allow Procter & Gamble to Print from Smartphones." http://news.xerox.com/news/new-xerox-mobile-print-solution-158013 (accessed May 6, 2010).
33. Dziedzic, B. (2010). "Xerox and P&G—What It Takes to Be a 'Dynamic Duo.'" http://realbusinessatxerox.blogs.xerox.com/2010/12/13/xerox-and-pg-percentE2 percent80 percent93-what-it-takes-to-be-a-percentE2 percent80 percent9Cdynamic-duo percentE2 percent80 percent9D/#.Udr9uebD_cd (accessed April 25, 2011).
34. (Xerox Corporation 2010). "Procter & Gamble Case Study: P&G Had 45,000 Print Devices in 200 Locations Worldwide. We Delivered a New, Improved Process." http://www.xerox.com/downloads/usa/en/gdo/casestudies/P_G_LR.pdf (accessed July 27, 2013).
35. (year). "Xerox and Cisco to Form Alliance to Deliver Cloud Services; Combine Network Intelligence and Print Management." http://newsroom.cisco.com/press-release-content?type=webcontent&articleId (accessed July 27,2013).
36. (Xerox Corporation,). "Leading the Way with Managed Print Services." http://services.xerox.com/managed-print-services/industry-analysis/enus.html (accessed July 27, 2013).
37. (Xerox Corporaton). "Xerox Cited as a Leader in The Forrester Wave™: Managed Print Services." http://services.xerox.com/managed-print-services/industry-analysis/forrester-wave/enus.html (accessed July 27, 2013)

References

Brown, B., and Anthony, S. D. (2011). "How P&G Tripled Its Innovation Success Rate." *Harvard Business Review* HBR Reprint R1106C (http://hbr.org/product/how-p-g-tripled-its-innovation-success-rate/an/R1106C-PDF-ENG. Accessed June 29, 2011

Doz, Y., and Hamel, G. (1998). *Alliance Advantage: The Art of Creating Value through Partnering*. Boston, MA: Harvard Business School Press.

Hoecht, A., and Trott, P. (2006). "Innovation Risks of Strategic Outsourcing." *Technovation* 26 (5–6): 672–81.

Prahalad, C. K., and Ramaswamy, V. (2004). *The Future of Competition: Co-creating Unique Value with Customers*. Boston, MA: Harvard Business School Press.

Rothenberg, S. (2007). Sustainability through Servicizing. *MIT Sloan Management Review* 48 (2): 82-91. - DONE).

Roser, T., DeFillippi, R., and Samson, A. (2012). "Managing Your Co-creation Mix: Co-creation Ventures in Distinctive Contexts." *European Business Review* 25 (1): 20–41.

CHAPTER 8

The Role of Open Innovation in Business-University R&D Collaborations

Ravi Chinta and Refik Culpan

Introduction

The role of universities in the development and transmission of new knowledge has been well recognized. Many cutting-edge scientific inquiries and innovations—including stem-cell applications, alternative energies, social networking, and cloud computing—have emerged as a result of university research endeavors that are often conducted in collaborations with businesses. With the widespread adoption of open innovation by business firms, universities have become a hub of new knowledge generation and have been instrumental in the development of new products and technologies.

Basically, research collaborations between businesses and universities have been a common endeavor for many years to expand knowledge and thereby to develop new products and technologies. And because of the increasing popularity of open innovation (OI) in recent years, these kinds of collaborative efforts have gained renewed momentum. As businesses have realized the limitations of internal R&D (closed innovation), they have sought the resources and capabilities of other parties, where universities have taken on vibrant roles. For example, Gerard George, Shakar A. Zahra, and D. Robley Wood, Jr., (2002) report that an analysis of two thousand alliances undertaken by 147 biotechnology firms shows that companies with university linkages have lower R&D expenses while maintaining higher levels of innovative output. Next, we will review the historical development of business-university R&D collaborations to understand the evolution of these relationships.

Historical Development

Universities have been involved in collaboration with industry ever since they were established. Though universities mostly engage in the development of basic knowledge, academic research has also had a practical side that has led universities to collaborate with industry. The Hatch Act of 1887 in the United States established land-grant state universities with a clear intent to develop and disseminate knowledge that resulted from academic research (Rosenberg and Nelson, 1994). While several entrepreneurial efforts by the universities helped farmers and manufacturers through extension services in the late nineteenth and early twentieth centuries, the pace of university-industry collaboration was quite slow until the end of World War II. Shane (2004) documents the accelerated pace of technology commercialization from universities during 1945–80, but those efforts were still limited to a few universities, and the phenomenon of university-industry collaboration was not widespread. The commercialization of academic research was still viewed with skepticism by academics during this period (Lee, 1998). Despite this skepticism, research collaborations between businesses and universities have only accelerated over time, partly aided by government regulations conducive to collaborations.

The Bayh-Dole Act of 1980 was a watershed moment in the history of university-industry collaboration in the United States. The Bayh-Dole Act, an amendment to the Patent and Trademark Law, reallocated the federal rights to intellectual property (IP) emanating from federally funded research to the universities that conducted the research. The idea was that the new IP policy would foster greater university-industry collaboration. While universities that owned the IP rights would earn royalties, the firms that licensed the IP would negotiate exclusive rights to the IP and also have further access to university resources. Within ten years after the passage of the Bayh-Dole Act, more than one thousand university-industry research centers were established within universities (Cohen, Florida, and Goe, 1994). Since 1980, the incentives provided by the Bayh-Dole Act have resulted in a five-fold growth in university patenting and a significant rise in spin-offs from universities (Shane, 2004). A self-reinforcing virtuous cycle that Shane (2004) denominates the "contagion effect" has accelerated the discovery, transfer, and utilization of knowledge from universities to industry. To understand the partnership between universities and industry, one must first look at the evolution of the innovation process within firms.

Intrafirm Innovation Process

Innovation used to take place within the R&D departments of companies, some of which had massive corporate laboratories, such as Bell Labs, Xerox, and IBM; referred to as *closed innovation* in the literature, much of the R&D took place within the firm, though many ideas may have come into the firm from outside. The prevailing philosophy was that without full control the company did not or could not advance the ideas to commercialization. As a corollary, firms adopting

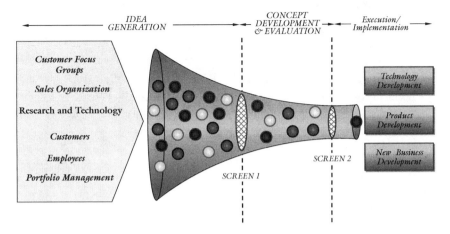

Figure 8.1   "Research to market" within a firm (Closed System)

closed business models tended not to utilize external sources by licensing in technology; they also tended not to allow other firms to exploit their knowledge, often adopting an internal policy not to license out their core technology. This closed innovation model is depicted in Figure 8.1.

An *open innovation* model is claimed to be more suitable or responsive to the internal and external flows of knowledge (and resources) than a closed innovation model, which concentrates on discovering and developing knowledge only within the limits of one firm (Chesbrough, 2003). Open innovation is a paradigm that assumes firms can and should use external ideas as well as internal ideas, and internal and external paths to market, as they look to advance their technology. According to one prominent scholar, by necessity, "the knowledge monopolies built by the centralized R&D organizations of the twentieth century have ended" (Chesbrough, 2003, 45). Reasons for this change are simple. Over time the costs and risks of the innovation process within the closed system increased dramatically, forcing the closed system to open up. A good example is that of the huge costs of new drug development.

High Costs of Discovery and the Emergence of Open Innovation in the Pharmaceutical Industry

The cost of pharmaceutical R&D has been skyrocketing. On average the cost of bringing an idea from the lab to the markets for a new drug is greater than one billion dollars (Siew, 2013). And yet, as pharmaceutical firms continue to toss around billions in search of the next blockbuster, the number of drug approvals is diminishing. Even more worrying is the fact that only two out of ten approved drugs generate revenues that recoup or exceed R&D costs. This means that the blockbuster model is becoming unsustainable. Not only are new drugs becoming prohibitively expensive, but worldwide public expectations are also pushing for lower drug prices due to the macroeconomic slowdown and to make health care more affordable for the public. Additionally, price erosion due to generic drugs and global companies from low-cost nations such as India are further forcing pharmaceutical firms to reduce their R&D costs. In response, the pharmaceutical industry has begun to change its existing paradigm of relying solely on in-house R&D to embracing open innovation as the new paradigm. That is, innovation is no longer confined to the R&D department within a firm. Particularly, developments in information and communication technology have made it easier to collaborate or jointly innovate. New and profitable ideas come from many sources—namely, suppliers, academia, competitors, customers, and so forth. Bringing external knowledge to the company is not a substitute but a complement to internally developed knowledge. It simply enhances the innovation efficiency of the firm. The differences between the closed and open innovation models are compared in Table 8.1.

The open innovation model, as a response to increasing costs of discovery, has led to cost reductions, access to new ideas, risk reduction, and an expansion of R&D funding to and from multiple sources (Chesbrough, 2003; Sisodiya,

Table 8.1 The Comparison of Closed and Open Innovation

	Closed Innovation	*Open Innovation*
Knowledge input: the best source of knowledge for innovation	The best knowledge is in-house based.	The best knowledge is found either inside or outside the firm.
Generating innovation	Firm discovers, develops, and ships R&D by itself.	It is seen that external R&D can create significant value and internal R&D is needed to claim some portion of that value.
The importance of proprietary nature and origination of innovation	The proprietary nature and origination of discoveries are seen as a way to become a first-mover.	The origination of innovation is secondary to the question of who is able to commercialize an innovation first.
The source of value	The value of first-mover advantage is emphasized.	The value of good business models is emphasized over the first-mover advantage.
Competition	The number and quality of ideas are emphasized in competition.	The best use of internal and external ideas is emphasized in competition.
Intellectual property (IP)	IP is controlled so that competitors cannot profit from it in any case.	IP is seen as a source of profit, and others are allowed to license it or buy it. Also, the firm is willing to buy others' IP if it looks attractive.

Adopted from Chesbrough, 2003, p. xxvi, and Bellantuono et al., 2013, p. 560.

Johnson, and Grégoire, 2013). While this transformation from a closed system to OI models is shaping the corporate world, universities have been undergoing a different evolution, but with the same result—that is, pushing the universities toward OI models. This overall trend toward OI can also be observed in business-university collaborations. To illustrate this collaboration, we will review the evolution of the research functions of universities next.

Evolution of the Research Roles of Universities

In their mission statements, universities across the world highlight the contributions of research, teaching, and service. For the purpose of this chapter, we will, however, primarily focus on the research roles of universities. For example, many prestigious academic institutions engage in cutting-edge research activities. In these endeavors, recently, numerous universities are reaching out to outside entities in such ways that can be explained in an OI model. For a university, external engagement denotes the efforts of the academic institution to interact with its appropriate communities around intellectual, educational, social, cultural, economic, and technological development (Gutteridge, 2007).

The late Ernest Boyer, former president of the Carnegie Foundation for the Advancement of Teaching, redefined the scholarship roles of universities in his 1990 monograph *Scholarship Reconsidered*. Boyer (1990) proposed a new paradigm of scholarship with four interlocking parts. The first area of the new paradigm is the *scholarship of discovery*, which takes the position that research is at the very heart of academic life. In addition to discovery, the second area, the *scholarship of integration*, is also necessary to develop creative people who go beyond isolated facts, who make connections across disciplines, who help shape a more coherent view of knowledge and a more integrated, more authentic view of life. The third category, the *scholarship of application*, is the ability to relate theory and research to the realities of life. The last category, the *scholarship of teaching*, is the ability not only to discover, integrate, and apply knowledge, but to inspire future scholars in the classroom as well. Boyer spoke of an urgent need—a moral imperative—for higher education to transform the way it fulfills its longstanding contract with America, to improve the society we live in. In particular, the *scholarship of application*, when catalyzed by the impetus given by the promulgation of the Bayh-Dole Act of 1980 (discussed above), led to university technology transfer programs across the United States. As universities discover new knowledge, patents are filed to create intellectual property rights, which are then transferred to outside entities for further development. The university technology transfer process is depicted in Figure 8.2.

As Figure 8.2 shows, not all discoveries go through the patenting process, which costs the universities filing fees and subsequent maintenance fees. Furthermore, not all patents get licensed or sold outright for down payments plus royalties or upfront payments. The feedback loops reveal the dynamic and complex nature of the intrauniversity patent management system that is institutionalized in university technology transfer offices. Thus the OI model is structurally

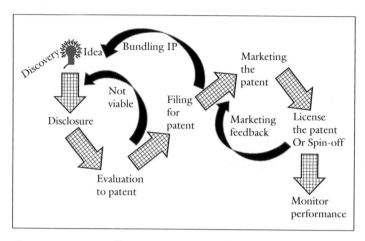

Figure 8.2   University Technology Transfer Process

embedded within the universities by the university technology transfer offices, which seek out and engage outside firms in the transfer and utilization of knowledge generated within the universities. In short, the vibrancy of the OI model for university-industry collaboration directly correlates with the presence of a university technology transfer office.

Mutual Benefits for Universities and Industry in R&D Collaborations

Fostering open innovation means nurturing networks, exchanging ideas, and sharing knowledge outside of a given system as well as within. Innovation networks, such as links to suppliers and technical institutes, are increasingly important to organizational innovation efforts (Dankbaar, 2003; Colin and Ja-Shen, 2013). Companies continuously seek to innovate more quickly and more effectively both within and often beyond their core markets and product lines. This has resulted in the practice of open innovation, wherein firms recognize that all components of an innovation do not need to come from within, that they can accelerate their own efforts or perhaps even broaden the scope of these efforts by acquiring some of the required technology externally. The benefits of business-university collaboration in these knowledge explorations were defined by Delphine and his colleagues (2012), but we have enhanced their list. The benefits can be summarized as follows: business-university collaboration (1) leverages funds from other sources, (2) utilizes leading science and faculty resources in universities, (3) shortens time to market, (4) reduces the costs of R&D projects, (5) mitigates the risk of failure in innovation, (6) clarifies intellectual property rights for participants, (7) allows for a broader portfolio of R&D projects, (8) improves companies' innovation efficiency, (9) establishes more extensive networks for alliances, and (10) develops a relative competitive advantage in growth.

While the benefits are clearly apparent, several problems lurk beneath the surface, and some of these are described next.

Potential Problems in University-Industry R&D Collaboration

While university-industry collaboration is touted as universally beneficial to all parties, some problems, concerns, and unintended consequences can arise from such collaboration. First, as university-industry collaborations increase, it is estimated that 10 percent of all US academic funds now come from industry, and the total amount of such funds is growing (Auranen and Nieminen, 2010). Such a trend leads to the budgetary dependence of universities on commercial organizations so that sponsoring companies may dictate the priorities of universities. This is the reason why commercial R&D is viewed with suspicion by some academics who claim that the commercialization of university research dilutes the main mission of universities. Second, there are long-established concerns about publication delays while a company examines a discovery's commercial potential. Legislation is under way now to allow 60–90 days as a reasonable waiting time for such evaluation before the path is cleared for publication. Third, the very idea of commercial interests being integrated into the university mission may create conflicts with respect to its main mission of teaching and research. Faculty entrepreneurs may neglect their academic duties to further their personal gains from entrepreneurial activities. Powell and Owen-Smith (1998) found that academics shifted some of their effort and creativity away from their academic work toward their companies. Fourth, there is a problem concerning the arcane area of "background rights," where a university is pressured to allow a collaborating company rights to core technologies that the university developed earlier in some other university projects sponsored by others, including the federal government. Incremental funding is given by the collaborating company only if the university gives the company the full value of the core inventions. In short, a core relationship could significantly limit corollary relationships in the future. There is no easy answer to this conundrum. Fifth, there is wide variation in the research costs used in university-industry collaborations, due primarily to the vastly different cost structures of research universities. While the Association of University Technology Managers (AUTM) is leading an effort to standardize these research costs, no standards have emerged yet. Current recommendations urge universities to charge federal rates for indirect costs. Sixth, and related to ongoing research projects, tensions arise when university researchers develop materials and techniques that they want to develop to be patented for exclusive IP rights, allowing only restrictive use of the new knowledge, while the collaborating companies may want to use those techniques more freely, with little or no royalty payments. The example of the University of Illinois (UI) and Netscape is instructive in this regard. UI wanted to restrict the use of its Mosaic patents, while Netscape wanted to freely build on it. The irreconcilable conflict became so acute that when Jim Clark became the CEO of Netscape, the firm completely eradicated all code pertaining to the original UI Mosaic code. Also, Marc Andreessen, the founder of Netscape and a UI alumnus, publicly stated that he would not give a single dime of donation to the university (Reid, 1997). Distinctions between what is public interest and what is private interest become muddier in university-industry collaborations, as research, by definition, produces results that are hard to compute a priori and can often be known only post hoc. In summary, the university-industry collaborative space is one of alliances with companies, and the networks that result are dynamic processes in which prior history (path-dependent processes) significantly affects the behavior of the universities engaged in the collaborative space. Seventh, given the importance of knowledge flows between companies, as seen in the literature on open innovation, there is always partner uncertainty (i.e., a problem of imperfect knowledge as one is not sure if one has the right partner), which can only be resolved after the fact. Aggravating this problem is the fact that prior relationships (social capital) can impede the potential for variation in subsequent relations in OI models. Social capital is the value within social-structural relationships that a firm can mobilize to make possible the achievement of certain ends that would not be attainable in its absence (Coleman, 1990).

Despite the problems listed above, the longer-lasting positive consequences of university-industry collaborations include the academic knowledge spillovers discussed next.

Academic Knowledge Spillovers

University-industry collaboration, as one of the carriers of knowledge spillovers from universities, leads to regional economic development. Within the literature, various empirical studies found evidence for the presence of knowledge spillovers from universities (see Doring and Schnellenbach, 2006, for an overview; see Fritsch and Slavtchev, 2007, for an example of innovation in space). It is noteworthy that these knowledge spillovers can be localized (within the local region) or supraregional (over long distances).

Universities are assumed to be important sources and also drivers of knowledge spillovers due to their explicit focus on the generation and diffusion of knowledge. To understand this phenomenon better, three well-known examples from the United States, the United Kingdom, and France are briefly described next.

Stanford and the University of California–Berkeley, in the United States

Both Stanford University and UC Berkeley played significant roles in the development of Silicon Valley into the success story that we all recognize today. Stanford University was founded in 1891, and right from its beginning, university-industry collaboration was emphasized. For example, in 1908 Stanford research commercialized vacuum tubes as a way to intensify electrical signals. Firms such as Hewlett Packard, SUN Microsystems, Varian, Litton Engineering, Fairchild Semiconductors, and Cisco were born at Stanford University. UC Berkeley, with 20 Nobel Prize winners, has also been a leading world center for knowledge creation. UC Berkeley alumni Andy Grove and Gordon Moore founded Intel. In

1951, Stanford University opened the Stanford Industrial Park—a creation that was unique for its time.

Cambridge, in the United Kingdom

Cambridge University is one of the most renowned universities in the world that has made a conscious decision to nurture university-industry collaboration. A number of high-tech spin-offs and consulting firms emerged from Cambridge University's competences in the areas of electronics, instrument development, and computing. Not only have new ventures sprung out of the university, but also many entrepreneurs from other parts of the United Kingdom chose to locate in the university area to collaborate with Cambridge University. The university thus became a magnet with its knowledge spillovers.

Sophia Antipolis University, in France

In 1965, Sophia Antipolis University was founded in Nice, France. In 1974, an incubator promoting university-industry collaboration, the Sophia Antipolis Science Park, was set up. Large firms such as France Telecom, IBM, and Texas Instruments located on the site. Of the firms located on the site, the information, computers, and telecommunications (ICT) sector accounted for 65 percent, and the health sciences sector accounted for 20 percent, with more than 50 percent coming out of the university as spin-offs (Sophia Antipolis, 2013). Today, the university campus benefits from the presence of 1,300 companies in the near vicinity, with co-location as its main driver of open innovation. Sophia Antipolis is a laboratory of twenty-first-century companies and an exceptional knowledge community.

It must be noted that, while the above examples illustrate university-industry collaboration through OI models, they are also strongly aided by government support. The next section discusses the expanded scope of OI models that include universities, industry, and government.

Government Role and the Triple-Helix Model of Open Innovation

The *triple helix* is the most well-known framework used to describe collaboration between universities, policy institutions, and industry (Etzkowitz and Laydesdorff, 2000; Leydesdorf and Meyer, 2003). Specifically, the term *triple-helix model of open innovation* denotes the multiple reciprocal relationships among three institutional sectors—government, industry, and university (Viale and Campodall' Orto, 2000; Leydesdorff and Meyer, 2003). To be sure, the stream of research based on the triple-helix model reveals that "university-industry-government interactions" at the regional level are not an entirely new phenomenon. The triple helix is a spiral model of the university-industry-government relationships as one of relatively equal, yet interdependent, institutional spheres that overlap and support each other. For example, the postwar "Route 128" high-tech conurbation can be traced to policy initiatives in the 1930s and even to the founding of the Massachusetts Institute of Technology (MIT) in the mid-nineteenth century

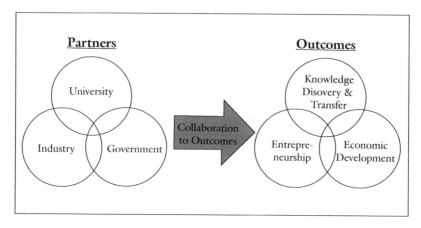

Figure 8.3 The Triple-Helix Model of Open Collaboration
Source: Partner collaborations above suggested by Tether and Tajar (2008); outcomes added by authors

for the purpose of infusing industry with new technology. What is new is the spread of technology policy to virtually all regions, irrespective of whether they are research or industrially intensive. See Figure 8.3 for the triple-helix model.

The intention of the triple-helix model is to shape the regional innovation environment, which consists of the set of political, industrial, and academic institutions that, by design or by unintended consequences, work to improve local conditions for innovation. The cooperative arrangements between universities, industry, and governments are resulting in greater social capital and networking relationships that go beyond the mere funding of university research. The next section discusses the various forms of OI models involving universities, industry, and governments.

A Revised Model for Business-University R&D Collaboration

The era of massive corporate laboratories, such as Bell Labs, where innovation took place within a firm, has now passed. The closed system of innovation described at the beginning of this chapter has been replaced by a more porous system wherein the "idea-to-market" journey takes place in partnership with many outside parties throughout the innovation process. Research across multiple business segments has identified a number of practices that firms have adopted to identify external technology to thereby bolster their own innovation processes. These practices could be described in a framework for categorizing the different methodologies and organizational structures for reducing uncertainties in the idea-to-market journey with the use of external partnerships (Witzeman et al., 2006). Although a variety of OI models define the practice of open innovation (Lichtenthaler, 2008), Fraser (2008) aptly points out a variety of stages and sponsors in the idea-to-market process. The participants, at least for funding purposes, change throughout the journey. We must note that while universities play vital roles in the first two stages—namely, basic research and proof of concept—it is not uncommon to see some universities even engaging in the early stages of technology development and product development through venture capital funding. The gap between the creation of intellectual property and its translation into products and processes has been called "the valley of death." (Murphy and Edwards, 2003) The use of public resources to reduce risk in the development of new technology has long been accepted in the agricultural, military, and health sectors. In recent decades, federal, state, and local governments have created a variety of mechanisms to encourage knowledge-based economic development. These initiatives include the supply of bridging funds, grants, and matching funds to support R&D and access to participation in joint projects with government laboratories. Public venture capital is a subset of *public investment,* a rationale for the support of various government initiatives that enhance the health, education, and welfare of the population. Universities are participating more in such triple-helix engagements. One good example is that of the Pittsburgh High Technology Council with participation from Carnegie Mellon University and the University of Pittsburgh. The interface between industry and universities is of worldwide interest in the promotion of technological change in many industries. The reasons for this interest are quite evident.

Collaborative partnerships have become strategic assets for companies that face diminishing in-house research expenditures, increasingly rapid and uncertain technological change, and increasingly intense international competition. As innovation moves outside of a single organization, lateral relationships across boundaries, rather than hierarchical bureaucratic structures, become more important. At the same time, universities are increasingly seeking out partnerships with outside entities to discover and transfer new knowledge. Adding to this mix of forces are governmental emphases on regional economic development. To analyze both of these developments and understand their future development, a new pattern of open innovation models is needed, as far as business-university collaborations are concerned. Open innovation, by definition, springs from resources external to a given system in combination with complementary resources that are internal to the system. When universities engage with industry and governments, the collaboration manifests in the following ways, as shown in Table 8.2.

Table 8.2 Open Innovation Model of Industry, University, and Government

Flows in OI Model	*Industry ↔ University*	*Government ↔ University*
Money flow	Industry-sponsored research	Government grants for research
Talent flow	Faculty/students joining industry	Faculty joining government agencies
Intellectual property rights (IP) flow	Rights of first refusal; University technology transfer	Bayh-Dole Act transferring rights to universities
Permanent infrastructure	Capital projects for laboratories; endowed research chair-ships	Capital projects for science parks; university-based incubators

Money, talent, IP, and infrastructure are not merely bilateral open innovation mechanisms present in the triple-helix model of open innovation. Specialist knowledge providers, such as consultancies and private research organizations, participate in this multiparty mix of open collaboration. The distinctions between public science (universities and governmental research laboratories) and private enterprise (industry and consultancies) are blurred in OI models in mutually beneficial partnerships. Universities are evolving from merely performing conventional research and education functions to serving as innovation-promoting knowledge hubs through incubators, science parks, and technology centers that spawn new businesses. Universities are also getting into seeding new start-up businesses with funding through university-linked venture capital funds. The first of these funds was started in 1974 when Boston University established the Community Technology Fund to invest in Boston University spin-off companies (Roberts and Malone, 1996). Many other universities began to follow Boston University's example, establishing their own directly managed venture capital funds. In 1988, Harvard University established Medical Science Partners, a venture capital entity to invest in companies that would commercialize technology developed at the university (Matkin, 1990). Since venture capital funds often co-invest with other venture capital funds, this development must still be seen as open collaboration and not as vertical integration on the part of universities. Shane (2004) details the extent and depth of university spin-offs as a burgeoning trend in the university-industry collaboration realm. Universities have thus expanded their scope of collaboration and are now actively engaging in academic, educational, entrepreneurial, venture capital, industrial, and public spheres.

In a reevaluation of business-university R&D collaboration, we expand the traditional dual business-university relationship and the triple-helix model (Etzkowitz and Leydesdorff, 2000; Leydersdorff and Meyer, 2003). Additionally, we combine industry-university-government collaboration and revise the idea-to-market model (Fraser, 2008) by changing a couple stages of its value chain and including multiple partnerships (e.g., more than one university, suppliers, and customers, in addition to the conventional triple players). In doing so, we considerbusiness-university-government involvements in an open innovation context. This revised model of business-university R&D collaboration captures the dynamic and multiplayer involvement of the initiation and development of an idea into a final product or technology. Unlike previous explanations, our model recognizes knowledge creation and sharing among partners, which may include nontraditional participants, such as suppliers, angel investors, venture capitalists, customers, and even competitors. This new interpretation of business-university R&D collaboration asks for value creation for new products and technologies that may require contributions from multiple sources, such as firms, suppliers, customers, and even sometimes competitors. Furthermore,it could be sponsored by the firm and/or partly by a university, angel investor, or venture capital. Thus, we offer a broader interpretation of business-university R&D collaboration by including such various parties as universities, firms, and government agencies for potential benefits of innovation that could be influenced, created, and managed by these multiple partners. We must note, however, that every innovation project does not necessarily require the involvement of all the parties, and the traditional triad (university-business-government) model and the idea-to-market model, as applied to business-university R&D collaboration, should be reconsidered and the potential contributions of other resourceful partners in the R&D process should be taken into account.

University-Industry Collaboration outside the United States

While much of the above discussion pertains to university-industry collaboration within the United States, similar patterns of increased collaboration exist in other countries as well. Wengenroth (1995) and Gustin (1975) traced the development of the chemical industry in Germany in the nineteenth century to university-based research. Despite similarities, significant differences prevail across nations when it comes to university-industry collaboration. Across nations, two major alternative approaches to university rights to intellectual property (IP) exist. In some countries, like Sweden and Germany (continental Europe), IP rights belong to the inventors of the technology, whereas in other nations, like the United States and the United Kingdom, IP rights belong to the university in which the invention was created. Goldfarb and Henrekson (2003) point out that the commercialization of IP is greater when the IP rights are owned by the universities than when they are owned by inventors. The progression of universities from the initial stages of research (knowledge discovery) toward the commercialization end (with spin-offs and science parks) is evident in advanced nations, such as the United States, Canada, and Western Europe. However, in emerging nations, such as China, the evolutionary pattern is the reverse. For example, science parks in China are serving as seedbeds of innovation with the chief impetus coming largely from local governments attracting universities and research institutions to economic zones, such as Shenzen and Beijing.

Unresolved Conundrums and Guidelines in University-Industry Collaboration

Thus far we have covered the multifaceted nature of university-industry collaboration in a descriptive manner. Yet several conundrums remain unresolved and warrant some suggestions to make the prevailing OI models more effective. Without claiming to be comprehensive, several specific issues are discussed next to provide some guidance.

Exclusive licensing by universities results in the effective marketing of IP rights but limits the potential for the greater utilization of the IP by a wider set of firms (Lee, 2009). It is well known that IP negotiations can act as a barrier to initiating new collaborations (Burnside and Witkin, 2008). The trade-offs that exist must be evaluated in detail. Hence, universities should assess licensing transactions using a more expansive scope of analysis. We recommend exclusive licensing for university spin-offs but nonexclusive licensing for other licensing transactions. By definition, open innovation contracts are evolving, and the *flexibility* that can allow for the building of newer relationships is the rule in cooperation for innovating, despite what contract law may suggest concerning tightly limiting the room for redefinitions and rework (Nystén-Haarala, Lee, and Lehto, 2010). That is, the strategic governance of IP rights is a sine qua non for successful university-industry open innovation.

The *division of royalties* between an inventor and his or her department and the university affects the pace of licensing and commercialization activity. It has been empirically shown that the greater the inventor's share of the licensing royalties, the slower is the pace of commercialization activity (DiGregorio and Shane, 2003). We suggest, therefore, that one must increase the university's share of licensing royalties so that institutional support for licensing IP is enhanced.

University culture should promote a consultative and support role for the university licensing office that will reduce the bureaucratic burdens of licensing activities for the university researchers. *Sharing success stories* and integrating these successes into the folklore of the university must be a regular activity in sustaining the entrepreneurial spirit within academia. Examples from MIT and Columbia University showcase the infectious nature of prior successes in spawning the seeds of innovation in subsequent periods. The sharing of knowledge across organizational boundaries and the formation of trusted relationships are keys to sustained collaboration. Hence, universities should devote resources to developing and coordinating *transorganizational communities of innovation* (TCIs). TCIs are not project-specific initiatives but are programs that promote interorganizational dialogue. TCIs could take the form of regional innovation summits or topic-oriented conferences or community participation in metaplanning for economic development. Universities have assumed an expanded role in science- and technology-based economic development that has become of interest to developing regions as well as to leading innovation locales. The Georgia Institute of Technology (Georgia Tech), as a knowledge hub, is an apt example in this sense (Youtie and Shapira, 2008).

Furthermore, we should note that international policies for open innovation are also available from international organizations such as the Organization for Economic Cooperation and Development (OECD Report, 2008). However, guiding principles on how such international guidelines for open innovation can be implemented nationally are missing. Also, recognizing that OI models involve the collaborative engagement of multiple partners across many stages in the idea-to-market journey, we suggest that *some guidance* is required, such that "gatekeepers" must act as champions in the implementation of each stage (much like *milestones serve as guidepost* in long and complex project management schemes). There is no single leader, but a number of leaders who hand off the baton to subsequent leaders.

Future Outlook for University-Industry Collaboration

It is clear that many organizations engaged in closed innovation systems in the past have now increasingly adopted open innovation. As the traditional thinking about internal and secretive R&D activities has changed, at least for a considerable number of business firms, the future outlook for university-industry collaboration is brighter. The emergence of OI models is breaking down the traditional roles that have been assumed by universities and industry in their R&D collaborations. As suggested by several authors (Normann and Ramírez, 1993; Alexander and Martin, 2013; Janeiro, Proenca, and Goncalves, 2013), our revised model in Figure 8.4 shows that the future outlook of open innovation models involves the transformation of traditional value chains into dynamic value networks.

Our broader interpretation of open innovation, as applied to university-industry collaborations, is not merely a change from bilateral to multiparty alliances, but also includes the dynamic and changing participation of industry players even within bilateral collaborations. For example, an initial business partnership may be supplanted by new business partners as old alliances die out and new partnerships form. Metaphorically, what we suggest is a paradigm change from structured bilateral value chains of predetermined, mutually beneficial exchanges to dynamic, multiparty, often not predetermined structures resembling value networks that at times contain unpredictable eddy currents in the evolution of university-industry collaborations. We detail the nature of these eddy currents next.

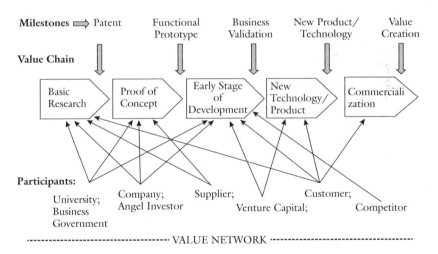

Figure 8.4 "Business-University Collaborations in Value Networks"

Note: Based on "Sequential model of development and funding" by John Fraser (2008), "Communicating the Full Value of Academic Technology Transfer: Some Lessons Learned," *Licensing Journal* 28 (1): 4, and the American Association for the Advancement of Science articles.

The variety of OI models reflect (1) greater numbers of partners, (2) greater numbers of stages in the idea-to-market journey, (3) greater numbers of complementary assets, (4) more bundling or repackaging of noncommercial IP, (5) more use of territorial exclusivities, (6) more product life cycle (PLC) linkages, and (7) more linkages of universities directly with customers and end users in the marketplace. In short, the value chains of innovation that were earlier self-contained within the universities or within firms have now become value networks, as shown in Figure 8.4. As Spithoven (2013) suggests (and as we suggested in our revised model), open innovation is a dynamic process with the involvement of multiple actors, who may have heterogeneous interests, warranting new governance mechanisms. Our open innovation–based model calls for the participation of multiple partners working in concert to traverse the idea-to-market journey. The number of stages in the idea-to-market journey is no longer strictly linear and forward directed, but circular in some stages (much like eddy currents in a laminar flow), especially when failures, either technological or market based, occur. A number of complementary assets (knowledge, financial, regulatory, etc.) come together in the OI model; and sometimes these assets come from nontraditional sources (e.g., universities provide the funding or infrastructure or firms provide the R&D resources). Novel techniques in IP management, with the slicing and dicing of IP domains (e.g., territorial exclusivity or cross licensing), will allow the greater diffusion of newly discovered technologies. As the frontiers expand for university-industry collaboration in multifaceted ways, universities are going through significant internal adaptations and changes that allow multiparty collaborations in a networked fashion.

We argue that university-industry open innovation will become more dynamic and complex as the sources of innovation get even more diversified. For example, crowdsourcing with free and open source code development in the software industry is a current trend (von Hippel and von Krogh, 2003). Bloodgood (2013) suggests that it is very difficult to capture the value created by a solution when many firms are exposed to the problem and the solution. The participation of other stakeholders—such as the general public or peers or other noncorporate actors whose main interest is the creation of IP, but not IP rights—will, if widespread, radically shake up the OI model discussed above, which has IP rights management as a foundation in the idea-to-market journey (Creative Commons website; Benkler and Nissenbaum, 2006; Howe, 2006). In networked innovation, as discussed by Valkokari and his colleagues (2009), R&D consortia involving many universities and multiple firms work in an open innovation context. To avoid the suboptimal performance of the network, which may arise from the potentially opportunistic behavior of single companies or company coalitions in the network and the associated free-riding problem, jointly agreed upon innovation-incentive mechanisms need to be designed so that each company is encouraged to utilize their best knowledge in the collaboration rather than keeping that information private (Jarimo, 2008). Also, value-creating networks sometimes disengage and lose voluntary networks with no profit motive (Tapscott and Williams, 2006). When one invokes the notion of cocreation in open innovation, the traditional roles assigned to universities, industry, and other participants get even blurrier. This is the new challenge in an OI model used in networked innovations. Another fascinating aspect, and still in an inchoate state in our understanding, is the effect of our collective existence on our individual perceptions, known as *stigmergy*. According to Elliot (2007), "Stigmergic collaboration arises when two or more people utilize some form of material media for the encoding of their collective creative endeavor" (108). It is closely related to *distributed cognition*, a term that describes a situation in which environment functions as a part of a cognitive system. Thoughtful reflection of stigmergy in OI models would lead one to accept the fact that an OI model needs to be context specific and that an ecosystem, an interdependencies of partners, would determine the efficacy of the model under consideration. Stigmergy has been proposed to be a partial explanation for the success of open source software (den Besten, Dalle, and Galia, 2008). "The Solution Revolution" (Eggers and Macmillan, 2013) reveals just such a burgeoning new economy, where players from across the spectrum of universities, business, government, philanthropy, and social enterprise converge to solve big problems and create public value. By erasing public-private sector boundaries, the solution economy is unlocking trillions of dollars in social benefit and commercial value. In short, OI models will indeed evolve to become very diverse in variety; therefore, open innovation requires networks, like communities of practice (Snow and Culpan, 2012; Wenger, 1998).

Concluding Thoughts

In this chapter, we have traversed the evolutionary path that transformed some closed innovation models into open innovation models. At the heart of closed innovation models was the premise that control of valuable resources is one of the most potent sources of competitive advantage organizations can possess. Changes in the environmental (technological and regulatory) conditions led to accelerated collaboration between universities and industries, leveraging the traditional roles played by them into synergistic resonance. Open innovation as the means for university-industry collaboration reflects multiple partnerships in complex and dynamic, rather than hierarchical, relationships among important partners who may have valuable inputs into the innovation process. Although the role of government(s) in this university-industry R&D collaboration has been described by the triple-helix model, by expanding the idea-to-market model, we considered potential contributors beyond this triad of university-business-government. While earlier closed innovation was characterized by greater control and reliance on in-house resources, open innovation is more complex as an iterative, multiagent system that involves internal and external, multidirectional knowledge spillovers.

We argue that the traditional roles of universities and industry are changing within the open innovation paradigm. The simple conventional assumption was that knowledge is created in academia and subsequently transferred to enterprises for further development and commercialization. A more granular understanding warrants an appreciation of the roles of businesses and universities in their interactions with other concerned parties, such as governments, suppliers, financial sponsors, and even competitors, as we depicted in Figure 8.4. Knowledge management for businesses is concerned with creating and identifying (research and search), translating and sharing (development), and exploiting (commercializing) knowledge with the dual objectives of value creation and value capture. Knowledge management for universities is concerned with knowledge creation (research and development), knowledge transfer (teaching), and knowledge utilization (service), while a network of payers (e.g., firms, governments, suppliers, angel investors, venture capitalists) provide support for that creation, transfer, and utilization. Conceptually, the transformation of closed innovation to open innovation is a paradigmatic change in one's view of resources, expanding from predominantly in-house resources to "network resources" (Gulati,, 2007; Normann and Ramírez, 1993). *Network resources* are defined as resources that accrue to a firm from its ties with external constituents—including (but not limited to) partners, suppliers, customers, and universities—and thus exist outside the firm's boundaries. However, the web of interfirm relationships will inevitably make university-industry collaboration more complex. The increased importance of knowledge management (discovery, transfer, and utilization) and the particular role of the university in the incubation of technology-based firms have given business-university collaborations a more prominent place in the context of open innovation.

University spin-offs (i.e., academic entrepreneurship), research consortia (i.e., multiple universities working together, as in genetic mapping), shortened product life cycles that necessitate different approaches to IP rights, globalization that requires territorial IP rights management, open source coding that lessens the need for IP rights, cloud computing with open architecture, and social entrepreneurship by universities that create value with a minimum of or no value capture are only some of the interesting ramifications of the new paradigm of open innovation that defines university-industry collaborations. Considering university-industry collaboration in the context of OI will help us understand and manage such collaborations better and will lead to the effective development of new technologies, products, and business models in the future. However, to this end, we need more comprehensive OI models, beyond the current ones examined here, to be developed in order to better explain the changing business environments and networks (or ecosystems) for knowledge creation, transfer, and utilization. Such models should explicate the roles of network members (e.g., business, university, governments, customers, suppliers, angel investors, venture capitalists, novel financing sources, etc.) involved in this process. In understanding and managing such knowledge networks effectively, the suggestions that we offered above will be useful. Nonetheless, we welcome further research and new explanations or expansions to our suggestions in advancing business-university R&D collaborations in the future. We hope that our revised framework offered here will stimulate such research endeavors while our suggestions will be useful for the main actors—businesses and universities in R&D collaborations.

References

Alexander, A. T., and Martin, D. P. (2009). "Intermediaries for Open Innovation: A Competence-Based Comparison of Knowledge Transfer Offices Practices." *Technological Forecasting and Social Change* 80:38–49.

Auranen, O., and Nieminen, M. (2010). "University Research Funding and Publication Performance-An International Comparison." *Research Policy* 39:822–34.

Bellantuono, N., Pontrandolfo, P., and Scozzi B. (2013). "Different Practices for Open Innovation: A Context-Based Approach." *Journal of Knowledge Management* 17:558–68.

Benkler, Y., and Nissenbaum, H. (2006). "Commons Based Peer Production and Virtue." *The Journal of Political Philosophy* 14:394–410.

Bloodgood, J. (2013). "Crowdsourcing: Useful for Problem Solving, but What about Value Capture?" *Academy of Management Review* 38:455–57.

Boyer, E. L. (1990). *Scholarship Reconsidered: Priorities of the Professoriate: Special Report.* Princeton, NJ: The Carnegie Foundation for the Advancement of Teaching.

Burnside, B., and Witkin, L. (2008). "Forging Successful University-Industry Collaborations." *Research-Technology Management* 51:26–30.

Chesbrough, H. (2003). *Open Innovation: The New Imperative for Creating and Profiting from Technology.* Boston: Harvard Business School Press.

Cohen, W., Florida, R., and Goe, W. R. "University-Industry Research Centers in the United States." Unpublished paper, Carnegie-Mellon University, Center for Economic Development, H. J. Heinz III School of Public Policy and Management, Carnegie Mellon University, Pittsburgh, PA, 1994.

Coleman, J. S. (1990). *Foundations of Social Theory.* Cambridge, MA: Harvard University Press.

Colin, C. J. C., and Ja-Shen, C. (2013). "Breakthrough Innovation: The Roles of Dynamic Innovation Capabilities and Open Innovation Activities." *The Journal of Business and Industrial Marketing* 28:444–54.

Creative Commons website. http://creativecommons.org

den Besten, M., Dalle, J. M., and Galia, F. (2008). "The Allocation of Collaborative Efforts in Open-Source Software." *Information Economics and Policy* 20:316–22.

Dankbaar, B. (2003). *Innovation Management in the Knowledge Economy.* In Series on Technology Management, vol. 7. London: Imperial College Press.

Delphine, M., Kaltenbach, P., Line, B., Valérie, M., and Fabbri, J. (2012). "Open Innovation: Putting External Knowledge to Work." *Supply Chain Management Review* 16:42–48.

DiGregorio, D., and Shane, S. (2013). "Why Do Some Universities Generate More Startups Than Others?" *Research Policy* 32:209–27.

Doring, T., and Schnellenbach, J. (2006). "What Do We Know about Geographical Knowledge Spillovers and Regional Growth? A Survey of the Literature." *Regional Studies* 40:375–95.

Eggers, W. D., and Macmillan, P. (2013). *The Solution Revolution: How Business, Government, and Social Enterprises Are Teaming Up to Solve Society's Toughest Problems.* Boston: Harvard Business Press Books.

Elliot, M. (2007). "Stigmergic Collaboration: A Theoretical Framework for Mass Collaboration." PhD diss., Centre for Ideas, Victorian College of the Arts, The University of Melbourne. http://www.springerlink.com/content/2538k675375g4337/fulltext.pdf. (Accessed March 25, 2014).

Etzkowitz, H., and Leydesdorff, L. (2000). "The Dynamics of Innovation: From National Systems and 'Mode 2' to a Triple Helix of University-Industry-Government Relations." *Research Policy* 29:109–23.

Fraser, J. (2008). "Communicating the Full Value of Academic Technology Transfer: Some Lessons Learned." *The Licensing Journal* 28:1–10.

Fritsch, M., and Slavtchev, V. (2007). "Universities and Innovation in Space." *Industry and Innovation* 14:201–18.

George, G., Zahra, S. A., and Wood, Jr., D. R. (2002). "The Effects of Business-University Alliances on Innovative Output and Financial Performance: A Study of Publicly Traded Biotechnology Companies." *Journal of Business Venturing* 17:577–609.

Goldfarb, B., and Henrekson, M. (2003). "Bottom-Up versus Top-Down Policies towards the Commercialization of University Intellectual Property." *Research Policy* 32:639–58.

Gulati, R. (2007). *Managing Network Resources: Alliance, Affiliations, and Relational Assets*. Oxford: Oxford University Press.

Gustin, B. (1995). *The Emergence of the German Chemical Profession, 1790–1867*. PhD dissertation, University of Chicago.

Gutteridge, T. (2007). "Outreach and Engagement: Afterthought or Strategic Priority?" *Mid-American Journal of Business* 22:5–6.

Howe, J. (2006). "The Rise of Crowdsourcing." *Wired*, June 14. http://www.wired.com/wired/archive/14.06/crowds.html. (Accessed March 29, 2014).

Jarimo, T. (2008). "Innovation Incentives and the Design of Value Networks." DSc thesis, Espoo, Helsinki University of Technology.

Janeiro, P., Proenca, I., and Goncalves, V. C. (2013). "Open Innovation: Factors Explaining Universities as Service Firm Innovation Sources." *Journal of Business Research* 66:2017–23.

Lee, N. (2009). "Exclusion and Coordination in Collaborative Innovation and Patent Law." *International Journal of Intellectual Property Management* 3:79–93.

Lee, Y. S. (1998). "University-Industry Collaboration on Technology Transfer: Views from the Ivory Tower." *Policy Studies Journal*, 26:69–84.

Leydesdorff, L., and Meyer, M. (2006). "Triple Helix Indicators of Knowledge-Based Innovation Systems (Introduction to the Special Issue)." *Research Policy* 35:1441–49.

Lichtenthaler, H. (2008). "Open Innovation in Practice: An Analysis of Strategic Approaches to Technology Transactions." *IEEE Transactions on Engineering Management* 55:148–57.

Matkin, G. (1990). *Technology Transfer and the University*. New York: Macmillan.

Murphy, L. M., & Edwards, P. L. (2003). *Bridging the valley of death: Transitioning from public to private sector financing*. Golden, CO: National Renewable Energy Laboratory.

Nystén-Haarala, S., Lee, N., and Lehto, J. (2010). "Flexibility in Contract Terms and Contracting Processes." *International Journal of Managing Projects in Business* 3:12–22.

Normann, R., and Ramírez, R. (1993). "From Value Chain to Value Constellation: Designing Interactive Strategy." *Harvard Business Review* 4:65–77.

OECD Report. (2008). *Open Innovation in Global Networks*. OECD Press.

Powell, W., and Owen-Smith, J. (1998). "University and the Market for Intellectual Property in Life Sciences." *Journal of Policy Analysis and Management* 17:253–77.

Reid, R. (1997). *Architects of the Web*. New York: John-Wiley and Sons.

Rosenberg, N., and Nelson, R. (1994). "American Universities and Technical Advances in Industry." *Research Policy* 23:323–48.

Shane, S. (2004). *Academic Entrepreneurship: University Spin-Offs and Wealth Creation*. Northampton, MA: Edward Elgar.

Siew, A. (2013). "Pharma Embraces Open Innovation." *Pharmaceutical Technology* 25:6–8.

Sisodiya, S. R., Johnson, J. L., and Grégoire, Y. (2013). "Inbound Open Innovation for Enhanced Performance: Enablers and Opportunities." *Industrial Marketing Management* 42:836–48.

Snow, C. C., and Culpan, R. (2012). "Open Innovation through a Collaborative Community of Firms: An Emerging Organizational Design." In T. K. Das (ed.), *Strategic Alliances for Value Creation*, 279–300. Charlotte, NC: Information Age Publishing, Inc.

Sophia Antipolis. (2013). "Garbejaire, the Inner Residential Community." Wikipedia. http://en.wikipedia.org/wiki/Sophia_Antipolis. (Accessed March 30, 2014).

Spithoven, A. (2013). "Open Innovation Practices and Innovative Performances: An International Comparative Perspective." *International Journal of Technology Management* 61:254–73.

Tapscott, D., and Williams, A. D. (2006). *Wikinomics: How Mass Collaboration Changes Everything*. New York: Penguin Group.

Valkokari, K., Paasi, J., Luoma, T., and Lee, N. (2009). "Beyond Open Innovation—The Concept of Networked Innovation." In Proceedings of the 2nd ISPIM Innovation Symposium, New York City.

Viale, R., and Campodall'Orto, S. (2000). "Neocorporations or Evolutionary Triple Helix? Suggestions Coming from European Regions." Presented at the Third Triple Helix Conference, Rio de Janeiro.

von Hippel, E., and von Krogh, G. (2003). "Open Source Software and the 'Private Collective' Innovation Model: Issues for Organization Science." *Organization Science* 14:209–23.

Wengenroth, U. (1995). "Natural Sciences and the Chemical Industry in Germany—Preconditions and Mechanisms of Their Rise in the 19th Century." *Historishce Zeitschrift* 260:922–24.

Witzeman, S., Slowinski, G., Dirkx, R., Gollob, L., Tao, J., Ward, S., and Miraglia, S. (2006). "Harnessing External Technology for Innovation." *Research-Technology Management* 49:19–27.

Youtie, J., and Shapira, P. (2008). "Building an Innovation Hub: A Case Study of the Transformation of University Roles in Regional Technological and Economic Development." *Research Policy* 37:1188–204.

Wenger, E. (1998). *Communities of Practice: Learning, Meaning, and Identity*. Cambridge: Cambridge University Press.

CHAPTER 9

The Big Data Lever for Strategic Alliances

Mariann Jelinek, Steve Barr, Paul Mugge,
and Richard Kouri

Globalization, Innovation, and "Big Data"

From the mid-1990s, many US firms began outsourcing formerly internal activities, while academics like J. Brian Quinn of Dartmouth asserted that a firm should develop world-class capabilities for core capabilities but seek world-class outsiders to accomplish everything else. First, parts manufacturing, then more knowledge-based tasks, and finally innovation itself were outsourced, in search of strategic advantage (Quinn, 1999, 2000; Quinn and Hilmer, 1994). Displacing the long trend of internalized functions for greater control that began in the nineteenth century (Chandler, 1977), increasing externalization of noncore activities has characterized the twenty-first century.

Outsourcing spans a host of activities and organizing forms, from one-time transactions to long-term relational engagements. "Simple" strategic alliance partnerships, multipartner alliances, joint ventures, joint R&D activities, consortia, comarketing arrangements, licensing, minority equity alliances, and supply chain contracts are all examples. Such activities acquire particular importance with innovative products, processes, or market entries: these are all explicitly beyond the focal firm's initial expertise and are thus fraught with uncertainty and risk. Seeking unfamiliar expertise in a partner for the missing elements seems promising—but also risky.

Identifying appropriate partners is itself a challenge: "world-class" is a moving target; technology change and entrepreneurship raise new opportunities in far-flung locales, even as new discoveries change what may be possible. State-of-the-art innovation can entail identifying partners in novel technologies and strategic arenas, as well as new geographic areas (Culpan, 2002; Doz and Hamel, 1998;

Doz, Santos, and Williamson, 2001). Moreover, since these alliances are "strategic," firms must assess likely strategic effects and interactions—like the impact on existing partners and rivals, for example.

Thus open innovation decisions are not only important and uncertain; they also inhabit decision territory unfamiliar to the decision maker. In such territory, heroic assumptions of omniscience and information availability enshrined in rational decision theory are misleading. Behavioral decision research reveals that actual human decision making enjoys no such benign conditions (March and Simon, 1959; Simon, 1950, 1957). Instead, in the highly uncertain and risky strategic decisions open innovation demands, human decision makers often lack needed information. Time and cost constraints can limit information gathering, and decision makers have limited ability to process information, reducing their ability to evaluate complex alternatives. In response, decision makers satisfice, choosing the first available alternative that meets the minimum requirements of their most important stakeholders.

Decision makers rely more on shortcuts as uncertainty and perceived risk increase or as the resources and efforts required by the decision process escalate (Maule, Hodgkinson, and Bown, 2003). These shortcuts, used by experts and novices alike, reflect assumptions about relationships among underlying decision factors. These shortcuts, as heuristics and biases—that is, "simplifying strategies" deployed to decrease required cognitive effort—degrade decision quality (D. Kahneman, Slovic, and Tversky, 1982; Tversky and Kahenman, 1982; Tversky and Kahneman, 1974).

Behavioral decision-making research literature[1] reveals a range of decision shortcomings, along with decision tools that can mitigate their impact on decision quality. But no genuine integration has linked behavioral decision theory with this descriptive approach to understanding strategic decision processes in general, nor those concerning open innovation. *Big data analytics* (BDA) can be considered a contemporary support for the necessary multiple stages of the decision process: problem definition, information gathering, information processing, analysis of alternatives, and selection among alternatives.

But despite "big data" search's promise, many remain skeptical about big data hype and disappointed in the massive amounts of irrelevant, obvious, or tangential data of little use for decisions. More and better data, and the incisive analysis of it, could offer superior strategies and new insights—if subject-matter experts' knowledge can be brought to bear, if their cognitive shortcomings can be mitigated, and if decision traps can be addressed.

This chapter will describe a directed form of BDA that systematically creates domain-specific search templates for more cogent problem definition, better information gathering and processing, and clearer presentation of choice options. These techniques help to overcome the limits that heuristics and biases impose. Further, the resulting curated libraries of timely, relevant data can be rapidly updated and rapidly searched to answer a wide range of domain-related questions, bolstering subject-matter experts' (SMEs') analysis. Combined with structured decision models, for example, through procedures like the *technology education and commercialization* (TEC) algorithm (Markham et al., 2000; Markham et al., 2002) and *analytical hierarchy process* (AHP) (Saaty, 2012), these approaches offer nuanced, evidence-based decision support.

The directed BDA platform process we shall describe enhances strategic alliance decisions by significantly increasing the quality of each of the five decision stages. This is especially important in decisions involving strategic alliances for open innovation, where uncertainty and risk loom large and unaided decision processes are especially vulnerable to the simplifications of heuristics and biases.

We begin with a discussion of open innovation's strategic challenges, incorporating behavioral decision theory insights into the limits of human decision making. Next, we will describe in some detail the directed BDA platform process developed by the Center for Innovation Management Studies (CIMS) at North Carolina State University and how it mitigates strategic risks and behavioral decision traps. We illustrate with examples from company clients' solutions to real-world problems using real-world data. These examples offer vivid proofs of concept; they underpin important lessons learned and point to further research.

Open Innovation and Big Data

While "we now live in a global economy," centuries-old networks of trade and cooperation that source ingredients, commodities, or components from abroad have long been a hallmark of civilization. Neither outsourcing, nor collaboration, nor even big data are new, precisely; each has seen earlier instantiations. *Outsourcing*, for example, is defined as the contracting out of some business process to another person or firm and is little different from buying parts or subassemblies or expertise from an outside source.

Firms have long contracted for specialist expertise, from accounting and legal services to equipment specification and installation supervision, and for innovation help. Booz Allen Hamilton was among the first formal business consultation services, in the 1910s and 1920s; McKinsey and Co., founded in 1926, today serves "two-thirds of the Fortune 1000." Major accounting firms initially offered specialist expertise in accounting, while other specialist services—think logistics, from UPS; aircraft engine maintenance, from Delta Airlines; engine makers, like GE or Pratt & Whitney; or specialists like Chromalloy—enable firms with expertise to expand lines of business and clients to access superior capability. Components or subassemblies also might involve close cooperation (extensively documented for the auto industry in Womack, Jones, and Roos, [1990]). while underlying-technologies confluences have led to cooperation among firms in the chemicals and pharmaceuticals industries (Culpan, 2002; Rabinow, 1996).

"Open innovation" covers a range of collaboration modes, including partnerships, joint ventures, collaborative R&D, comarketing, license agreements, minority equity alliances, and various supply chain arrangements (Culpan, 2011). Firms may bring in outside ideas, components, products, or expertise at any point in the value chain for some, much, or even all of the needed links—and they have done so for some time. What is different today? Increasingly complex products embed increasing amounts of knowledge, *requiring* collaboration—particularly where genuine innovation is at issue, a point to which we shall return—and especially in fast-paced innovation environments. Moreover, partners may be anywhere on the planet.

Big data constitutes a special case, requiring a definition. What is "data" can change from one era to the next, as can the concept of what is "big." So, for example, a recent article noted that statisticians have worked with "big" data for centuries: Kepler's detailed astronomical records were "big" for their time, and very large linguistic data sets go back nearly eight hundred years (Arbesman, 2013). In contemporary usage, "big data" emphasizes the broad availability of substantially larger amounts and types of data via the Internet, digital recording devices and memories, and burgeoning computer analytical capabilities. Still, many uses of big data today seem parochially confined to targeting existing customers (sending more emails to past clients or website visitors) or analyzing a firm's internal data for optimization (Manyika et al., 2011). Executives who find little value in generalized searches are skeptical of big data benefits. Yet despite the title "Think Big Data is All Hype? You're Not Alone," BDA seems to be attracting customers (Hesseldahl, 2013).

How, then, is today's big data truly different? First, it is "bigger," measured in exabytes (IDC estimates 13,000 exabytes—1 exabyte is one quintillion bytes—by 2020).[2] Online shopping generates vast information about users' habits from their search terms, enabling Amazon to infer their likely interests on the fly. Google processes over a billion searches *per day* in the United States alone—and stores them for subsequent mining. Perhaps more importantly, while accessible data formerly meant "numbers," new types of sensors, larger storage and memory capacity, and faster computers now digitize an array of data types, most particularly unstructured data—text and images, for instance—as well as locational information, music, colors, and more. In 2000 only a quarter of the world's information was digital; today, "less than two percent of all stored information is nondigital" (Cukier and Mayer-Schoenberger, 2013).

Both the kinds of data and their availability have escalated, feeding a trend toward the "datafication" (Cukier and Mayer-Schoenberger, 2013) of almost everything, opening new prospects for innovative uses for that "datafied everything." Examples range from molecular-level genomic data on infectious agents, enabling the identification of the multiple, interacting genes involved in tuberculosis (TB) resistance (Yong, 2013) or cancer (Williams, 2013); or massive amounts of collision data from the Large Hadron Collider at CERN to confirm the identification of the Higgs Boson (Boisot et al., 2011); to locational data on customers proximity to, say, restaurants. With these expansions, contemporary big data offers not just "more of the same," but new strategic capabilities from new kinds of data.

Yet many firms remain focused on internal data: videos of customers queuing in line at a hotel, or analyzing call center voice-tone data, or micromanagement of fuel use for efficiency improvements (Davenport and Dyché, 2013). Such operational improvements can help, but external data supports more important decisions, including strategic repositioning in changing environments—especially for open innovation.

Procter & Gamble famously announced that 50 percent of its new product ideas came from outside the company (Huston and Sakkab, 2006; Sakkab, 2002), enabling P&G to exploit internal development and consumer marketing capabilities and shocking observers who considered innovation sacrosanct. Yet P&G's announcement reflected contemporary technology realities. Many complex products (like the iPhone, new medical diagnostic "lab-on-a-chip" products, or even the VISA credit card system) meld numerous advanced capabilities beyond any one firm's: despite P&G's excellent internal capabilities, far more scientists, researchers, and idea generators reside *outside* the company.

New markets too often demand fresh expertise. Strategic alliances (including partnerships, joint ventures, joint R&D, comarketing, license agreements, minority equity alliance, supply chain contracts) offer needed elements. For-profit companies, NGOs and not-for-profits, and even governments increasingly collaborate to achieve their goals, tapping into external resources, contacts, and capabilities. Leveraging internal capabilities and resources by accessing missing ones, or having outsiders perform "downstream" activities like marketing and distribution, makes sense, but it is not easy.

In each instance, a focal company must find candidates for partnership or potential technologies or inviting markets that may be distant and unfamiliar. Both appropriate criteria and information may be scarce, and where genuine innovation is involved, decision makers may have to tool up in conceptually distant knowledge domains. These are not new problems: a decade ago Procter & Gamble concluded that global technology transfer was highly inefficient, too often dependent on "'Who do you know?' and 'How good is your Rolodex?'" (Sakkab, 2002, 43).

Internet-based intermediaries for open innovation seemed an exciting new resource, beginning with sites like Yet2.com (of which P&G was a founding sponsor in 1999) and InnoCentive (founded in 2001). By 2005, two editors at *Wired* had coined the term "crowdsourcing" (Safire, 2009), reflecting new collaboration possibilities. By 2013, one innovation website lists some 25 intermediary sites[3] offering variants on crowdsourcing for both technology and market intelligence. Problem solved? Maybe not. Effective outsourcing management still poses such challenges that it can constitute a competitive advantage in the form of "combinative capabilities" (Kogut and Zander, 1992; Zander and Kogut, 1995), often based on underlying firm capabilities (Ellonen, Wikstrom, and Jantunen, 2009).

Neither Markets nor Hierarchies

Achieving such innovation potentials requires locating *appropriate* innovation resources to access expertise and intellectual property beyond the firm. Even very large firms now turn to licensing, outsourcing, and, increasingly, strategic alliances for open innovation (P&G, Apple, and IBM are merely three examples).

Many contemporary products depend on highly complex components (for example, consumer electronics) (Hagel III, Brown, and Jelinek, 2011); difficult-to-master manufacturing activities, as with flat-screen displays (Murtha and Lenway, 1994); an ongoing stream of new product ideas, like P&G (Huston and Sakkab, 2006); or access to formerly untapped markets, like numerous foreign firms entering China (see Doz and Hamel, 1998; Doz et al., 2001). These firms collaborate, practicing some variant of open innovation.

Simple insourcing of components or raw materials—procurement—can typically be managed contractually. What is exchanged and, often, the price are routinely known matters where numerous sources exist. The parties agree to terms, specified a priori (although specifications may be contingent, as in ongoing commodity deliveries, where price and quantity may vary), and contracts may be extended indefinitely. Beyond such simple transactions, establishing the relationship becomes more complicated because its terms are indeterminate, uncertain, or altogether unknown.

Theory offers few managerial options. *Behavioral controls* specify requisite behavior, monitoring compliance through close supervision and assessment of behavior (Cheng and McKinley, 1983). *Output controls* monitor results but require clear standards (Thompson, 1967) and observed, measurable outcomes (Eisenhardt, 1985; Ouchi, 1979). Where output cannot be measured and behavior cannot be monitored, *input controls* rely on social suasion and group pressure (Ouchi, 1979), resource sharing and socialization (Govindarajan and Fisher, 1990), and carefully managed hiring, training, and selection (Snell, 1992).

What happens when the shared activity addresses "strategic" activities—innovation on core products or processes, for instance, where project failure might cause the demise of the firm and where innovation pushes the edge of the state of the art and neither party has complete knowledge? Under such conditions, many traditional control levers for managing risk are unavailable—so the cognitive limits of decision makers become central. How can managers exert any meaningful control over activities beyond their legitimate authority to give orders, beyond their capability to specify inputs, behaviors, or outputs, beyond their knowledge base (or, often, anyone else's)? How can they avoid the decision traps inherent in human cognitive limits? Early decision errors have major impact on what control systems may be required later to implement and maintain the strategic alliance. Errors in forming open innovation alliances can even lead to failure.

Such strategic collaborative activities cannot be codified in a contract: neither inputs, procedures, outcomes, nor market values can be reasonably forecasted. Nor are important actors employees of the focal firm; those nominally in charge cannot select, train, reward, or sanction employees of a collaborating firm. Nor will critical players (or their firms) typically be acquired. Further, the parties cannot fall back on a shared company culture: their decision paradigms may differ radically. Forming such alliances is a major source of uncertainty and risk for open innovation strategies, and well-managed, directed BDA can mitigate strategic decision traps.

Directed BDA for Executing Open Innovation: Varieties and Procedures

Three archetypes of open innovation have been identified: *inside-out*, bringing ideas to the market by licensing or selling to others; *outside-in*, integrating outsiders' knowledge or capabilities with internal capabilities; and *coupled processes*, utilizing both inside-out and outside-in, for example, via strategic alliances (Gassmann and Enkel, 2004). The decades-old emphasis on licensing by IBM, Texas Instruments, and many others is *inside-out*: revenues are realized from technologies or intellectual property the firm elects not to pursue. P&G's widely admired "Connect and Develop" approach is principally *outside-in*: it links outside product ideas, packaging options, and new technologies to the company's own expertise in development and marketing. IBM's "First-of-a-Kind" (FOAK) collaborative development projects are *coupled processes*, initially of a one-off nature (Frederich and Andrews, 2010). Ongoing relational network alliances, like Apple's, are *coupled processes* that endure over time, over multiple innovation projects.

Inside-out open innovation may well subsume to a marketing problem: making the available technology or product known to potentially interested parties via prior connections or perhaps on a site like Yet2.com or Innovation Exchange (which describes itself as an "online open innovation marketplace"). But a more targeted search, for parties active in relevant markets or interested in related technologies, promises better results, by identifying partners with the interests and expertise to value what is on offer. Both outside-in and coupled-process open innovation underscore the importance of *appropriate* partners even more clearly—the relationship may be closer, the stakes and the risks higher, and proprietary technologies and core markets are at issue.

Cognitive Limits, Heuristics, and Decision Traps

Decision makers rarely follow the prescriptive decision models, nor do they enjoy the luxuries of complete information and unlimited resources these models imply. Instead, they satisfice (March and Simon, 1959; Simon, 1956, 1957), managing their limits by choosing the first available alternative that meets the minimum requirements. We selectively focus our discussion on those heuristics and biases particularly relevant to strategic alliance formation in the highly uncertain, unstructured environment of open innovation. Our aim is to demonstrate how a directed BDA process can mitigate these particular hazards to enhance decision quality.

Faced with great uncertainty, ambiguity, and overwhelming amounts of information that cannot readily be assessed, strategic decision makers considering open innovation turn to shortcuts to simplify, reducing an unmanageable problem to one they can solve. Consciously or unconsciously, they often limit the amount of information considered. If needed information is not available, decision makers use such information as they have, referring to recent or especially vivid memories to assess probability that an event will occur (availability bias). They may attend only to what is familiar, literally *not seeing* the incongruent or unexpected (Bruner and Postman, 1949–50). They may "pre-decide" or anchor their decision and seek or attend to only information confirming their initial understanding (Maule et al., 2003; Svenson, 1999). This in turn can encourage a kind of "cognitive inertia"—retaining an older, perhaps obsolete mental model of the strategic situation they face.

Among the key problems impeding better strategic decisions, then, are the *lack of information needed* to define the problem or criteria; *time and cost constraints* that limit information gathering; and a *limited ability to hold information in mind and process it*, making it *harder to evaluate alternatives*—all exacerbated by natural cognitive limits and human responses to complex, unfamiliar situations. Two consistent themes emerge from the behavioral decision literature: decision makers will attempt to reduce perceived uncertainty in their decision process to minimize their perceived risk, and they will attempt to reduce cognitive effort required to gather, process, and interpret data (Kahneman et al., 1982; Tversky and Kahenman, 1982). Decision makers exhibit "bounded rationality"—limits to their ability to search for all relevant information, process it consistently, and draw impartial, logical conclusions. Open innovation decisions are especially vulnerable because the use of shortcuts to simplify increases as uncertainty and risk increase.

The *availability heuristic* induces decision makers to misjudge the likelihood or importance of an event, relying on similar occurrences that are readily "available" in memory. What is highly personally relevant, vivid, or emotional is most available, whether or not memory reflects actual likelihood or importance or even accuracy. The availability heuristic also drives what information is considered.

The *representativeness heuristic* leads decision makers to misevaluate event likelihood or causal relationships, instead following their stereotypes of similar occurrences even when the information is insufficient or better information exists. These heuristics suggest that decision makers' information search and processing are often seriously limited. One bias affects decision makers' tendency to ignore existing base-rate data when considering risky decisions, for example, overestimating chances of success, regardless of fact. Another bias leads them to routinely ignore sample size, even though statistical sampling suggests that outliers are more frequent in smaller data sets. The third bias is misconception of chance, ignoring its role and likelihood. The fourth bias ignores regression to the mean despite its statistical validity: decision makers subject to this bias assume that temporary, unusual outcomes will continue, rather than revert to long-term averages. These shortcuts drive decision makers to rely on a few small, favored bits of data, assuming them to reliable and valid reflections of all relevant data. Unaided human decision makers are poor judges of statistical reality.

The *anchoring and adjustment heuristic* leads to a trial decision that dominates subsequent thinking: the final decision will deviate very little from the first. The anchor seems to reduce uncertainty by providing a reference point against which to evaluate later information; but adjustments, if any, tend to be much smaller than warranted by the data. Moreover, interactive effects among heuristics can further limit decision processes, particularly in unstable, unfamiliar, complex environments, like those typical of open innovation.

Risk perceptions and framing, the primary modes through which cognitive heuristics affect decision making, are particularly likely in open innovation. Decision makers are especially likely to perceive risk and, as a result, especially likely to frame their decisions in ways vulnerable to inadequate search, rejection of nonconfirming data, anchoring, misjudgment of risk and failure to reassess on subsequent data, and biased assessments of alternatives. Thus viable options can be dismissed while a first impression based on inadequate information endures or potential gains and losses can be seen differently, although they are logically equivalent (Kahneman and Tversky, 1979). These decision traps virtually ensure poor decisions by limiting the impact of evidence.

Well-structured, directed BDA directly acts to mitigate the biases relevant to open innovation, including framing biases. Computers serve as extensions of human information search and processing capabilities (Donald, 1991), and directed BDA is an elaboration of that linkage. Naïve BDA produces "more information" but risks simply overwhelming decision makers, inviting all of the biases and heuristics we have discussed. To effectively address cognitive limits, something more is needed: a focused, directed, and targeted BDA that produces highly relevant data, along with the means to evaluate, interpret, and transform that data into actionable information.

A timeline of strategic alliance development, from finding needed resources through evaluating prospects and choosing among options (see Figure 9.1),

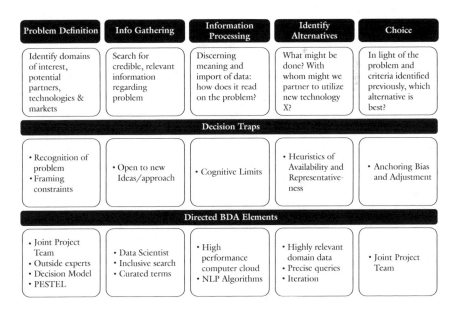

Figure 9.1   Decision Stages: Timeline of Strategic Alliance Formation

schematically depicts how the directed BDA platform process assists open innovation. The challenge is knowing what is available and where: potential partners and technologies may reside in hitherto unknown "spikes" of capability (Hagel III et al., 2011; Hagel III and Brown, 2005), in unanticipated places (Culpan, 2002; Doz and Hamel, 1998; Doz et al., 2001). "Who's in your Rolodex?" is unlikely to help. Strategic alliance isn't about *the* needle in a haystack containing many; it is about finding *appropriate* needles—and then assessing candidates to choose well among them.

CIMS[4] Big Data Analytics Process

Since 2008, CIMS has conducted enhanced technology and market searches using natural language processing machines to analyze unstructured text data—the kind of information that resides on the Internet in websites, blogs, wikis, research papers, and presentations. Much of companies' internal information (e.g., customer satisfaction reports, engineering notebooks, project management reports, call center logs, and other operational data) is also stored as unstructured text data. Using IBM's "Watson" software technology hosted on North Carolina State University's high-performance servers, a powerful analytics platform helps companies sift through massive amounts of data—previously unaffordable, if not physically inaccessible—to answer strategic questions.

Computers parse, filter, and index unstructured text to assign meaning and context to the data, precisely "reading" millions of documents in accordance with specific rules. Unlike humans, computers don't suffer from biases or take shortcuts; their cognitive capacity is virtually unlimited. But first, people must articulate the terms of interest and associations between the terms, typically in a customized client workshop, using a standardized approach to address known limits in human decision processes.

Finding Needed Resources: Using the Directed BDA Platform Process

Big data's first and most obvious application is in finding needed innovation resources "anywhere." With most of the world's information available in digital form, identifying novel technologies, processes, materials, and practices is vastly easier, faster, and more inclusive than in the days of "Who's in your Rolodex?" Directed BDA search eliminates information constraints by addressing the entire Internet via targeted search terms, exploiting the burgeoning data availability. Such a search also facilitates the identification of newly emergent resources, whether those are emerging "spikes" of design and manufacturing expertise, university research programs, or public-private partnerships. But broad Internet accessibility must be coupled with *targeted* search terms and sources to sift through literally millions of potential hits to select those of genuine merit, lest masses of irrelevant or tangential data overwhelm decision makers. Targeted search facilitates the critical transformation of massive amounts of *data* into potentially actionable *information.*

Partnership Possibilities

Lacking needed expertise (or having insufficient internal resources), firms seek external resources for open innovation. Who has the needed technology or expertise? Where are the partners? Using special software,[5] CIMS directed BDA (DBDA) deploys guided dictionaries of search terms, including likely names (e.g., of relevant universities, companies, NGOs, or researchers), technical terms, technology features, relevant journals, and companies, across a limited set of URLs for initial queries. These dictionaries can be constructed by client SMEs, in collaboration with outsiders, or initially derived automatically from a small number of high-interest articles, whose keywords, references, and topics themselves serve as initial search terms. Queries guided by such dictionaries yield high-potential, curated libraries of indexed hits (including websites, conference proceedings, published articles, abstracts, seminars, and more). SMEs can rapidly search these with combinations of terms to winnow down to a much smaller number of very high interest items for examination.

Identifying possible resources can be straightforward (e.g., Which researchers are publishing on topic X?), but more interesting searches are less intuitively obvious and thus more likely to be of strategic value. Software tools enable SMEs to discern early-stage technologies in development, prioritize market possibilities, and identify emerging trends. These searches utilize tools for mining the domain-relevant data that directed search produced—cross-referencing terms and ideas of interest and exploring where they occurred—to go well beyond current-product/current-customer searches, internal information for optimization, or the stereotypical misunderstanding of BDA as "just Google on steroids." Inclusive Internet searches based on *curated* terms (whether suggested by SMEs or derived from relevant, advanced publications) instantly obviate the biases and simplifying heuristics humans typically use to lower perceived risk and information overload. Such searches encourage interesting questions because they enable rapid, repeated searches of highly domain-relevant data that require little cognitive effort, time, and expense. We turn now to specific, detailed examples of how well-focused, highly specific BDA searches mitigate the risks and hazards of open innovation decisions.

Tackling TB

The Clinton Health Access Initiative (CHAI) is a nongovernmental organization focused on health care that collaborates with other NGOs, pharmaceutical companies, and governments to expand access to life-saving health care. CHAI sought strategic insight into possible novel TB diagnostics and therapeutics. A joint project team (JPT)—consisting of CHAI and outsider SMEs, some from CIMS—participated in a workshop to identify an initial research question: "What is the market potential for new TB diagnostics and therapeutics in specific CHAI countries?" The JPT SMEs crossed organizational and disciplinary boundaries (e.g., marketing, public health, tuberculosis, information science, strategy), reducing the likelihood of overly constrained thinking. Together, they suggested dictionary search terms and 50 high-quality seed URLs for the initial search, thought likely read on market size and potential for TB diagnostics by country. Web-crawlers[6] were instructed to link down four levels within sites and make up to ten jumps from each seed URL to gather the information found at these connected locations. Some 800,000 files were gathered, each typically containing between ten and two hundred web pages.

ICA crawlers then "parsed, indexed, and filtered" this corpus of data, based on the 39 custom dictionaries developed by the JPT. Dictionaries included high-potential domain-relevant search terms (here, terms related to TB diagnostics, therapeutics, incidence, co-morbidities, research issues, and so on). A total of 280,000 parsed, indexed, and filtered files resulted, all with high probability of relevance to the queries of interest. This curated collection, hosted on a dedicated server,[7] was available to the JPT 24 hours a day, seven days a week for SME searches. This inclusive, indexed search library of 280,000 files avoided the "Rolodex problems" of limited personal knowledge resources and constrained familiarity, but it was still far beyond any expert's ability to assess. DBDA analytical tools enable SMEs to rapidly construct still tighter sampling and still more focused searches by mining the library for items of more immediate relevance and clicking through to examine those of interest. An example will illustrate.

A search for novel TB diagnostics reduced the indexed library by applying "2013" as a filter, thereby reducing the number of files slightly, to 263,000. (This slight reduction shows that most library items were very recent.) Searching with a combination of dictionaries, like **Disease Foundations**[8] (a list of research-funding organizations) and **Biomarkers** (a list of biological indicators of disease or health), substantially reduced the number of files, to 23,000, while revealing what the grants-making organizations were currently funding. Examining this smaller set using software analytics revealed the highest frequency match of terms across these items to be **Welcome Trust** $\times$ **miRNA** = 15,000 files: Welcome Trust is actively funding microRNA research, a current hot topic.

One form of microRNA (miRNA) appears in exhaled air, a transmission mode for TB: searching manually for "exhaled air" showed 76 relevant items in the set. Eight of the first ten files mentioned one paper, "A Blood Based 12 miRNA Signature . . . for Alzheimer's Disease," another disease so notoriously difficult to diagnose that it is presently diagnosed only from postmortem tissue samples. A quick read of the abstract of this paper revealed that the authors had discovered a set of 12 miRNAs in blood-borne exosomes that were unique to Alzheimer's patients, enabling in vivo diagnosis.

To an informed expert, this suggested that miRNA was a highly interesting biomarker capable of diagnosing disease and might be interesting for TB diagnostics as well (especially latent TB, which is also difficult to diagnose). Since TB is transmitted by exhaled droplets containing the bacterium, exhaled air as a medium for exosomes—cell-derived vesicles present in many, if not all, biological products, including blood, urine, sweat, saliva, and exhaled air—was of very high interest as a potential novel TB diagnostic pathway. The SMEs also recognized that TB microRNA exosomes in exhaled air would avoid some serious problems with current TB diagnostics (where infant and child patients cannot easily produce sputum or where immune-compromised patients do not produce antibodies, for example).

Following the trail of exhaled exosomes revealed several articles using exosomes found in exhaled air to diagnose lung cancer and chronic obstructive pulmonary disease (COPD). However, *no* articles addressed microRNA from TB in exhaled air: thus the biology suggested a promising yet unexplored area for further research, while also identifying *microRNA* as a new keyword for monitoring. These articles were all published in the four months prior to the search, and one, having just been posted online, was not yet available in print: this highly timely search required under ten minutes.

Furthermore, another quick search of the same database also revealed nearly six thousand articles relevant to hepatitis, testifying to the power of such a database to leverage confluences in technology and biology: because miRNA "reads" on multiple diseases, it offers a novel pathway into a broad range of diagnostics. This broader, more general-purpose insight across a targeted domain of disease underlines how DBDA supports a range of SME "deep dives" into relevant, detailed information adjacencies.

Directed BDA inquiry leverages SMEs: this search highlights their critical role to ensure highly focused searches, first via the creation of appropriate dictionaries and then by further querying retrieved, indexed libraries to identify immediately relevant information for action. Searches of the same database by other SMEs identified other, broader issues, such as an emerging regional TB-HIV epidemic in sub-Saharan Africa (important because TB and HIV are mutually synergistic), the roots of that epidemic in South African mines (where migrant miners, far from home, visit brothels and are exposed to HIV, while their occupational exposure to silica dust makes them more susceptible to TB), and the epidemiology of transmission (as the migrant miners return to their home villages). These searches also identified an emerging cross-border collaboration across the region to share information resources to target the epidemic—with implications for CHAI's internal organization and information sharing, and for alliance partners.

Both very tightly targeted searches (miRNA) and more contextual searches (epidemiology of growing TB-HIV incidence in sub-Saharan Africa) are supported by the same curated, filtered, parsed, and indexed library, which multiple SMEs can search simultaneously. The searches can reveal potential partners for alliance with CHAI, such as NGOs with similar TB focus, NGOS and foundations addressing health care in the region, and researchers targeting exosomes and miRNA (including both university and institute researchers, as well as pharmaceutical companies, some of which are already CHAI partners). Organizations active both by country and in strengthening regional health delivery and information systems are now visible, including newly active collaborative government organizations across the region targeting TB and HIV.

Assessing Strategic Options

Another CIMS client sought insight to prioritize potential research targets. Where should they focus their R&D, given limited resources? How could they leverage expertise in vaccine development for viral diseases, and which held most promise? Their search around mosquito-borne viral diseases needed to include prevalence data, implications such as the DALY index,[9] prevalence of travel to the affected areas, time to market, and cost implications. Once search terms and likely URLs were identified, discussion of preliminary data suggested factors that could be differentially weighted, with implications systematically discussed by SMEs. Analysis of market landscapes for dengue and dengue hemorrhagic fever, West Nile virus, chikungunya fever, yellow fever, and Japanese encephalitis produced good estimates of vaccine markets for all five. Based on this market research and timing, pricing, and cost assumptions, decision makers identified dengue vaccine as their priority. No vaccine existed for dengue, which is a serious problem in China, India, Australia, and the Caribbean. Recently, indigenous cases have been documented by the CDC in Florida.[10] Climate change may expand vector territories and the relevant market geography, intensifying its importance. The firm targeted dengue R&D and announced preclinical success with a dengue vaccine in early 2013.

Strategic Options Identification

Another client sought to identify and prioritize companies interested in pharmacogenetics of the central nervous system (CNS) in China. Potential partners might be researching a variety of biomarkers, so decision makers wished to identify all the biomarkers focused on specified indications of interest and all organizations in China working in pharmacogenetics. Directed BDA search identified targets, supported prioritization by highlighting research activity, and produced contact information for 46 high-potential partner companies using biomarkers in projects for nonpain CNS indications, including oncology, inflammation, and nutraceutical evaluation. Because searches can be conducted in languages besides English, searches of foreign-language sites are convenient.

Directed BDA's carefully curated libraries of highly targeted information help uncover strategic options, some logical extensions of present activities (termed "adjacencies") and others farther afield. Inclusive, unbiased searches are especially valuable where technology convergence renders formerly disparate areas of research and discovery unexpectedly relevant, as with computers and telecommunication. "Smartphones" are, in fact, computers—but they now also incorporate television, music, instructional media, photos, and more. Apple's iPhone displaced former cell phone market leaders Nokia and Motorola, even though Apple is a "computer company," not a telephone company, nor a music company (although today, iTunes dominates global music distribution). In the worlds of biology, medicine, and chemistry, the evolution toward molecular and nano-level analysis has brought formerly distant disciplinary areas into close adjacency, as in the microRNA example.

Discussion and Conclusions

Cognitive biases and heuristics constitute well-documented hazards for effective decision making, particularly in uncertain, complex, information-constrained, and ambiguous situations like those involved in strategic alliances for open innovation. It is easy to understand that inadequate information or framing a new problem in older domain terms can lead to "fighting the last war," a failure to see disconfirming information or recognize its significance. Limits to what can be held in mind at one time for consideration (Miller, 1956) can exacerbate a tendency to give greater weight to recent insights, facts, or conclusions.

Each of these limitations to unaided decision making can be mitigated by targeted assistance, extending human capability in much the same way that written notes expand memory beyond our brains. Cognitive limits can be remedied by search protocols and decision-support approaches that address them directly. CIMS directed big data analytics (DBDA) extends the expertise of SMEs and mitigates human limits to strategic decision making by bringing directed big data search and analytics to bear, as Table 9.1 illustrates.

The potential for identifying new technologies, partners, markets, materials, or production techniques bodes well for far more proactive strategy—if the cognitive biases and heuristics that limit the consideration of new possibilities can be overcome. BDA and Internet searches clearly provide *more* data; *directed* BDA driven by a cross-disciplinary SME team provides *better, curated data*. SMEs both assess and make use of this data—mining the library, supported by software tools for further filtering and inquiring into topics of interest. These tools easily expand the domain-relevant searches SMEs can do, thus leveraging their capabilities.

Directed BDA requires care and attention to the human dynamics, as well as the information dynamics. Creating a joint project team to manage and evaluate the search process helps to keep it honest by incorporating helpfully divergent views to broadly frame an initial query and search-term dictionaries. Client perspectives are first captured by depicting the existing strategic frame in the format of the analytical hierarchy process (AHP) template, incorporating major factors currently recognized as affecting the client's strategy (Saaty, 2012).[11] Preliminary search terms can be derived from the client's website, well-respected journal articles on the topics of interest, and the like. Then client SMEs critique and elaborate the AHP.

Form a Strong JPT

Even excellent recommendations, not seen as legitimate and relevant by those who must eventually make the decision, will languish. Legitimacy and acceptance are not merely functions of outside expertise; instead, the credibility and stature of the recommenders within the organization is essential. Thus the JPT cannot be simply outsiders, however skilled, nor should it be overly focused by discipline. Instead, a heavyweight team (Clark and Wheelwright, 1992) of cross-disciplinary, experienced, and respected client SMEs, enriched by outside SMEs, assures legitimacy and credibility. (An outside TB control officer joined

Table 9.1 Elements of the CIMS 8 - Step Directed BDA Process

Step	Element	Description
1. Project Selection	a. Joint Project Team	The 8-step process is led by a heavyweight team, the Joint Project Team (JPT). The JPT is "heavyweight" in two respects: First, team members are highly respected, seasoned client managers. Hence, besides their domain expertise, they wield significant organizational influence. Second, heavyweight team leaders are ultimately accountable for the decision, exert direct control over the team and are responsible for integrating their inputs to make the decision. Consensus is sought, but is not necessary. (Kim B. Clark and Steven C. Wheelwright, California Management Review, vol. 34, no. 3, Spring 1992.)
	b. Outside Experts	To help the JPT, CIMS provides outside experts to work on the BDA project. These people are equally heavyweight in their respective fields and offer an un-biased and objective viewpoint that an organization may lack.
	c. Data Scientists	CIMS also provides Data Scientists (specially trained MBA and Ph.D. students) for the duration of the project. The Data Scientists help prepare and operate the CIMS Big Data Analytics Platform.
2. Frame (and Reframe) the Decision	a. Initial Decision Model (Unweighted)	A Decision Model is a graphical representation of the problem (or decision). It depicts the contributing factors, and their relationship in a hierarchical fashion, facilitating their analysis for making the decision. An Initial Decision Model captures "where the company" is at the outset: its strategic commitments and behavior, as derived by CIMS from client websites, for example.
	b. PESTEL Analysis / Decision Model Workshop	In a structured and highly-facilitated Decision Model workshop, designed to expand perspectives on the problem, CIMS faculty guides the JPT in a PESTEL Analysis. The PESTEL Analysis develops an external view of the context in which the organization operates in six major areas: Political, Economic, SocioCultural, Technological, Environmental, and Legal. Data examination drives the workshop discussion to develop shared understanding and insight as to the potential, most likely, and most important effects expected in these areas for the organization, its customers, competitors, and other stakeholders. These external market factors should always be made part of the Decision Model.
	c. Elaborated Decision Model (Weighted)	A weighted decision modeling technique, the Analytical Hierarchy Process (AHP) to represent an Elaborated Decision Model, incorporating preliminary search results with JPT intuitions and expertise. AHP allows the JPT to assign importance , or weight, to contributing decision factors. Spending time to think, discuss, and diagram the Decision Model helps the team to visualize the problem; It forces strategic debate; and this discussion assists the JPT to form consensus over what's important and what's not.

(Continued)

Table 9.1 Elements of the CIMS 8 - Step Directed BDA Process

Step	Element	Description
		The Elaborated Decision Model directs the BDA project. It is used to construct the Decision Criteria, Dictionaries, information Sources, and Rules (Steps 3,4, and 5) used by the NLP computers to search, crawl, parse, filter, and index the data (Step 6); it is used to determine the sufficiency of the data (Step 7); and it is used at the end of the process to visualize the findings that led to the decision in (Step 8). Note: A number of software packages are available to create a Decision Model. (See list of concept and mind mapping software applications at http://en.wikipedia.org/wiki/List_of_concept-_and_mind-mapping_software)
3. Create Dictionary of Key Terms	Search Terms	A Dictionary consistst of key terms (single words or phrases) that are associated with a particular domain. Some terms are common synonyms, but others are the domain-specific "professional language" appropriate to the query. For example, the domain of Tuberculosis Diagnostics would involve terms, like "infectious disease" and "lung disease", but it might also involve terms, like "mycobacterium", "latent TB", "co-morbidity", "multi-disease resistance", "extreme disease resistance", etc." NLP programs will use all the terms to search for and analyze information. Note: A preliminary set of dictionaries can be automatically constructed where NLP computers "parse" (i.e. break into nouns, verbs, adverbs, etc.) an article by a prominent author that "reads on" the problem to be solved, or a client website. It is then an easy task to pick out the most frequently used words the author used to describe a situation. JPT members then suggest missing or alternative search terms.
4. Identify Sources	Information Sources	Information Sources consist of locations that likely contain creditable information relevant to the decision. This information can reside on the internet in the form of company websites, academic websites, government websites, conference proceedings, blogs, wikis,and social media sites Relevant iInformation may also reside in data warehouses inside the company in Call Center logs, Product Quality reports, Customer Satisfaction reports, etc. Preliminary Information Sources become the "seed" sites for the NLP computers to begin their crawls. The NLP computers crawl the seed sites, and they can also be instructed to search adjacent sites and links to distant sites. This "deep web" crawling ability provides comprehensive information regarding the domain and related knowledge areas.

(Continued)

Table 9.1 Elements of the CIMS 8 - Step Directed BDA Process (*Continued*)

Step	Element	Description
5. Search (Automation)	Data Collection	Multiple search engines crawl and scrape the data sources defined in Step 4, creating a raw data collection that can easily exceed 100 million documents. NLP algorithms then parse, filter, and index this data collection in accordance with the Dictionaries developed in Step 3. The resulting curated data collection is presented back to the JPT for real-time analysis and reporting. Note: Collections can be programmed to automatically recrawl the sources at designated frequencies (e.g., once every second or once a year). Each recrawl gathers only the data that is new or changed, creating big data "movies". Using advanced analytical functions, e.g. Time Series, and Trend Analysis, the NLP computers can spot inflections in the data and issue alerts to the JPT to emerging trends and changing BDA from an ad hoc activity to an ongoing discourse with real-time data.
6. Design Rules	Query Rules	Applying Information Science to the search, Data Scientist guide analysis of the collection, designing Query Rules that instruct the NLP computers as to which terms to use to analyze data. Rules can be constructed to compare entire dictionaries, or individual key words and phrases. A rich set of Boolean functions allows the Data Scientist to create "aggregate" rules to combine queries and "mash up" data from millions of previously unrelated documents. Rules represent the "logic" behind the analysis and can be saved, shared, and reused from session to session. Rules in conjunction with additional search words or phrases open the curated database to revealing, detailed "mining."
7. Assess Data	a. Data and Decision Sufficiency Test	The jPT and Data Scientists examine the data to determine its sufficiency for making a decision, scoring for its amount, timeliness, and relevance to the initial query. More sophisticated models can be constructed to examine these factors, as well as the type and source of the data collected (e.g. government, academic, social media, business press, as well as the data internal to the company, etc.). Examination of these initial results can suggest further routes of inquiry: new search terms and new data sources, for example.
	b. Iteration	If the collection is determined to be insufficient, Steps 3 through 7 are repeated in attempt to find the evidence needed to satisfy the initial query's decision criteria. The assessment may also identify flaws in the Elaborated Decision Model itself. Because of the new insights invariably gained from BDA changes to the Model may take the form of adding entirely new decision criteria. At a minimum it may cause the JPT to assign a different importance (weight) to the factors. In these cases Steps 2–7 are repeated. In essence, this step puts the JPT's initial understanding of its domain to the test of real world evidence.

(Continued)

Table 9.1 Elements of the CIMS 8 - Step Directed BDA Process (*Continued*)

Step	Element	Description
8. Score Data on Criteria	a. Decision Support	The JPT read items of interest and discuss the information collected that either supports or refutes each factor in the Decision Model. A pairwise comparison of factors is repeated until the decision outcome becomes apparent as the evidence speaks. Real differences of opinions are noted. While convergence is sought, ultimately the JPT leader makes his/her decision.
	b. Visualization	The decision - and the factors that contributed to it—can be displayed graphically on a dashboard. A number of graphics packages are available for this purpose and Data Scientists can help with this task. CIMS recommends plotting complex strategic decisions in this manner so that the JPT, and ultimately the organization, can readily see the data pattern(s) that support the decision.

the CHAI project, for instance.) Since strategic alliance and open innovation decisions are by their nature large, messy, and complex, resources should also include information specialists. The JPT chooses the research question.

"Frame the Decision" (Step 1) with a Physical Diagram (Decision Model)

Time spent framing the decision is time well spent, since inadequate framing is a critical decision hazard. Facilitated discussion among the multidisciplinary JPT members frames the decision in a structured, hierarchal decision model, with a single clear purpose for the decision and important factors affecting the decision—technology, resource constraints, or regulatory requirements, for example—identified. Factors point to domain areas for search, with decision criteria specified. A well-structured decision model helps keep the JPT coordinated and will help make new relevant data evident. Formally framing the decision in this manner brings order to decision making while it avoids anchoring biases, since incoming data may change this model. The decision frame's factors, and the URLs and search terms derived from them, guide the automated DBDA search process to create the database.

BDA Is Not a Linear Process—Expect to Iterate (Steps 2–7)

The single largest benefit of big data analytics is new learning, driven by new insights arising from the data. These insights can challenge the JPT's original judgments and change their decision model, adding entirely new decision criteria or reassessing the original decision criteria, as unforeseen factors emerge from the data. Such revisions are central to evidence-based strategic decisions and illustrate how cognitive biases can be overcome in uncertain, risky decisions. JPT members can be more confident that their decisions rest on a broad, objective search of relevant domains that incorporates unanticipated links and adjacencies not evident to unaided decision makers.

Of the many software packages available to structure and diagram decisions, we prefer the AHP, a weighted decision-modeling technique that allows the JPT to break complex decisions down into contributing factors. An initial preference or weight is assigned to these factors via systematic, pairwise comparisons. AHP is particularly useful for DBDA because it incorporates both qualitative and quantitative data. AHP also facilitates the rapid examination of changed factor weightings via computer support in live discussions.

The risks and uncertainties of open innovation strategic alliances have much to do with information: where to find partners or possibilities, how to contact them, how they might be assessed against one another in light of strategic interests. Directed BDA bolsters decision quality by providing *more* and *better data* that is *relevant to the specific decision domain* of interest. The automated search process uses the SME-generated search term dictionaries and URLs, plus the links discovered in search, to execute an objective, inclusive, domain-relevant search with prima facie legitimacy. The DBDA's *curated* database is available for deeper analysis by SMEs, via a host of supporting analytics.

These processes enable strategic decision makers to ground their choices in up-to-date, relevant, objective evidence, overcoming information insufficiency in both quantity and quality. The search is inclusive, so representativeness heuristics are overcome; it is objective, so anchoring, adjustment, and availability heuristics are mitigated. A planned sequence of evolving decision models, taking into account new data discovered in the search, helps to avoid premature closure and framing hazards. Coupling this data with the structured decision model, decision makers' decision constraints and uncertainties can be mitigated. In short, BDA directly leverages SME expertise to reduce uncertainty and risk in strategic alliance-formation decisions, supporting better strategic decisions.

Notes

1. For a contemporary summary of cognitive limits for strategic decisions, see Bazerman, M. H., and D. A. Moore, *Judgment in Managerial Decision Making* (New York: Wiley, 2012).
2. See http://www.emc.com/leadership/digital-universe/iview/big-data-2020.htm (accessed September 8, 2013).
3. See http://www.ideaconnection.com/outsourcing/, which lists some 25 "open innovation intermediaries," web-based connection resources, including InnoCentive, Yet2.com, NineSigma, and Chaordix.
4. CIMS, The Center of Innovation Management Studies (CIMS), located at the Poole College of Management, NC State University: initially founded 30 years ago as an NSF-funded Industry-University Collaborative Research Center, CIMS continues today as an industry-funded research collaborative.
5. IBM's Content Analysis (ICA) software crawls the web, searching instances of relevant terms, following website links down (specified numbers of levels), capturing

content; then the software eliminates duplicates and filters, parses, and indexes the resulting hits to create a searchable database.

6. IBM Content Analysis (ICA) software.
7. In NC State's High Performance Computing Lab.
8. Search parameters are in **bold face.**
9. The *disability-adjusted life year* (DALY) is a measure of overall disease burden, expressed as the number of years lost due to ill-health, disability, or early death (Wikipedia). (Please include a URL and access date.)
10. See http://miami.cbslocal.com/2013/08/31/more-cases-of-dengue-fever-in-south-florida/ (Please include an access date.)
11. AHP captures high-level factors (e.g., "technology"); then discussion fleshes these out (e.g., genomics or miRNA) in greater detail and specificity.

References

Arbesman, Samuel. (August 16, 2013). "Five Myths about big Data." *Washington Post.* http://articles.washingtonpost.com/2013-08-16/opinions/41416362_1_big-data-data-crunching-marketing-analytics. (Accessed August 16, 2013).

Boisot, Max, Nordberg, Marcus, Yami, S., and Nicquevert, B. (2011). *Collision and Collaborations: Organizational Learning in the ATLAS Experiment at the LHC.* Oxford: Oxford Univerity Press.

Bruner, Jerome S., and Postman, Leo. (1949–50). "On the Perception of Incongruity: A Paradigm." *Journal of Personality* 18(September 1949–June 1950): 206–23.

Chandler, Jr., Alfred D. (1977). *The Visible Hand: The Managerial Revolution in American Business.* Cambridge: Harvard University Press.

Clark, Kim B., and Wheelwright, Steven C. (1992). "Organizing and Leading 'Heavyweight' Development Teams. *California Management Review* 34 (3): 9–28.

Cukier, Kenneth Neil, and Mayer-Schoenberger, Viktor. (2013). "The Rise of Big Data: How It's Changing the Way We Think about the World." *Foreign Affairs Vol. 92, No. 3* (May/June).

Culpan, Refik. (2002). *Global Business Alliances: Theory and Practice.* Westport, CT: Quorum Books.

Culpan, Refik (ed.). (2011). *Multinational Strategic Alliances* :Haworth Press, Binghampton, NY.

Davenport, Thomas H., and Dyché, Jill. (2013). "Big Data in Big Companies: International Institute for Analytics." Research report, SAS: URL: http://www.sas.com/reg/gen/corp/2266746)

Donald, Merlin. (1991). *Origins of the Modern Mind: Three Stages in the Evolution of Culture and Cognition.* Cambridge, MA: Harvard University Press.

Doz, Yves L., and Hamel, Gary. (1998). *The Alliance Advantage.* Boston, MA: Harvard Business School Press.

Doz, Yves, Santos, Jose, and Williamson, Peter. (2001). *From Global to Metanational: How Companies Win in the Knowledge Economy.* Boston, MA: Harvard Business School Press.

Ellonen, Hanna-Kaisa, Wikstrom, Patrik, and Jantunen, Ari. (2009). "Linking Dynamic-Capability Portfolios and Innovation Outcomes." *Technovation* 29 (11): 753–62.

Frederich, Mary Jo, and Andrews, Peter. (2010). *Innovation Passport: The IBM First-of-a-Kind (FOAK) Journey from Research to Reality.* Upper Saddle, NJ: IBM Press- Pearson PLC.

Gassmann, Oliver, and Enkel, Ellen. (2004). *Towards a Theory of Open Innovation: Three.* Paper presented at the *R&D Management Conference*, Lisbon, Portugal, July 7–9, 2004.

Hagel III, John, Brown, John Seeley, and Jelinek, Mariann. (2011). "Relational Networks, Strategic Advantage: New Challenges for Collaborative Control." In S. B. Sitkin, L. B. Cardinal, and K. Bijlsma-Frankema (eds.), *Organizational Control.* Cambridge, UK: Cambridge University Press, pp.251–300.

Hagel III, John, and Brown, John Seely. (2005). *The Only Sustainable Edge: Why Business Strategy Depends on Productive Friction and Dynamic Specialization.* Boston: Harvard Business School Press.

Hesseldahl, Arik. (2013). "Think Big Data Is All Hype? You're Not Alone." All Things D. http://allthingsd.com/20130819/think-big-data-is-all-hype-youre-not-alone/ Accessed June 9, 2014.

Huston, Larry, and Sakkab, Nabil. (2006). "Connect and Develop: Inside Procter & Gamble's New Model for Innovation." *Harvard Busiess Review* 23 (3): 58–66.

Kahneman, D., Slovic, P., and Tversky, A. (1982). *Judgment under Uncertainty: Heuristics and Biases.* Cambridge: Cambridge University Press.

Kahneman, Daniel, and Tversky, Amos. (1979). "Prospect Theory: An Analysis of Decision under Risk." *Econometrica* 47 (2): 263–92.

Kogut, Bruce, and Zander, U. (1992). "Knowledge of the Firm, Combinative Capabilities and the Replication of Technology." *Organization Science* 3 (3): 383–97.

Manyika, J., Chui, M., Brown, B., Bughin, J., Dobbs, R., Rosburg, C., and Hung Byers, A. (2011). "Big Data: The Next Frontier for Innovation, Competition, and Productivity." *McKinsey Global Institute.* : McKinsey & Company, New York, 1–143.

March, James G., and Simon, Herbert A. (1959). *Organizations.* New York: John Wiley and Sons.

Markham, S. K., Baumer, D., Aiman-Smith, Linda, Kingon, Angus, and Zapata, Michael. (2000). "An Algorithm for High Technology Engineering and Management." *Journal of Engineering Education* 89 (209), 209-218.

Markham, Steven, Kingon, Angus, Lewis, R., and Zapata, M. (2002). "The University's Role in Creating Radically New Products." *International Journal of Technology Transfer and Commercialization* 1 (1–2): 163–72.

Maule, A. John, Hodgkinson, Gerard P., and Bown, Nicola J. (2003). "Cognitive Mapping of Causal Reasoning in Strategic Decision Making." In D. Hardman and L. Macchi (eds.), *Thinking: Psychological Perspectives on Reasoning, Judgment and Decision Making*, 253–72. Chichester, UK: John Wiley & Sons.

Miller, G. A. (1956). "The Magic Number Seven Plus or Minus Two: Some Limits on our Capacity to Process Information." *Psychological Review* 64 (2): 81–97.

Murtha, T. P., and Lenway, S. A. (1994). "Country Capabilities and the Strategic State: How National Political Institutions Affect Multinational Corporations' Strategies." *Strategic Management Journal* 15 (Special Issue): 113–29.

Quinn, James Brian. (1999). "Strategic Outsourcing: Leveraging Knowledge Capabilities." *Sloan Management Review* 44 (4): 9–22.

Quinn, James Brian. (2000). "Outsourcing Innovation: The New Engine of Growth." *Sloan Management Review,* 41(4): 13–28.

Quinn, James Brian, and Hilmer, Frederick G. (1994). "Strategic Outsourcing." *Sloan Management Review* 35 (4): 43–55.

Rabinow, Paul. (1996). *Making PCR: A Story of Biotechnology.* Chicago: University of Chicago Press.

Saaty, Thomas L. (2012). *Decision Making for Leaders: The Analytical Hierarchy Process for Decisions in a Complex World*, 5th ed. Pittsburgh, PA: RWS Publications.

Safire, William (February 5, 2009). "Fat Tail," in On Language. *New York Times Magazine*, p. MM24.

Sakkab, Nabil Y. (2002). "Connect & Develop Complements: Research and Development at P&G." *Research Technology Management* 45:38–45.

Simon, Herbert A. (1950). *Administrative Behavior*. New York: Macmillan.

Simon, Herbert A. (1956). "Rational Choice and the Structure of the Environment." *Psychological Review* 63:129–38.

Simon, Herbert A. (1957). *Models of Man: Social and Rational*. New York: Wiley.

Svenson, O. (1999). "Differentiation and Consolidation Theory: Decision Making Processes before and after a Choice." In P. J. H. Montgomery (ed.), *Judgment and Decision Making: Neo-Brunswikian and Process-Tracing Approaches*, 175–97. Mahweh, NJ: Erlbaum.

Tversky, Amos, and Kahenman, Daniel. (1982). "Judgments of and by Representativeness." In D. Kahenman, P. Slovic, and A. Tversky (eds.), *Judgement under Uncertainty: Heuristics and Biases*. (84-100).New York: Cambridge University Press. Tversky, Amos, and Kahneman, Daniel. (1974). "Judgement under Uncertainty: Heuristics and Biases." *Science* 185:1124–31.

Williams, Ruth. (2013). "Different Cancers, Same Mutations: Scientists Document Common Genetic Alterations in Cancers of Different Origins." *The Scientist*. URL: http://www.the-scientist.com/?articles.view/articleNo/37661/title/Different-Cancers--Same-Mutations/; accessed June 9 2014.

Womack, James P., Jones, Daniel T., and Roos, Daniel. (1990). *The Machine That Changed the World*. New York: Rawson Associates.

Yong, Ed. (2013). "Genomes Reveal Roots of TB Drug Resistance: Tuberculosis Strains Evolve by Gradually Acquiring Subtle Mutations." *Nature Nature News* doi:10.1038/nature.2013.13645 (URL: http://www.nature.com/news/genomes-reveal-roots-of-tb-drug-resistance-1.13645; accessed June 9, 2014).

Zander, U., and Kogut, Bruce. (1995). "Knowledge and the Speed of the Transfer and Imitation of Organizational Capabilities: An Empirical Test." *Organization Science* 6:1–17.

CHAPTER 10

Open Innovation and KIBS Start-Ups: Technology- and Market-Based Alliance Portfolio Configurations

Brian V. Tjemkes, Eduard H. de Pinéda,
Marc D. Bahlmann, Ard-Pieter de Man,
Alexander S. Alexiev

Introduction

Firms are increasingly relying on combining internal resources with external knowledge to sustain firm renewal, which has led to open innovation being considered critical to a firm's competitive advantage (Chesbrough, 2003). Successful open innovation produces first-mover advantages, superior financial returns, market growth, and market share (Lichtenhaler, 2011). In particular, knowledge-intensive business services (KIBS) start-ups—defined as "[new] expert companies that provide services to other companies and organizations" (Toivonen, 2006, 2)—rely on open innovation, as it is their primary knowledge input and output (Gallouj, 2002). However, KIBS start-ups are exposed to extant uncertainty because they face risk in the form of liability of newness, liability of smallness, and fundamental uncertainty. This uncertainty can be mitigated via a firm's portfolio of alliance relationships (Ozcan and Eisenhardt, 2009).

Open innovation at the firm level manifests through two distinct processes, which are often referred to as *outbound exploitative* and *inbound explorative* innovation. Prior literature on innovation and learning has emphasized the importance of combining both processes in a balanced manner (e.g., He and Wong, 2004; Jansen, Van Den Bosch, and Volberda, 2006; Lavie, Stettner, and Tushman, 2010). However, analyzing innovation exclusively in terms of inbound exploration and outbound exploitation will create ambiguities, given that both concepts can be performed at numerous firm functions (Salinger, 1989), including upstream activities, such as R&D, and downstream activities, such as marketing. Allocating exploratory and exploitative learning to both downstream and upstream functions adds a certain nuance that has been structurally overlooked in the exploration-exploitation debate and provides a more fine-grained view on realizing ambidexterity (Garcia and Calantone, 2002; Gupta, Smith, and Shalley, 2006).

Researchers are increasingly adopting the alliance portfolio perspective in order to explain a variety of firm performance outcomes (Lavie and Rosenkopf, 2006), including innovation. Although prior studies have identified relevant and used equivalent portfolio-configuration dimensions, they have also reported conflicting results. For example, whereas Stefan Wuyts and Shantanu Dutta (2012) found that alliance portfolio *diversity* exerts a U-shaped effect on innovation performance, Leon Oerlemans, Joris Knoben, and Marthinus Pretorius (2013) reported an inverted U-shaped effect between alliance portfolio diversity and both exploration and exploitation outcomes. Such conflicting findings create an obstacle when theorizing the role that alliance portfolio configuration plays in terms of reaching a state of ambidexterity, which can be defined as reaching an optimal balance between exploratory and exploitative outcomes. This issue is particularly salient in the context of KIBS, as such firms should configure their alliance portfolio in order to support their exploratory and exploitative innovation objectives simultaneously.

To address these issues, the present study aims to disentangle the relationship between alliance portfolio configuration and ambidexterity, while recognizing that knowledge-intensive business services' (KIBS) alliance portfolios are manifested in both the upstream and downstream domain. To this end, we conducted four case studies of innovative KIBS start-ups that use their alliance portfolio to explore and exploit in both upstream and downstream domains. This method derived two types of open innovation activities: (1) seeking ambidexterity by exploration in the upstream and exploitation in the downstream domain (henceforth, *technology-based innovation*) and (2) seeking ambidexterity by exploitation in the upstream and exploration in the downstream domain (henceforth, *market-based innovation*). The results indicate that if optimal performance (that is, ambidexterity) is to be realized in either type of innovation orientation, certain alliance portfolio configuration parameters—most notably, alliance portfolio diversity—must be taken into account.

This study contributes to the open innovation literature by showing that, by taking downstream and upstream functions into account, research on subtypes of knowledge-intensive business services' alliance portfolios reconciles the alleged incompatibility of simultaneous exploration and exploitation. In so doing, we overcome issues of simplification, such as one-dimensional and aggregated portfolio configurations (Wassmer, 2010). The present study also enriches the alliance portfolio literature by highlighting how portfolio configurations that differ in terms of diversity and size can foster either technology- or market-based innovations in a KIBS context.

The remainder of this chapter is structured as follows. We start with a theoretical background that sketches the research context and core logic, and provides knowledge of the concepts applied in the study. We then describe the research methodology, including the research design, operational definitions, data collection, and data analysis. Third, the case study results are provided and propositions are developed. The final part of this chapter provides the discussion, the implications of the study, future research, and conclusions.

Theoretical Background

Open Innovation, Exploration, and Exploitation

Firms across industries are increasingly embracing the concept of open innovation (Chesbrough, 2003), which we define as "systematically relying on a firm's . . . capabilities of internally and externally carrying out the major technology tasks . . . across the innovation process" (Lichtenthaler, 2008, 148). The adoption of open innovation practices can be seen as a break from traditional approaches to innovation, which tended to be more internally oriented (Ahlstrom, 2010; March, 1991). As such, the concept of innovation can be turned into a continuum, one end of which is characterized by much more closed approaches and the other end of which comprises very open approaches (Trott and Hartmann, 2009). Therefore, open innovation should be understood as combining internal innovation activities with external ones (Chesbrough, 2003).

In open innovation literature, this distinction has become known as the *outside-in* (or inbound) process versus the *inside-out* (or outbound) process. An outside-in approach to open innovation involves opening up the innovation process to exploratory learning by acquiring new knowledge from external partners. A firm using an inside-out approach engages in exploitative learning with external partners, for instance through licensing technology (Lichtenthaler, 2011). Interorganizational relationships, such as alliances, represent a prime source of open innovation practices because they allow organizations to extend their internal knowledge base (Grant and Baden-Fuller, 2004). Therefore, the open innovation concept should be seen as a trend toward becoming involved in interorganizational innovation (Vanhaverbeke, Van de Vrande, and Chesbrough, 2008), while also relying on intraorganizational innovation processes in order to ensure sufficient absorptive capacity (Cohen and Levinthal, 1990).

Nowadays, many firms rely on inbound, exploratory processes of innovation as well as outbound, exploitative processes (Lichtenthaler, 2011). Successfully engaging in both exploratory and exploitative learning simultaneously is challenging but critical (March, 1991; Gupta et al., 2006). On the one hand, knowledge exploitation enables organizations to acquire "reliability in experiences," leading to increased "productivity, refinement, routinization, production, and elaboration of existing experiences" (Holmqvist, 2003, 99). Knowledge exploration, on the other hand, allows organizations to develop "variety in experiences" (ibid.) by experimenting and innovating, thereby complementing the limitations of knowledge exploitation. Where past literature has tended to treat the exploration-exploitation dichotomy as an "either-or" decision (He and Wong,

2004), open innovation research seeks to integrate both processes of innovation. Essentially, firms that seek to enhance both inbound, exploratory and outbound, exploitative innovation are confronted with the challenge of building a portfolio of alliances that can fulfill both objectives (Wassmer, 2010).

Open Innovation through Alliances: An Alliance Portfolio Perspective

An alliance portfolio enables a firm to focus on its core competences while accessing external resources through alliance partners (Wassmer, 2010), and also to mitigate strategic uncertainty (Eisenhardt and Schoonhoven, 1996). A firm thus may proactively configure an alliance portfolio in order to attain its strategic goals. A prominent part of the literature focuses on portfolio size (Ahuja, 2000; Hoffmann, 2007), portfolio structure (Ahuja, 2000), and both relational and partner characteristics (Hoffmann, 2007; Lavie, 2007). Recently, an additional approach has been added to this list of configuration-based perspectives, focusing on the diversity of alliance portfolios and its relationship to firm performance (Jiang, Tao, and Santoro, 2010; Wuyts and Dutta, 2012).

Achieving alliance portfolio diversity depends on what type of partners are incorporated in the portfolio and, related to this, what type of portfolio orientation is required in order for the focal firm to achieve its open innovation goals. Following Ruihua Joy Jiang and colleagues (2010), we have approached alliance portfolio diversity as a multidimensional construct, defined as the degree of variance in partners, functional purposes, and governance structures of the alliances. *Partner diversity* captures the variance in resources and capabilities as well as knowledge and technologies, while *functional diversity* captures the variance in the functional background of alliances in terms of value chain activities, and *governance diversity* captures the variance in the governance type of the alliances involved (Jiang et al., 2010; Goerzen and Beamish, 2005). All three types of alliance portfolio diversity are inherently and simultaneously present in any given alliance portfolio and are expected to influence both inbound exploratory and outbound exploitative innovation processes.

Inbound exploratory learning inherently aims to achieve discontinuous learning and experimentation (Simsek, 2009), which implies a dependence on variation or diversity rather than uniformity. Therefore, exploratory learning is expected to thrive when supported by an alliance portfolio characterized by high levels of diversity. The potential value of diversity in relation to explorative learning lies in the following two points. First, a focal firm with an alliance portfolio characterized by partner diversity is expected to reach more heterogeneity in its problem-solving arsenal (Simsek, 2009), as it is allowed to consider multiple perspectives in its search for a solution. Second, this will enable the organization to develop more advanced capabilities when dealing with a wide range of perspectives. A set of heterogeneous contacts (that is, contacts holding varying social positions and characteristics) broadens the scope of knowledge available. This contrasts sharply with an alliance portfolio made up of relatively homogeneous organizations, such as when all organizations are active in the same industry.

Such a scenario would not allow the focal firm to consider multiple perspectives on an issue, as alliance portfolio members would be more likely to regard their environment similarly (Simsek, 2009); this would limit the focal firm's potential for explorative learning.

Exploitative learning differs fundamentally from explorative learning and should be addressed accordingly. As noted above, exploitative learning is characterized by routinized, standardized learning processes because it aims to refine and extend existing technologies or capabilities. When considering the characteristics of exploitative, outbound innovation, it is important to realize that "exploiting interesting ideas often thrives on commitment more than thoughtfulness, narrowness more than breadth, cohesiveness more than openness" (March, 1991, 280) and therefore requires an efficient portfolio organization characterized by centralization and tight cultures (Jansen et al., 2006). A high level of alliance portfolio diversity is likely to conflict with the production of an efficient portfolio aimed at exploitative learning. The reason for this is to be found in the difficulty and complexity of governance associated with high levels of alliance portfolio diversity. Processes of inbound exploitation are likely to be hampered by the presence of procedural differences (Simsek, 2009), and it is more difficult to monitor and manage advances in the network. Also, the costs of knowledge integration are likely to rise with an increase in portfolio diversity, which implies a shift away from the desired level of portfolio efficiency required for successful knowledge exploitation.

Seeking Ambidexterity in the Upstream and Downstream Domains

Given that all learning actions of a firm can be abstracted to exploration and exploitation, all of a firm's functions can be condensed into two core elements: upstream and downstream (Kwok and Reeb, 2000). *Upstream firm functions* are defined as those "that involve the production of a good" (Salinger, 1989, 374), whereby a *good* is defined as "a scarce economic resource" in the broadest sense of the word, rather than just tangible manufactured goods. *Downstream firm functions* are defined as those "involving the buyer-seller relationship" (ibid.), including marketing, sales, and distribution. This distinction between upstream and downstream domains enables us to distinguish between two types of innovation: technology-based and market-based (see Figure 10.1).

Akin to the notion of inbound exploration and outbound exploitation, technology-based innovation combines upstream exploratory learning and downstream exploitative learning (Garcia and Calantone, 2002). Exploratory learning on upstream functions requires complex basic research. As such, the creation of state-of-the-art technology requires significant investments, and innovation outcomes are unstable (Damanpour, 1991). Some technology-based innovations can provide the basis for new technological platforms, while others are technological dead ends. Those that do succeed as the bases for new platforms may vie to become the dominant design and become widely accepted industry standards (Anderson and Tushman, 1990). Technology-based innovations on the

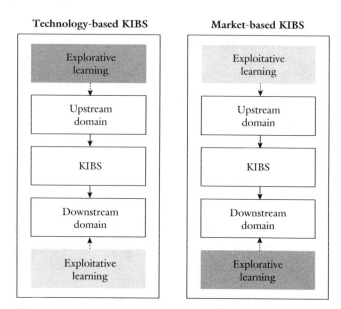

Figure 10.1 Technology- and Market-Based KIBS

downstream side are achieved through a market push strategy, through which firms can often draw on available markets with existing customers and proven and commercially available marketing tools.

Market-based innovation involves the creation of a new market (Garcia and Calantone, 2002) and the combination of downstream exploration and upstream exploitation. Downstream exploration is less complex than the upstream exploration associated with technology-based innovation and involves connecting the supply and demand of unconnected parts of the value chain (Bresser, Heuskel, and Nixon, 2000), as opposed to the often intangible, tacit, complex, uncertain, unstable, and costly process of new technology development. Although market-based innovations are risky, given that firms can only *estimate* the size of new markets (Hamel and Prahalad 1994), new market offerings can only be successful if they offer new segments of value in comparison to matured markets. Upstream exploitation occurs through a market pull strategy, which is created in a relatively straightforward manner, technology-wise, using existing off-the-shelf technologies.

The above suggests that the distinction between upstream and downstream innovation offers several advantages for firms as they create stability in the learning balance (that is, ambidexterity) of the firm. The first advantage is that firms generating new knowledge via explorative learning on either upstream or downstream functions may experience a first-mover advantage. Second, technology-based or market-based innovation is developed and commoditized more rapidly than radical innovation (that is, explorative upstream and downstream learning), as these two innovation types involve single-sided exploitation. This point appears to be imperative as the frequency with which firms innovate is correlated to firm performance (Soni, Lilien, and Wilson, 1993); a continuous stream of innovations enables a firm to stay ahead of its competition. It is especially relevant to KIBS, as service innovations are difficult to secure via intellectual patent protection due to the classic characteristics of services (Fitzsimmons and Fitzsimmons, 2006).

It remains unclear how inbound explorative and outbound exploitative learning can be optimally produced simultaneously by actively and purposefully addressing alliance portfolio configuration. Distinguishing two domains in a firm's alliance portfolio (that is, upstream and downstream functions) makes it possible for firms to pursue both types of innovation in either the upstream or downstream domain. Rather than pursuing both by means of one integral alliance portfolio, ambidexterity is achieved across the upstream and downstream domain. To explore this issue further, we have developed the following research question:

How can KIBS configure their alliance portfolios in the upstream and downstream domains in order to realize ambidexterity and successfully develop and commoditize technology-based or market-based innovations?

Methods and Case Description

To answer the research question, we have adopted an exploratory case study approach. According to Kathleen Eisenhardt (1989) and Robert Yin (2003), there are three reasons why this design is appropriate for theory building and for answering the research question: (1) it helps to answer "how" questions; (2) it mobilizes numerous observations on complicated processes; and (3) it attracts meaning from a variety of interconnected levels of analysis. We followed case study research procedures to ensure the validity of the research design (Eisenhardt, 1989; Yin, 2003). More specifically, based on our research question, we developed a semistructured interview guide (i.e., indicators), we created a rich data set by means of interviews and documents, and we moved from data to theory building following case study guidelines.

Research Setting

We conducted four case studies of KIBS. Each company depicts a recent Dutch-based start-up that built its core competence on information and communication technology (ICT) and operates internationally. The companies are relatively small and young (operating for between six months and two years). As in many alliance studies, the partners' real names cannot be revealed, even though doing so would have enhanced the methodological rigor of the study. Also, in our study, the real names of companies are not revealed for the purpose of confidentiality.

There are four main reasons why these four cases are appropriate for the purpose of this study. First, in keeping with our definition of KIBS, each company depicts a business service company in which knowledge constitutes a critical input as well as output. Second, consistent with our KIBS classification, two companies engage in technology-based innovation, as they compete in existing markets with newly developed technologies (that is, software). Two other companies engage in market-based innovation, as they create a new market by bundling and connecting existing technologies. Third, we selected a high-performing and a low-performing company for each innovation type. Fourth, these cases were appropriate because the research team had good access to the companies involved.

Data Collection

The data was collected retrospectively by means of interviews based on a semi-structured interview guide (see Appendix 1). Such retrospective data collection reduced the danger of data overload and collection of unusable data (Poole et al., 2000). However, documenting cases retrospectively also has certain disadvantages. For instance, respondents tend to filter out events that are less relevant to them or that render their story less coherent (ibid.). In order to improve the validity of these retrospective reports and prevent respondent bias, we applied the following strategies. First, the data was triangulated using interviews and documents. Second, the informants were asked to reflect on concrete situations (that is, portfolio dimensions) rather than abstract concepts, in order to reduce the risk of cognitive bias and impression management (Miller, Cardinal, and Glick, 1997). Third, we verified individual reports by posing similar questions to different informants.

Each interview was conducted face-to-face and in the native language of the interviewee in order to maximize his or her ability to express thoughts, feelings, and opinions (see Table 10.1 for an overview). All interviews were conducted with individuals who had extensive knowledge of the firm's strategy, such as founders, CEOs, CTOs, and business development managers. The average length of the interviews was 90 minutes. All of the interviews were taped and transcribed in order to increase the verifiability of the research and to make it possible to analyze the collected data in a systematic manner. At this stage, we

Table 10.1 Overview of Interviewees

#	Ref	Firm[1]	Position
1	A1.	VC3world	Founder/CEO
2	A2.	VC3world	CTO
3	B1.	H&L	Cofounder/CFO
4	B2.	H&L	Business developer
5	B3.	H&L	Buyer
6	C1.	FINFAST	General manager
7	C2.	FINFAST	Business developer
8	D1.	FINLEG	Business developer & head of market surveillance
9	D2.	FINLEG	Business developer & head of market surveillance

[1]The real names of companies are kept confidential.

reexamined all available documents to verify whether the content of the interviews was consistent with that of the documents and also to support the perceptions of the interviewees regarding the reliability of their perceptions. When discrepancies occurred among the data sources, the respondents were contacted for additional information.

Data Analysis

The research consisted of two phases. During the first phase, semistructured interviews were held with the purpose of constructing the alliance portfolio. We also gathered relevant documents to ensure data triangulation (Yin, 2003). As

Table 10.2 Indicators of Key Variables

Variable	Indicator	Example quote
Performance	The success of the company, including innovation, is captured by growth, profit, turnover, etc.	"We are not self-sufficient . . . If we're not able to cover our costs we won't survive as . . . Well, then maybe the community as well will disappear." (A1)
Alliance portfolio size	The number of alliances a focal firm has and the size of the alliances gives an indication of the size of the alliance portfolio	"To do this you need a number of players." (D1) "Our business works, because we actively build and invests in our partners." (B1)
Industry diversity	Industry diversity within a firm's alliance portfolio; determined by the main industry focus of a partner	"To make this work, we need to work with [upstream] partners that have experience in the financial industry, otherwise it would be too complex." (D2)
Nationality diversity	Nationality diversity within a firm's alliance portfolio; determined by the nation in which the headquarters is located	"The probability that you partner with an international company is greater than partnering with a domestic one. Some larger traders operate in the Netherlands, but the key ones operate in London." (D1)
Organizational diversity	Organizational size differences within a firm's alliance portfolio; determined by the relative size of a partner (turnover, employees)	"The larger a supplier [upstream], more power it has. We break with industry conventions, larger suppliers are reluctant to work with us." (B3)
Functional diversity:	Functional diversity within a firm's alliance portfolio, if an alliance is characterized as upstream or downstream	"We developed our primarily technology in-house, some help from externals, but now we partner primarily with two financial institutes [upstream] and a client [downstream]." (C1)
Governance diversity	Governance diversity within a firm's alliance portfolio; examples of governance forms are, for example, contractual or equity alliances	"Our [downstream] supplier relationships are based on goodwill. Although, we recognize the risk of liability suits, we just have a simple contract." (B2)

Sources: Jiang et al., 2010; Oerlemans et al., 2013; Ozcan and Eisenhardt, 2009; Wassmer, 2010.

interviewees described the alliance portfolios, we asked additional "why" and "how" questions in order to obtain a better view of the consequences of the portfolio configuration. Table 10.2 provides an overview of indicators and examples quotes. To ensure construct validity, Robert Yin (2003) suggests data triangulation with secondary data; whenever possible, the researcher rechecked the data via websites or external documents.

During the second phase, we examined the data and moved from data analysis to theory building. Consistent with case study research recommendations (Yin, 2003), we adopted a two-step data analysis procedure. In the first step, each member of the research team analyzed the data individually. Comparing the results revealed some initial discrepancies, which were resolved by returning to the data, contacting the interviewees, and conducting discussions. In the second step, we moved to a more theoretical level, building on the data and the results of the first step to arrive at an explanatory framework that enabled us to answer the research question. As data analysis progressed, we also contrasted the findings with prior literature, which led to certain propositions.

Findings

This section describes each case company's background, business service innovation, and portfolio configuration. Figure 10. 2 illustrates each case's alliance portfolio configuration.

Market-Based Innovation Cases

Case 1: VC3world
VC3world (Venture Capital 3rd World) was formally established in 2011 and provides an online media and communication platform to mediate between investors and entrepreneurs in Africa. Whereas microfinancing has been successfully implemented in Africa, VC3world's owners identified a persistent financial need among start-up entrepreneurs, so it mediates between venture capitalists and African entrepreneurs who require investments ranging from $10,000 to $1 million. The company is best characterized as a KIBS with market-based innovation. It uses existing and commercially available technologies, such as LinkedIn, WordPress, and Ning, to offer a new and innovative service to African entrepreneurs. As one interviewee stated: "We basically started building the network on social media channels, like LinkedIn and Twitter and Facebook and platforms like this . . . We've leveraged open-source WordPress and platforms as much as we're able to do that . . . The investor is someone who is willing to become sort of an active coach, an active partner in building a new company. That's something that is still very nascent in the African context" (A1).

The online mediation technology has been transformed into a business service concept that is offered to potential users, entrepreneurs, and venture capitalists. However, although it has entered the market, start-up performance remains behind expectations. More specifically, the company remains dependent on

10.2a VC3world: Market-based KIBS / low performance

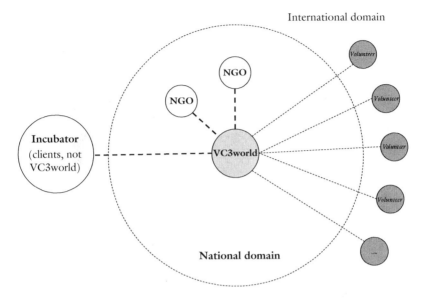

10.2b H&L: Market-based KIBS / high performance

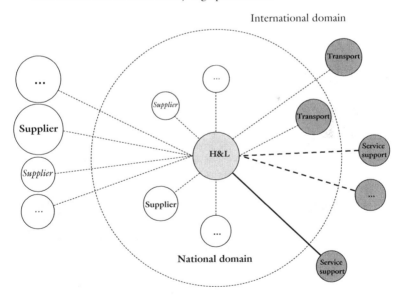

Figure 10.2   Alliance Portfolio Configurations

Note: Size of partner firm(s) circle depicts organization size; white circle depicts upstream partner, gray circle depicts downstream partner; dotted line depicts nonequity relationship; solid line depicts equity relationship; thickness of the line represents the degree of integration between the focal firm and the partner; ". . ." depicts multiple similar partners are part of the alliance portfolio.

10.2c FINFAST: Technology-based KIBS / low
performance

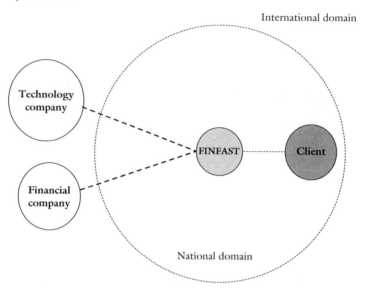

10.2d FINLEG: Technology-based KIBS / high
performance

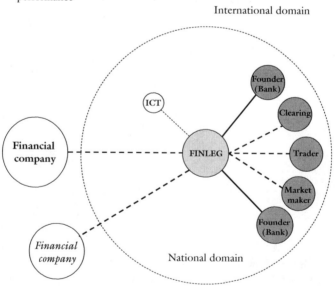

Figure 10.2   Alliance Portfolio Configurations

external funding. As the CEO stated: "Our monthly burn rate is still too high, we are not self-sufficient" (A1).

Figure 10.2a contains the visualization of VC3world's alliance portfolio. Three alliances that have been created with upstream partners enable VC3world to develop and market its online mediation technology. Two of those alliances are with domestic nongovernmental organizations (NGOs) and are governed by simple nonequity contracts. These alliances contributed knowledge about African contacts and local contacts, as well as start-up funding for VC3world. In the international domain, the company created one nonequity alliance with an incubator that provides venture capital, thus providing funds to be used by start-up African entrepreneurs.

The downstream domain of the alliance portfolio consists primarily of informal relationships with volunteers and officers who actively approach clients. These partners represent VC3world in local markets. Although VC3world recognized the importance of creating a large set of potential entrepreneurs, the sheer size of the African continent was too large to cover; each country has unique characteristics, and a "one-size-fits-all" approach was unlikely to work. Despite this barrier, VC3world considered its network of representatives and users (that is, clients) as an important source of information. The rationale behind the decision to enter the market with volunteers promoting VC3world's online service is explained as follows: "You know, we try to cover as many different industries in Africa as possible, to get the word out and create momentum for the site. We are an early-stage startup; we only can afford to have a limited focus. As such, we use officers, clients that volunteer" (A2).

Consequently, VC3world experienced serious difficulties in terms of expanding its market. Promising downstream partners demanded that the technology work flawlessly and felt it was too risky to ally with a start-up venture. Despite being confronted with limited possibilities for partnerships with other (large) firms, VC3world decided to launch and expand its platform. As one interviewee stated: "I think one of the things that we've tried to do is to avoid partnerships in the early stages to some extent, because they can also be extremely distracting if they're not part of the core of what it is that you're trying to do. I've tried a similar partnership [venture capital] with an organization in Uganda that didn't work out" (A1).

In summary, VC3world successfully developed a new online mediation technology for use in Africa. Its alliances with upstream partners enabled it to source the knowledge it required to enhance the online platform. However, launching the technology via a surplus of informal downstream relationships inhibited its performance. This suggests that the portfolio configuration appears to be inconsistent with VC3world's strategy, which could inhibit the company's effort to successfully achieve ambidexterity in its alliance portfolio configuration and market its service.

Case 2: H&L
H&L was established in mid-2011 by a venture capitalist who takes innovative Internet concepts that have been used successfully by rivals in other geographical

markets and launches them in carefully selected geographical markets. H&L offers an online store for customers interested in home and living products, the foundation of which was adopted from a US-based online web shop. H&L applies a "flash sale" business model, which means that products are only on sale for one week. H&L can be considered highly successful due to its rapid growth since its launch; it currently has approximately three million active members and forecasts predict a steady increase in members. H&L is best characterized as a market-based KIBS because it engages in explorative learning (launching a new online web-shop concept) in the downstream domain and engages in exploitative learning in the upstream domain (leveraging existing web-shop technology). The following statements were made by two interviewees: "H&L is good at using a fragmented market to create a new business model enhanced via social media and a high community-based feeling . . . There are fashion firms that sell some home and living products, but we are the first with a specific focus on home and living" (B2). "We use a ready-made program, XCart [off-the-shelf web shop]; it has certain limitations as it is built to be used by smaller firms and is not optimized for larger organizations. I think HQ intends to enhance the software package" (B3).

Figure 10.2b visualizes the alliance portfolio. The alliance portfolio within the national domain consists of multiple upstream ties (suppliers) that are governed via nonequity agreements. H&L's success results from the quality and quantity of procured products, hence the large number of suppliers. H&L attempts to diverge from traditional business models; as such, it has forged flexible nonequity relationships. It also seeks to avoid complex contracts in order to be able to react quickly to competitors' moves. Internationally, H&L seeks to procure its resources locally, also through nonequity partnerships. As one interviewee stated: "The Belgian market is being addressed by H&L Netherlands; this is due to synergy reasons, as both are neighboring countries, are relatively small, and have a common language. You can see this in various countries, including the Scandinavian countries—Sweden, Norway, and Finland—and Switzerland is being served by Germany" (B1).

H&L's alliance portfolio is moderately diverse in terms of the organizational size of its partners, specifically upstream. Large-sized suppliers are reserved about partnering with H&L, as its ambitions of becoming the largest home and living website involve breaking with traditional industry conventions. Suppliers of industry incumbents prefer to use traditional channels, instead of participating in new and relatively unknown Internet-based retailing.

At the national domain, H&L has also forged two medium-sized downstream alliances. It has one nonequity partnership with a transport company that delivers large items, while the other alliance is with the venture capitalist and is governed via an equity investment. Part of the contract is a service level agreement stipulating that the partner will enable H&L to procure services, such as office space, customer service, support advisory, technical support, and logistics. In the international domain, H&L has multiple downstream nonequity relationships with other subsidiaries that are part of the mother company. H&L has also forged an alliance with an internationally operating transport company that specializes in small-sized products; this partner accounts for 80 percent of the transport volume of H&L.

In summary, H&L experienced a successful launch of its web shop. Consistent with its focused international strategy, the alliance portfolio configuration supports its market-based innovation. The surplus of nonequity upstream relationships with suppliers enables it to enhance its technology while securing the provision of content (that is, products). Simultaneously, the downstream alliances with distributors (across countries) enable H&L to market its service flexibly and efficiently. The large size of the alliance portfolio contributed to H&L's success, as did its ability to balance upstream and downstream activities. As one of the cofounders stated: "You want to be the largest and the first. If you're the largest, you can sign better contracts with the suppliers [upstream], you get more traction with your members [downstream]. The more traction you get with your members, the better contracts you'll get with your suppliers, it's reciprocity between the two" (B1).

Technology-Based Innovation Cases

Case 3: FINFAST

FINFAST introduced an "all-in-one" finance solution for corporate and small-sized firms. Its technology-based service offers a cloud-computing solution that enables clients to access their financial management system 24 hours a day with any type of Internet-ready device (i.e., mobile phone, laptop, tablet, etc.) from any location in the world. By so doing, FINFAST optimizes a company's payments, cash management, and treasury decisions. This newly developed "off-the-shelf" program is stable for extreme amounts of financial traffic and allows for rapid implementation. To date, however, the program has only been in use by one client. As development of the technology primarily occurred in-house without support from large investors and only a limited number of technology partners, the program was brought slowly to market. FINFAST's business service is best characterized as a technology-based innovation that involves limited explorative upstream learning and exploitative downstream learning. As one interviewee stated: "Our added value is that we can run massive amounts of volume without trouble; that's our unique selling factor . . . So we don't use any middle-software like other applications, and removing the middle-ware is the key to our solution . . . We have got heavy competition, we are ahead on the market of worldwide payment traffic" (C1).

Figure 10.2c illustrates the alliance portfolio. FINFAST has a small alliance portfolio, as it developed its innovative technology primarily in-house. This was done for two reasons. First, the building blocks of the system had been developed in the preceding years by another company owned by the same owners as FINFAST, and FINFAST continued with further developing this technology internally. Second, because FINFAST encountered resistance by (competing) financial institutions, who considered the new technology an industry threat, its opportunities to forge alliances to enhance this technology were limited.

In the national domain, FINFAST forged a nonequity partnership with a large company operating in the energy sector. That is, this partner is a client and adopted the program. In the international domain, FINFAST has two nonequity upstream alliances with two large technology firms, one of which has substantial experience in the financial industry. These partners were selected for their expertise and primarily to obtain legitimization. As one interviewee put it: "And on the bottom left side [of the company's website] you see 'Powered by' [partner X]; such an association with an established partner legitimizes what we do as a company; there is not a single company that doesn't work with this partner in Japan . . . We have a good relationship with this partner because they possess the platform for finance" (C1).

In summary, FINFAST developed a new business-service concept based on technology developed in-house. After the product-development phase, two upstream alliances were forged to access knowledge and obtain legitimacy. Downstream, it only created one alliance, which represents a relationship with a client. Though the business concept has been successfully developed, diffusion among clients remains rather low. As such, FINFAST has been unable to balance explorative upstream learning with exploitative downstream learning. It has also been unable to configure a supporting alliance portfolio configuration.

Case 4: FINLEG

FINLEG was founded in 2009 as a joint venture by two financial services organizations that saw an opportunity due to the introduction of new legislation known as the "Markets in Financial Instruments Directive" (MiFID), which deregulated financial markets by stipulating that smaller retail investors should have choice when placing financial orders. This opened up an opportunity in the trade for derivatives, which was till then monopolized by industry incumbents. To enter the derivatives market (i.e., trading , clearing, completing a derivative transaction), FINLEG developed, among others, "Smart Order Routing," a technology that organizes price comparison and the routing of financial orders to the best broker or bank for execution. This allows FINLEG to provide clients with the best prices. FINLEG successfully developed the new technology and enjoyed strong financial performance. It processed 2.5 million transactions in 2011 alone and has become a serious rival to established financial institutions. FINLEG depends on explorative learning in the upstream domain, as the technology required to develop the Smart Order Router System is unique. It depends on exploitative learning in the downstream domain, as the market for financial derivatives is already served by competitors. As two interviewees said: "A broker [via its Smart Order Router] searches for the best price for stocks; multiple parties can do that, but it can search as the only one in Europe for derivatives" (D1). "We are the first in Europe that starts the competition with markets that already exist for more than 100 years" (D2).

Figure 10.2d illustrates FINLEG's alliance portfolio. The firm has multiple upstream partnerships in the national and international domains. In the international domain, FINLEG forged partnerships with two similar financial services–oriented organizations, which provided knowledge that was critical for the construction and enhancement of the technology required to build the Smart Order Router. These critical technical alliances were sourced from outside the Netherlands because FINLEG was looking for proven and validated technology, but in its absence it allied with experienced companies. It also forged an alliance with an established company that provided much-needed knowledge about the design of websites for financial firms. As two interviewees put it: "They [the technical partner] were also the only one; we conducted research into who could supply the technology [Smart Order Router]. No one could because it was completely new, but this technical partner possessed experience with derivatives, which was rare . . . We have a license for the software; we think of something and they build it and in return we get a license, so we actually rent it" (D1). "And to bring everything together you need a platform and that's the other technical partner. Even though they are not a shareholder, you could see them as a very important player because they possess the technology that makes the trade work, they deliver the matching engine" (D2).

In the national domain, FINLEG created three downstream nonequity alliances with four financial institutes. It also established equity ties with the founding partners. These partnerships are necessary to execute financial transactions. That is, each partner fulfills a specific downstream function, which is necessary to complete a financial transaction. As the following quote states: "To achieve this [the success of FINLEG], you need different industry partners: you need a market-maker, you need an order flow provider. It doesn't matter if its institution flow or retail flow, you need flow from end investors and you need high-quality partners to do the roll-over. And you need a clearing house to check the trades for derivatives" (D1).

In summary, FINLEG successfully built and marketed a technology-based innovation. In doing so, it engaged in upstream explorative learning with various partners, with different competences in the financial industry. This allowed FINLEG to reengineer procured knowledge into a new technology. Via carefully selected downstream alliances, it was also able to successfully sell and deliver its service to clients. As such, it created a balance between the exploitative upstream and explorative downstream functional domains.

Discussion

The purpose of this study was to explore how start-up KIBS can configure their alliance portfolio configurations in order to achieve a balance between explorative and exploitative learning (that is, ambidexterity). Four KIBS start-ups (two market-based and two technology-based) proved to be good showcases for this purpose. With limited resources, these KIBS have successfully developed their innovation-based services, yet at varying performance levels. A comparison of the findings has enabled us to provide details on alliance portfolio properties that have enabled or inhibited the KIBS to overcome the hurdles of simultaneous exploration and exploitation.

Table 10.3 Cross-Case Comparison

	VC3world	H&L	FINFAST	FINLEG
KIBS context				
Innovation type	Market-based	Market-based	Technology-based	Technology-based
Service	Online mediation platform	Online web shop	Online financial management	Financial trade and order technology
Innovative capability	Capability to leverage externally acquired knowledge	Capability to leverage externally acquired knowledge	Capability to internally develop knowledge	Capability to integrate externally acquired knowledge
Alliance approach	Reactive partnering, closed portfolio	Proactive partnering, open portfolio	Reactivepartnering, closed portfolio	Proactive partnering, open portfolio
Performance	Underperformance	Superior performance	Underperformance	Superior performance
Strategy	Shotgun approach, trial and error	Focused approach, systematic	In-house, trial and error	Focused approach, systematic
Alliance portfolio				
Portfolio size	Small	Large	Small	Large
Industry diversity	Moderate	High	Low	Low
National diversity	Moderate	High	Moderate	High
Organizational diversity	High	Moderate	Low	Moderate
Governance diversity	Low	Moderate	Low	Moderate
Functional domain				
Upstream domain	Heterogeneous; supplementary partners, strong	Homogenous; supplementary partners, weak	Homogenous; supplementary partners, strong	Heterogeneous; complementary partners, strong
Downstream domain	Surplus of informal partners	Heterogeneous, complementary partners, mixture of strong and weak	Only one formal partner (client)	Homogenous, supplementary partners, mixture of strong and weak
Ambidexterity	Unbalanced alliance portfolio configuration	Balanced alliance portfolio configuration	Unbalanced alliance portfolio configuration	Balanced alliance portfolio configuration

Cross-Case Comparison

Table 10.3 provides an overview of the findings. A common feature of the four cases is that their core competences are built around matching internally developed knowledge with externally acquired knowledge to develop and market an innovative ICT-based business service. All of the cases possessed a business idea that had been developed in-house; additionally they all had identified a market opportunity and possessed in-house knowledge and (to varying degrees) the capability to access, acquire, and use external knowledge. However, we also identified several salient differences in the organization of the KIBS.

The results indicate that two cases (H&L and FINLEG) approached partnering proactively, selecting alliance partners carefully based on internal needs and managing them systematically toward their objectives. These alliance processes contributed to the construction of a coherent alliance portfolio. In contrast, the two other cases (VC3world and FINFAST) adopted a reactive partnering approach and experienced difficulties in attracting and bonding with alliance partners. Consequently, their ability to build a supportive alliance portfolio was impeded. The results also indicate that the high-performing KIBS adopted a focused strategy that they implemented systematically, whereas the KIBS with low-performing strategies showed elements of trial and error. One explanation could be that both H&L and FINLEG received external support to organize their primary internal processes. For example, H&L's mother company (i.e., an equity-based relationship) provided office space and other (downstream) services. Overall, we propose that these organizational properties enabled the high-performing KIBS to develop a foundation upon which ambidexterity could be achieved. Therefore, we offer the following initial proposition:

Proposition 1: Irrespective of innovation type, for a KIBS start-up, its ability to realize ambidexterity increases when it (a) possesses a capability to acquire, integrate, and use external knowledge, (b) proactively approaches partnering, (c) formulates and implements a focused strategy, and (d) receives external support to build the internal organization.

By distinguishing between the upstream and downstream domains, on the one hand, and between high and low performance, on the other, we were able to disentangle the portfolio-configuration dimensions necessary to achieve ambidexterity and successfully develop and commoditize market-based and technology-based innovations.

Market-based innovations in a KIBS context imply that a company focuses on creating new business services that fulfill market needs. Creating a new market benefits from temporary (and therefore explorative) knowledge of multiple merchants, as such benefits provide the input necessary to make the creation of new markets successful. In order to create momentum and a sufficiently large offering, it is necessary to have an alliance portfolio that consists of exploitative/supplementary upstream and explorative/complementary downstream partnerships.

In the upstream domain, the creation of a market-based innovation requires less complex knowledge, as the desired technology has been developed by other companies. As such, supplementary upstream alliances are sufficient—that is, partnerships that provide (technological) resources that reinforce the core competence of a KIBS. For example, H&L (a high-performing firm) forged upstream alliances with suppliers primarily driven by flexibility and agility motives; apart from knowledge concerning the quality and quantity of products, limited knowledge was exchanged. Similarly, though to a lesser extent, VC3world (a low-performing firm) forged upstream alliances to enhance and provide legitimization to their "off-the-shelf" technology. Thus, knowledge transfer, to the extent that a company uses upstream partners to improve an existing technology, is limited. Therefore, a nonequity governance structure is preferable as such structures require less organizational resources to manage. In addition, organizational integration with a partner is less of a concern, as flexibility reflects a key motive to establish supplementary partnerships.

With downstream alliances, a shift of focus toward the commoditization of the innovation occurs through the use of existing, openly available technologies, such as websites and apps. This requires that a market-based KIBS possess knowledge about market dynamics and opportunities and that they forge complementary alliances with partners who are closely connected to clients—that is, partnerships that provide (marketing and sales) resources that enable a KIBS to improve its core competence and enter or create new markets. Alternatively, KIBS may seek to contact clients directly and obtain customer feedback. For example, H&L (high-performing) developed high-quality partnerships with local and European transport companies in order to secure the reliability of web-ordered products. In addition, they forged multiple alliances that enable it to deliver high-quality service support. In contrast, VC3world's (low-performing) market approach entailed an informal network of loosely coupled volunteers and representatives. This comparison suggests that downstream explorative learning requires a systematic set of (organizationally integrated) partners that reinforce and complement the firm's core competence. In sum, we offer the following proposition:

Proposition 2: A market-based KIBS start-up's ability to realize ambidexterity increases when it (a) possesses a large set of alliance partners; (b) forges a set of supplementary upstream technology partners, which operate in a similar or adjacent industry, originate in different countries, and are connected via nonequity relationships; and (c) forges a set of complementary downstream partners that have experience in creating/entering new markets, provide marketing and sales resources, and are connected via nonequity and equity relationships.

A high-performing technology-based KIBS requires complex information and extensive knowledge transfer in order to build a new business service. Building a new technology benefits from temporary (and therefore explorative) knowledge of existing or proven technologies, as such know-how and know-what provide the input necessary to make the technology successful. In order to create new technologies and market them successfully, it is necessary to have an alliance portfolio that consists of explorative/complementary upstream and exploitative/supplementary downstream partnerships.

Our findings indicate that complementary upstream alliances that are well developed (i.e., organizationally integrated) enable these KIBS to successfully proceed from testing and prototyping to commercializing. That is, technology-based innovation originates from collaborations with partners operating in the same industry or adjacent industries (nationality may vary), which provide unique and scarce (technological) resources to develop the new technology. For example, FINLEG's (a high-performing firm) decision to partner with two financial organizations with extensive experience in handling financial transaction enabled it to develop its Smart Order Router technology. In contrast, FINFAST (a low-performing firm) developed the technology in-house and only used upstream partners for incremental enhancements. Firms creating technology-based innovations can extend their knowledge and search for exploration within industries as long as they respect the copyright and patent restrictions of such knowledge. Technology-based innovations require large amounts of complex knowledge, which increases the likelihood of allying with larger organizations that are more likely to possess the required knowledge. Partnering with established companies may also offer legitimization advantages.

The exploitative learning on the downstream side involves commercially available marketing and distribution partners that tend to be governed by nonequity agreements. Developing a substantive set of supplementary downstream partners increases the likelihood of commercial success—that is, partnerships that provide (marketing and sales) resources that enable a KIBS to leverage its core competence in existing markets. This requires investments from the KIBS in their downstream domain, which may conflict with their primary focus on technology development. However, refraining from exploitative learning (for example, by absorbing customer feedback directly or indirectly through alliance partners) may lead to a service that is technologically superior but not commercially viable. For example, although FINFAST developed a viable technological innovation (a cloud computing–based financial solution), its market approach was impeded by a lack of supplementary partners to actively promote its service and/or provide customer feedback. In contrast, FINLEG built a systematic set of supplementary, highly organizationally integrated partners, which enabled it to effectively enter different markets. This suggests that creating a set of partners with extant experience and marketing power is critical, as market presence and customer feedback are critical conditions for technology-based innovation. In summary, we offer a final proposition:

Proposition 3: The ability of a technology-based start-up KIBS to realize ambidexterity increases when the KIBS (a) possesses a large set of alliance partners; (b) forges a set of complementary upstream technology partners, which operate in a similar or adjacent industry, originate in different countries, and are connected via nonequity relationships; and (c) forges a set of supplementary downstream partners that operate in existing markets, provide marketing and sales resources, and are connected via nonequity and equity relationships.

Implications, Limitations, and Future Research

In this chapter, we have formulated an answer to our research question: how can KIBS configure their alliance portfolio in the upstream and downstream domains in order to realize ambidexterity and successfully develop and commoditize technology-based or market-based innovations? Our results indicate that distinguishing between the upstream and downstream domains, while accounting for explorative and exploitative learning, enables us to provide details on distinct alliance portfolio properties that support ambidexterity.

Theoretical Implications

We have validated the open innovation perspective (Chesbrough, 2006; 2003) by providing a tentative insight into the conditions of alliance portfolio configuration (i.e., diversity dimensions) under which a desired state of ambidexterity could be attained, such that explorative and exploitative learning (both of which are integral parts of open innovation initiatives) are optimally produced. We have also expanded the literature in this field by showing how a knowledge-intensive business services' context and different alliance portfolio configurations, while taking into account the upstream and downstream functional domain, affect explorative and exploitative learning differently and simultaneously. Specifically, a focal firm faces the challenge of designing its portfolio configuration in a manner that is analogous to the concept of domain separation (Lavie and Rosenkopf, 2006). This requires that management regard a focal firm's alliance portfolio as a multidimensional phenomenon, especially when viewed from a diversity perspective. The present chapter has made an initial effort in order to fill this lacuna.

Second, we have advanced the alliance portfolio literature by showing that alliance portfolio configuration entails a complex, multidimensional role for the concept of portfolio diversity in the advancement of simultaneous explorative and exploitative learning. Whereas prior studies have adopted a one-dimensional or aggregated view on alliance portfolios (Wassmer, 2010), these case study results indicate that the possibility of creating and sustaining a situation of ambidexterity exists when KIBS distinguish between and proactively select and manage alliance relationships across upstream and downstream domains. That is, KIBS may forge, upstream or downstream, supplementary alliances—in which partners contribute similar resources and offer feedback—to realize exploitative learning processes. Alternatively, they may establish complementary alliances—in which partners contribute new resources and participate in (joint) learning opportunities—to realize explorative learning processes.

Third, we have contributed to the KIBS literature (Toivonen, 2006) by showing that KIBS start-up success, captured by successful market-based or technology-based innovation, depends to some extent on a company's internal organization and its ability to manage its set of alliance relationships. Successful start-up KIBS are able to reconcile the pressure to build a core competence and use upstream and downstream partners to exploit it. In addition, we show that founding conditions are critical. A focused strategy, partnering, and securing external funding and/or organizational support improves a KIBS firm's chances to successfully develop and market a technology-based business service.

Managerial Implications

Gassman, Enkel, and Chesbrough (2010) found that the process by which firms manage open innovation is still characterized more by trial and error than by professional management. However, the present study has shown some lessons that managers can put into practice. First, the case studies show it is vital for a firm to align its portfolio strategy with the alliance portfolio configuration. More specifically, if a KIBS seeks to innovate in both the upstream and downstream domains, it is necessary to establish appropriate portfolio configurations in order to facilitate these innovation objectives. As these case studies have shown, neglecting this issue is likely to result in suboptimal returns in either the upstream or downstream innovation domain.

Second, the case studies demonstrate that it makes sense to distinguish upstream from downstream activities, as well as upstream from downstream alliance partners. The upstream-downstream domains offer managers the opportunity to pursue intrinsically different types of innovation, while ensuring optimal performance in terms of creating an ambidextrous portfolio. Moreover, the case studies hint at the importance of managing both domains purposefully and proactively in order to sustain firm performance (for example, turnover, market growth, etc.).

Finally, the cases suggest the importance of integral governance of the alliance portfolio. Upstream and downstream domains must be balanced, as both domains are interdependent to some extent and serve to attain specific strategic objectives, which, together, help a firm achieve its overall strategic goals. Thus, malfunctioning alliances in one domain may frustrate the functioning of alliances in the other domain. A holistic understanding of how the portfolio should be governed, configured, and managed is in order.

Limitations and Future Research

The present study has certain limitations. First, the findings are limited to the context of start-up KIBS, specifically those for which IT constitutes a critical resource. This limits the external validity of the findings (Gibbert et al., 2008). Therefore, future research could consider different types of KIBS, as well as other industries, in order to verify the conclusions drawn in the present study. Second, we have only focused on two types of innovation: technology-based and market-based. Future research could contrast our findings with KIBS engaged in radical innovation, such that they adopt exploration in both upstream and downstream activities. Alternatively, our findings may be contrasted with KIBS that adopt exploitation in upstream and downstream activities. Third, the cross-sectional nature of our investigation has prevented us from exploring portfolio evolution. Contingent on the development state of an innovative business concept, different partnerships could be required. Adopting a longitudinal approach would also make it possible to track the evolution of the alliance portfolio.

Concluding Remarks

In this chapter, we have shown that technology-based and market-based KIBS require different alliance portfolio configuration to successfully develop and commoditize innovations. Interorganizational learning, either downstream or upstream, is critical to a firm's success. However, we do not suggest that managers should engage in partnerships to an unlimited extent. Managers of KIBS should attempt to avoid myopic partnering when engaging or participating in open innovation initiatives. Open innovation initiatives should be aligned with corporate strategy, and alliance portfolio strategy and configuration should be instrumental to corporate strategy.

Appendix: Semistructured Interview Guide (Short Version)

Innovation

Market Innovation
- Does your organization commercialize products and services that are completely new?
- Does your organization frequently utilize new opportunities in new markets?
- Does your organization regularly use new distribution channels?
- Does your organization frequently make small adjustments to markets for existing products and services?
- Does your organization expand services for existing clients?

Technology Innovation
- Does your organization's performance depend on newly developed technologies?
- Does your organization increase economies of scales in existing for technical products and services?
- Does your organization expand services for existing clients using new technologies?
- Does your organization develop products and services that are completely new to our organization?

Alliance Portfolio
- Could you describe the partners used in service innovation projects?
- Could you describe the alliances that this company has?
- Which service innovations were developed in recent years in collaboration with these alliance partners?
- How does the current alliance portfolio perform in terms of innovation and learning?

Partner Diversity Domain
- How would you describe the type of partners in the alliance portfolio (e.g., customers, suppliers, competitors, etc.)?

Functional Domain
- Could you describe the goal/function of the alliances of innovation partners of the firm, and what was their outcome?
- What value do these alliances add to the innovation process or project?

Governance Domain
- What type of governance form do you use with your alliance partners (e.g., contractual, equity stake)?
- Why was an equity or nonequity governance form chosen (e.g., control, knowledge sharing)?
- How do you judge whether this alliance is successful (e.g., output, process)?

References

Ahlstrom, D. (2010). "Innovation and Growth: How Business Contributes to Society." *Academy of Management Perspectives* 24 (3): 11–24.

Ahuja, G. (2000). "Collaborative Networks, Structural Holes, and Innovation: A Longitudinal Study." *Administrative Science Quarterly* 45:425–55.

Anderson, P., and Tushman, M. (1990). "Technological Discontinuities and Dominant Designs: A Cyclical Model of Technological Change." *Administrative Science Quarterly* 35 (4): 604–33.

Bresser, R. K. F., Heuskel, D., and Nixon, R. D. (2000). "The Deconstruction of Integrated Value Chains: Practical and Conceptual Challenges." In R. K. F. Bresser, M. A. Hitt, R. D. Nixon, and D. Heuskel (eds.), *Winning Strategies in a Deconstructing World*, 1–21. Chichester, UK: Wiley.

Chesbrough, H. (2003). *Open Innovation: The New Imperative for Creating and Profiting from Technology*. Boston: Harvard University Business School Press.

Chesbrough, H. (2006). *Open Business Models: How to Thrive in the New Innovation Landscape*. Boston: Harvard Business School Press.

Cohen, W. M., and Levinthal, D. A. (1990). "Absorptive Capacity: A New Perspective on Learning and Innovation." *Administrative Science Quarterly* 35 (1): 128–52.

Damanpour, F. (1991). "Organizational Innovation: A Meta-analysis of Effects of Determinants and Moderators." *Academy of Management Journal* 34:555–90.

Eisenhardt, K. M. (1989). "Building Theories from Case Study Research." *Academy of Management Review* 14 (4): 532–50.

Eisenhardt, K. M., and Schoonhoven, C. B. (1996). "Resource-Based View of Strategic Alliance Formation: Strategic and Social Effects in Entrepreneurial Firms." *Organization Science* 7 (2): 136–50.

Fitzsimmons, J. A., and Fitzsimmons, M. J. (2006). *Service Management: Operations, Strategy, Information Technology*, 5th ed. New York: McGraw-Hill Irwin.

Gallouj, F. (2002). *Innovation in the Service Economy: The New Wealth of Nations*. Cheltenham, UK: Edgar Elgar.

Garcia, R., and Calantone, R. (2002). "A Critical Look at Technological Innovation Typology and Innovativeness Terminology: A Literature Review." *Journal of Product Innovation Management* 19 (2): 110–32.

Gibbert, M., Ruigrok, W., and Wicki, B. (2008). "What Passes as a Rigorous Case Study?" *Strategic Management Journal* 29 (13): 1465–74.

Goerzen, A., and Beamish, P. W. (2005). "The Effect of Alliance Network Diversity on Multinational Enterprise Performance." *Strategic Management Journal* 26 (4): 333–54.

Grant, R. M., and Baden-Fuller, C. (2004). "A Knowledge Accessing Theory of Strategic Alliances." *Journal of Management Studies* 41 (1): 61–84.

Gupta, A. K., Smith, K. G., and Shalley, C. E. (2006). "The Interplay between Exploration and Exploitation." *Academy of Management Journal* 49 (4): 693–706.

Hamel, G., and Prahalad, C. K. (1994). *Competing for the Future*. Boston: Harvard Business School Press.

He, Z.-L., and Wong, P.-K. (2004). "Exploration vs. Exploitation: An Empirical Test of the Ambidexterity Hypothesis." *Organization Science* 15 (4): 481–94.

Hoffmann, W. H. (2007). "Strategies for Managing a Portfolio of Alliances." *Strategic Management Journal* 28 (8): 827–56.

Holmqvist, M. (2003). "A Dynamic Model of Intra- and Interorganizational Learning." *Organization Studies* 24 (1): 95–123.

Jansen, J. J. P., van den Bosch, F. A. J., and Volberda, H. W. (2006). "Exploratory Innovation, Exploitative Innovation and Performance: Effects of Organizational Antecedents and Environmental Moderators." *Management Science* 52 (11): 1661–74.

Jiang, R. J., Tao, Q. T., and Santoro, M. D. (2010). "Alliance Portfolio Diversity and Firm Performance." *Strategic Management Journal* 31:1136–44.

Kwok, C. C. K., and Reeb, D. M. (2000). "Internationalization and firm Risk: An Upstream-Downstream Hypothesis." *Journal of International Business Studies* 31:611–29.

Lavie, D. (2007). "Alliance Portfolios and Firm Performance: A Study of Value Creation and Appropriation in the U.S. Software Industry." *Strategic Management Journal* 28:1187–212.

Lavie, D., and Rosenkopf, L. (2006). "Balancing Exploration and Exploitation in Alliance Formation." *Academy of Management Journal* 49:797–818.

Lavie, D., Stettner, U., and Tushman, M. L. (2010). "Exploration and Exploitation within and across Organizations." *Academy of Management Annals* 4:109–55.

Lichtenthaler, U. (2008). "Open Innovation in Practice: An Analysis of Strategic Approaches to Technology Transactions." *IEEE Transactions on Engineering Management* 55:148–57.

Lichtenthaler, U. (2011). "Open Innovation: Past Research, Current Debates, and Future Directions." *Academy of Management Perspectives*, February, 75–93.

March, J. G. (1991). "Exploration and Exploitation in Organizational Learning." *Organization Science* 2 (1): 71–87.

Miller, C. C., Cardinal, L. B., and Glick, W. H. (1997). "Retrospective Reports in Organizational Research: A Reexamination of Recent Evidence." *Academy of Management Journal* 40:189–204.

Oerlemans, L. A. G., Knoben, J., and Pretorius, M. W. (2013). "Alliance Portfolio Diversity, Radical and Incremental Innovation: The Moderating Role of Technology Management." *Technovation* 33 (6–7): 234–46.

Ozcan, P., and Eisenhardt, K. M. (2009). "Origin of Alliance Portfolios: Entrepreneurs, Network Strategies, and Firm Performance." *Academy of Management Journal* 52 (2): 246–79.

Poole, M., Van de Ven, A., Dooley, K., and Holmes, M. (2000). *Organizational Change and Innovation Processes: Theory and Methods for Research*. Oxford: Oxford University Press.

Salinger, M. A. (1989). "The Meaning of "Upstream" and "Downstream" and the Implications for Modeling Vertical Mergers." *Journal of Industrial Economics* 37 (4): 373–87.

Simsek, Z. (2009). "Organizational Ambidexterity: Towards a Multilevel Understanding." *Journal of Management Studies* 46 (4): 597–624.

Soni, K., Lilien, G. L., and Wilson, D. T. (1993). "Industrial Innovation and firm Performance: A Re-conceptualization and Exploratory Structural Equation Analysis." *International Journal of Research in Marketing* 10:365–380.

Tether, B. S. (2005). "Do Services Innovate (Differently)? Insights from the European Innobarometer Survey." *Industry and Innovation* 12 (2): 153–84.

Toivonen, M. (2006). "Supporting the Development of KIBS with a Research-Based Policy: Activities Initiated in Finland." XVI International Conference of RESER, September 2006, Lisbon.

Trott, P., and Hartmann, D. (2009). "Why 'Open Innovation' Is Old Wine in New Bottles." *International Journal of Innovation Management* 13 (4): 715–36.

Vanhaverbeke, W., Van de Vrande, V., and Chesbrough, H. (2008). "Understanding the Advantages of Open Innovation Practices in Corporate Venturing in Terms of Real Options." *Creativity and Innovation Management* 17 (4): 251–58.

Wassmer, U. (2010). "Alliance Portfolios: A Review and Research Agenda." *Journal of Management* 36 (1): 141–71.

Wuyts, S., and Dutta, S. (2012). "Benefiting from Alliance Portfolio Diversity: The Role of Past Internal Knowledge Creation Strategy." *Journal of Management*. doi: 10.1177/0149206312442339.

Yin, R. K. (2003). *Application of Case Study Research*. Thousand Oaks, CA: Sage Publications.

CHAPTER 11

R&D Partnership Portfolio Strategies for Breakthrough Innovation: Developing Knowledge Exchange Capabilities

Scott Mooty and Ben Kedia

In competitive business environments, partnerships and alliances are formed for the purposes of innovation because the technological, capital, and intellectual resources necessary to first research and then develop complex product, service, organization, and platform innovations rarely reside within the legal boundaries of a single firm (Grant and Baden-Fuller, 2004). Influential and leading firms that compete with multiple platforms are often the strategic center of numerous alliances and partnerships (Kedia and Mooty, 2013). From the perspective of these center, or focal, firms, the aggregation of these present and past partnerships and alliances form an alliance portfolio and an interactive resource from which new ideas and knowledge may be drawn (Dhanaraj and Parkhe, 2006; Wassmer, 2010). As such, focal firms seek ways to develop innovation-management functions and capabilities that ensure the collaborations of the alliance portfolio possess the competencies necessary to create a range of product, system, and organizational innovations (Laursen and Salter, 2006; Maula, Keil, and Salmenkaita, 2006; O'Connor, 2008). These innovation functions and capabilities encompass several critical and interrelated tasks, which include fostering, improving, and maintaining the relationships between the partnership through the processes related to research and development (Kale, Dyer, and Singh, 2002) and managing the intellectual property and knowledge that flows between the partners (Kyriakopoulos and De Ruyter, 2004). Other, more complicated tasks include identifying and building the necessary capabilities that allow the focal firm and its alliance partners to access and exchange knowledge resources between one another and the members of the focal firm's alliance portfolio, enhancing knowledge flows and understandings within the collaboration (Fjeldstad et al., 2012; Grant, 1996; Heimeriks, Klijn, and Reuer, 2009). The development and sophistication of these capabilities enable the firms' partnerships to be more efficient, effective, and responsive to customer and market demands (Hoffman, 2007; O'Connor et al., 2008). However, advances in online communication technologies, platforms, and forums—allowing for the efficient widespread solicitation, collection, and distribution of information and knowledge beyond the partnership, alliance, and alliance portfolio boundaries (Jeppesen and Fredricksen, 2006; Jeppesen and Lakahani, 2010)—have emerged and coalesced into new organizational forms called *meta-organizations* (Gulati, Puranam and Tushman, 2012). The prominence of these meta-organizations is reshaping the ways focal firms approach open innovation practices and alliance portfolios (Faraj, Jarvenpaa, and Majchrzak, 2011; Fjeldstad et al., 2012; Gulati, Puranam, and Tushman, 2012).

Meta-organizations represent networks of secondary and nonbinding interactive resources for information and knowledge that may be integrated with the open innovation practices of the alliance portfolio (Kogut, 2000). Meta-organizations exist in digital and conventional forms. Examples of digital meta-organizations include firm-sponsored user forums, independent electronic forums that address technology fields and interests common to the focal firm, and "innovation malls," such as Innocentive.com, where companies post scientific problems seeking solutions from at-large participants (Faraj, Jarvenpaa, and Majchrzak, 2011; Pisano and Verganti, 2008; Yoo et al., 2012). More conventional meta-organizations include geographic clusters in which the focal firm or its partners may be located and professional organizations and communities of practice of which the partners or their employees may be members. The digital meta-organizational tools allow the focal firm and its users, cohorts, and other independent parties (including other firms) that have no formal obligation to the focal firm forums to post, store, retrieve, examine, and verify ideas, concepts, and solutions pertinent to innovation and new product development (Baldwin and von Hippel, 2011; Bogers, Afuah, and Bastian, 2010).

In addition, scholars and professionals have embraced the idea that open innovation practices involving the systematic absorption, exploration, retention, release, and exploitation of information and knowledge within and across defined organizational boundaries present beneficial opportunities and managerial challenges for research and development (R&D) activities (Lichtenthaler, 2011). The opportunities result from the ability to access and integrate the broad and deep knowledge that resides in the alliance portfolio and meta-organizations. The challenges occur as complexities arise when this broad and deep knowledge is identified and integrated in uncommon and unfamiliar circumstances (Carlile and Rebenstich, 2003). From the perspective of the focal firm, open innovation practices create four distinct knowledge flows between the alliance, alliance portfolio, and meta-organization boundaries as depicted in Figure 11.1.

In brief, the first knowledge flow involves the absorption and exploration of inbound information—knowledge and intellectual property obtained from partners, users, and competitors to enhance and improve products, platforms, or

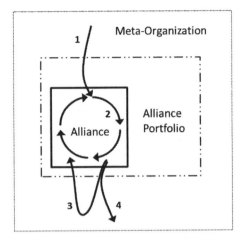

Figure 11.1   Open Innovation Knowledge Flows Relative to Alliance Boundaries

systems in development (Laursen and Salter, 2006; Lichtenthaler and Lichten-thaler, 2009). The second knowledge flow is internal to the partnership and con-sists of the processing and synthesis of the retained information—knowledge and intellectual property imported from outside the partnership and developed within the partnership (Almirall and Casadesus-Masanell, 2010). The third knowledge flow is associated with the selective release of information—knowledge and intel-lectual property to the alliance portfolio membership and meta-organization to produce feedback, and additional knowledge and intellectual property critical to advancing an innovation's development (Chesborough, 2003; Vanhaverbeke and Cloodt, 2006; West, 2006). The fourth is associated with the selective release and sale of information, knowledge, and intellectual property by the focal firm and its active partners for exploitation by other key partners, users, and com-petitors to generate revenues from the products, platforms, and systems of the collaboration; to create complimentary products and innovations enhancing the value of the products, platforms, and systems of the collaboration; or to create entirely new products that better meet user needs (Alexy, George, and Salter, 2013; Boudreau, 2010; Faraj, Jarvenpaa, and Majchrzak, 2011).

The purpose of this chapter is to explore how focal firms may strategically utilize partnerships and alliances, alliance portfolios, and meta-organizations in an open innovation context to improve the consistency and success of break-through innovation initiatives. Our main thesis draws upon the inbound, inter-nal feedback and outbound information flows supported by open innovation practices in the context of alliance portfolios and meta-organizations. We posit focal firms choosing to engage in open R&D alliances may be more consistent in the development of breakthrough innovations when those projects are man-aged in the context of a firm's alliance portfolios (Hoffman, 2007) and the meta-organizations (Gulati, Puranam and Tushman, 2012) in which the focal firm and its portfolio are centered, relative to the inbound, internal, feedback, and outbound knowledge flows that occur during each phase of the innovation development process (O'Connor, 2006; Ahuja, Lampert, and Novelli, 2013). However, success and consistency are only possible when the dynamic capabilities of the partnership in managing the complexities arising from knowledge exchange and integration are appropriate to the innovation's stage of development and commensurate with the demands of the innovation project itself (Carlile, 2004; Grant, 1996; Helfat and Raubitschek, 2000). This is particularly difficult when breakthrough innovations are considered. By definition, breakthrough innovations require the creation of knowledge domains and lexicons that enable knowledge exchange concurrent with their development (Nonaka, 1994; Verganti, 2011). The knowledge exchange capabilities are part of those domains and lexicons and must be co-developed to realize success in the present initiative and consistency in the development of associated and future innovation projects.

In the next section, we present and explain an integrative framework (drawing its inspiration from the four knowledge flows noted above), three progressively sophisticated knowledge exchange capabilities adopted from Carlile (2004), and four phases of the innovation development process based on the work of Gina C. O'Connor and her colleagues (i.e., O'Connor, 2006; O'Connor et al., 2008), which we modify and extend.

In brief, the integrative model depicted in Figure 11.2 suggests that the knowledge flows are distinct in each phase of the innovation development process. In addition, the knowledge domain boundary of the partnership starts broadly and then focuses as the innovation is developed and commercialized. Once commercialized, outside input and interactions with clientele begin to erode and broaden the knowledge domain boundary, as interactions with users and modifications to the innovation occur. Furthermore, the knowledge exchange capabilities necessary for efficient and effective knowledge exchange vary, requiring the most

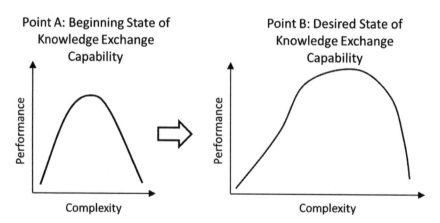

Figure 11.2 Beginning and Desired States of Knowledge Exchange Capability

Note: Adopted from Ahuja and Lampert (2001), Laursen and Salter (2006), and Sampson (2007)

sophisticated capabilities at the inception and after commercialization of the breakthrough innovation project.

Next we briefly define *breakthrough* and *open innovation*, distinguishing between the two constructs. We then examine how complexity arises during the course of search activities in the alliance, alliance portfolio, and meta-organizational contexts. The knowledge exchange capabilities are then defined, followed by a detailed explanation of the innovation development process, emphasizing the activities of the four open innovation knowledge flows illustrated in Figures 11.1 and 11.2 above. We conclude with a brief discussion summarizing the chapter and how this framework extends the open innovation literature.

Defining Breakthrough Innovation and Open Innovation

Innovation is often defined as the recombination of knowledge in new and commercially viable ways (Schumpeter, 1934). By this classical definition, the knowledge elements and domains utilized in the development of an innovation are assumed to exist. Therefore, the task set before innovators is to explore and exploit new ways in which the elements of existing knowledge domains may be combined so that they are commercially viable and profitable to the partnership. However, this definition is insufficient, as knowledge is frequently created as part of the innovation process.

Breakthrough innovations are innovations that require knowledge be created and linked together with other new or existing knowledge in a commercially viable way that either disrupts an existing market or industry and/or spawns new markets and industries (Ahuja and Lampert, 2001; Anderson and Tushman, 1990; Verganti, 2011). There are two classifications of breakthrough innovation: (1) those based on newly created technology and inventions (Fleming and Sorenson, 2004) and (2) those based on the unique and novel combinations of existing technologies and knowledge (Henderson and Clark, 1990).

Breakthrough innovations that are based on new technologies and inventions are rare and require the development of concepts, ideas, and terminology to describe the technology, resulting in new knowledge domains. This type of breakthrough innovation is conceptually similar to the radical innovations described in Henderson and Clark's (1990) typology of four different types of technical innovation. Successfully implemented breakthrough innovations of this type tend to establish new dominant designs and create new sets of core product-design languages (lexicons) linked together with a new user interface (Henderson and Clark, 1990). These new knowledge domains often supplant existing knowledge domains, resulting in structural changes to existing alliances, alliance portfolios, and familiar business practices (O'Connor, 2008). Finally, the locus of radical innovations may include traditional R&D efforts internal to a lead or focal firm, or traditional and nontraditional partnerships that emphasize basic research, observation, and invention, such as partnerships with entrepreneurs, independent inventors, research institutions, and universities (Kedia and Mooty, 2013).

Breakthrough innovations that combine existing knowledge and technology in unique and novel ways, changing the structure of existing product solutions and the manner in which users interface with it, also require the creation of new knowledge (Garcia and Calantone, 2002; Henderson and Clark, 1990). The new knowledge explains how the disparate knowledge elements integrate, as well as how other products and systems may be configured or developed to produce and complement it (O'Connor, 2008). Breakthrough innovations of this type are conceptually similar to the architectural innovations described by Henderson and Clark (1990). This second type is more common and emphasizes the creation of knowledge regarding the systems that connect different existing knowledge domains, the complementary and accessory product innovations associated with the innovation, and how the innovation is produced, distributed, and understood by the customer. Thus, this second type of breakthrough innovation involves the creation of new business knowledge and can be highly disruptive to existing products and industries.

Open innovation may be defined as the acts of "systematically performing knowledge exploration, retention, and exploitation inside and outside an organization's boundaries throughout the innovation process" (Lichtenthaler, 2011, 77). In this definition, *boundaries* may be interpreted as relating to the legally defined extents of a firm, alliance, or alliance portfolio. For instance, relative to the focal firm, the boundary in question is its legal boundary. Relative to an established and enduring alliance, the boundary in question is that of the contracts and agreements defining the alliance itself. To an alliance portfolio, boundary refers to the active and ongoing alliances of a focal firm and, at least, the frequent partners of its past alliances that are likely to be called upon in future alliances. These explicit and legally defined boundaries may also serve as proxies to conceptualized boundaries, such as knowledge domains.

Knowledge domains, or the intellectual spaces of an organization, may be associated with each of the three organizational boundaries described above and that of the meta-organization that surrounds them. These knowledge domains that reside inside and outside any particular organizational boundary are often very different, holding knowledge in disparate technologies, as well as expertise in the development of new products, their marketing, and creating businesses associated with the innovations (Gerbert, Boerner, and Kearney, 2010; O'Connor et al., 2008). Breakthrough innovations may occur when elements of these knowledge domains are combined in unique and new ways to realize new products and services of commercial value. As such, the activities of absorption, exploration, retention, release, and exploitation—associated with open innovation—describe the integration processes of various knowledge domains across organizational boundaries. However, where breakthrough innovation is concerned, these activities may be driven by the necessity to create knowledge. Thus we amend the definition of open innovation for the purposes of this chapter. *Open innovation* is the systematic and integrative acts of knowledge creation, absorption, exploration, retention, release, and exploitation, inside and outside an organization's boundaries throughout the innovation process.

Search Activities, Innovation Performance, and Complexity

Understanding the challenges presented by open collaborative relationships between a focal firm and its various partners is key to understanding how breakthrough innovations may be achieved and how the complexities that thwart these efforts arise (Duysters and Lokshin, 2011). Knowledge exchange and integration is difficult in the context of a firm, much less in the context of a collaboration comprised of disparate partners and other contributors (Jiang, Tao, and Santoro, 2010). Despite the challenges, there are several benefits realized by exchanging and integrating knowledge originating from inside and outside the alliance. These benefits include, but are not limited to, (1) decreasing the time to market for a new product or service innovation (Deeds and Hill, 1996; Eisenhardt and Tabrizi, 1996; Kessler and Chakrabarti, 1996), (2) increasing the effectiveness of the ultimate innovation by accurately matching the performance attributes of the innovation's technology to user needs (Govindarajan, Kopalle and Danneels, 2011), and (3) decreasing the costs associated with the innovation cycle (Mansfield, 2008). Ideally, a balance should be achieved between the capabilities of knowledge exchange with the complexities resulting from the exchange of knowledge, relative to performance.

Research dealing with the integration of knowledge domains frequently finds an inverted U-shaped relationship between the intensity of knowledge exchange activities and performance, as depicted on the Point A side of Figure 11.3.

The complexities of knowledge exchange arise when the information and knowledge necessary to develop the innovation is new and unfamiliar to the focal firm. This occurs by degree, in two forms originating from different conditions: (1) technological novelty, when the innovation under development is based on a technology or invention that is unfamiliar to the partnership, and (2) knowledge domain disparity, when the innovation under development is not based on a technology or invention but is instead based on the new and unique combination of information and knowledge from different knowledge domains. Thus, from the perspective of the focal firm, complexity arises as novelty and disparity associated with each condition increases.

Deep search, commonly referred to as *search depth*, involves the continued and repeated mining of existing intellectual spaces for knowledge used to foster innovations (Ahuja and Lampert, 2001; Katilla and Ahuja, 2002). Within an alliance setting, search depth manifests when focal firms repeatedly utilize the same partners over the course of several alliance projects to realize efficiencies (Sampson, 2007). However, over time the efficiencies diminish as the technology on which the innovation is based becomes obsolete, the number of new applications for the innovation dwindles, and the innovation is challenged by competing innovations (Laursen and Salter, 2006). Breakthrough innovations realized from deep organizational search are rare and are most often associated with large firms (such as Dow Corning, 3M, DuPont, and BASF) that possess robust basic research capabilities, as well as dedicated formal structures and systems that allow the firms to commercialize the innovations (O'Connor, 2008). Firms that invent or

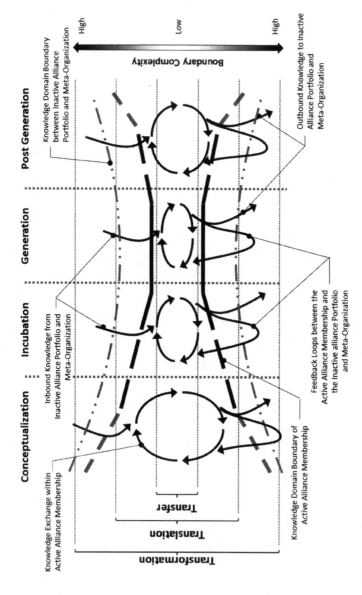

Figure 11.3 Conceptual Framework of Knowledge Exchange for Breakthrough Innovations Utilizing Open Innovation Practices

discover a new technology but do not possess the capabilities to commercialize the innovation often rely on partners that have such capabilities, and vice versa. Other firms emphasize a different approach.

Established firms more frequently realize innovation performance benefits from *broad search* activities that tap and integrate knowledge domains that are new or novel to the focal firm itself (Ahuja and Lampert, 2001) but are not new to other firms or in other industries. The point of maximum innovation performance via broad search, or *search scope*, is achieved when the knowledge domains tapped are disparate enough to have a moderate degree of novelty to each other, yet similar enough such that the lexicons associated with each may be translated, allowing knowledge exchange to occur efficiently and effectively (Ahuja and Lampert, 2001; Laursen and Salter, 2006). However, the most beneficial search approach, and particularly germane to this chapter, is when established firms engage in search scope and search depth activities simultaneously.

The joint and systematic pursuit of both forms of open search within the context of alliance portfolios and meta-organizations often results in the creation of new knowledge (Ahuja and Lampert, 2001; Capaldo, 2007). Search scope and search depth activities are separate, orthogonal theoretical constructs, but complementary, and in alliance and alliance portfolio settings, each is essential to the other. When new knowledge must be created, search depth activities often allow for more intense search scope activities, and search depth activities often allow for more intense search scope activities relative to the knowledge creation that is essential to breakthrough innovations. For example, search scope is important to breakthrough innovations that are based on radical technologies when the need to describe a new invention, technology, or device function is aided by referencing distant elements of an existing knowledge domain beyond the bounds of the focal firm and project alliance, such as in the alliance portfolio and meta-organization (O'Connor et al., 2008). In such instances, the knowledge domains developed in conjunction with the technology or invention through search depth are informed by and integrated with outside knowledge, forming new knowledge. Conversely, search depth is important to breakthrough innovations that are based on the unique combination of existing knowledge domains as the need arises to understand and describe the combination's business applications. Search depth aids this type of knowledge creation by referencing obscure elements of the knowledge domain residing within the bounds of the focal firm, its alliance partners, and conceptually congruent meta-organizations during the innovation development process (O'Connor et al., 2008). In such instances, the knowledge domain developed in conjunction with the unique combination of existing knowledge domains is informed and integrated with knowledge of the partnership, creating new knowledge (Ahuja and Lampert, 2001). Thus, breakthrough innovations may be initiated by search depth or search scope activities, but within an alliance portfolio environment, the use of both is likely necessary to generate the new knowledge required for breakthrough innovations. Focal firms that possess or develop capabilities to form and maintain open alliances that search broadly, as well as form and maintain open alliances that search deeply over the course of the innovation process, may be able to increase both the range and amplitude of those benefits, as depicted in the Point B portion of Figure 11.2 (Gupta, Smith, and Shalley, 2006; Raisch et al., 2009).

Knowledge Exchange Capabilities

The effective and efficient movement, combination, and integration of knowledge in the portfolio context is contingent on the capabilities of the partnership to manage complexity arising from knowledge exchange across organizational and conceptual boundaries (Dhanaraj and Parkhe, 2006; Ozcan and Eisenhardt, 2009; Powell, Koput, and Smith-Doerr, 1996). Complexity arises when the knowledge domains sourced by the focal firm, its partners, and the meta-organization in the innovation process are unfamiliar and incongruent and do not overlap. Complexities also arise, sometimes exponentially, when the knowledge domains do not exist and need to be co-developed with the innovation. Thus, as complexity increases, so must the sophistication of the knowledge exchange capability. As such, we adopt Carlile's (2004) framework for managing knowledge exchange across boundaries. The framework delineates three progressively sophisticated knowledge exchange capabilities—transfer, translation, and transformation capability—each of which builds upon the other and addresses increasingly difficult complexities associated with technical and organizational boundaries of breakthrough innovations in the portfolio context. These knowledge exchange capabilities are dynamic and may be co-developed with the knowledge domains of breakthrough innovations throughout the innovation development process.

Transfer Capability

Transfer capability is necessary when there is a low degree of novelty and complexity arising from the lack of incongruence between accessed knowledge domains. In such instances, collaborators need only move or transfer knowledge, as common and similar definitions and meanings exist between the collaborators. Within the portfolio context, transfer capability is most applicable when knowledge exchange occurs between longstanding and familiar partners that share repeated experiences. The technical and business knowledge that resides in the conceptual and organizational domains of the collaborators associated with the innovation project is very similar and shared. Such collaborations are primarily formed to compete on the basis of scale and economy and, when not associated with breakthrough innovations, are narrowly focused on incremental and limited modular innovations associated with new product development, production, and operations. In addition, the partners are likely to have highly defined roles relative to the product lines and businesses of the focal firm and will have likely committed considerable resources to the ongoing operations and innovation platforms supported by the focal firm. Therefore, transfer capability enables the exploitation of understood and codified knowledge; however, it is necessary but insufficient when exploration is required to find and integrate disparate technological and business knowledge domains (Carlile, 2004).

Transfer capability is limited, but it is utilized in all phases of the innovation development process. As we will discuss below, part of the purpose of the other two knowledge exchange capabilities—translation and transformation—is to manipulate and synthesize knowledge from disparate knowledge domains so that it may be codified, enabling simple transfer among partners and, ultimately, to clientele. This process is depicted in the integrative framework by the narrowing of the active and inactive knowledge domains of the alliance portfolio from the conceptualization to the development phases of innovation. Furthermore, knowledge transfer is essential once the initial and successive conceptual and business boundaries of breakthrough innovation are delineated if the collaboration is to license or spin out intellectual property, seeking the development of complementary products that enhance the value and usability of the breakthrough innovation. If the knowledge is not codified and defined, it is difficult to set parameters for its intellectual property value for licensing (West, 2006). Codified and easily transferable knowledge also simplifies the experience for the user and may possibly limit infringements and deter misapplication of the technology and business knowledge, minimizing risks associated with the release of such knowledge and information (West, 2006). Thus when the new knowledge domains and capabilities associated with the breakthrough innovation are developed to the point at which they achieve congruence with the existing knowledge domains or are clearly delineated to the point at which they clearly define the breakthrough innovation with a new and understandable lexicon, knowledge flows effectively and efficiently in and out of the R&D partnership.

Translation Capability

Translation capability is necessary when there is a moderate degree of complexity arising from partial incongruence between the accessed knowledge domains. In such instances, the collaborators must interpret and translate knowledge, as they do not fully share common meanings, definitions, and lexicons of understanding. The meanings, definitions, and lexicons the collaborators do share often become the basis for translation, allowing for the manipulation and synthesis of knowledge. Within the alliance and portfolio context, translation capability is most applicable when there is some diversification within the alliance and linkages to the meta-organization. Such alliances are likely to be composed of longstanding and frequent partners, as well as new partners that provide different and diverse technical and business knowledge for the innovation project (Frey, Lüthje, and Haag, 2011). Collaborations of this type are formed primarily for the purposes of modular and minor architectural innovations to existing products and product platforms. Focal firms that rely on these types of alliances often compete via planned, periodic platform improvements to capture market share relative to rivals. Examples of such firms include video game console manufacturers (e.g., Sony, Nintendo, and Microsoft), microchip manufacturers (e.g., Intel and AMD), and automobile manufacturers (e.g., GM, Toyota, and Mercedes). Competitive advantage generated by these and similar focal firms depends on developing generational products and new models at specified intervals. Each successive generation builds upon existing knowledge and incorporates some new knowledge, improving the performance of their respective platforms by adding and augmenting features. The new knowledge and technologies that are included frequently do not dramatically alter the platform or design of the product; rather, the new knowledge and technology help to evolve the product. In some instances, the evolutionary step is dramatic. Thus, translation capability enables the limited exploration and assimilation of knowledge domains beyond the existing knowledge domains associated with the product platform, allowing for the relatively rapid exploitation of that acquired knowledge. Like transfer capability, translation capability is necessary but insufficient for breakthrough innovation.

For breakthrough innovation to occur, technical and business knowledge from inside and outside the knowledge domain of the alliance portfolio must be translated to produce shared meaning and understandings. This translated knowledge need not be fully codified initially, but instead it represents an identifiable bridge or pathway between the disparate knowledge domains associated with a breakthrough innovation prior to and during the development of the lexicon. Such knowledge may be exchanged and understood between active and engaged actors inside and outside the alliance portfolio boundaries, by decoding and interpreting the meanings and values. In order to do this, the actors must be grounded in their respective knowledge domains and have some understanding of the shared and commonly understood elements between their own and the source's knowledge domain. These commonly understood elements allow knowledge and information to span two knowledge domains and to be relevant in each. Translation capability may be utilized throughout an innovation development process, but it is most prominent in the incubation and postdevelopment phases.

Transformation Capability

Transformation capability is necessary when there is a high degree of complexity arising from high levels of incongruence between the accessed technological and business domains, or the lack of a significant and identifiable knowledge domain associated with a new invention or scientific discovery. To realize innovations in such cases, collaborators must reinvent their own technical and business knowledge domains or create new technical and business knowledge domains associated with the innovation, as the existing meanings, definitions, and lexicons of understanding shared between the partners are inadequate and inappropriate to the innovation or simply do not exist.

At best, the shared meanings and understandings of the collaborators that do exist provide a basis for analysis and analogy to develop meanings, definitions, and understanding. At worst, the existing knowledge domains act as a barrier, blocking the development of knowledge and understanding relative to the innovation. In either case, the existing knowledge domains of the focal firm and its partners require change and are at risk, as is the well-being of the actors and collaborators invested in and dependent on those domains that may be in question (Carlile, 2004).

Alliances formed to develop transformation capability draw membership from varied and dissimilar contexts. The membership balance of such alliances is frequently weighted heavily to nontraditional partners of the focal firm, rather than long-held and frequent partners. These nontraditional partners are likely to include universities and research institutions, inventors, entrepreneurs, and lead clientele. The transformative alliance may also draw heavily on the meta-organization, in particular the knowledge embedded in geographic clusters, communities of practice, the focal firm's own internal discussion boards, and carefully selected digital forums. The frequent and closely held partners invited to such alliances often possess or provide access to unique knowledge, capabilities, and expertise that aid the collaboration.

The unique knowledge, capabilities, and expertise brought to bear in the new alliance will likely not have been applied and used in previous alliances with the focal firm. Rather, the unique knowledge, capabilities, and expertise may be utilized in the other alliances or within the obscure confines of the partners' R&D functions. When this occurs, some risks associated with nontraditional partners may be averted, as there may be a mutual and tacit understanding between the partners on how the project interaction is to proceed, due to their familiarity, but knowledge and information relative to breakthrough innovation will still have to be created and integrated. Conversely, the established partners may also represent an impediment to the transformative alliance, as the established partners are likely heavily invested in existing relationships that may be upset by the new knowledge and capabilities. However, if a closely held partners are committed to the breakthrough innovation and, more importantly, embraces the disruption associated with it, those partners may prove to be an indispensable allies in the innovation development process. Unique knowledge, capabilities, and expertise essential to transformation capability may also be sourced from the focal firm's own R&D function. As we stated above, focal firms can generate inventions and the new knowledge associated with them (Katilla and Ahuja, 2002). Within the bounds of a transformative alliance, any esoteric and obscure knowledge is selectively revealed for the purposes of finding its best use and application (Alexy, George, and Salter, 2013; Licthenthaler, 2010). As such, this knowledge and expertise represents the initial state of the as-yet-to-be-developed knowledge domain of the breakthrough innovation.

The purpose of transformation capability relative to breakthrough innovation is to produce a working knowledge domain of the emerging breakthrough innovation (Carlile, 2004). This working knowledge domain may draw upon distant domains to create analogies and schemata, laying the groundwork for more sophisticated and nuanced understandings and the development of the innovation's applications. Knowledge exchanged with these characteristics is far from concrete and is often conceptual in nature. Thus, transformation capability is most associated with the conceptualization phase of the innovation development process.

Furthermore, transformation is the only capability of the three that involves significant levels of knowledge creation. Breakthrough innovation cannot occur without the creation of knowledge. Therefore, transformation capability is the essential knowledge exchange capability relative to breakthrough innovation. However, transformation alone is insufficient to realize breakthrough innovations. Transformation must be used in conjunction with translation and transfer capabilities to realize breakthrough innovations throughout the innovation development process.

Innovation Development Process

Our treatment of the innovation development process delineates four phases: conceptualization, incubation, generation, and postgeneration. The first three phases are attributable to the models promoted by Gina O'Connor and colleagues (i.e., O'Connor 2006, 2008; O'Connor et al., 2008; O'Connor and Rice, 2013). Our postgeneration phase is an extension of the O'Connor models and is inspired by the Gulati, Puranam and Tushman's (2012) paper on meta-organizations and Bogers, Afuah, and Bastian's (2010) work on the user's role in innovation development. The conceptualization phase encompasses the invention, discovery, and initiation of the innovation, as well as the first speculations of its uses and applications. The incubation phase involves experimentation, testing, and trials of various forms of the innovation, allowing for the exploration of the potential uses and applications without significant commitment to the commercialization of the project applications. The generation phase includes a commitment to at least one of the previously explored applications and the acceleration of businesses and models that lead to the application's commercialization. The postgeneration phase refers to the time period that begins immediately after the commercialization and release of the innovative application. This phase may involve both proactive and reactive actions: proactive in the sense that interaction with the users and the market brings serendipitous realizations that the innovation has the potential for additional applications, which may or may not have been explored in the previous phases of the innovation development process (Bogers et al., 2010); reactive in the sense that interaction with users and the market for a particular application may be improved, is not well received, or may simply be a failure. Regardless of the ultimate outcome of breakthrough innovation, each phase of the innovation development process places different demands on the knowledge exchange capabilities as they are co-developed as part of the knowledge domain and lexicon relative to the breakthrough innovation. As we will discuss in detail below, alliance portfolio strategies deployed in the early research phases are different from the strategies deployed in the development and postdevelopment stages of the innovation process.

Knowledge exchange capability development is enabled and accelerated by the knowledge flow internal to the active knowledge domain of the alliance portfolio and across the active and inactive alliance portfolio knowledge domain boundaries to the meta-organization by means of open inbound, feedback and outbound knowledge flows in each of the four phases of the innovation development process (O'Connor, 2006; O'Connor et al., 2008; Ahuja, Lampert, and Novelli, 2013). The active and inactive knowledge domain boundaries illustrated by the centered constricting and darkening dashed-to-solid lines and framed by the gray double-dotted and dashed lines, respectively, are significant in that all of the knowledge resources of the alliance portfolio membership are not active and fully engaged during the innovation development process. Rather, the intellectual spaces and resources necessary for firms and partners to realize a breakthrough innovation must exceed the actual knowledge embodied in the innovation (Madhaven and Grover, 1998) and act as a reservoir of expertise to be tapped when unforeseen challenges and serendipities arise (Austin, Devin and Sullivan, 2012). Furthermore, the implicit and overall goal of each phase is to create usable knowledge that may further the breakthrough innovation's development in the next phase. In practice, the knowledge that is developed must be made more lucid, defined, and codified with each phase, thus making it more commercializable and transferable and utilizing less sophisticated knowledge exchange capabilities as the project progresses. This is illustrated by the narrowing of both the active knowledge domain and inactive knowledge domain boundaries to the development phase in the framework. Finally, the equal widths of each phase in the figure are not intended to imply that each phase takes an equal amount of time. This is done for graphical purposes. In reality, the duration of each phase is likely to vary considerably.

The sections that follow describe each of the four phases of the innovation development process—conceptualization, incubation, generation, and postgeneration—and are summarized in Table 11.1.

Each phase description begins with a brief explanation of its purpose and goal relative to the other phases and then discusses the boundary conditions of the knowledge domain boundary associated with the active alliance membership. These boundary conditions and the resultant level of complexity affect which of the knowledge exchange capabilities are most important for the successful completion of the phase. Finally, we discuss each of the four open innovation knowledge flows relative to the phase and give general examples of activities that may be associated with knowledge exchange capability in each phase. These examples are far from complete and are not prescriptive, but they were chosen to highlight key features and possibilities that are important to the development of knowledge domains and knowledge exchange capabilities associated with breakthrough innovation.

Conceptualization

The first phase of the innovation development process is the conceptualization phase. The goal of the phase is to produce concepts of the innovation, its applications, and its commercial potential (O'Connor, 2006; O'Conner et al., 2008).

Table 11.1 Summary of Activities Associated with the Innovation Development Process

	Conceptualization	Incubation	Generation	Postgeneration
Goal	To create knowledge that has not been seen before to solve an unforeseen or unaddressed problem of industry, relative to the industry	To create a viable prototype that meets technical and business viability concerns; in instances where the solution is so new, the viability of market creation must also be evaluated	To introduce and explain innovation with initial complementary innovations presenting a guiding framework for future collaborations while maintaining the collaborators' interests	To monitor and scan partner feedback, customer inputs, and unsolicited ideas for future business opportunities; selectively disclose additional knowledge as needed to capture secondary rents
Boundary Condition of the Active Alliance Membership Knowledge Domain	Vague and undefined; high degree of novelty arises primarily from the central technical and business opportunities of the potential innovation	Framed but not fully defined; considerable but lessened novelty from the central technology and business propositions; increased novelty arises from new partners, complimentary technologies and their associated business interests	Formed and defined; reduced intraorganizational novelty due to the solidification of the partner structure and the familiarization with the developed knowledge of the innovation; extraorganizational novelty arises as the innovation is commercialized, introduced, and encountered by users, would-be partners, and other entities	May remain fully defined; but form likely to expand and become less defined with time as application of core technology and business model occurs in different and sometimes unanticipated settings by partners, new partners, and outside-of-industry users
Knowledge Exchange Capability	Transformation—high novelty and complexity	Translation—moderate novelty and complexity	Translation to Transfer—moderate to low novelty and complexity	Transfer (possible Translation)—low to moderate novelty and complexity
Inbound Knowledge Activities	Spin-in and absorption of ideas, inventions, technologies, data, information, and knowledge from research institutions, experts, futurists, entrepreneurs, suppliers, start-ups, and users via licensure, investment, acquisition, scanning, hiring of human capital, partnership/alliance formation, or simple information uptake	Spin-in of complementary technologies and business expertise to resolve design and business implementation issues; extraorganizational collaborators include research institutions, partners not associated with innovation, competitors, or non-associated firms—possibly in other industries	Spin-in of market knowledge and initial user, partner, outside firm, and industry feedback, as the innovative innovation enters the market; acquire rights to complementary information, ideas, and technologies that further the innovation performance and provide added growth and value	Spin-in of emergent information, data, and knowledge from users, partners, start-ups, and would-be partners enabling the extension, expansion, or an alternative application of the innovation; moves should be selected to sustain or replace the innovation with the next generation

Knowledge Exchange Activities within the Alliance Portfolio Knowledge Domain	Creation of knowledge lexicon to describe and delineate nascent technological and business opportunities of a potential innovation; a result of the absorption of knowledge, sense making, intense internal circulation of data and information between partners, and technical knowledge production	Experimentation with a working lexicon to establish the likely boundaries of the technical and business innovation application; integration of new innovation technology and business opportunities with existing and captured technology and businesses that are evaluated, pursued, catalogued, held, or dismissed	Codification and deployment of a practical lexicon defining the initial technological and business applications of the innovation, their use, and the appropriability regime for their use	Continued evaluation and refinement of the existing applications in the context of market viability evaluations, new opportunities, and co-developed technologies; may also revisit those associated ideas and propositions shelved and delayed in earlier phases as technologies and knowledge emerge allowing for opportunities to be realized
Feedback Activities	Calculated release of information and knowledge to select actors to fill knowledge domain gaps and resolve difficult integrations	Calculated release of information and knowledge to select actors to gain insights on technical and business applications of innovation	Utilization of meta-organizational tools to solicit comments and feedback on existing innovations and aggregate insights for future innovations	Utilization of meta-organizational tools to solicit comments and feedback on existing innovations and aggregate insights for future innovations
Outbound Knowledge Activities	Selective spin-out of knowledge, information, and ideas and nascent innovation knowledge to possible partners regarding the technological and business opportunities of the proposed innovation via invitation, design competition parameters, and innovation malls (to garner feedback)	Spin-out, sale, or licensure of noncore technical knowledge to evaluate potential commercialization modes for that knowledge; recipients include patent brokers, suppliers, competitors, and other entities	Spin-out, sale, or licensure of technical and innovation knowledge to secure financial benefits, complementary efficiencies, create market share and momentum, and define alternative business opportunities; recipients include suppliers, select customers, competitors, and other firms	Select-spin out, if not full divestiture, of innovation technology and knowledge to sustain existing innovation, create greater opportunities for regeneration, or devalue the existing innovation in anticipation of next generation; recipients include suppliers, users, partners, competitors, and other firms external to the industry

Concepts are developed as the focal firm and its partner's progress through sub-processes beginning from the point of scientific discovery and invention or the identification and integration of disparate technologies and knowledge domains. The phase culminates in the articulation and elaboration of a nascent and emerging knowledge domain and lexicon relative to the innovation and the knowledge exchange capabilities to move and manipulate that knowledge.

Scientific discovery and invention refer to the realization of a new technology, process, or substance through research. Examples of scientific discoveries include new chemical compounds, alloys, and gene sequences. Thus, scientific discoveries represent the most basic and fundamental origins of innovation, as at the point of their discovery, they may have no known commercial application and an extremely limited knowledge domain. Invention refers to the unique and novel devices, methods, compositions, and processes resulting from research, necessity, and sometimes serendipities found by the focal firm, its partners, and other organizations, such as clientele and research institutions. Inventions are more complete than scientific discoveries and may be based on scientific discoveries. Unlike scientific discoveries, the initial applications for invention are more likely to exist, but the commercial viability of those applications is most likely undetermined. Identification and integration refer the recognition that different ideas and elements of existing products and technologies may be compatible and combined for the purposes of innovation in unique and novel ways. Identification presumes that the partnership possesses or may access the requisite knowledge bases, skills, and expertise to recognize and visualize the possibilities associated with unique and novel combinations.

Such abilities also suggest that the breadth and depth of the partnership's knowledge, skills, and expertise are significant and appropriate for the innovation project. The intellectual breadth of the resources allows the collaborators to examine a broad range of possibilities, finding unique possibilities for innovation. The depth of the resources allows the collaborators to visualize the applications of the innovation relative to ongoing and present business practices and user and market demands. Like identification, integration presumes that the partnership may access the requisite knowledge bases, skills, and expertise, but the breadth and depth of these abilities allows the partnership to synthesize information and knowledge from new and disparate knowledge domains to describe and define the conceptual combinations. Together, these activities that are employed to conceptualize the breakthrough innovation also create the nascent and emerging knowledge domains associated with the innovation and are evident in boundary conditions of the phase and the knowledge exchange capabilities requisite for the four knowledge flows associated with open innovation.

Knowledge Domain Boundary and Knowledge Exchange Capabilities during Conceptualization

The knowledge domain boundary of the alliance at the beginning of the conceptualization phase is likely to be very wide, vague, and undefined. As the phase progresses to conceptualize the innovation, the technical specifications, its potential applications, and its commercial prospects, the knowledge domain will narrow and become more apparent and defined. This progression is illustrated by the narrowing and darkening of the knowledge domain boundary of the active alliance membership illustrated in Figure 11.2. As such, all three knowledge exchange capabilities will be necessary during the conceptualization phase, but emphasis will be on the development of transformation capability.

The complexities associated with conceptualization are likely to be very high as the focal firm and its partners are likely to engage several different outside and inside actors via multiple knowledge flows (Gerbert, Boerner, and Kearney, 2010), constituting high degrees of search depth and scope. As this occurs, the partnership will be highly reliant on the transformation of its own knowledge domain to receive and understand the information from these various sources. With any success, the focal firm and its partners will broaden the collaboration's knowledge domain and improve the core competencies of the alliance membership. Thus the lessons of these activities may carry over to other initiatives or to future collaborations associated or similar to the breakthrough innovation initiative.

Inbound Knowledge during Conceptualization
The qualities and types of information and knowledge absorbed via inbound flows during conceptualization are largely dependent on the manner in which the partnership approaches the breakthrough innovation. However, the function of each one of these actions is to bring new knowledge into the alliance that is either utilized for the basis of the innovation or helps the focal firm and its partners discern the ambiguities associated with the innovation and create the fledgling knowledge domain and capabilities associated with it. When the collaboration is pursuing innovation by means of discovery and invention, the inbound information flows are likely to involve the collection of theoretical and basic research findings. This may be as simple as reading journals or purchasing basic research data sets pertaining to the materials, processes, and procedures under investigation. Other information may come from consultations with scientists, researchers, and experts of related processes and materials. These activities may result in the formation of partnerships and alliances with research institutions, universities, firms dedicated to basic research, inventors, and scientists. If the information or knowledge is sourced from a firm, the focal firm is likely to invite the firm into the alliance or, if the resources are available, acquire the firm. When the collaboration is pursuing innovation by means of invention, the inbound knowledge flows are likely to include any or all of the above information and knowledge flows related to discovery, as well as the purchase of licenses to existing technologies and inventions and the technical parameters of materials and processes needed to construct a proof-of-concept model associated with the invention. Innovation by means of the integration of knowledge domains is likely to include the purchase of licenses, as well as consultations with inventors, entrepreneurs, and futurists, and the formation of alliances with distant and unfamiliar partners not formerly associated with the

alliance portfolio. The focus of this exercise is broad search and integration. This may involve both the identification of possible combinations and the search for knowledge and information that binds the concept together in a manner that is discernible to both the collaborators working on the project and those evaluating the project's progress.

Internal Knowledge Circulation during Conceptualization

Internal knowledge circulation during the conceptual phase is primarily concerned with the creation of the knowledge domain and lexicon to describe and delineate the technological and business opportunities of the innovation. This involves *sense making*, the intense circulation of data and information between partners and technological knowledge production. *Sense making* refers to the ability to describe new and previous unknown phenomena by means of analogy and reference to unrelated fields of knowledge (Weick, Sutcliffe, and Obstfeld, 2005). This occurs when an actor encounters a phenomena or technology that is unfamiliar and begins to develop patterns of language and meaning that create basic understanding. Relative to breakthrough innovation in the conceptualization phase, sense making is particularly germane to the discovery and integration of disparate knowledge domains. These sense-making exercises enable intense circulation of the nascent knowledge between partners and help create the framework for the knowledge exchange capabilities necessary to move the knowledge during conceptualization and future phases. The result of internal knowledge circulation should be the establishment of the early knowledge exchange capabilities and conceptual understanding between partners of the innovation's technical aspects and with some initial ideas of the innovation's business potential.

Feedback during Conceptualization

Activities and associations made in attempts to acquire feedback during conceptualization are similar to those of the inbound innovation flows. The goal of soliciting feedback is to gain outside perspective and knowledge that advances the development of the knowledge domain and the knowledge exchange capabilities. Feedback is likely to include many, if not all, of the relationships associated with inbound knowledge flows. The difference between the two is the calculated release of information and knowledge related to the innovation project to the actors of the alliance portfolio and meta-organization. This may occur in different ways, depending on the objectives of the focal firm and its partners. Discrete disclosures will most likely occur to previous partners of the alliance portfolio or to hired consultants and supported research professionals bound by contract not to divulge proprietary knowledge and information pertaining to the innovation in development. Open disclosures during conceptualization involve solicitation of assistance by means of design competitions (Lampel, Jha, and Bhalla, 2012; Terwiesch and Yu, 2008), requests for proposals, and the use of innovation malls (Pisano and Verganti, 2008) seeking knowledge and information from the meta-organization. In total, these activities are designed to inform the activities of the internal knowledge circulation flow.

Outbound Knowledge Flows during Conceptualization
Outbound knowledge flows from the partnership are limited during the conceptualization phase. As we will see in later phases, outbound innovation flows usually concern the sale and licensure of information, knowledge, and technologies associated with the breakthrough innovation. At this early stage, the knowledge domain is not developed and codified enough to sufficiently enable this activity, but this is not to say a sale cannot happen. The sale may prove to be the divestiture of properties and personnel from the endeavor after the focal firm or its partners determine that pursuit of a particular technology or process is unrelated to their business goals or is unattainable in the desired time frame with their current resources and capabilities.

Incubation

The incubation phase involves experimentation, testing, and trials of various forms of the innovation, allowing for the exploration of the potential uses and applications without significant commitments. The goal of experimentation and testing is to identify at least one prototype that is technically viable and meets the business concerns of the focal firm, its partners, and the likely clientele (Grönlund, Sjödin, and Frishammar, 2010; O'Connor, 2006; O'Conner et al., 2008). This prototype captures and embodies the working knowledge domain and knowledge exchange capabilities of the breakthrough innovation. Furthermore, the prototype also signifies the maturation and advancement of the innovation's knowledge domain from a concept to a tangible and transferable state, utilized in the commercialization and establishment of the innovation upon introduction. The experimentation and testing of the innovation occurs in the partnership and across boundaries, utilizing the alliance portfolio networks and meta-organization tools. Within the open innovation context, these early engagements with potential clientele and users help to guide the innovation's development, explore its potential uses, and identify potential markets, some of which would not have been recognized otherwise (Baldwin and von Hippel, 2011; Bogers et al., 2010). The experimentation and testing also help the focal firm identify and establish the supply chain and value networks necessary to produce the application. Thus, the end of the incubation phase represents the end of most research activities associated with the R&D partnership.

Knowledge Domain Boundary and Knowledge Exchange Capabilities
during Incubation
The knowledge domain boundary of the active alliance members will continue to become more focused and defined during the incubation phase. As the phase progresses, experimentation and testing will produce knowledge as to which forms of the innovation and its applications are viable and which are not, given the current resources of the focal firm and its partners. The applications that are determined to be not viable are not necessarily discarded, but are more likely stored in the organizational memories of the focal firm, its partners, the alliance

portfolio, or the elements of the meta-organization engaged during the current and previous phases of the innovation development process. Furthermore, experimentation and testing may also identify complementary innovations that add value to the breakthrough innovation or create other markets entirely. This progression and solidification of the knowledge domain is illustrated in Figure 11.2 by the narrowing and darkening of the knowledge domain boundary of the active alliance membership. Though incubation activities are likely to utilize all three knowledge exchange capabilities early in the phase, the overall emphasis will be on translation. This is because the experimentation and testing will develop an increased understanding of the innovation and define its potential as well as its limits and constraints. The prototypes and models produced through incubation enable the exchange of knowledge between technically savvy first users and clientele, who, by means of the meta-organizational tools, have likely influenced the innovation's development to this point and increase the likelihood for initial success. The net effect is that complexity is reduced and the knowledge domains and knowledge exchange capabilities are matured, allowing for more focused and specific activities between the focal firm and the various present and future collaborators associated with the innovation. Additionally, the prototypes and models produced during the phase enable the establishment of the licensure and appropriability structures that allow for the production of codified knowledge necessary for the outbound knowledge flows and sharing of rents.

Inbound Knowledge during Innovation
The types of knowledge absorbed via inbound flows during the incubation phase are dependent on the testing and experimentation activities and approaches selected by the focal firm and its partners. The collaborators may choose to serially pursue the applications of the innovations based on an order of priority determined in feasibility studies, or the collaborators may have the resources to establish multiple and sometimes competing alliances to pursue applications for the innovation. The serial approach produces focused alliances and invites inbound information and knowledge streams from selected actors of the alliance portfolio and meta-organization. The broadcast approach produces multiple low-risk and low-commitment alliances and invites waves of information and knowledge from the alliance portfolio and meta-organization. The first approach suffers from a lack of variety in inbound knowledge. The latter may create too much variety and prove difficult to manage. However, if the partnership has sufficient knowledge exchange capabilities that allow the collaboration to quickly filter and absorb the information, resulting in synthesis, the second approach is likely to accelerate the innovation development process.

Internal Knowledge Circulation during Incubation
Internal in-alliance knowledge circulation during incubation is primarily concerned with the testing and experimentation of the developing knowledge domains and lexicons to establish the limits and boundaries of the technical and business applications of the innovation. Like the conceptualization phase,

incubation also involves sense making, but in this phase the focus of the activity is centered on the applications and business propositions of the innovation. As such, the partnership must determine which prospective applications should be pursued, cataloged, held, or dismissed. The cataloged and held applications often represent the opportunities that are not yet plausible with current technologies. However, the partnership may be aware of other technologies, inventions, and applications under development that may make the prospects plausible in the future. The dismissed applications may be candidates for sale as outbound knowledge activities. Internal circulation also focuses on the integration of new technology and business opportunities with captured technology and businesses. This activity produces new knowledge associated with the businesses and applications of the innovation. As such, these activities are central to the development of the prototypes used as the starting point of the generation phase.

Feedback during Incubation
Feedback activities during the incubation phase are similar to those of the conceptualization phase. However, the purpose of the feedback in the incubation phase is to gain insights and perspectives on the technical and business applications of the innovation, not the technical and integrative origins of the innovation. Entities engaged during this phase are likely to shift away from basic research entities, as the partnership begins to focus on suppliers, manufacturers, and lead clientele. As such, the prototypes produced by incubation are likely to reflect the resources currently available in the alliance portfolio, the meta-organization, and the needs of active and interested users and clientele. Feedback will also help the focal firm and its partners evaluate the viability of the proposed applications. In addition, and because the knowledge domain of the innovation is more concrete and defined, the feedback process is more likely to identify complementary and alternative applications and technologies compatible with the innovation.

Outbound Knowledge during Incubation
Outbound knowledge flows during incubation are likely to pertain to the sale or licensure of noncore technical knowledge to suppliers, manufacturers, and other firms. The sale of this knowledge signifies the maturation of the innovation and its imminent introduction. Other outbound information and knowledge released during incubation might include beta programs and programing code to open source developers that will create complementary applications and software relative to the innovation. Recipients of outbound knowledge likely include patent brokers, suppliers, competitors, and potential collaborators.

Generation

The generation phase involves the introduction and commercialization of the new innovation. The goal of the phase is to introduce the breakthrough innovation to the users and clientele and explain the parameters and guiding framework that allow the establishment of complementary innovations and future collaborations associated with the breakthrough innovation. The establishment of these guidelines shifts much of the onus of knowledge creation from the partnership to the users, clientele, and complementary innovation developers residing in the alliance portfolio and meta-organization. Set up properly, the parameters and framework will protect the business interests of the focal firm and its closest partners, while allowing a clear platform for the users, clientele, and complementary innovators to innovate and interact with the primary innovation and its developers (O'Connor, 2006; O'Conner et al., 2008).

Knowledge Domain Boundary and Knowledge Exchange Capabilities during Generation

The knowledge domain boundary of the active alliance membership will be highly defined and remain focused during the generation phase. The alliance structure will change as the emphasis moves away from research and experimentation to development and commercialization. As such, the membership of the active partnership will change, minimizing the relationships with the basic research-oriented partners and expanding relationships with partners that will help to bring the innovation to the market. Despite these changes, overall complexity will continue to fall as the knowledge exchange capabilities are developed and matured. The complexities that arise are brought about by the integration of complementary innovations with the breakthrough innovation, and from the perspective of the users, clientele, and complementary innovation developers not involved in the innovation's development as they encounter it for the first time. These clientele and users may have difficulty absorbing the unfamiliar knowledge associated with the breakthrough innovation.

Though transformation and translation capability may periodically be called upon to address issues arising from the migration of the innovation into different businesses and industries, the main knowledge exchange capability utilized in generation is transfer. Transfer is possible because complexities associated with the exchange of knowledge are minimal between the active alliance members. At this point, the focal firm and its partners have established routines, procedures, and a common lexicon for communications relative to the breakthrough innovation. The knowledge domain associated with breakthrough innovation will be modified in time, but in this phase, which includes the introduction of the innovation, little modification will occur unless there are unexpected circumstances associated with the introduction.

Inbound Knowledge during Generation

Inbound knowledge during generation involves the observation of user and developer activities associated with the innovation and the acquisition of technologies, processes, knowledge, and firms that are complementary to the innovation. Not all users, clientele, and complementary developers will directly communicate and provide feedback to the focal firm and its partners. These users and clientele are more likely to use any number of third-party forums, blogs, and other digital boards to post opinions, reviews, and their displeasure with the innovation. The focal firm and its partners often benefit by scanning and observing the interactions on these digital meta-organizational tools. Some users and clientele will discuss additional uses and applications for the innovation that may lead to the viable applications of the technology associated with the innovation. Others will provide insights on the innovation's use that lead to improvements or the establishment of complementary innovations. The focal firm may also seek to harvest via acquisition the firms that were started by utilizing the selective release of information, technology, and knowledge in the incubation phase.

Internal Knowledge Circulation during Generation
The internal knowledge circulation activities during the generation phase involve the codification and deployment of a practical lexicon defining the initial technological and business applications of the innovation, its use, and the appropriability regime for its use. Codification of the technological applications simply defines the innovation's limits and performance attributes. *Business applications* refer to how the innovation may be utilized by its users to generate revenues. *Use* simply refers to what the innovation does relative to other products, procedures, and systems. The *appropriability regime* clearly defines how the revenues will flow from the users to the partnerships as a result of the innovation. Together, these activities create the framework by which users, clientele, partners, competitors, and other organizational entities will interact with the innovation, applying it in different contexts and generating royalties for the partnership.

Feedback during Generation
Feedback during generation is largely a function of the meta-organizational tools and support services deployed with the innovation. Though these tools often do not explicitly request feedback, the existence of such tools and their associations to the innovation provide a convenient location for users and clientele to express opinions and commentary about the innovation. Many firms currently sponsor message forums that allow users to post questions and comments relative to an introduced product or service. These forums also allow users to discuss the product or service experience and potential improvements to the innovation. Collectively, they act to solicit, collect, catalog, and store the feedback for use in improvements to the innovation and for insights to additional innovations both complementary and independent of the breakthrough innovation.

Outbound Knowledge during Generation
Outbound knowledge flows during the generation phase involve the licensure and sale of technical and business knowledge relative to the innovation. These sales occur to secure financial benefits, create complementary efficiencies, create market share and momentum, and define alternative business opportunities. Purchasers of the licenses include suppliers, select customers, competitors, and other firms.

Postgeneration

The postgeneration phase involves both the activities that improve and sustain the initial innovation and the observation of the business environment to determine the needs and opportunities for future innovations based on the knowledge domain of the breakthrough innovation and other technologies and integrations (Bogers, Afuah, and Bastian, 2010; Gulati, Puranam, and Tushman, 2012). Improvements and activities to sustain the innovation are often based on partner feedback, customer inputs, and unsolicited ideas (Alexy, Criscuolo, and Salter, 2012). The goal of the phase relative to the innovation is to remain viable. The goal of the phase relative to the partnerships is to remain competitive. As such, remaining competitive may not include maintaining the innovation. An option in this phase is the divestiture of the innovation and its intellectual properties if evaluation finds the circumstances unsustainable.

Knowledge Domain Boundary and Knowledge Exchange Capabilities during Postgeneration

The knowledge domain boundary of the active alliance membership may remain fully defined, but it is more likely to broaden and become less defined with time as the application of the core technology ages and is adopted and applied by different users in different settings and circumstances. The boundary may also be loosened as the focal firm continues to release once-proprietary information and knowledge about the core knowledge domain to additional users and clientele. Though this may occur gradually, the cumulative effect may change the innovation entirely over time. The cumulative effect and volume of the user-inspired modifications may also create greater complexities for the focal firm and necessitate the use of translation and, eventually, transformation capability.

Inbound Knowledge during Postgeneration

Inbound knowledge activities associated with the postgeneration phase are likely to mirror the observation and acquisition activities associated with the inbound knowledge during the generation phase. However, there may be more and additional emphasis on the spin in of unsolicited emergent information, data, and knowledge from users, partners, start-ups, and would-be partners, enabling the extension, expansion, or alternative applications of the innovation (Alexy, Criscuolo, and Salter, 2012). Though there are many factors involved with this, the availability of such information depends on whether the innovation was indeed successful, capturing significant market share and being utilized by multiple users, clientele, and firms in other industries. This may also be a function of the innovation's duration in the industry, allowing other firms and users to become familiar with the innovation and its knowledge domains over time such that they seek additional features and applications for the innovations. Moves based on inbound information of this type should be carefully evaluated and approached. Though the overall volume of the demand could be large, the overall innovation improvements could be small and inconsequential, making the decision to improve the established product or service a nonissue. However, the demand and needs of the evolving clientele and the current architecture of the innovation may not be compatible, and the focal firm should carefully evaluate the situation to determine if the innovation should undergo breakthrough improvements or be replaced by the next generation of the innovation; or they may search and determine whether another solution is more appropriate for the problems identified by the unsolicited inbound knowledge flows and feedback.

Internal Knowledge Circulation during Postgeneration
Internal knowledge circulation during the postgeneration phase can be multifaceted. In addition to the evaluation of unsolicited information absorbed by the partnerships, the collaborators may choose to revisit applications of the innovation that were held or shelved during earlier phases. These shelved and held applications may provide better answers to the demands and needs of the actors requesting changes to the current innovation. The shelved and held applications of the innovations may also be the basis for value-adding and sustaining complementary innovations (Faems et al., 2010). The stored applications may also be the basis for the next generation of the breakthrough innovation. The partnership should also continue to evaluate the present innovation and its improvements, but at this point, the evaluation may include the sustainability of the innovation and routes to divestiture.

Feedback during Postgeneration
Like the feedback during generation, feedback during postgeneration is largely a function of the meta-organizational tools and support services deployed with the innovation. In postgeneration, however, the feedback tools are likely to lose the capacity to produce quantities of novel information if the innovation's applications and design remains static. The users of such tools are likely to be longtime users and, as such, offer little in the way of new and novel information relative to improving the innovation. There will be a few new participants and late adopters that may impart knowledge and information important to future generations of the innovation. However, these contributions may be sporadic at best. Thus the feedback loop may lose its effectiveness over time, effectively accessing the same knowledge domains and users repeatedly and yielding less impactful results with each engagement.

Outbound Knowledge during Postgeneration
Postgeneration outbound knowledge flows will be similar to the outbound knowledge activities during the generation phase. However, subtle strategies may be enacted to prepare the industry and clientele for future innovations and generations of the current innovation. As in other phases, the focal firm may elect to selectively spin out innovation technology and knowledge to sustain the innovation. However, this activity may be approached systematically in a way that ultimately devalues the current innovation and prepares the industry and clientele for a planned new generation of the innovation. When this

occurs, the partnership seeks ways to regenerate, altering core competencies and beginning the innovation development cycle anew. The focal firm may also seek divestiture of the innovation. In this case the focal firm may be seeking exit from the industry or market, or it may have a new product or technology under development that will supersede and supplant the current innovation. If either is the case, the focal firm may have to alter its knowledge domain and core competencies to accommodate and retain the rents from the superseding innovation.

Discussion

In this chapter, we have suggested that single firms are usually not endowed with the requisite broad and sophisticated knowledge domains necessary to realize breakthrough innovations consistently, efficiently, or effectively, as is often required in competitive business environments (Kedia and Mooty, 2013). To counter this, firms frequently form partnerships with other entities to pursue innovation initiatives, and research of these phenomena suggests that this approach has yielded considerable success. Firms that compete in multiple industries utilizing several platforms often find themselves at the center of alliance portfolios. These alliance portfolios are a resource from which the broad and sophisticated knowledge necessary for breakthrough innovations may be drawn. However, the environment from which the broad and sophisticated knowledge is drawn has been enhanced and expanded by the emergence of meta-organizations that both enable and complicate breakthrough innovation development.

Open innovation practices allow partnerships to create, explore, retain, release, and exploit knowledge effectively and efficiently in the context of alliance portfolios and meta-organizations (O'Connor, 2006; O'Connor et al., 2008). Thus, focal firms choosing to engage in open R&D alliances may be more consistent in the development of breakthrough innovations when those projects are managed in the context of a firm's alliance portfolios (Hoffman, 2007) and the meta-organizations (Gulati, Puranam and Tushman, 2012) in which the focal firm and its portfolios are centered. Open innovation practices may be expressed in terms of knowledge flows of inbound, internal, feedback, and outbound knowledge across the organizational and conceptual boundaries of the partnership, alliance portfolio, and meta-organization in each phase of the innovation development process (O'Connor, 2006; Ahuja, Lampert, and Novelli, 2013). However, success and consistency are only possible when the dynamic capabilities of the partnership in managing the complexities arising from knowledge exchange and integration are commensurate with the demands of the innovation and appropriate to its stage of development (Carlile, 2004; Grant, 1996).

By definition, breakthrough innovations, which require the creation of new knowledge domains, are based on new technologies or unique and novel combinations of knowledge and possess the potential to disrupt existing industries and/or create new ones. The knowledge exchange capabilities associated with breakthrough innovations are co-developed and co-evolved with the requisite knowledge domains by means of organizational learning associated with the construction of and engagement with individual partnerships, alliances, alliance portfolios, and interfaces and procedures of meta-organizations over the course of the innovation development process (Heimeriks, Duysters, and Vanhaverbeke, 2007). When the breakthrough innovation is based on new technology or invention, the knowledge domain and lexicon associated with it is incomplete and centers on the technical capabilities and parameters of its performance. At its inception, the knowledge domain and lexicons associated with the potential applications of a new technology or discovery may not exist. Any knowledge of the innovation's potential and commercialization that does exist is mostly conceptual and speculative in nature and exists in forms that are difficult to move. When breakthrough innovations are based on unique and novel combinations of existing knowledge, the sourced knowledge domains may provide insight into the applications and commercialization of the new innovation. However, these insights will not be specific to the unique and novel combination. Knowledge of the unique and novel combinations' applications may be evident and, in fact, obvious but still must be developed and matured. As such, the new knowledge domains and lexicons relative and specific to the unique and novel combination's applications must be co-developed with the capabilities to exchange that knowledge. In either case, when the dynamic knowledge exchange capabilities are mature and sufficient relative to the co-developed knowledge domains and lexicons, efficient and effective knowledge exchange and integration may occur to the benefit of the focal firm, the partners, and the innovation itself. When the dynamic knowledge exchange capabilities are immature and insufficient, the project is likely to progress slowly, stall, unravel, and may ultimately fail. However, within the context of alliance portfolios, failure may not only be tolerated, it may be expected and necessary to the long-term development of a breakthrough innovation and the capabilities that will sustain the focal firm as it juggles and reconfigures alliances to capitalize on the lessons learned from those failures.

The knowledge generated from the experience of the development of knowledge domains and associated exchange capabilities does not evaporate with the completion of the breakthrough innovation project, regardless of its success or failure. When breakthrough innovation development is attempted in the context of alliances, alliance portfolios, and meta-organizations utilizing open innovation practices, the lessons from the experience are often and frequently captured, absorbed, embedded, and cataloged by the collaborative actors and participants, by means of the digital and traditional functions of the alliance portfolio and meta-organization (Lichtenthaler and Lichtenthaler, 2009). Therefore, if a focal firm attempts multiple breakthrough innovation development projects, it will accumulate these experiences over time, and organizational learning will likely occur as the knowledge domains and lexicons of the breakthrough innovation attempts, successful or not, are stored, referenced, and used for future and successive innovations.

Conclusion

With a few exceptions discussed and integrated above, the open innovation literature to date has focused on relatively minor modular and incremental innovations. However, competitive business environments are increasingly dependent on strategies that include competition by means of more substantial and breakthrough innovations. Firms competing in these environments are rapidly developing systematic and structured capabilities to realize these types of innovation, but there are still great variations in their success. In most instances, focal firms are not consulting textbooks or journals to develop these capabilities. They are learning to develop the capabilities via multiple experiences coupled with trial and error. They have also learned that the knowledge necessary for effective and efficient innovation does not reside in a single firm but is dispersed within the bounds of various organizational entities and individuals. To truly be successful and consistent in the development of substantial and breakthrough innovations, focal firms must be willing to engage these entities on various fronts, opening up the innovation process. The novel framework we have presented partially illustrates this process, which allows for failure as integral to organizational learning. Much more research is needed to flesh out the model and complete the picture. However, we conclude that our model begins to bring together many of the necessary components to realize a rich and robust theory explaining how firms may realize breakthrough innovations more reliably.

References

Ahuja, G., and Lampert, C. M. (2001). "Entrepreneurship in the Large Corporation: A Longitudinal Study of How Established Firms Create Breakthrough Inventions." *Strategic Management Journal* 22 (6–7): 521–43.

Ahuja, G., Lampert, C. M., and Novelli, E. (2013). "The Second Face of Appropriability: Generative Appropriability and Its Determinants." *Academy of Management Review* 38 (2): 249–69.

Alexy, O., George, G., and Salter, A. (2013). "Cui bono? The Selective Revealing of Knowledge and Its Implications for Innovative Activity." *Academy of Management Review* 38 (2): 270–91.

Alexy. O., Criscuolo, O., and Salter, A. (2012). "Managing Unsolicited Ideas for R&D." *California Management Review* 54 (3): 116–39.

Almirall, E., and Casadesus-Masanell, R. (2010). "Open versus Closed Innovation: A Model of Discovery and Divergence." *Academy of Management Review* 35 (1): 27–47.

Anderson, P., and Tushman, M. L. (1990). "Technological Discontinuities and Dominant Designs: A Cyclical Model of Technological Change." *Administrative Science Quarterly* 35:604–33.

Austin, R. D., Devin, L., and Sullivan, E. E. (2012). "Accidental Innovation: Supporting Valuable Unpredictability in the Creative Process." *Organization Science* 23 (5): 1505–22.

Baldwin, C., and von Hippel, E. (2011). "Modeling a Paradigm Shift: From Producer Innovation to User and Open Collaborative Innovation." *Organization Science* 22 (6): 1399–417.

Bogers, M., Afuah, A., and Bastian, B. (2010). "Users as Innovators: A Review, Critique, and Future Research Directions." *Journal of Management* 36 (4): 857–75.

Boudreau, K. J. (2010). "Open Platform Strategies and Innovation: Granting Access vs. Devolving Control." *Management Science* 56 (10): 1849–72.

Capaldo, A. (2007). "Network Structure and Innovation: The Leveraging of a Dual Network as a Distinctive Relational Capability." *Strategic Management Journal* 28: 585–608.

Carlile, P. R. (2004). "Transferring, Translating, and Transforming: An Integrative Framework for Managing Knowledge across Boundaries." *Organization Science* 15 (5): 555–68.

Carlile, P. R., and Rebentisch, E. S. (2003). "Into the Black Box: The Knowledge Transformation Cycle." *Management Science* 49 (9): 1180–95.

Chesborough, H. (2003). *Open Innovation: The New Imperative for Creating and Profiting from Technology.* Boston: Harvard Business School Press.

Deeds, D. L., and Hill, C. W. (1996). "Strategic Alliances and the Rate of New Product Development: An Empirical Study of Entrepreneurial Biotechnology Firms." *Journal of Business Venturing* 11 (1): 41–55.

Dhanaraj, C., and Parkhe, A. (2006). "Orchestrating Innovation Networks." *Academy of Management Review* 31 (3): 659–69.

Duysters, G., and Lokshin, B. (2011). "Determinants of Alliance Portfolio Complexity and Its Effect on Innovative Performance of Companies*." *Journal of Product Innovation Management* 28 (4): 570–85.

Eisenhardt, K. M., and Tabrizi, B. N. (1995). "Accelerating Adaptive Processes: Product Innovation in the Global Computer Industry." *Administrative Science Quarterly* 40 (1): 84–110.

Faems, D., De Visser, M., Andries, P., and Van Looy, B. (2010). "Technology Alliance Portfolios and Financial Performance: Value-Enhancing and Cost-Increasing Effects of Open Innovation*." *Journal of Product Innovation Management* 27 (6): 785–96.

Faraj, S., Jarvenpaa, S. L., and Majchrzak, A. (2011). "Knowledge Collaboration in Online Communities." *Organization Science* 22 (5): 1224–39.

Fleming, L., and Sorenson, O. (2004). "Science as a Map in Technological Search." *Strategic Management Journal* 25 (8–9): 909–28.

Fjeldstad, Ø. D., Snow, C. C., Miles, R. E., and Lettl, C. (2012). "The Architecture of Collaboration." *Strategic Management Journal* 33 (6): 734–50.

Frey, K., Lüthje, C., and Haag, S. (2011). "Whom Should Firms Attract to Open Innovation Platforms? The Role of Knowledge Diversity and Motivation." *Long Range Planning* 44 (5): 397–420.

Garcia, R., and Calantone, R. (2002). "A Critical Look at Technological Innovation Typology and Innovativeness Terminology: A Literature Review." *Journal of Product Innovation Management* 19 (2): 110–32.

Gebert, D., Boerner, S., and Kearney, E. (2010). "Fostering Team Innovation: Why Is It Important to Combine Opposing Action Strategies?" *Organization Science* 21 (3): 593–608.

Grant, R. M. (1996). "Prospering in Dynamically-Competitive Environments: Organizational Capability as Knowledge Integration." *Organization Science* 7 (4): 375–87.

Grant, R. M., and Baden-Fuller, C. (2004). "A Knowledge Accessing Theory of Strategic Alliances." *Journal of Management Studies* 41 (1): 61–84.

Govindarajan, V., Kopalle, P. K., and Danneels, E. (2011). "The Effects of Mainstream and Emerging Customer Orientations on Radical and Disruptive Innovations." *Journal of Product Innovation Management* 28 (S1): 121–32.

Grönlund, J., Sjödin, D. R., and Frishammar, J. (2010). "Open Innovation and the Stage-Gate Process: A Revised Model for New Product Development." *California Management Review* 52 (3): 106–31.

Gulati, R., Puranam, P., and Tushman, M. (2012). "Meta-organization Design: Rethinking Design in Interorganizational and Community Contexts." *Strategic Management Journal* 33 (6): 571–86.

Gupta, A. K., Smith, K. G., and Shalley, C. E. (2006). "The Interplay between Exploration and Exploitation." *Academy of Management Journal* 49 (4): 693–706.

Heimeriks, K. H., Duysters, G., and Vanhaverbeke, W. (2007). "Learning Mechanisms and Differential Performance in Alliance Portfolios." *Strategic Organization* 5 (4): 373–408.

Heimeriks, K. H., Klijn, E., and Reuer, J. J. (2009). "Building Capabilities for Alliance Portfolios." *Long Range Planning* 42 (1): 96–114.

Helfat, C. E., and Raubitschek, R. S. (2000). "Product Sequencing: Co-evolution of Knowledge, Capabilities and Products." *Strategic Management Journal* 21 (10–11): 961–79.

Henderson, R. M., and Clark, K. B. (1990). "Architectural Innovation: The Reconfiguration of Existing Product Technologies and the Failure of Established Firms." *Administrative Science Quarterly* 35: 9–30.

Hoffmann, W. H. (2007). "Strategies for Managing a Portfolio of Alliances." *Strategic Management Journal* 28 (8): 827–56.

Jeppesen, L. B., and Frederiksen, L. (2006). "Why Do Users Contribute to Firm-Hosted User Communities? The Case of Computer-Controlled Music Instruments." *Organization Science* 17 (1): 45–63.

Jeppesen, L. B., and Lakhani, K.R. (2010). "Marginality and Problem-Solving Effectiveness in Broadcast Search." *Organization Science* 21 (5): 1016–33.

Jiang, R. J., Tao, Q. T., and Santoro, M. D. (2010). "Alliance Portfolio Diversity and Firm Performance." *Strategic Management Journal* 31 (10): 1136–44.

Kale, P., Dyer, J. H., and Singh, H. (2002). "Alliance Capability, Stock Market Response, and Long-Term Alliance Success: The Role of the Alliance Function." *Strategic Management Journal* 23 (8): 747–67.

Katila, R., and Ahuja, G. (2002). "Something Old, Something New: A Longitudinal Study of Search Behavior and New Product Introduction." *Academy of Management Journal* 45 (6): 1183–94.

Kedia, B. L., and Mooty, S. E. (2013). "Learning and Innovation in Collaborative Innovation Networks." In B. L. Kedia and S. C. Jain (eds.), *Restoring America's Global Competitiveness through Innovation*, 3–27. Cheltham, UK: Edward Elgar.

Kessler, E. H., and Chakrabarti, A. K. (1996). "Innovation Speed: A Conceptual Model of Context, Antecedents, and Outcomes." *Academy of Management Review* 21 (4): 1143–91.

Kogut, B. (2000). "The Network as Knowledge: Generative Rules and the Emergence of Structure." *Strategic Management Journal* 21 (3): 405–25.

Kyriakopoulos, K., and De Ruyter, K. (2004). "Knowledge Stocks and Information Flows in New Product Development*." *Journal of Management Studies* 41 (8): 1469–98.

Lampel, J., Jha, P. P., and Bhalla, A. (2012). "Test-Driving the Future: How Design Competitions are Changing Innovation." *Academy of Management Perspectives* 26 (2): 71–85.

Laursen, K., and Salter, A. (2006). "Open for Innovation: The Role of Openness in Explaining Innovation Performance among UK Manufacturing Firms." *Strategic Management Journal* 27 (2): 131–50.

Lichtenthaler, U. (2011). "Open Innovation: Past Research, Current Debates, and Future Directions." *The Academy of Management Perspectives* 25 (1): 75–93.

Lichtenthaler, U. (2010). "Technology Exploitation in the Context of Open Innovation: Finding the Right 'Job' for Your Technology." *Technovation* 30 (7): 429–35.

Lichtenthaler, U., and Lichtenthaler, E. (2009). "A Capability-Based Framework for Open Innovation: Complementing Absorptive Capacity." *Journal of Management Studies* 46 (8): 1315–38.

Madhavan, R., and Grover, R. (1998). "From Embedded Knowledge to Embodied Knowledge: New Product Development as Knowledge Management." *The Journal of Marketing*: 62 (4):1–12.

Mansfield, E. (1988). "The Speed and Cost of Industrial Innovation in Japan and the United States: External vs. Internal Technology." *Management Science* 34 (10): 1157–68.

Maula, M. V. J., Keil, T., and Salmenkaita, J.-K. (2006). "Open Innovation in Systemic Innovation Contexts." In H. Chesborough, W. Vanhaverbeke, and J. West (eds.), *Open Innovation: Researching a New Paradigm*, 241–57. New York: Oxford University Press.

Nonaka, I. (1994). "A Dynamic Theory of Organizational Knowledge Creation." *Organization Science* 5 (1): 14–37.

O'Connor, G. C. (2006). "Open, Radical Innovation: Toward an Integrated Model in Large Established Firms." In H. Chesborough, W. Vanhaverbeke, and J. West (eds.), *Open Innovation: Researching a New Paradigm*, 62–81. New York: Oxford University Press.

O'Connor, G. C. (2008). "Major Innovation as a Dynamic Capability: A Systems Approach*." *Journal of Product Innovation Management* 25 (4): 313–30.

O'Connor, G. C., Leifer, R., Paulson, A. S., and Peters, L. S. (2008). *Grabbing Lightning: Building a Capability for Breakthrough Innovation.* John Wiley and Sons.

O'Connor, G. C., and Rice, M. P., (2013). "New Market Creation for Breakthrough Innovations: Enabling and Constraining Mechanisms." *Journal of Product Innovation Management* 30 (2): 209–27.

Ozcan, P., and Eisenhardt, K. M. (2009). "Origin of Alliance Portfolios: Entrepreneurs, Network Strategies, and Firm Performance." *Academy of Management Journal* 52 (2): 246–79.

Pisano, G. P., and Verganti, R. (2008). "Which Kind of Collaboration Is Right for You?" *Harvard Business Review* 86 (12): 78–86.

Powell, W., Koput, K., and Smith-Doerr, L. (1996). "Interorganizational Collaboration and the Locus of Innovation: Networks of Learning in Biotechnology." *Administrative Science Quarterly* 41 (Mar.): 116–45.

Raisch, S., Birkinshaw, J., Probst, G., and Tushman, M. L. (2009). "Organizational Ambidexterity: Balancing Exploitation and Exploration for Sustained Performance." *Organization Science* 20 (4): 685–95.

Sampson, R. C. (2007). "R&D Alliances and Firm Performance: The Impact of Technological Diversity and Alliance Organization on Innovation." *Academy of Management Journal* 50 (2): 364–86.

Schumpeter, J. A. (1934). *The Theory of Economic Development.* Cambridge, MA: Harvard University Press.

Terwiesch, C., and Xu, Y. (2008). "Innovation Contests, Open Innovation, and Multi-agent Problem Solving." *Management Science* 54 (9): 1529–43.

Vanhaverbeke, W., and Cloodt, M., (2006). "Open Innovation in Value Network." In H. Chesborough, W. Vanhaverbeke, and J. West (eds.), *Open Innovation: Researching a New Paradigm*, 258–81. New York: Oxford University Press.

Verganti, R. (2011). "Designing Breakthrough Products." *Harvard Business Review* 89 (10): 114–20.

Wassmer, U. (2010). "Alliance Portfolios: A Review and Research Agenda." *Journal of Management* 36 (1): 141–71.

Weick, K. E., Sutcliffe, K. M., and Obstfeld, D. (2005). "Organizing and the Process of Sensemaking." *Organization Science* 16 (4): 409–21.

West, J., (2006). "Does Appropriability Enable or Retard Open Innovation?" In H. Chesborough, W. Vanhaverbeke, and J. West (eds.), *Open Innovation: Researching a New Paradigm*, 109–33. New York: Oxford University Press.

Yoo, Y., Boland, R. J., Lyytinen, K., and Majchrzak, A. (2012). "Organizing for Innovation in the Digitized World." *Organization Science* 23 (5): 1398–408.

CHAPTER 12

Corporate Groups and Open Innovation: The Case of Panasonic in Japan

Hiroyuki Nakazono, Takashi Hikino, and Asli M. Colpan

Introduction

This chapter examines the struggling transformation process of a Japanese corporate group from its conventionally adopted closed technological innovation model to open innovation. The chapter incorporates the structural feature of *corporate groups*, an operational model characteristic of large Japanese companies, as the critical mediating variable that influences the organizational choice of conventional closed and novel open innovation processes. The corporate group is the organizational design implemented by a firm with the strategy of related diversification that adopts the consequential structure of multidivisional form but recognizes the strategic and operational autonomy of those operating divisions.

We take Panasonic Corporation as the subject of analysis as that company represents one of the most active corporate groups in Japan in terms of its diversification into related business activities and also expansion into overseas markets. The company also exemplifies the decentralized structural design in which many of the company's operations are organized as either sovereign product divisions or separate legally independent subsidiaries with strategic and managerial autonomy as if they formed an equity alliance or a network structure with free-standing firms, which is a typical distinction of large and established firms in Japan.

Panasonic, previously named Matsushita Electric Industrial Company (until 2008), is a comprehensive electronics manufacturer and one of the largest enterprises in that industry in the global market.[1] The electronics industry of Japan faced some of particularly large changes in its economic environment and experienced dramatic challenges in international competition. Since the industry adapted the conversion to the digitization of electronics technology around 2000, Panasonic began reforming its structural and operational design by going through a fundamental reorganization of its entire corporate group. This modification had become necessary in order to centralize and integrate the resources that had been accumulated in the center yet dispersed among operating divisions and subsidiaries. This overall integration and utilization of resources within the whole Panasonic group eventually meant the renewed commitment to a closed innovation model within individual operating units that would give the company a temporary recovery in market competitiveness and financial performance.

Panasonic, however, lost its competitive power in changing market environments, especially after the "Lehman Shock" in 2008. By holding on to a closed innovation model, the group company basically could not adapt to the shifting market and technological conditions. Although Panasonic has since 2008 aimed at integrating its conventional model of R&D with open innovation, it has not succeeded in that conversion process to date. Why has Panasonic not been able to effectively shift to an open innovation model? What is the role of the organizational structure and design of the corporate group in this attempt? The present chapter attempts to answer these critical questions.

The chapter is organized as follows. The following section summarizes the conceptual framework and research context regarding corporate groups and technological innovation in Japanese enterprises. The second section describes the transformation of the organizational structure and R&D processes of the Panasonic corporate group. Concentrating on the focal interest described above, the third section then analyzes the development of Panasonic's innovation model since its heyday of division-focused closed innovation. The final section defines Panasonic's failure in formulating a process to promote open innovation beyond group boundaries.

Conceptual Framework and Research Context

The Corporate Group Structure and Technological Innovation

Research involving the corporate group structure and technological innovation of a company has lately been the popular subject of academic inquiry that takes business groups in a late-industrializing economy as its focus. Examples of such business groups include Japanese *keiretsu*, South Korean *chaebol*, the business houses in India, and the *grupos economicos* in Latin America. A business group is typically described as the amalgamation of legally independent companies through equity and/or nonequity ties (such as managerial interlocks). The general feature of business groups in those emerging economies is that they represent technologically unrelated diversification, and they are usually, but not always, held under the control of families (Colpan and Hikino, 2010; Khanna and Yafeh, 2007).

In contemporary Japan, there are two different business groups, but they represent interrelated sets of organizations. First is the business network, where large companies hold each other's equity but do not have any controlling entity, such as a headquarters or holding company at the top. A typical example is the Mitsubishi group of companies. It is argued that these networks have been weakened in Japan in recent decades, especially after the 1990s when Japan entered its economic recession that has lasted for more than two decades (Lincoln and Shimotani, 2010). The second type is the so-called corporate groups, in which equity- and otherwise-tied companies are organized around a core parent company. The companies in this type of group are autonomous in their operations, and they are also mostly operating in businesses that are related to the parent company. One example of such groups is the Panasonic group, where the parent company is in the electronics business and its more than six hundred independent subsidiaries and affiliated companies are operating in technologically related businesses under the ownership of various equity stakes of the parent company, Panasonic Corporation. This second type of group consists of dominant large enterprises in today's Japanese economy (Lincoln and Shimotani, 2010). As such, they are the focus of this present study.

What influence, then, does such a group structure have on the technological innovation process of the group companies? Michael Hobday and Asli M. Colpan (2010) argue that business groups facilitate innovation by providing "innovation infrastructure" (a term coined by Mahmood and Mitchell [2004]), which consists of critical assets, including financial and human resources, knowledge sourcing, and vertical intermediation. Firms in a business or corporate group exploit such assets for the successful innovation of group members. Group membership, for instance, permits member companies to tap into intragroup capital markets. As a result, groups can easily allocate resources to new innovative projects, especially when the external capital markets are less developed (Khanna and Tice, 2001; Mahmood and Mitchell, 2004). In a study of European firms, Sharon Belenzon and Tomer Berkovitz (2010) show that group-affiliated firms are more innovative than standalone companies.

Group-affiliated firms may also be in an advantageous position to source the required resources for innovation as the other member firms may relatively easily provide the skills, equipment, and other resources that are readily available within the group (Chang, Chung, and Mahmood, 2006; Hobday and Colpan, 2010). While Masatoshi Fujiwara (2007) found different patterns of technology transfer between the related diversified groups and the unrelated diversified groups in Japan, the exact nature of those differences is, however, still not that clear. Furthermore, technology transfer within the group network occurs in a way similar to that of open innovation, where independent and autonomous divisions and subsidiaries within the group may provide the necessary knowledge to the focal firm or other operating units belonging to the group. The case of the Panasonic group, as described below, however, shows how such intragroup inflow and outflow of technological knowledge can sometimes result in organizational conflicts as the group concurrently embraces open innovation.

Institutional Settings and Open Innovation in Japan

The general characteristic of large Japanese companies should be described in order to comprehend the institutional context of their attempted conversion into a model suitable to open innovation. Open innovation represents a theoretical framework in which external knowledge is utilized and combined with a firm's internal R&D activities to come up with commercializable products or processes (Chesbrough, 2003; Lee et al., 2010; Takeishi, 2010). It is mostly based on the US business environment and economic structure (see Figure 12.1). The US economy is known to be equipped with such transfirm resources as abundant venture capital, plentiful start-up businesses, and mobile and talented human capital (Chesbrough, 2003; Chesbrough, 2006a; Nakazono, 2013). In Japan, although start-up businesses have been developing and talented entrepreneurs are increasing , their number, level, and characteristics remain limited in comparison to the economic settings in the United States, which are surely more conducive to open innovation (Chesbrough, 2013; Motohashi, 2008). An argument persists among Japanese scholars that open innovation does not effectively fit into the Japanese settings because of a unique institutional environment in Japan that is different from those of the United States (Itami, 2009; Niwa, 2010). Furthermore, as Japanese companies have grown by the accumulation of internal resources and by the practical use of those resources, previous studies suggest that the companies may not actively utilize external resources beyond the firm itself even when they become available (Odagiri, 1992; Yoshihara et al., 1981).

Therefore, Japanese companies have conventionally followed the constricted model of closed innovation by developing and holding on to intrafirm technological resources and capabilities. However, they have historically been quite active in some aspects of open innovation, such as the deployment of some of internally developed technological resources outside of the firm. It is common for large Japanese firms to establish subsidiaries or form joint ventures for commercializing those resources instead of selling off underutilized and idle resources to outside parties in the market. It is actually one of the general features of large Japanese firms that pile up numerous subsidiaries by spin outs and split offs from the original parent company (Shiba and Shimotani, 1997). Chesbrough (2006b) actually acknowledged these oft-cited cases of spin-offs from a parent company that represent the entry strategy to a new market as the basis of one form of open innovation processes among Japanese companies.

Theoretically, then, a product subsidiary remains closely tied to its parent company in terms not only of equity holdings, but also of technological interconnectedness, as it is usually spun off based on the R&D activities committed by the parent firm that commits to related diversification (Kikutani and Saito, 2006b). In Japan, however, the stock listing of both parent and subsidiary companies on the same exchange is commonly observed (Colpan and Hikino, 2010). The relationships between the parent company and its product subsidiaries often become somewhat distant as the subsidiaries start having their own public shareholders,

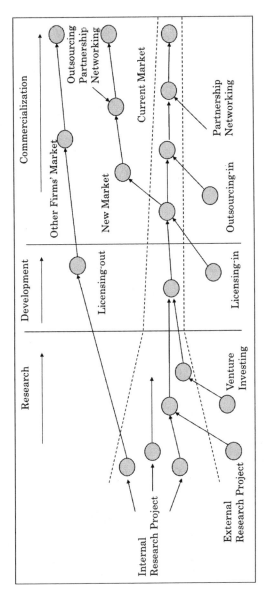

Figure 12.1 The Open Innovation Process

Source: Based on Lee et al. (2010), p. 292, with modifications by the authors.

whose voice has to be heard by the management of the subsidiaries even when it conflicts with the parent company (Kikutani and Saito, 2006a).

This mechanism of strategic and operational autonomy on the part of the product divisions and especially subsidiaries forms the potential basis of the *group-encompassing* innovation. Group-encompassing innovation can be considered a semiopen form of innovation since the technological inflow and outflow is open to the other group companies but closed to outside group parties. Some Japanese companies, however, also attempted to actively incorporate full open innovation as well, although this form of innovation remains still uncommon in Japan, as Chesbrough (2013) concluded.

To contrast the problematic case of Panasonic group on which we focus in the present chapter, we present the case of Osaka Gas and Fuji Film, whose collaborations represent a rare example of open innovation. Osaka Gas was one of the first Japanese companies that deployed open innovation. It established the Open Innovation Office within its Technology Strategy Division in 2008 and designated specific employees in charge of open innovation at individual R&D departments. In hosting the matchmaking meetings between the company and possible providers of the necessary technology, the Open Innovation Office was responsible for locating the outside supplier, which was to provide the required technology that had been requested by various R&D departments. Through the wide and positive publicity that Osaka Gas enjoyed, the company established its reputation in terms of its commitment to open innovation; and thus the matchmaking meetings were able to attract an increasing number of outside companies that could provide the potentially useful technology to Osaka Gas. Consequently, in 2011, for instance, when individual R&D departments of Osaka Gas requested 54 different technological items that could be introduced from outside of the company, the Open Innovation Office successfully matched all of those requests with outside suppliers of technology (Kawai, 2010).

Another case is Fuji Film, one of the major competitors in photographic film and equipment, along with Eastman Kodak, once the mighty crown of this particular industry in the global market. As was usual with Japan's photography-related companies, Fuji Film effectively transformed itself into one of the market leaders in digital cameras through the utilization of technological and marketing competencies that the enterprise gained in its conventional businesses. By deploying resources and competencies in fine chemicals, the company has expanded into cosmetics businesses and successfully entered into pharmaceutical fields, especially in antibacterial drugs. As Fuji Film aimed further into other market segments in pharmaceuticals, where its technological competencies stand beyond its current resources and capabilities, the company aggressively formed strategic alliances with Toyama Chemical, an established medium-sized pharmaceutical firm strong in antibiotics, and acquired Perseus Proteomics, a biotech start-up business that had originated in Tokyo University's Laboratory for Systems Biology and Medicine. Fuji Film has thus become one of the prominent cases of the active utilization of external resources beyond the corporate group boundaries (Asaba and Ushizima, 2010; Nakazono, 2012). In contrast to the case of Osaka Gas and Fuji Film, Panasonic's attempts to shift toward the open innovation model remain problematic, and they are described below to illustrate the contexts, rationales, and challenges in that process.

The Developmental Analysis of the Panasonic Case

Overview of the Panasonic Management and R&D Organization

The case of Panasonic is especially striking for its dynamic interaction between the changes of its corporate group structure and the shifts in its R&D organization. Panasonic is a diversified electronics manufacturer that originated in 1918 and was long known as Matsushita Electric Industrial Company. In 2008 the firm adopted the present corporate identity of Panasonic Corporation to unify its global brand name under "Panasonic." And by its shift to multidivisional structure in 1933, the company was actually one of the pioneers in adopting such a structural form in Japan. By the time Yoichi Morishita became president of Panasonic Corporation in 1992, Panasonic had established the operational principle of the divisional management organization that held the independent responsibility in strategic implementation as well as the part of strategic formulation as long as that particular division remained profitable. In order to secure that free hand of divisional sovereignty, the division management had to continuously invest in R&D to develop new products. As each operating division and subsidiary had their own product life cycles, the operating units, seeking promising opportunities in new products, started strategizing product diversification (Kodama, 2007). (See Figure 12.2 for the organization chart of the Panasonic group with operating divisions, product subsidiaries, and affiliates.) With the growing demand in domestic as well as international markets until the early 1990s, the rivalry among operating divisions enhanced the competitive power for the whole group at Panasonic. In the recessionary times since then, however, the rivalry between individual operating units has had a negative impact as they tightly protected their technological knowledge stemming from their internal R&D activities. Of course, the exclusive utilization of technological knowledge by operating units and their unwillingness to share such knowledge with other units worked against the basic interest of the whole Panasonic group. Since the major competitive advantages of the corporate group derive from the shared resources across operating units in technological knowledge and brand names, such noncollaborative behavior among operating units resulted in a suboptimal level of competitiveness and a lower level of profitability for the whole group.

The technological environment of growing electronics digitization naturally changed the dynamics of decentralized R&D and consequently financial performance when the negative outcomes of intragroup competition between operating units became evident. While developmental resources are distributed across the operating divisions and subsidiaries within the vast Panasonic group, the corporate headquarters remained incapable of integrating all of those resources. Therefore, in 1992 the corporate headquarters attempted to centralize R&D

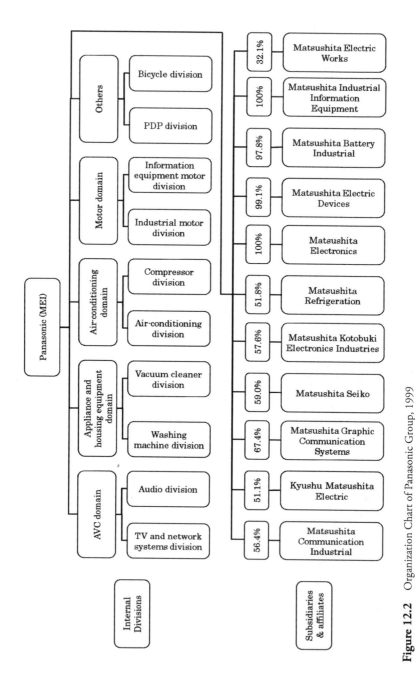

Figure 12.2 Organization Chart of Panasonic Group, 1999

Source: Information compiled from Kodama (2007), p. 51, and various Panasonic Corporation sources.

organizations at least partially by creating the "President's Project for the Whole Panasonic Corporation." This project was a development scheme led by the group headquarters that confiscated a part of the product development authority, which operating divisions and subsidiaries had previously held. The technical section of the corporate headquarters took charge of the mid- and long-term projects exceeding one year for commercial production in the Information Technology Equipment Division, while that division continued to be in charge of the projects that could come up with commercial products within one year (Kawai, 1996). However, as long as the business of significant operating subsidiaries, such as Matsushita Communication Industrial and Kyushu Matsushita Electric, remained profitable enough, the centralizing measure that the corporate headquarters attempted to institute did not produce an effective impact across the whole group (McInerney, 2007).

However, the turning point came in 2001 when the collapse of the IT bubble seriously affected Panasonic's financial standing and forced the company to integrate and utilize the intragroup technological resources that were scattered across the operating divisions and subsidiaries. The measure was intended to cut burgeoning costs by eliminating overlapping investment in R&D and other functions across the operating units. It was also regarded as a strategic response to come up with new products by more effectively mobilizing the intragroup resources. As long as the integration and rationalization of the R&D processes went as planned, it sounded natural to the management in the headquarters to commit to the basic reorganization without adding more costs for product development. This line of group-wide reorganization toward integration and unification—designated as the "Nakamura Reform," which was led by Kunio Nakamura, who assumed Panasonic's presidency in 2001—revived the company, which had strategically struggled ever since the early 1990s, when the Japanese economy fell into its distressing recession (Itami, 2007; Tobita, 2010). Nakamura surely knew the challenging environment and the urgent necessity for the corporate restructuring, especially in product development, that the Panasonic group was facing. He stated, "When the economy was growing rapidly, independent operations in the group encouraged good competition, but now we need to cut redundancy to cope with a digital consumer electronics era that requires a huge R&D cost."[2] Nakamura swiftly reorganized the major business subsidiaries—such as Matsushita Electronics Industry, Matsushita Communication Industrial, and Kyushu Matsushita Electric—one after another into a wholly owned subsidiary. Subsequently, Panasonic reorganized the whole group into 14 business domains and reclassified each operating division or business subsidiary into one of the domains. (See Table 12.1 for the changes in the organization structure of Panasonic group.) The central R&D laboratory was abolished and then reorganized as the separate and independent R&D facilities at the level of each domain, which would be coordinated by the R&D administration department of the headquarters (Kodama, 2007; Nishiguchi, 2009).

It is critical to note once more that the Nakamura Reform created the R&D model that became theoretically open within the entire Panasonic group, which

Table 12.1 Changes in Panasonic's Corporate Group Structure

Year CEO	Establishment	Wholly owned (consolidated) subsidiaries	Absorption and internalization
1995 Morishita			Matsushita Household Equipment
2000 Nakamura	Matsushita Plasma Display	Matsushita Refrigeration	
2001			Matsushita Electronics
2002	Toshiba Matsushita Display Technology	Matsushita Communication Industrial, Kyushu Matsushita Electric, Matsushita Seiko, Matsushita Kotobuki Electronics Industries, Matsushita Graphic Communication Systems	
2003	Matsushita Toshiba Picture Display	Matsushita Electronic Components, Matsushita Battery Industrial	
2004		Matsushita Electric Works (Consolidated), Pana Home (Consolidated)	
2005			Matsushita Industrial Information Equipment
2007 Otsubo		Matsushita Toshiba Picture Display	
2008			Matsushita Refrigeration, Matsushita Battery Industrial
2009		Sanyo Electric (Consolidated)	
2011		Matsushita Electric Works, Sanyo Electric	
2012			Matsushita Electric Devices

Source: Information gathered from various Securities reports of Panasonic Corporation.

was a step forward relative to the segmented R&D organization within individual operating divisions and subsidiaries. Yet, the reorganized R&D system did not go far enough to tap into external resources beyond the whole Panasonic group.

The wholesale reorganization of the corporate group was meant to integrate technology scattered across the corporate group. The Panasonic headquarters designated the domain-level R&D laboratories as the "core technology platform" and rebuilt them into an R&D organization that collaborates within individual domains and with operating units in other domains, all of which were to be coordinated from above by the R&D administration department in the group headquarters (Kodama, 2007). Within the "core technology platform," the technological blocks that the whole corporate group possessed were concentrated to reclassify and reformulate each of those blocks into separate technological domains. Thanks to the Nakamura Reform, the integration and unification of dispersed technology was achieved to establish an effective development organization. It was conceived as the coherent integration of growth strategy at the group-headquarters level and technology policy at the operating-unit level (Nishiguchi, 2009). Panasonic could then intensively invest its group-level developmental resources in implementing specific strategic products designated as "V(ictory) Goods." Thanks to this round of reorganization of the R&D model, Panasonic successfully launched such products as the digital camera Lumix and the PDP television Viera. It is thus generally recognized that the reorganization of the entire Panasonic group, which Nakamura instituted, achieved a certain level of corporate and financial success in turning around the troubled company in the first half of the 2000s (Kishimoto, 2007; McInerney, 2007).

However, Panasonic became engulfed in the downturn of businesses again in the second half of the 2000s, especially after the Lehman Shock in 2008. (See Figure 12.3 for the struggling financial performance of the company since 2008.)[3] Both macroeconomic and microeconomic factors were responsible for the lagging business results of Panasonic, and the entire consumer electronics industry of Japan, for that matter. First, the continuous recession of the Japanese economy, the volatile demand movements of advanced industrial nations, and the rapid expansion of emerging markets all created a taxing environment for Japan's established large manufacturers, such as Panasonic. On the microeconomic side, the notable rise of the competitive power of East Asian large

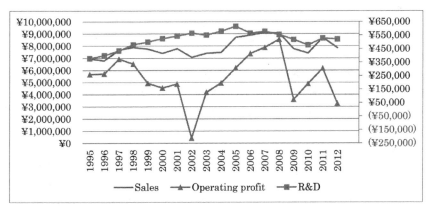

Figure 12.3   Financial Performance and R&D Investment of Panasonic, 1995–2012

Source: Securities reports about Panasonic Corporation.

enterprises, particularly Samsung and LG, of South Korea, started challenging the once-dominant position of Panasonic and other Japanese firms, like Sony and Sharp, in the domestic market of Japan and more so in international markets.

In response to such fundamental changes in the economic environment, Panasonic, under the strong and capable leadership of Nakamura, initially established the "Promotion Center for Industry-University Collaboration" in 2003. Since those days, the R&D department of the corporate headquarters has played the central role in adapting the open innovation model. Panasonic consecutively founded the "Tokyo R&D Center" for collaborating with governmental and academic research institutions to develop advanced technology in 2008 and the "Innovation Promotion Center" encompassing the entire group organization under the R&D department of the corporate headquarters in 2010. Since these organizations were established as a response to environmental changes, they assumed the primary role of achieving a synergistic effect through the reorganization of the whole group structure and operation to advance cooperation between cross-industrial domains within the group. The ultimate mission of the new group-level organizations was defined as technical development that should lead to a global innovation (Motohashi, Ueda, and Mitsuno, 2012). In order to advance its new open innovation model, Panasonic actively participated in such interfirm organizations as the "Japan Open Innovation Forum" of Nine Sigma Japan, an independent company that specialized in the promotion of various innovations. Panasonic also committed to open innovation forums founded by NEDO, an independent government agency established by the New Energy and Industrial Technology Development Organization legislation (Chesbrough, 2013). Through participating in private and government-led open innovation schemes, Panasonic gradually accumulated the knowledge needed for a shift from its conventional closed innovation model. Nevertheless, as will be explained in the next section, the process to incorporate open innovation processes remained limited.

Transformation of the Corporate R&D Organization toward Openness

At the Panasonic corporate group, as described previously, with the philosophy of independent management responsibility, operating divisions and business subsidiaries historically were in charge of their own R&D planning and execution. Naturally, operating domains ultimately overlapped with each other, as long as each domain attempted the maximization of growth and profitability on its own. Various means were introduced and intragroup organizations established in order to overcome these operational troubles. Ironically, this whole process of combatting the interdivisional conflicts eventually led to the developments of the R&D organization at the whole group level.

In 1982, Panasonic established the "New Media Strategic Committee," a group-level organization across all product divisions and subsidiaries and intended to promote a flexible environment for new media businesses. In order to not only coordinate the R&D efforts between the intragroup divisions and subsidiaries, but also to actively propose advanced R&D schemes to them, Panasonic reorganized the "New Media Strategic Committee" to establish the "Promotion Office for Significant Business Domains" in 1988. Emphasizing the role of this R&D model, the entire organization of R&D was reconstructed. The abolished departments were the conventional arrangements based on the sequential phases of R&D processes, such as the "Technology Headquarters," "Research Center for Semiconductors," and "Promotion Headquarters for Businesses." Newly instituted departments were such R&D organizations as "Information and Communications Research," "Visual and Audio Research," and "Semiconductor Research" (Kawai, 1996).

Next, in 1990 Panasonic founded the "Group-Encompassing Project Scheme for New Products," which was supposed to function as an intermediary for the procurement of necessary technology to relevant operating units within the Panasonic group. In order to materialize the effective utilization of technological resources across the operating units within the group, in 1992 the company also introduced the "Group-Wide President Project," reflecting an unconventional philosophy of independent responsibility on the part of operating divisions and subsidiaries. Moreover, Panasonic pushed the headquarters-led formulation of technology strategy further to exercise the allocation of technical resources under the central control of the "Group-Wide Committee for Research and Development" (Kawai, 1996). Before this drive toward R&D centralization, technology strategy had remained the responsibility of product divisions and subsidiaries, while the group headquarters was in charge of the group-level overall strategic decisions (Nishiguchi, 2009). The Group-Wide Committee for Research and Development was expected to resolve this issue of the incoherence of general and technological strategic responsibilities within the Panasonic group.

Panasonic then went even further in introducing the practice of open innovation in 1995, when the company started engaging in a joint development project with Plasmaco, a New York–based firm that was established in 1987 under the leadership of Dr. Larry F. Weber, to come up with plasma display panels that could operate with alternate current electricity (AC-PDP). Panasonic itself had committed to plasma display using direct current electricity (DC-PDP) because technologically the latter was presumed doable while the former had faced some engineering difficulties. As the difficulties were gradually resolved, Panasonic decided to form an alliance with Plasmaco in order to keep pace with the development of AC-PDP, which was technically superior to DC-PDP. Ultimately, the Panasonic-Plasmaco alliance resulted in the acquisition of Plasmaco by Panasonic in 1996 (Shibata, 2012).

Overall, however, Yoichi Morishita, who had become the president of the company in 1992, attempted to concentrate his efforts to take a tighter grip of the entire group. He eventually gave up on the principle of open innovation, as well as group-wide technological development, as he started investing little of his spare time in the activities of the group-wide R&D committee, and ultimately the committee itself became dysfunctional (Tateishi, 2001). The subsequent reform in the R&D organization for the entire Panasonic group that Morishita attempted constituted a return to the pre-1988 model in which the whole organization was reconstructed based on an R&D flow-oriented process starting from the "Technology and Basic Nature Headquarters," through the "Research Headquarters," and ending in the "Development Headquarters" (Kawai, 1996).

The group-wide reorganization launched in 2002 commanded the clear and basic philosophy of eliminating overlapping businesses across product divisions and group-affiliated subsidiaries, putting together and concentrating managerial resources (especially those in product development), and integrating and unifying all the functions related to development, production, marketing, and sales.[4] The R&D organization became the "Platform-Based Development Model." Understandably, in the midst of the critical confusion and its resolution in strategic and administrative philosophy and organization, the flow-oriented R&D system would once again be converted to the product domain–based R&D organization after this round of integration and centralization.

However, Panasonic maintained an R&D organization that was not assured intragroup resources and business domains. The "Center for Industry-University Collaboration" was established in 2003 and became an intermediary between the university community and the whole group. Then, in 2008 Panasonic founded the "Tokyo R&D Center," which cooperated with external research institutions—such as third parties in related domains, ministries and government offices, and universities—in order to promote high-technology development together.[5] The company moved further by founding the "Innovation Promotion Center" for advancing development projects with critical importance or high urgency in 2010. This institution, in addition to the usual function of product development in general, possessed the specific mission of integrating former subsidiaries and competitors, such as Panasonic Electric Works and Sanyo Electric, into the whole Panasonic corporate group organization and of combining the R&D resources scattered across operating divisions and subsidiaries.[6]

Since 2011, Panasonic has committed to the reform of the R&D department of the corporate headquarters. For this purpose, the "Device Systems Development Center," "Material and Process Development Center," and similar organizations were established at the headquarters level. The major purpose of these organizations was to maximize synergy in the three major operating units: Panasonic Electric Industrial, the headquarters unit that functions as an operating-holding company; Panasonic Electric Works; and Sanyo Electric. The last two were major operating companies, large in size and listed in stock exchanges. By doing so, technological competitiveness was expected to be enhanced. This goal was intended to be achieved by creating new businesses, developing products with novel ideas, and furthering advanced research and development by accelerating resource sharing across group divisions and subsidiaries.[7] In 2012, Panasonic installed the "Open Innovation Promotion Section" within the R&D department of the corporate headquarters along this line of advancing the model of open innovation, as illustrated in Figure 12.4.[8]

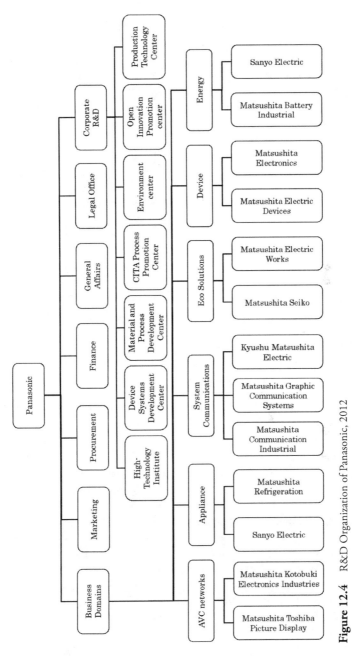

Figure 12.4 R&D Organization of Panasonic, 2012

Source: Information gathered from Kodama (2007), p. 56, and Japanese Securities reports (2005–12), modified by the authors.

Open Innovation within the Corporate Group Structure

Changes of Innovation Processes

What kind of influence has the integration of the Panasonic corporate group and its changes to R&D organization had on the firm's innovation processes? Here, an analysis could be made in three chronological phases: (1) the conventional structure of the corporate group and the decentralized management and R&D organization, (2) the transition to a more integrated model of corporate organization and R&D conduct starting in 2000, and (3) the resulting organizational and administrative structure with more integrated and concentrated resources at the corporate-group level.

First, the decentralized managerial structure that Panasonic had long nurtured and had led to duplicating and overlapping business and product domains among its operating units. Within those product markets, individual divisions and subsidiaries naturally competed against each other as they aimed to maximize market share and enhance financial performance on their own. Allegedly, those operating divisions and subsidiaries treated technology and pertinent information, especially about products, as strictly confidential, and leaking to other operating units was unthinkable (Kodama, 2007). In order to solve such a sectionalist dilemma, Panasonic consecutively introduced various measures for changing the R&D organization, but, as long as the operating units had final decision-making authority about product development, such reforms did not bring about satisfactory group-level integration. Each operating division and business subsidiary continued to invest in their own R&D and product developments and sales and marketing of products. Since Panasonic headquarters still respected the independence and responsibility of management at every operating unit, this consequently resulted in "closed innovation within operating units."

Next, starting in 1988 the development of the structural integration of the Panasonic corporate group eliminated the duplication of business domains among principal operating divisions and subsidiaries, which transformed Panasonic's organization of R&D activities, making them more open and accessible across the operating units. With this change, the divisions and subsidiaries could now actually utilize the technological resources accumulated beyond their own units within the Panasonic group. The company furthered this shift toward the group-wide sharing of technological knowledge by structuring a universal platform for the whole group organization. Furthermore, by establishing the group-encompassing marketing headquarters, the sales channel of audio-visual and home electronics within the domestic market was transferred from individual business units to the single Panasonic organization (Fukuchi, 2007). The R&D model thus basically became "open" beyond individual operating divisions and subsidiaries but still remained "closed" within the entire Panasonic corporate group.

Finally, the Panasonic corporate group has lately committed to the wholesale utilization of intragroup technology across the operating divisions and subsidiaries, while it has actively started seeking resources beyond the group boundaries.

The trend of the group-wide employment of intragroup resources was accelerated after the Panasonic group internalized Panasonic Electric Works and Sanyo Electric, two manufacturing giants that had been associated with the Panasonic group as wholly owned subsidiaries. In the meantime, the practical utilization of external technology beyond the group boundaries has gradually progressed in new business fields, such as robotics, in which the Panasonic group and its constituent operating units did not possess proprietary competitive resources.

Panasonic Corporate Group and Innovation Processes

The basic principle for Panasonic's shift to open innovation has been to seek technological resources that had not been developed within the whole corporate group. One typical example of Panasonic's commitment to open innovation was its entry into the new field of robotics business. In 2009 Panasonic headquarters founded the "Open Laboratory," with access for outside parties, such as medical experts, university and academic organizations, research institutions, parts suppliers, and other interested organizations. Each of these external organizations was allowed to utilize Panasonic's facility for their own needs, including component-engineering development and technical improvements. Often an outsider actually visited the open laboratory, where technical information was exchanged and the commercialization of products was arranged between Panasonic and interested outside parties.[9]

In the proprietary electronics businesses that constituted the major business sector of the Panasonic group, by contrast, innovation activity was based on the synergy within the group and still remained far more common than the utilization of open innovation processes beyond the group boundaries. For example, in the air purifier business, the "Alleru-Buster" antiallergy technology that Panasonic Electric Industrial (the group's main operating unit) owned and the "Nano-E" technology that its major heavy-equipment subsidiary (Panasonic Electric Works) developed were successfully integrated to bring technological and commercial achievement.[10] For the reorganized Panasonic group, the creation of synergistic effects has become critical between the headquarters unit and its former subsidiary, Panasonic Electric Works. Nakamura summarized this issue by claiming: "Matsushita Electric Industrial owns network as well as semiconductor technology, while Panasonic Electric Works possesses superior capability to make high quality living. We shall be able to create something better if these companies work together side by side" (Kodama, 2007, 82).

However, the actual process for creating intragroup technological sharing between member firms turned out to be challenging. The examples of failure to achieve the synergistic effects within a group were numerous. In the process of transforming newly acquired Sanyo Electric into a new operating subsidiary to materialize synergetic results, the case of battery-related technology represents the difficulties of strategic and operational integration. Although Panasonic was aiming at achieving synergistic outcomes with Sanyo Electric in lithium ion batteries, the fundamental principles and practical approaches for

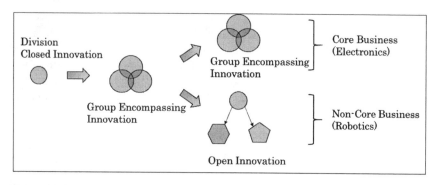

Figure 12.5 Transformation of the Innovation Process of Panasonic

the commercialization of battery technology differed, in fact, between Panasonic and Sanyo, which made the mutual use of the technology virtually impossible (Okumura, 2012).

Consequently, in its core businesses in which Panasonic has long nurtured its own idiosyncratic way of nurturing technology and developing products, its collaboration with other organizations outside the group, especially those in other industries and business sectors, has rarely been materialized. Adjustments for operative integration within the whole Panasonic group have become an urgent, yet time-consuming and difficult, task for the top management in the group headquarters. In spite of its urgency, the acquisition of external technological knowledge and resources through open innovation processes has been a secondary consideration.[11] Because of its emphasis on within-the-group innovation and product development, Panasonic has underutilized external resources beyond the group boundaries. Consequently, it could not fully exploit its links with such technology sources as Nine Sigma Japan in an active manner.[12]

In summary, as depicted in Figure 12.5, the Panasonic group still fundamentally holds on to the semiopen and group-encompassing model of R&D at the entire group level. It partially exploits open (outside-the-group) innovation processes for its noncore businesses, where the group has not yet developed adequate capabilities across its business domains.

Group-Encompassing Innovation as an Obstacle to Open Innovation

Panasonic seriously started shifting toward the practical use of open innovation only after the big economic shock in 2008, as mentioned above. The substantial shift in the macroeconomic and competitive environment, particularly in electronics business sectors, changed the market demand, while leading to the emergence of competitive suppliers in emerging markets. In particular, the digitization of electronic technology has reduced the barrier to entry for the industry and induced new competition, which has resulted in stiff price competition between established and newly emergent firms (Nishiguchi, 2009; Suzuki, 2008).

As the Panasonic corporate group conventionally valued the Japanese markets as both the supply base and product outlet, it has not quite nurtured the competitive resources that can be effectively deployed in international, especially in emerging, markets. As such, even had Panasonic shifted its geographical focus toward emerging markets, especially in the largest mass-product segment with low value added in those markets, the Panasonic Group would have fallen short in marketing competencies that were abundantly available beyond the group boundaries. The top priority remained to establish a coalition among operating units belonging to different product domains in order to create a synergistic effect through internal resources within the group (Motohashi et al., 2012). As Campbell and Goold (1998) pointed out, pursuing synergy among operating divisions and subsidiaries had been the immediate objective, rather than seeking other strategic options. In fact, the development of synergistic results between Panasonic Electric Works and Sanyo Electric, which were then transformed into wholly owned subsidiaries, was the foremost objective.[13] Although Panasonic had philosophically transformed itself to appreciate the significance of open innovation, it continued to utilize a semiopen innovation model within the group (Niwa, 2006).

In contrast, with the emergence of new businesses and technologies, such as robotics, the product division of the company could have incorporated advanced technologies from external sources to launch new products and cut costs. Ironically, it could neither capitalize on the internal member firms within the Panasonic group nor secure adequate investment funding from the group headquarters (Sekiya, 2012). Since the corporate group members were not interested in the robotics business, Panasonic's business division dealing with robotics could have sought necessary technological resources from external parties (Christensen, 1997; Spithoven, Vanhaverbeke, and Roijakkers, 2012).

Conclusion

Responding to the shift in technological and market environments since the 1990s, Japan's corporate groups reoriented their strategy in terms of product portfolio and geographical scope and also restructured their organizational design to be more tightly integrated between operating units to maximize the effective use of accumulated resources. While this process of strategic reconsideration and organizational consolidation was a necessary and appropriate measure in the new and more competitive environment, the process has turned out to be inadequate due to the disparate operational processes that individual divisions and subsidiaries had developed.

This chapter singled out the major characteristics of the basic changes in innovation processes and the R&D organization of Panasonic that had become a focal issue in the context of the comprehensive restructuring at the entire group level. Among many options for strategic and operational reforms, Panasonic headquarters had to commit much of its efforts to the concentration and integration of technological resources at the whole group level, which were all scattered across the decentralized R&D model that was carried out at individual product divisions and subsidiaries.

Consequently, practical and effective resources beyond the group boundaries ultimately were underutilized or even neglected. In spite of the availability of useful external resources, the Panasonic group has devoted much of its energies to internal reorganization rather than external resource utilization. Ultimately, Panasonic headquarters has compromised by taking group-encompassing R&D efforts, which go beyond the original boundary of the main operating companies, as a substitute to genuine *open* innovation.

In summary, our analysis demonstrates that Panasonic fell into a dilemma between structural decentralization and operational integration - two opposing organizational processes at the level of the whole corporate group, which eventually has prevented the company from adopting an open innovation model. This dilemma manifests the lock-in mechanism that the company experienced when it attempted to maximize intragroup resources by integrating the group's structure. This in turn prevented Panasonic's shifting to open innovation, which in principle goes against the intragroup functioning of tight networks. Overall, although Panasonic has arranged a mechanism of open innovation within group boundaries, it has failed to formulate a process to promote genuine open innovation beyond group boundaries. This de facto continuous policy of maximizing the effective use of intragroup technological assets may be a rational response to changing macroeconomic and competitive environments since the company invested huge amounts of financial and human resources at the group level and across the individual operating units. Although this seems to be a short-term solution, a more flexible and coordinated utilization of resources beyond the group boundaries could have yielded more competitive and operational advantages since new efficient and effective technologies are disbursed across Japanese and global companies.

As the case of Panasonic illustrates, although there is a trend toward open innovation in many Japanese companies since the 2000s, it encounters the ambiguity and dilemma of centralization versus decentralization of R&D along other organizational functions. After examining these issues, we can draw the conclusion that open innovation movement should be assessed in the context of corporate and national cultural and economic environments. Thus, we argue that open innovation represents the contextual characteristics of firm locations, which engender differences in the applications of open innovation such that open innovation at Japanese corporate groups develops gradually when compared to that of Western companies.

Notes

1. In this paper, Matsushita Electric Industrial is referred to as "Panasonic" until otherwise specified.
2. Hara, Yoshiko, "Japanese Giant to See Red Ink for First Time in over 50 Years," *Electronic Engineering Times*, January 14, 2002, 12.

3. Sekiya (2012) argued that Panasonic concentrated its investment from 2000 to 2010 into a limited scope of business domains, while remaining businesses have gotten left out of additional investment. This is especially so about the foreign operations of Panasonic. The company's time horizon has become shortsighted without the long-term view of the entire Panasonic group.

4. "Reorganization of MEI Groups," Panasonic news release, April 26, 2002.

5. "Reorganization and Staff Reassignment," Panasonic news release, March 31, 2008.

6. "Fourteen heads of R&D Talk on the Secret Plan That Will Challenge New Fields," *Nikkei Electronics*, August 23, 2010, 48–49.

7. "Reorganization and Staff Reassignment," Panasonic news release, December 27, 2011.

8. "Reorganization and Staff Reassignment," Panasonic news release, September 28, 2012.

9. Refer to "Opening Up the Inner Shrine," *Nikkei Business*, March 29, 2010, 24–25.

10. "The Craftsmanship beyond the Wall of the Operating Division," Nikkei BP Net, April 18, 2006. http://www.nikkeibp.co.jp/style/biz/feature/panasonic/060418_5th/. (Accessed 3/11/2013)

11. Interview with Panasonic's corporate R&D researcher, July 8, 2013.

12. Interview with Panasonic's corporate R&D researcher, July 8, 2013.

13. Interview with Panasonic's corporate R&D researcher, July 8, 2013.

References

Asaba, S., and Ushizima, T. (2010). *The Essentials of Management Strategy*. Tokyo: Yuhikaku (in Japanese).

Belenzon, S., and Berkovitz, T. (2010). "Innovation in Business Groups." *Management Science* 56:519–35.

Campbell, A., and Goold, M. (1998). "Desperately Seeking Synergy." *Harvard Business Review* 76 (5): 131–43.

Chang, S. J., Chung, C. N., and Mahmood, I. P. (2006). "When and How Does Business Group Affiliation Promote Firm Innovation." *Organization Science* 17 (5): 637–56.

Chesbrough, H. W. (2003). *Open Innovation: The New Imperative for Creating and Profiting from Technology*. Boston: Harvard Business School Press.

Chesbrough, H. W. (2006a). "Open Innovation: A New Paradigm for Understanding Industrial Innovation." In H. W. Chesbrough, W. Vanhaverbeke, and J. West (eds.), *Open Innovation: Researching a New Paradigm*, 1–14. Oxford: Oxford University Press.

Chesbrough, H. W. (2006b). "The Open Innovation Model: Implications for Innovation in Japan." In D. H. Whittaker and R. E. Cole (eds.), *Recovering from Success: Innovation and Technology Management in Japan*, 129–44. Oxford: Oxford University Press.

Chesbrough, H. W. (2013). "Open Innovation: Implications for Japanese Innovation." *Annual Report on Japanese Silicon Valley Innovation Forum 2013*. http://ww.info.com/searchw?qkw=annual+report+on+japanese+silicon+valley+innovation+forum+2013&cb=34&affid=19&cmp=4063. (Accessed 10/1/2013)

Christensen, C. M. (1997). *The Innovator's Dilemma: When New Technologies Cause Great Firms to Fail*. Boston: Harvard Business School Press.

Colpan, A. M., and Hikino, T. (2010). "Foundations of Business Groups: Towards an Integrated Framework." In A. M. Colpan, T. Hikino, and J. R. Lincoln (eds.), *The Oxford Handbook of Business Groups*, 15–66. Oxford: Oxford University Press.

Fujiwara, M. (2007). "Toward the Research on Innovation Mechanism of Diversified Firm: Integrating Resource-Based-View and Innovation Research." *Kyoto Sangyo University Social Science Series* 24:139–51.

Fukuchi, H. (2007). "Consumer Electronics Sales and Marketing Reform." In H. Itami, K. Tanaka, T. Kato, and M. Nakano (eds.), *Management Revolution at Matsushita Electric Industrial*, 96–132. Tokyo: Yuhikaku (in Japanese).

Hobday, M., and Colpan, A. M. (2010). "Technological Innovation and Business Groups." In A. M. Colpan, T. Hikino, and J. R. Lincoln (eds.), *The Oxford Handbook of Business Groups*, 763–82. Oxford: Oxford University Press.

Itami, H. (2007). "The Significance of Nakamura-Reform." In H. Itami, K. Tanaka, T. Kato, and M. Nakano (eds.), *Management Revolution at Matsushita Electric Industrial*, 1–20. Tokyo: Yuhikaku (in Japanese).

Itami, H. (2009). *Promoting Innovation.* Tokyo: Nikkei (in Japanese).

Khanna, T., and Tice, S. (2001). "The Bright Side of Internal Capital Markets." *Journal of Finance* 56:1489–531.

Khanna, T., and Yafeh, Y. (2007). "Business Groups in Emerging Markets: Paragons or Parasites?" *Journal of Economic Literature* 45 (2): 331–72.

Kawai, K. (2010). "Salaried Entrepreneurs and the Internalization of Technology Market: A Case Study on Open Innovation by Osaka Gas." *Hitotsubashi Business Review* 60 (2): 56–71 (in Japanese).

Kawai, T. (1996). *Strategic Organizational Innovation: A Comparison of Sharp, Sony and Matsushita.* Tokyo: Yuhikaku (in Japanese).

Kikutani, T., and Saito, T. (2006a). "Economic Analysis of Becoming Wholly-Owned Subsidiary." Working paper, Graduate School of Economics, Kyoto University, J-53 (in Japanese).

Kikutani, T., and Saito, T. (2006b). "Reorganization of the Business Structure from the Perspective of Business Groups." Working paper, Graduate School of Economics, Kyoto University, J-54 (in Japanese).

Kishimoto, T. (2007). "Nakamura-Reform from the Perspective of Profit Margins." In H. Itami, K. Tanaka, T. Kato, and M. Nakano (eds.), *Management Revolution at Matsushita Electric Industrial*, 229–56. Tokyo: Yuhikaku (in Japanese).

Kodama, K. (2007). "Reorganization of Business Structure." In H. Itami, K. Tanaka, T. Kato, and M. Nakano (eds.), *Management Revolution at Matsushita Electric Industrial*, 49–94. Tokyo: Yuhikaku, (in Japanese).

Lee, S., Park, G., Yoon, B., and Park, J. (2010). "Open Innovation in SMEs: An Intermediated Network Model." *Research Policy* 39 (2): 290–300.

Lincoln, J. R., and Shimotani, M. (2010). "Business Networks in Postwar Japan: Whither the *Keiretsu*?" In A. M. Colpan, T. Hikino, and J. R. Lincoln (eds.), *The Oxford Handbook of Business Groups*, 127–56. Oxford: Oxford University Press.

Mahmood, I. P., and Mitchell, W. (2004). "Two Faces Effects of Business Groups on Innovation in Emerging Economies." *Management Science* 50 (10): 1348–65.

McInerney, F. (2007). *Panasonic: The Largest Corporate Restructuring in History.* New York: Truman Talley Books.

Motohashi, K. (2008). "Growing R&D Collaboration of Japanese Firms and Policy Implications for Reforming the National Innovation System." *Asia Pacific Business Review* 14 (3): 339–61.

Motohashi, K., Ueda, Y., and Mitsuno, M. (2012). "The New Trend on Open Innovation in Japan." RIETI policy discussion paper, P-015 (in Japanese).

Nakazono, H. (2012). "Strategic Function of the Platform in Open Innovation." MBA dissertation, Osaka University, Japan.

Nakazono, H. (2013). "Chesbrough's 'Open Innovation': Survey Study towards the Development of Open Innovation." *Doshisha Business Review of Graduate Students* 47 (2): 76–107 (in Japanese).

Nishiguchi, Y. (2009). *Open Integrated Business Management System.* Tokyo: Hakuto Shobo (in Japanese).

Niwa, K. (2006). *Technology Management.* Tokyo: University of Tokyo Press (in Japanese).

Niwa, K. (2010). *Innovation Strategy.* Tokyo: University of Tokyo Press (in Japanese).

Odagiri, H. (1992). *Growth through Competition, Competition through Growth.* Oxford: Oxford University Press.

Okumura, H. (2012). *Panasonic to an End?* Tokyo: Toyokeizai (in Japanese).

Sekiya, N. (2012). "Corporate-Level Strategy of Panasonic." In T. Numagami (ed.), *Strategic Analysis Vol. 2*, 153–90. Tokyo: Toyokeizai (in Japanese).

Shiba, T., and Shimotani, M. (1997). *Beyond the Firm: Business Groups in International and Historical Perspective.* Oxford: Oxford University Press.

Shibata, T. (2012). "Building Parallel Development for Technological Transition." *Organizational Science* 46 (2): 53–63 (in Japanese).

Spithoven, A., Vanhaverbeke, W., and Roijakkers, N. (2012). "Open Innovation Practices in SMEs and Large Enterprises." *Small Business Economics* 41 (3): 537–62.

Suzuki, Y. (2008). "Digitalization of Product Technology and Time-Based Competitive Strategy: Organizational Capability Building in Matsushita Electric Industrial Co., Ltd." *Doshisha Business Review* 60 (1–2): 18–43 (in Japanese).

Takeishi, A. (2010). "Open Innovation: Mechanisms and Challenges for Success." *Hitotsubashi Business Review* 60 (2): 16–26 (in Japanese).

Tateishi, Y. (2001). *Sony and Matsushita.* Tokyo: Kodansha (in Japanese).

Tobita, T. (2010). "An Analytical Viewpoint of Management Control System to Increase Corporate Value: The Change of Corporation View and the Influence of Management Accounting in 2000s." *The Journal of Professional Accountancy* 1:37–52 (in Japanese).

Yoshihara, H., Sakuma, A., Itami, H., and Kagono, T. (1981). *The Diversification Strategy of the Japanese Firm.* Tokyo: Nihon Keizai Shinbun Sha (in Japanese).

CHAPTER 13

Open Innovation Ecosystems in the Software Industry

Mehmet Gençer and Beyza Oba

Introduction

Computers have an increasing variety of uses in virtually every aspect of our personal life and work-related activities. Children from early ages play games on tablets, Grandma uses a small digital device to track her blood pressure, and parents work with smartphones and laptops during their commutes. A common characteristic of computers is that, for the most part, they rely on software to accommodate different uses.

Computer software is a bunch of bits and bytes, which enables information processing in computer hardware and performs various tasks. Nowadays, one can put several gigabytes of software on a tiny device; thus, even a commonplace software product can be very complicated.[1] Furthermore, since software products are digital themselves, the products and their features can penetrate markets relatively fast and do so on a global scale. These large scales and scopes of complicated and interconnected engineering works behind software production presents its peculiar character when compared with other industries. The software industry not only produces for numerous and various uses, but also it comprises complicated and "big" information-processing machines, which need to be continuously and rapidly reengineered to keep up with ever-changing business and consumer demands. Thus, the nature of both computer hardware and software and the work behind them shapes many aspects of the industry.

Approaches to the issue of innovation are deeply influenced by the industry's peculiar characteristics. A software-producing firm (this may include hardware firms that need to deliver homemade software embedded in their products or firms that provide services powered with software they produce themselves) creates added value by designing and implementing parts of a big and complicated system whose overall functioning requires many other parts coming from other manufacturers. Nowadays such systems also must interact and be compatible with other computer systems and devices through the Internet or cabled and wireless connections. These requirements generally impose an "open" attitude upon firms in the industry, which is driven by vertical interdependence among firms in the creation and functioning of their products. Open source software is the earliest example of an approach to innovation that exhibits the main features of what we now term *open innovation* and that has been explicitly identified and widely practiced in the whole industry.

This chapter gives an overview of the case for open innovation in the software industry: why and when open innovation is appropriate, the history behind its emergence, and how it is applied today. We first summarize the characteristics of the software industry with references to its history and evolution. Today there are some segments of the industry whose contexts are suitable for open and collaborative innovation. We generalize these contextual characteristics and discuss how these characteristics make certain subcontexts suitable for open innovation practices, with examples of its application. Similarly, we also present other subcontexts that are less suitable for open innovation. Following this analysis, we review historical patterns of open innovation in the software industry up to today, laying out archetypes of strategic alliances and presenting commonalities among contemporary open innovation practices against this background. Finally, we discuss possible directions toward which the software context and strategic alliance patterns and practices within are expected to evolve in the near future.

Software Industry: Characteristics and Evolution

In the late 1990s, the software industry was characterized by two dominant worlds, named "Cathedral" and "Bazaar" by Eric Raymond (2001). These two archetypes were totally separate worlds with different, even contrasting, production modes, philosophies, governance mechanisms, and innovation practices. In this earlier paradigm, big firms like IBM, Sun, and Microsoft were much closer to closed innovation practice, where they developed software within their boundaries with their own staff and then commercialized those products. In this way they were able to create and appropriate economic value. In this mode of production, the initial development costs were very high whereas costs of software copies were very low. Big firms were able to realize supply-side economies of scale (West and Gallagher, 2005), which led to the rigid use of intellectual-property protection practices. In this model, firm returns were based on the production of a complete software product, which maximized switching costs for the customers. Firms were then able to increase their returns from the reproduction of their products, which were protected by copyrights, and by capturing markets characterized by repeat purchases of various components of the same product. This approach to production, product, appropriation, and commercialization gave rise to consolidation among firms, which led to high market shares and eventually the development of big firms. As is the case in other consolidated industries, knowledge production and sharing about the products and markets were confined to the boundaries of a single firm. This closeness in terms of knowledge production and its articulation provided a framework of closed innovation.

During the same period, open source software (OSS) projects like Apache and Linux were already utilizing another production mode and open innovation practices in various forms. OSS projects were different from the model developed by big firms in terms of their production mode, philosophy, and knowledge production approaches. Open source production is based on collaboration among distributed developers/users. Thus, the production of the software is modular and not confined to the boundaries of a single firm. As a consequence of the overlapping notion of users and developers, this mode of production supports differences in production methods, quality assurance, business functions utilized, and cost/revenue structures. First, a software package (with its complements) is not produced from beginning to end by a single firm, and thus the output does not belong to a single producer; yet in order to produce the software, source codes need to be shared. Such coproduction necessitates the free sharing of source code, which in turn renders copyrights irrelevant. Similarly, since the software package is not planned, designed, and produced by the same firm, quality checks are not done by this firm; rather, they are completed as the program develops by the users/developers. This approach facilitates a continuous innovation milieu, where software packages are developed, improved, and redesigned according to the needs of the users. In OSS projects, software manufacturing costs are driven primarily by access to talent rather than economies of scale.

Rapid growth in the global software industry (more than 50 percent between 1996 and 2000) created opportunities for big firms to expand their markets and operations (UNCTAD, 2012). However, with the existing business models in big firms, coping with the changes in demand structure and composition was nearly impossible; one of the major problems faced by these companies was the shortage of skilled developers (UNCTAD, 2012). Besides quick expansion, markets were characterized by rapid changes in software components/complements and a shortening of development cycles (especially due to the performance of OSS projects), which required quick responses with reliable software packages. Furthermore, with the widespread use of the Internet and the emergence of the World Wide Web (www), some deficiencies related to interoperability standards emerged; ensuring the smooth running of the Internet and the www entails collaboration and content exchange between many hardware and software platforms. The reaction of big firms to these new industry conditions was to shift their operations toward being system integrators and providers. Consequently a number of big players (e.g., Microsoft, IBM, Sun, and Apple) which traditionally favored closed systems, started to approach OS developers. Strategic alliances of various forms with OS projects provided resources and capabilities for the realization of this repositioning and were useful in reaching more users and more developers and in shortening new release cycles and rearranging quality assurance processes. Thus, in the early 2000s, the software industry was marked by alliance projects (like Linux, Apache, and Eclipse) backed by big corporations. But the process of this strategy turn was not so easy:

The problem for IBM, Apple and Sun was that by making source code freely available and modifiable, open source inherently reduced barriers to entry by rivals and switching costs by customers. So, despite the appealing logic of mutual adversaries ("the enemy of my enemy is my friend"), a pure open source strategy would eliminate each company's historic source of differentiation, their proprietary software. Each of the firms faced a dilemma of how to adapt an open source strategy suitable for their respective core competencies and resources. (West, 2003: 1269)

Nowadays, the software industry still has a significantly high growth rate of about 10 percent a year (UNCTAD, 2012), and the robustness of this industry creates risks even for the most established industry players; firm survival and growth is all about rapid and continuous innovation. Besides the high growth trend, several characteristic features mark the nature of work, competition, and innovation in the software products industry:

- Software products are purely digital artifacts. Thus the local or global markets present relatively low barriers, in terms of product delivery and marketing, for new entrants of all sizes.
- Software products are relatively harder to protect with patents. Therefore, the market position rests on continuous innovation, more so than on first-entry advantages.
- Software systems are becoming increasingly more complex (Sommerville et al., 2012), where a workable system is comprised of several subsystems coming from various manufacturers, each of which may change independently, even at time of release. This situation is turning software R&D into an evolutionary process rather than a planned and linear one. It also enforces proximity among industry players in various ways.
- All of the above still applies even when the software itself is not sold or distributed; furthermore, it is the basis of a value-added product or service, as in Software as a Service (SaS) or Platform as a Service (PaaS) business models.

In line with the changes in software products and the industry itself, new strategic patterns have emerged and been established; besides big firms and OSS projects, one of the emerging patterns in the last decade is strategic alliances between these two worlds. While combining the strengths of both worlds and leading to hybrid forms of organizing, producing, and governing, alliances provide a milieu for open innovation.

The computing industry, both hardware and software, has a well-established tradition of cooperation, which is an important element in the effectiveness of open innovation practices. Given the complexity of software systems, such interdependency among various producers (firms or individual developers) exerts deeper pressures to cooperate than in many other industries. Langlois's (1990) study on the microcomputer industry gives a striking example of how interdependence gives rise to strategies that blend competition and collaboration in novel ways. Langlois (1990) notes how IBM came up with the idea of PC architecture, a design that enabled consumers to combine IBM computers, through a standard interface, with parts coming from other manufacturers compatible with that interface. The architecture was extremely compelling for consumers, since it meant a plethora of parts manufacturers from all over the world would create lower-price alternative components that offered ways to combine machines according to specific requirements. IBM's strategic move against competitors like Apple and Atari, in 1980, was based "not from the focusing of its great internal capabilities, but rather from its willingness to abandon capabilities in favor of those in the external network" (Langlois, 1990: 97). Given the impact of such strategic innovations, the rest of the eighties and nineties witnessed numerous examples of industry collaboration to create standard hardware and software interfaces to accommodate strategies that acknowledge interdependence within the industry.

Similar examples of cooperation among ecosystem inhabitants can be observed in the software industry as well. Starting with the early years of computing, software has been a complementary product that increased the attractiveness of computers in the market. During these years, firms enjoyed the benefits of collaboration with UNIX—an operating system—which comprised the heart of any software system and allowed value-added software to be produced and run (McKusick and Kirk, 1999). Later, at the turn of the 1980s, the success of software products like VisiCalc signaled that software itself was an important source of value (Grad, 2007), and its production could be incorporated into other production strategies. As a result of these developments, vertical-integration strategy dominated the software industry, whereas the hardware industry was dominated by vertical interdependence. Consequently, different vendors provided software, data, and document formats, which were incompatible with each other and could be used for the development of reliable software packages. The computing industry from the 1980s on manifested mixed strategies of competition and cooperation. These strategies are shaped, on one hand, by the desire for horizontal and/or vertical control in terms of vendor lock-in and value-capture advantages (think of, for example, Microsoft) and, on the other hand, by more open approaches and open standards (like PC standard), which stimulate value creation through innovations.

Software Context and the Case for Open Innovation

Regardless of the industry, the sources of a firm's knowledge-creation capability and consequently its innovation performance are seen as closely dependent on its relations with other firms within the same business ecosystem. According to strategic management approaches, firms in the same industry must be different from each other in order to maximize their economic returns; the major source of this difference is market imperfections that should be removed by strategies that will overcome high entry barriers and reduced costs. Similarly, strategies that promote the development of inimitable resources and capabilities can create differences among firms that will lead to sustained competitive advantage. However, according to the knowledge-based theory of the firm differences among firms in the same industry can be explained as consequences of their strategic choices (Nonaka and Toyama, 2005); differences are the sources of economic capability. It is through conscious exploitation and management of these differences that a firm extends its capabilities beyond its own limited resources (Langlois, 1990). Knowledge is created by firms and individuals who interact with each other, either within a firm or beyond its boundaries, as competitors or collaborators. This perspective on how and why firms (co)evolve to be different is more visible in research streams in knowledge-intensive industries since knowledge creation is considered to be a process that works through interactions (Nonaka and Toyama, 2005). Thus, in a knowledge-intensive industry like software, part of a firm's value derives from its participation in networks with other firms (Kogut, 2000).

A considerable amount of research has been dedicated to the study of knowledge interactions *within* a firm and strategies for organizational and spatial designs to stimulate this cocreation. More recently, a research stream extends this abstract concept to include virtual, online spaces (Tee and Karney, 2010; von Krogh and Geilinger, 2014;). This research stream is largely based on the abstract notion of "ba," an extraorganizational or extradivisional space within which interactions underlying intra-/interorganizational knowledge-creation processes can take place (Nonaka and Konno, 1998). Today such interorganizational spaces are called "ecosystems," a term that emphasizes the coevolution of firms and cocreation of products and services.

The software industry provides several examples of strategic advantage stemming from the cooperation of firms and individuals for innovation; most of these cases relate to the adoption of innovation strategies linked to open source software (West, 2003). Apple, for example, has turned to an OS UNIX operating system to tap external innovations and better compete in the market. Among the industry's giants, Sun seemed very hesitant to adopt open source methods. IBM, however, has quickly evolved its strategy (Capek et al., 2005) and established strategic alliances with the open source community. By around 2005, there was widespread awareness of the potential of open source strategy, and it is worth noting that this predates the appearance of the *open innovation* concept as a blanket label for similar practices.

The major assumption in open innovation is that "useful information is widely distributed" (Chesbrough, 2006). Most of the characteristics of the software industry, as described in the previous sections, line up with this assumption. The fact that the bulk of input for software products is talent makes it possible for small firms (among larger ones) to create significant innovations. Conversely, On the other hand, difficulties in the nature of software patents (i.e., lack of patent protection) run rather contrary to open innovation concerns, simply rendering success in this industry more ephemeral and dictating continuous innovation for protecting one's position in the industry. Therefore, for firms in the software industry, there is a lot of useful information to be found in external sources. This information is quite widely distributed and, thus, presents a strong justification for *why* to get engaged in open innovation. Engagement in open innovation practices involves considerations related to how production is distributed, shared, and product complexity.

The software industry today is characterized by a distributed production mode; in contrast to similarly complicated products (such as, for example, an airplane), a software system is not—in the proper sense—designed as a whole or even tested extensively. Consider the act of viewing a web page on your computer. Your physical computer is among numerous models available. You might be running an alternative operating system on it (with a variety of software libraries) and using one of several web browser programs. Each of these software systems can have various versions/releases. Yours may be a unique combination. The web page you intend to browse contains several pieces of software code, along with content, and is expected to deliver a consistent and reliable experience to all users. The stability of this complex system of interactions between independently manufactured parts mostly rests on *standards* coming out of industry collaborations. Thus, standards play an important role in the industry in terms of providing product compatibility and shaping the competitive environment. Facilitating technology standards can lead to the creation of market dominance or the avoidance of a market battle for those who created them.

The standards that facilitate collaboration and product compatibility in most cases emerge out of the strategic and technological success of a single firm or an alliance of firms. Many electronics or communications standards come from nonprofit organizations, such as the Institute of Electrical and Electronics Engineers (IEEE) or the Internet Engineering Task Force (IETF), and play an important role in the functioning of the computing industry. However, most of these standards were developed as hardware or software platforms that were designed by a firm or public organization, whose success turned them into de facto standards. Microsoft's Windows operating system and Sun Microsystems's Java language are examples coming from private firms; Berkeley UNIX and the National Center for Supercomputing Applications (NCSA) Apache web server are examples from public organizations or universities.

In the software industry, platforms[2] are the main instrument for the continuance of standards. A successful standard platform facilitates modularity in innovation activity by the joint contributions of the platform sponsor and third-party contributors (Baldwin and Woodard, 2009). If implemented effectively, the technical architecture and the arrangement of intellectual property rights of a platform enables the development of complementary assets and allows reuse between vendors in the business ecosystem (West and Wood, 2013). For the participants in such ecosystems, "seizing opportunities frequently involves identifying and combining the relevant complementary assets needed to support their business" (Teece, 2003: 59). Once positive business feedback is created out of these complementarities, the advantage thus produced is amplified and leads to further support for the platform.

Some software platform standards come out of public organizations, such as the UNIX operating system, Apache web server, or GNU Compiler Collection. These platforms are created, sponsored, and initially supported in a nonbusiness context. However, changing industrial conditions may create opportunities for firms to derive value from such platforms. In most of these cases, the platform is governed cooperatively, by providing suitable software licensing schemes for for-profit players and participating in knowledge transfer and coendowment of the platform (Gençer and Oba, 2011a). Other standard platforms are initiated by innovative firms. The level and form of openness of the platform is related closely to how the firm views value-creation and value-capture opportunities through collaboration and asset complementarities in the ecosystem. In many cases, the "opening up" of a platform is processual rather than temporary, as it progresses through feedback from potential partners in the business ecosystem (Gençer and Oba, 2011a and 2011b).

The decision as to what level, degree, and form of openness a firm adopts in its software innovation strategy is based on intellectual property rights and product complexity. The leading industry firms' responses to the challenges and opportunities of open source innovation have varied, "depending on whether they had used software as a source of competitive advantage, and whether they retained other sources of competitive advantage" (West, 2003: 1277). IBM's embracing of open source and Microsoft's distancing itself from open source can be explained by this logic (West, 2003); in the case of IBM, open source technologies like UNIX stimulate the adoption of its hardware or system products, while in case of Microsoft, open source is in direct conflict with the software licensing fees upon which its business relies. The issue of open source innovation is further complicated by limitations on software patenting and, as a consequence, its licensing (Heller and Eisenberg, 1998; de Laat, 2005).

Capek's report (2005) on IBM's open source strategy further clarifies the applicability of open innovation strategy to the software industry. This strategy seems to be targeted at lower layers of the software technology stack,[3] where compatibility, rather than added value, is the major systemic factor. Conversely, the upper layers, such as domain-specific applications, that create added value are more compatible with closed, proprietary innovation strategies. The recent example of Android's rather fast rise in the mobile devices market also illustrates that the industry is more receptive to open innovation strategies where lower layers of the software stack are concerned. The long-enjoyed dominant position of Microsoft on the desktop PC segment of the market appears to be the very reason why its proprietary alternative to Android on the mobile platform has not been well received in the industry ecosystem.

Besides suitability in terms of its location in the software stack, there are also issues about the *applicability* of open innovation strategies for a specific firm. In many cases, the entire company culture and its strategic mind-set may be at conflict with open innovation and open source collaboration. Many firms are not equipped with management that has the understanding of how to replace customer lock-in when open technologies are to be adopted. After various successes and failures, firms in the industry are coming up with some novel solutions to this issue, which mainly aim at containing and delimiting openness in a manageable way. Some firms experiment with levels and degrees of openness in relation to a specific market niche. Others come up with innovations based on software architecture or dual licensing that allow them to open parts of their software and to pursue open innovation initiatives and attract partners, while at the same time protecting their core competences from imitation. In any case, be it to develop a synergistic relationship with an ally to go up against a common, strong competitor (e.g., Apple and IBM against Microsoft) or be it the desire to get a new software platform accepted in the industry ecosystem, firms are provided with ample motivation to turn to open innovation.

In an important but rather subtle way, the applicability of open innovation at a particular layer of the software stack is related to the complex nature of the software package. The interoperability of products in a complex system requires a lot of technical effort by firms to learn and utilize technology coming from others. There is an ample amount of open or available software out there. But such openness does not easily carry just any player to the innovative core. The very complexity of software systems renders such a journey to the core like a swim in a sticky ocean. Put simply, it takes a good deal of competence and a lot of effort to explore what is out there and what useful combinations are possible. Taken separately from the motivating factors for open innovation, this characteristic gives us the key to understanding *how* it is being done. There are certain software industry contexts within which establishing open ecosystems of innovation promises huge advantages to sharing the costs of innovation, while at the same time making these advantages more available to initiators and first movers. Therefore, the innovation prospects relies to some degree on possessing competence in open innovation practices and tacit knowledge of a particular technology, rather than simply relying on license agreements.

Subcontexts Less Suitable for Open Innovation

At the upper layers of the software stack, the innovation landscape changes. Software products in these layers are typically targeted at a market niche rather than a mass user base, and they have high added value as compared to those in the lower stacks. For example, it would be very hard for a firm producing ERP software to develop any business opportunities by opening all or parts of its software technology. The same logic applies for a company selling cloud or social network services. The market share of such companies increases by vendor lock-ins and by the control of add-on products or services. Since such upper layers of the software stack appear to be less suitable for open innovation practices, strategic alliances and asset complementarity are to be managed differently in each case.

However, some firms offering products and services for the upper layer seem to be experimenting and finding opportunities in open innovation strategy. These firms provide examples of the importance of delimiting open and closed innovation at this layer. The relatively recent concept of *crowdsourcing* fits well into describing opportunities driven by open innovation at the upper layers of the software stack. Exemplifying open innovation's root assumption that "useful information is widely distributed," many companies seek to enable a large number of potential innovators to contribute complementary innovations for their products or services. Many users create innovations with the sole purpose of solving their own problems. In some cases, such innovations have value for others as well. This situation presents the service or product provider with the opportunity to capture value from the crowd, or what Hippel, Ogawa, and de Jong (2011) call "consumer innovators." In order to exploit such opportunities, the provider needs to make its product or service more amenable to such innovation by, for example, opening its interfaces, publishing its interface specifications, making developer training materials more accessible, and so forth. Some examples are Google's map service and Facebook: both allow embedding and the reuse of services by third-party websites, which create further added value for customers, hence contributing to the acceptance of the backing platform.

In a similar vein, Gonçalves and Ballon (2011) report on the benefits of open platforms in mobile operators whose business is based on Software as a Service (SaaS) or Platform as a Service (PaaS) models, rather than selling software licenses in the traditional way. The emerging open innovation strategy in this business subcontext appears to include practices such as making network interfaces accessible and well documented. This allows customers and third-party providers to create some innovative add-ons, for example, by using the network interface of a GSM service provider to send SMS from a little program they've created. Similar practices can be seen in several examples at the upper layer, such as Facebook or Twitter enabling application developers with an open application programming interface (API). Therefore, at the upper layers of the software stack, there is still significant innovation capacity outside of firm boundaries, but it is sparser; its actualization requires specific tactics and usually occurs after a product is created.

The Practice of Open Innovation in Software: Strategies and Patterns

As with many other industries, the practices of exchanging or cocreating innovations existed in the computing and software industry long before these were systematically taken to the core of business strategies. Today, open innovation research classifies some of these practices as "inside-out" and "outside-in" (Chesbrough, 2003; Enkel et al., 2009; Spaeth, Stuermer, and von Krogh, 2010) models or strategies. Inside-out strategies commonly involve moving innovations out of a given firm's boundaries, either by licensing out products to capture value or by establishing spin-off firms to speed up product development (Spaeth, Stuermer, and von Krogh, 2010; West and Gallagher, 2006). Outside-in strategies are employed by licensing in products or acquiring small firms that have developed (or are in the process of developing) innovative products. Both of these strategies are essentially dyadic arrangements between firms. Beyond these now rather traditional arrangements, however, recent studies emphasize the importance of strategies based on the co-development of products and technologies (Chesbrough and Schwartz, 2007), which seems to move away from the firm-centric emphasis in most open innovation literature and also accommodates the logic of multilateral arrangements vis-à-vis the co-creation of technologies. It also fits well in relation to open source–based practices in the software industry. Here we present a short selection of these practices and point to strategic patterns that have emerged out of the software industry's past.

As discussed in the first section of this article, today's software landscape is characterized by three dominant business and thus innovation archetypes: closed innovation (mainly within the boundaries of a firm), open innovation (including open source projects), and hybrids (strategic alliances between firms and the open source community). However, in practice, these archetypes are not clearly separated from each other; as big firms do, the open source community, through various alliances, utilizes mixed innovation strategies (open and closed) leading to a rich variety of open innovation strategies.

The choice of cooperation for innovation—how it is going to be realized, at which technology levels, and with whom—is a strategic decision determined by the vision of management teams and is dependent upon an evaluation of risks and opportunities. Although distributing programs for free (i.e., freeware) is an old practice that is motivated by the need to develop a greater user base (whose value is captured by means of complementary products or versions of products with more features), IBM was one of the first commercial firms to experiment with these practices for the explicit goal of boosting innovation. Capek et al. (2005) describes an early experience within the company, in 1997, as follows: "One of our first and most memorable experiences with OSS followed the Jikes source code release. Within eight hours of the release, a programmer in California sent an e-mail to the Jikes authors containing a non-trivial enhancement to the compiler, one which required investing some time and effort to understand the code" (250).

This example highlights the potential for firms in value creation with open source–based practices. Encouragement coming from these experiences resulted in IBM and other firms taking more seriously the benefits of both reaching out to firms and professionals in the industry to co-develop innovations and also creating open innovation ecosystems to realize such goals. The increasing scales, success, and corporate involvement based in these ecosystems has resulted in the institutionalization of certain strategic and organizational patterns and governance structures (Gencer and Oba, 2011a, 2011b). Here we discuss the choice of open innovation strategies in relation to decisions about *what to* develop (i.e., which products and services), *how to* develop, and *with whom* develop.

As we have discussed before, the lower layers of the software technology stack provide more suitable contexts for open innovation strategies. In fact, the open source–based projects that have generated large revenues appear to be those at the lower layers, such as Linux, Apache, and Android (Fitzgerald, 2006). Therefore, collaboration at that level is an established pattern in relation to the "what to" question. There are numerous large-scale initiatives at this layer that seem to easily attract collaboration.

However, at the higher levels of the software technology stack, there is more reluctance to engage in open source innovation practices since software developed in these layers is designed to perform functions targeted for a specific application. These upper layers accommodate more traditional open innovation practices, such as licensing. However, as Fitzgerald (2006) notes, open source is becoming a valuable "brand," and many firms with products at different layers of the software technology stack are interested in leveraging this brand. Examples such as the Eclipse Project (aiming to produce developer tools) and Jquery (a toolkit for web applications) demonstrate that the industry's willingness to practice open source–based innovation at the upper layers is progressing, although it seems to be lagging behind that of the lower layers. Recently, many firms whose products or services are at the upper layers are blending crowdsourcing-based practices into open innovation strategies to expand innovation activities to users (individuals or small firms) and even to apply them within the firms themselves (Spector, Norvig, and Petrov, 2012).

In relation to *how to* apply open innovation, one needs to address a number of issues, such as sharing control, licensing schemes, governance, collaborative decision making, and trust. As the software industry has accumulated experience in open innovation, there emerge certain strategic patterns that address these issues (Gencer and Oba, 2011a). The general themes emerging seem to be (1) a formalizing of governance and decision practices within structures like foundations or steering committees, in contrast to the meritocratic style of community-based open source projects, and (2) the use of more liberal licensing to allow value capture, accompanied with tighter enforcement of these by parties involved on their contributions to avoid legal litigations. In community-originated examples, like Linux and Apache, firm involvement results in the creation of foundations and steering committees to apply these patterns and transfer of command to these structures. Corporate-led examples, such as Java and Eclipse, also move toward the same point, but from a different origin. Recent initiatives, like Android technology, appear to fit these emergent strategic patterns. This group of patterns is suitable in developing large-scale infrastructure-related software technologies at the lower layers of the software technology stack. In corporate-led cases (like Android and Eclipse), the game is usually initiated with a major contribution from a leading firm.

With whom to realize open innovation so that the returns of internal R&D investments and resources with external innovative potential can be balanced is another decision that requires managerial discretion. Open innovation strategies create opportunities either in terms of providing resources for improving products through collective contributions or by endowing a base for extending markets. Users and developers—individual or corporate—collectively develop products that can be used by all. This process of the collective production of software also enables the continuous improvement of product quality. Furthermore, the inclusion of users in the production process enables market extension: the visibility of the product increases, and, as is the case with spin-offs, noncommercial technology can find a milieu in which to flourish and expand.

The choice of partners seems to be driven by market dynamics, as well as factors relating to a firm's culture and whether it is at conflict with open innovation practices. In the Linux example, one can see extensive participation from the relevant segments of the industry regardless of firm culture, with the notable exception of Microsoft, whose market position is in direct conflict with the Linux ecosystem. One can see adversaries and allies on the same boat in such ecosystems. In the case of Android technology (which has gained extensive support in the industry), Nokia—a firm that is quite familiar with open source practices and is a leader in mobile devices technology—opted to stay out so as not to undermine its own technology. But later, unable to push its own technology forward fast enough to compete against Android, Nokia was forced to partner with Microsoft. In general, the domination of a powerful player in a particular market is the reason for collaboration of a critical mass of other players in open source–based innovation ecosystems.

Future Directions

Open innovation strategy in the software industry has entered into what we may call an "establishment" phase. Certain strategic practices addressing key innovation issues have proven effective and are being adopted by increasingly more players. This transition phase carries certain implications. The new situation is expected to exacerbate a competitive disadvantage among those that fail to embrace these strategies. Additionally, the implementation of open innovation strategies raises some questions regarding the manner and mechanisms through which cooperation can be established in a dis-integrated industry where production is distributed, products are complex, and innovation cycles are short.

As strategic practices in the industry move in this "more open" direction, new opportunities for open innovation emerge while some others disappear or lose impact. The direction of this move appears to be what Nalebuff and Brandenburger (1997) label as "co-opetition": collaborating for value creation and then competing to capture the value created. It is important to note that the positive perception that is developing about the emergent strategy is an important element of its success, in terms of convincing collaboration partners to engage in open innovation–based alliances. Equally important is the relative vacuum and competitive pressure this emergence creates on alternative strategies. A recent example of this is the success of Google's Android technology in contrast to alternative products from Microsoft and others. While these alternative products "technically" appear to be equally competent, due to certain strategies employed, they are unattractive for collaborators.

Adapting business strategies to exploit opportunities exposed by open source is a moving target. Besides the notable exception of Microsoft, all the big players in the computing and software industry appear to be seriously experimenting with open source strategies. In the meantime, success stories about firms developing or translating open source technologies (e.g., Apache, UNIX, Java) into products and services and, in turn, creating innovations and capturing significant value out of these innovations are inscribed in the memory of the industrial community (Behlendorf, 1999; Geer, 2005; Fitzgerald, 2006).

The challenges of open innovation strategy for big firms in the software industry seem to be rooted in balancing popularity and market coverage. If the products are popular, they will be demanded more, and in terms of mainstream strategy logic, firms can appropriate more value by protecting their products from competition by patents and licenses. However, the more their products are protected, the fewer users they will have, and this will increase their vulnerability in competition with open source products.

A distinguishing and enduring feature of open innovation in the software industry seems to be the involvement of user and software-developer communities in the process. Open source innovation is creating a strong feedback effect through which young and independent talent (students, entrepreneurs) are empowered to participate in the innovation process, with all the tools they need being available on a simple laptop computer, often at no cost. This is in strong contrast to the innovation requirements in, for example, a jet engine or the biotech industries, where one needs expensive setups to experiment with the development processes. This community-based landscape can be expected to continue to affect open innovation practices in the software industry for the foreseeable future.

In contrast to big firms, it is still unclear how open innovation can be employed by Small- and Medium-sized Enterprises (SMEs) and with what types of business models. Successful examples of national innovation systems, like the one developed in Finland, suggest that such employment may be highly dependent on local contexts, rather than large enterprises. Similarly there is little experience for the case of public sphere and not-for-profit organizations.

Notes

1. For example, Google's Android system for tablet PCs has over a million lines of program code (Source: retrieved July 19, 2013)
2. A platform is hardware, software, or a combination of both that sustains the smooth running and interaction of value-added software products. They set the standards around which appropriate software can be developed. Operating systems (Linux, Windows, etc.) and programming systems (Java, GCC [GNU C Compiler Collection]) are some examples.
3. A software technology stack can be best understood in comparison to something such as electricity technology. In electrical engineering, lower-level problems, such as the transfer of electricity, precedes other problems, such as turning the electricity into physical power with a motor. Similarly, for example, transferring data between two computers precedes whatever content is being transferred. In this example, Internet data communication standards are at the lower level of the technology stack. A webpage you are browsing may have more complex features (at the upper layer of the technology stack), which are less standardized and may work better on one computer than another.

References

Baldwin, C., and von Hippel, E. (2011). "Modeling a Paradigm Shift: From Producer Innovation to User and Open Collaborative Innovation." *Organization Science* 22: 1399–1417.

Baldwin, C., and Woodard, C. J. (2009). "The Architecture of Platforms: A Unified View." In A. Gawer (ed.), *Platforms, Markets and Innovation* (pp. 19–44).Nothrhampton, MA: Elgar Edward.

Bahrendorf, B. (1999). "Open Source as a Business Strategy." In C. DiBona, S. Ockman, and M. Stone (eds.), *Open Sources: Voices from the Revolution* (pp. 171–88). Sebastopol, CA: O'Reilly Media, Inc.

Capek, P., Frank, S. P., Gerdt, S., and Shields, D. (2005). "A History of IBM's Open-Source Involvement and Strategy." *IBM Systems Journal* 44: 249–57.

Chesbrough, H. (2006). "Open Innovation: A New Paradigm for Understanding Industrial Innovation." In H. Chesbrough, W. Vanhverbeke, and J. West (eds.), *Open Innovation: Reaching a New Paradigm* (pp. 1–15). New York: Oxford University Press.

Chesbrough, H. W. (2003). *Open Innovation: The New Imperative for Creating and Profiting from Technology*. Boston: Harvard Business Review Press.

Chesbrough, H., and Schwartz, K. (2007). "Innovating Business Models with Co-development Partnerships." *Research-Technology Management* 50 (1): 55–59.

Enkel, E., Gassmann, O., and Chesbrough, H. (2009). "Open R&D and Open Innovation: Exploring the Phenomenon." *R&D Management* 39 (4): 311–16. doi:10.1111/j.1467-9310.2009.00570.x.

Fitzgerald, B. (2006). "The Transformation of Open Source Software." *MIS Quarterly* 30: 587–98.

Geer, D. (2005). "Eclipse Becomes the Dominant Java IDE." *IEEE Computer Society Press* 38: 16–18.

Gençer, M., and Oba, B. (2011a). "Taming of 'Openness' in Open Source Software Innovation." European Group of Organizational Studies Colloquium in Gothenburg, Sweden.

Gençer, M., and Oba, B. (2011b). "Organizing the Digital Commons: A Case Study on Engagement Strategies in Open Source." *Technology Analysis & Strategic Management* 23 (9): 969–82.

Gonçalves, V., and Ballon, P. (2011). "Adding Value to the Network: Mobile Operators' Experiments with Software-as-a-Service and Platform-as-a-Service Models." *Telematics and Informatics* 28 (1): 12–21.

Grad, B. (2007). "The Creation and the Demise of VisiCalc." *IEEE Annals of the History of Computing* 29 (3): 20–31.

Heller, M., and Eisenberg, R. S. (1998). "Can Patents Deter Innovation? The Anticommons in Biomedical Research." *Science* 280: 698–701.

Von Hippel, E., Ogawa, S., and de Jong, J. P. J. (2011). "The Age of the Consumer-Innovator." *MIT Sloan Management Review* 53 (1): 27–35.

Kogut, B. (2000). "The Network as Knowledge: Generative Rules and the Emergence of Structure." *Strategic Management Journal* 21: 405–25.

von Krogh, G., and Geilinger, N. (2014). "Knowledge Creation in the Ecosystem: Research Imperatives." *European Management Journal* 32 (1): 155–163

de Laat, P. B. (2005). "Copyright or Copyleft? An Analysis of Property Regimes for Software Development." *Research Policy* 34 (10): 1511–32.

Langlois, R. (1990). "Creating External Capabilities: Innovation and Vertical Disintegration in the Microcomputer Industry." *Business and Economic History* 19: 93–102.

McKusick, M. K. (1999). "Twenty Years of Berkeley Unix: From AT&T-Owned to Freely Redistributable." In C. DiBona, S. Ockman, and M. Stone (eds.), *Open Sources: Voices from the Revolution* (pp. 31–46). USA: O'Reilly Media, Inc.

Nalebuff, B. J., and Brandenburger, A. M. (1997). "Co-opetition: Competitive and Cooperative Business Strategies for the Digital Economy." *Strategy & Leadership* 25 (6): 28–35.

Nonaka, I., and Konno, N. (1998). "The Concept of 'Ba': Building a Foundation for Knowledge Creation." *California Management Review* 40 (3): 40–55.

Nonaka, I., and Toyama, R. (2005). "The Theory of the Knowledge-Creating Firm: Subjectivity, Objectivity and Synthesis." *Industrial and Corporate Change* 14 (3): 419–36.

Raymond, E. S. (2001). *The Cathedral and the Bazaar: Musings on Linux and Open Source by an Accidental Revolutionary*. Sebastopol, CA: O'Reilly.

Sommerville, I., Cliff, D., Calinescu, R., Keen, J., Kelly, T., Kwiatkowska, M., McDermid, J., and Paige, R. (2012). "Large-Scale Complex IT Systems." *Communications of the ACM* 55 (7) 71. doi:10.1145/2209249.2209268.

Spaeth, S., Stuermer, M., and von Krogh, G. (2010). "Enabling Knowledge Creation through Outsiders: Towards a Push Model of Open innovation." *International Journal of Technology Management* 52 (3): 411–31.

Spector, A., Norvig, P., and Petrov, S. (2012). "Google's Hybrid Approach to Research." *Communications of the ACM* 55 (7): 34–37. dx.doi.org/10.1145/2209249.2209262.

Tee, M. Y., and Karney, D. (2010). "Sharing and Cultivating Tacit Knowledge in an Online Learning Environment." *International Journal of Computer-Supported Collaborative Learning* 5 (4): 385–413.

Teece, D. J. (2003). "Capturing Value from Knowledge Assets: The New Economy, Markets for Know-how, and Intangible Assets." In *Technology Management and Policy; selected Papers of David Teece* (pp. 47–75). USA: World Scientific Publishing Co.

United Nations Conference on Trade and Development (UNCTAD). (2012). *Information Economy Report: The Software Industry and Developing Countries*. United Nations Publications. http://unctad.org/en/PublicationsLibrary/ier2012_en.pdf (accessed April 26th, 2013).

West, J. (2003). "How Open Is Open Enough? Melding Proprietary and Open Source Platform Strategies." *Research Policy* 32 (7): 1259–85.

West, J., and Gallagher, S. (2008). "Patterns of Open Innovation in Open source Software." In H. Chesbrough, W. Vanhaverbeke, and J. West (eds.), *Open Innovation: Researching a New Paradigm* (pp. 82–106). USA: Oxford University Press.

West, J., and Wood, D. (2013). "Evolving an Open Ecosystem: The Rise and Fall of the Symbian Platform." In A. Ron, J. E. Oxley, and B. S. Silverman (eds.), *Collaboration and Competition in Business Ecosystems (Advances in Strategic Management, Volume 30)* (pp. 27–67). UK: Emerald Group Publishing Limited.

CHAPTER 14

The Challenges and Prospects of Open Innovation through Strategic Alliances

Refik Culpan

Introduction

It has been a decade since the concept of *open innovation* (OI) was first introduced in management literature and began to be practiced in organizations. Although it has provided new insights and useful directions in the management of innovation beyond company boundaries in the areas of new products, processes, and technologies, both researchers and practitioners still face some challenges that need to be addressed. In the past, in management literature, various popular trends, approaches, or techniques (like *sociotechnical systems* and *total quality management*) have been put forward; but, today, we hardly hear about them anymore. So we could aptly ask: is OI a fact or a fad? (Chesbrough and Brunswicker, 2014; Trott and Hartman, 2009). The pioneering scholars (Chesbrough, 2003; 2006; Gassmann and Enkel, 2010; West, 2003) of OI have convincingly argued that firms are heavily dependent upon the development and adoption of OI in products and processes for gaining competitive advantage and achieving above average returns. Today we live in an increasingly interdependent global business environment where almost no single firm, even one with vast resources, can afford to stay within its company boundaries and develop all of its R&D aims without collaboration with or help from external sources. Although OI sounds appealing in theory, a critical question is whether companies can embrace this approach by allocating their scarce resources, time, and energy, and especially how they can work with other potential firms by sharing their valuable intellectual properties. If firms perceive OI as a fashion in management that will fade away as time goes, they will likely stick to their conventional strategic ways and tools (i.e., closed innovation) in developing competitive products and technologies. However, the current business environment (i.e., technological advances and the globalization of business) and the practical competitive realities of business have taught us that companies can no longer afford to rely solely on their own sources for innovation. For example, Merck Corporation, a major US pharmaceutical firm, announced that it would cut its workforce by 81,000, or 20 percent, over the next two years. These cuts will especially curtail its R&D activities. Joseph Walker and Peter Loftus (2013), in a *Wall Street Journal* article, report that in recent years advancements in the understanding of genetics and biology have increasingly encouraged drug development, with many of the promising new drugs aimed at niche disease populations. These new drugs have been developed by smaller biotechnology competitors on the cutting edge of science. Moreover, this downsizing of its R&D department at Merck means that the company will either pursue a strategy of acquiring start-up companies that excel in cutting-edge research, instead of in-house drug developments, or collaborate with such external companies to develop new drugs. Either way, Merck is moving toward being a biotech venture capitalist. The company is putting greater emphasis on acquiring experimental drugs from outside the company, which will help it minimize costly research expense and unsuccessful new drug launches. For Merck, this reflects a strategy shift, from developing new drugs internally to seeking opportunities externally. It is also seeking interfirm partnerships in developing new drugs. Furthermore, Merck is not alone in this shift in R&D and product innovation ventures.

Another typical example of interfirm collaboration for OI is Blade.org, which was established by IBM and six other founding firms to promote the development and innovation of blade technology to help customers to meet the growing demands for their computer server needs in information technology systems (as noted in chapter 2). Blade.org, a collaborative community of firms, consists of governing members (i.e., IBM and the other six founding firms), sponsoring members (developers and distributors of Blade platforms), and general members (end-user firms). The purpose of Blade.org, as described by Snow and Culpan (2011), is to enhance the ongoing development of blade-based solutions that can be offered to the market in a timely fashion and that will increase customer confidence in the system. The Blade.org community was intended to achieve its purposes by including the provision of guidelines to member firms for designing their programs, developing their solutions, developing independent compliance testing procedures that member firms may use, hosting industrywide solution demonstrations and other marketing events, and incorporating member concerns and preferences into strategic initiatives that expand and improve the community.

The Blade.org case illustrates that IBM, along with its fellow founding firms, chose to form a collaborative community of firms focusing on accelerating the development and adoption of blade server solutions, rather than attempting to exploit the blade IP by itself (Snow and Culpan, 2011).

As the above cases and earlier studies (Chesbrough, 2003; Enkel, Gassmann, and Chesbrough, 2009; Gassmann and Enkel, 2010; von Hippel and Krogh, 2003) suggest, firms' openness can stimulate innovation by incorporating the resources and competencies of diverse complementary firms, leading to new products and processes that serve customer needs. Thus, OI, in conjunction with internal innovation, should be considered as a viable strategic tool that will continue to provide users with unprecedented benefits. Many companies are under a competitive pressure to look for novel ways of developing new products, services, or technologies, as attested to in previous chapters in this book. Not only has open innovation emerged as an effective paradigm to overcome in-house R&D complacency (Gassmann, Enkel, and Chesbrough, 2010), but also it has enabled firms to leverage distributed knowledge in innovation ecosystems for new value creation. In many ways, the open innovation paradigm creates an environment where firms can exploit and explore external sources of innovation through strategic alliances, collaborative partnerships, and/or knowledge and technology brokering.

Nonetheless, there are still some critical strategic questions that need to be answered to before business firms can fully utilize OI. For example, West and Gallanger (2006) identify three fundamental challenges for OI: finding creative ways to exploit internal innovation, incorporating external innovations into internal development, and motivating outsiders to supply an ongoing stream of external innovation. They also point out that the latter challenge presents a paradox as to why firms would spend their resources on R&D projects if the outcomes of such projects might benefit their rivals. Traditionally, companies tend to be conservative and secretive about their R&D activities since they consider such efforts as proprietary knowledge that will potentially lead to their competitive superiority against their rivals. However, as indicated by Culpan (2002) and Hamel and Prahalad (1989), collaborating with competitors may lead to win-win outcomes. Moreover, this conservative attitude has indeed been changing, as we will elaborate below.

In light of the studies reported in this book, we have identified some critical questions concerning OI concepts and applications, which will now be articulated and discussed.

Critical Questions Posing Challenges for OI

Some critical strategic questions concerning OI warrant the attention of both researchers and managers of innovation. To place OI into a proper perspective and comprehend its importance and effective applications, we need to tackle these questions. Thus, this chapter looks at OI concepts and applications from the perspective of the process of knowledge creation and development in the context of strategic alliances. First, it raises some questions that need to be addressed in light of emerging technologies, products, services, and markets and then discusses them in a conceptual framework.

1. How can OI be viewed in the business and management literature? What are the theoretical underpinnings of OI?

There are several theoretical explanations for OI; however, from a strategic management standpoint, we believe the resource-based view, the knowledge-based view, and the view of the dynamic capabilities of a firm offer the most relevant conceptual justifications for it. According to the strategic management literature, a firm's competitive advantage hinges upon how distinct the resources and capabilities or knowledge assets that the firm possesses are. Also, incorporating innovation into a firm's strategy largely determines the firm's profitability (or rents), as described in chapter 2, thus linking business strategy and innovation. Now let us look specifically at those theoretical bases of OI to understand its characteristics and dynamics.

Resource-Based View and Dynamic Capabilities of the Firm

As Grant (2008) acknowledges, in the 1990s, the role of resources and capabilities for firm strategy and the primary source of competitive advantage and profitability was recognized as a new perspective and has become known as the *resource-based view* of the firm. As proponents of this particular view, Barney (1991), Collis and Montgomery (1995), and Peteraf (1993) argue that the competitive advantage of a firm stems from the firm's possession and use of a unique portfolio of its resources and capabilities. Such valuable resources consist of the tangible (i.e., financial and physical), intangible (i.e., technology, reputation, culture), and human resources of a firm, while capabilities enable the firm to transform those resources into superior uses. In a similar fashion, Prahalad and Hamel (1990) describe such crucial capabilities as the "core competences" that provide competitive advantage for a firm over its rival by making a disproportionate contribution to ultimate customer value or to the efficiency with which that value is delivered. Furthermore, according to Teece (2009), "dynamic capability is the capacity of an organization to purposely create, extent, or modify its resources base" (4). Moreover, the concept of dynamic capability includes the capacity with which to identify the need or opportunity for change, formulate a response to such a need or opportunity, and implement a course of action. Looking with these lenses, Dyer and Kale (2007) define relational capabilities as follows: firms can create value from their strategic relationships by focusing on creating idiosyncratic combinations of resources and capabilities. They argue that the drivers of relational capabilities are relationship-specific assets that are usually built over time by systematic investments in a partnership (e.g., the collaborations between Japanese auto manufacturers and their suppliers), complementary capabilities (e.g., when one partner has a strong R&D orientation while another has commercialization skills), interfirm knowledge-sharing routines (e.g., establishing effective knowledge-transfer processes), and effective governance (e.g., alliances through contracts or ownership structures that effectively protect each side from the opportunistic behavior of the other). So, these four factors driving relational advantage and rents add a relational perspective to the resource-based view.

Knowledge-Based Views of the Firm and Knowledge Exploration and Exploitation

In addition, the knowledge-based view considers a firm's hold on a set of knowledge assets with the purpose of deploying these assets to create value. This approach can be deemed as an extension of the resource-based view of the firm defined previously, but it has some specific ramifications in terms of knowledge creation and sharing among firms. From a strategic viewpoint, Grant (2008) asserts that a firm's knowledge is valuable, effective, and a particularly interesting resource. It has certain properties, like being scare, and much of it is difficult to transfer and, in its complex forms, may be difficult to replicate. Moreover, the capabilities of a firm may be viewed as the manifestation of the knowledge of the organization. Thus, knowledge management offers valuable tools for creating, developing, maintaining, and replicating organizational capabilities. However, the type of knowledge—tacit (knowing how) versus explicit (knowing about)—becomes important in the transfer of knowledge from one organization to another. Tacit knowledge involves skills that are expressed through their performance, while explicit knowledge comprises facts, concepts, and sets of instructions. Since explicit knowledge can be coded, it is easier to transfer, but tacit knowledge cannot be codified, so it can be observed only through its application and acquired through practice; hence, its transfer between people (firms) is slow, costly, and uncertain (Grant, 2008). Thus, the transfer of tacit knowledge from one firm to another becomes a perplexing issue in strategic alliances and should be handled skillfully in the context of OI.

An important component of knowledge management is the understanding of processes of knowledge transfer and acquisitions. March (1991) identifies two major processes—knowledge exploration and knowledge exploitation. He considers the relation between the exploration of new possibilities and the exploitation of old certainties in organizational learning. Moreover, Spencer (1999) refers to knowledge exploration as "knowledge generation" and knowledge exploitation as "knowledge application." The former consists of knowledge creation and acquisition, while the latter involves knowledge integration, sharing, replication, storage, organization, measurement, and identification. In the OI context, firms could cocreate, transfer, and utilize such knowledge assets. In fact, the proponents of open innovation (Chesbrough, 2003; Enkel et al., 2009; Gassmann et al., 2010) recognize these processes through which new products, technologies, and business models can be developed.

Developing and acquiring knowledge through learning and integrating it into the organization is essential for creating innovative capabilities within a firm. Working with an open paradigm allows a firm to move away from an insular firm-centric model of innovation to one that seeks to exploit outside ideas and networks. In addition, opening to its environment exposes a firm to new knowledge and ideas that enhance the firm's capabilities and competencies. New knowledge and ideas lead to organizational learning, which can yield new sources of innovation and competitive advantage for the organization.

Overall, the theories described above underlie the conceptual bases for open innovation, and it would be useful to understand the rationalizations for OI and its relations to a firm's business strategy and competitive advantage. However, company resources, competencies, and knowledge bases have their limitations. In other words, almost no company possesses all the necessary competencies and knowledge assets that will lead to innovative products and technologies, which in turn provide the profits (or rents) that the firm is seeking. Thus, increasingly, firms need resourceful and capable partners for knowledge exploration (or generation) and exploitation (or application) for novel products and technologies in today's competitive world; that, in turn, necessitates open innovation models and modes.

Specifically, to develop organizational capabilities for innovation, it becomes necessary for organizations to strike a balance between exploratory and exploitative learning. In constantly changing or unstable environments, firms face the challenge of exploring new alternatives, redeploying existing resources, and developing new capabilities and routines. Without continuous organizational learning, open innovation is not implementable, and an organization is likely to be stagnant and fail.

2. Will OI replace closed innovation?

The question of closed versus open innovation and the choice between two opposing paradigms has been debated in the literature. Almirall and Casa-desus-Masanell (2010) aptly ask, when is open innovation superior to closed innovation? In answering this question, they conclude that an open approach to innovation allows a firm to discover combinations of product features that would be hard to envision in a confined environment. However, open innovation restricts the firm's ability to control the product's technological paths when partners have divergent goals. They suggest that the resolution of the trade-off between benefits of discovery and costs of divergence determines the choice between open and closed innovation.

Overall, we believe that two paradigms will continue to be employed simultaneously, and in fact they are complementary to each other, rather than one replacing the other. While firms continue to rely on in-house knowledge generation and innovation, they will seek opportunities to employ open innovation and benefit from collaborations with other knowledge sources, as knowledge has become increasingly disbursed globally and even across industry lines. Because of advances in technologies, market volatilities, and interdependencies among players in various industries (i.e., the role of complementors—outsourcing companies, financial institutions, technology providers, competitors, and customers), which can be viewed as an open ecosystem, we will witness the widespread utilization of OI among firms.

In their book, *The Agile Enterprise*, Pal and Lim (2005) contend that collaborative innovation allows firms to be responsive to customer needs and adaptive to market changes by collaborating with external partners to secure resources to meet the need for complex challenges and business processes. In addition, the agile firm is able to devise the most effective business process model to incorporate the information and knowledge available from the external context and utilize this process to develop dynamic adaptability in driving open innovation through continuous organizational learning. Furthermore, Chesbrough and Brunswicker (2013) show that large companies in Europe and the United States are increasingly using open innovation in their business practices.

Moreover, in his empirical research in the German chemical industry, Herzog (2011) found that as innovation force slowed down over the last 20 years, many chemical companies began to strive for implementing an OI strategy. He reported that German chemical companies have implemented open innovation concepts by setting up separate organizational units (e.g., Degussa's "Creavis Technologies and Innovation" or BASF's "Joint Innovation Lab"), which undertake innovative projects that cannot be operated by the focal firms' R&D departments alone (Herzog, 2011). Further, he argues that closed and open innovations involve two different corporate cultures, and the not-invented-here (NIH) syndrome may be an impediment in implementing open innovation strategy. Likewise, earlier, Chesbrough (2006) identified NIH syndrome as a major obstacle to the adoption of OI within organizations; he stated that such a syndrome is partly based on a xenophobic attitude, disliking and not trusting external ideas. This attitude of internal resistance to external new ideas happens to be a major hindrance to the implementation of OI; therefore, the organizational culture of a receiving organization needs to be changed to be more receptive for external innovations.

The new notion of the open innovation paradigm is in a sharp contrast to that of closed innovation, in which a company maintained complete control overall all aspects of the innovation process and discoveries were kept highly secret. Further, changes in society and industry, advances in information and communication technologies, and increasing globalization have led to the increased mobility of knowledge workers and the development of new financial structures, such as venture capital—forces that have caused the boundaries of innovation processes to start breaking up (Chesbrough, 2003).

Nonetheless, since open innovation has been around for some time now, probably we need more recent empirical studies comparing closed and open innovation practices with their outcomes (e.g.,competitive superiority and profitability) despite some measurement difficulties of core variables concerning both process and outcomes of innovations. , which need to be defined further and refined. Still, there have been an increasing number of conceptual and empirical studies (Chesbrough, 2006; Chesbrough and Brunswicker, 2013; Christensen et al., 2005; Lichenthaler, 2011; van de Vrande et al., 2009; West, 2003), including the ones in this book, making compelling arguments for the value of open innovation, which can be used in combination with in-house R&Ds.

3. Is OI appropriate for only certain industries?

We also need to assess whether open innovation is suitable only for particular industries—such as computer and information systems (CIS), biotechnology, and biochemistry, as discussed in previous chapters—or whether it can be employed across industries on a larger scale. Although the notion of OI applies to every business sector, it can be argued that it is more common in such industries as software development and biochemistry, as chapters 4 and 13 illustrate. Matzler and his colleagues (2014) assert that as organizations increasingly adopting Web 2.0 technologies, more collaborative opportunities emerge, leading to more open modes of strategizing, which is called *open source strategy* (Matzler calls it "open strategy"). Also, Chesbrough (2006) points out that it remains to be seen whether the concepts of open innovation can be applied to low-technology or more mature industries as well as it has been used in high-technology industries. Moreover, West (2003) asserts that computer platforms provide an integrated architecture of hardware and software standards as a basis for developing complementary assets. The most successful platforms were owned by proprietary sponsors that controlled platform evolution and appropriated associated rewards, but after examining three traditional vendors, he found that they experimented with hybrid strategies, which attempted to combine the advantages of open source software while retaining control and differentiation.

Actually, Chesbrough and Crowther (2006) demonstrated that early adopters of OI go beyond high-technology industries and include traditional and manufacturing industries. Furthermore, by analyzing the OI concept from an industrial-dynamics perspective, Christensen, Olesen, and Kjær (2005) argued that as the cooperative management of OI in regard to an emerging technology differed, the specific modes used reflected the companies' differing positions within the innovation system in question, the nature and stage of maturity of the technological system, and the particular value proposition purposed by the companies.

Thus, it can be argued that new OI applications have more commonly been used in CIS, pharmacology, and biochemistry so far, but they also have a great potential to be used in other industries, particularly in emerging industries that cross traditional industry boundaries, as demonstrated in chapter 4. It is conceivable that the need for OI applications will increase in the future because of the rapid advance in e-business technology, the increasing openness of the environment and society, increasing globalization, the blurring of technology and industry boundaries, and the rapid proliferation and popularity of social media and crowdsourcing.

4. Is OI only relevant in Western firms (e.g., US firms)?

We argue that contextual considerations, including national and corporate cultural environments and organizational paradigms, could influence the adoption and implementation of OI. As the authors of chapter 12 show in reference to Japanese corporate groups, particularly in the case of Panasonic Corporate Group, there are national and organizational impediments in utilizing OI across nations or organizations. The Panasonic case illustrates that a gradual adoption of

OI might be more appropriate in countries like Japan, where the economic system and corporate groups' influence do not particularly favor collaboration with external parties. A strategic shift from closed to open innovation may develop gradually as firms in such environments realize the benefits of open innovation while their internal R&D efforts prove unable to deliver desired results as they fall behind in the global competition in launching innovative products and technologies. Nonetheless, it must be noted that OI has been gaining momentum and has been welcomed by organizations in many countries, but such a shift in innovation endeavors requires a change in both managerial mind-sets and organizational paradigms and environmental conditions.

For example, after studying Chinese, Indian, and Brazilian multinational companies, Contractor (2013) identifies several possible location-specific assets of emerging market multinationals (EMMs), including the mind-sets of the top management of EMMs (such as long-term orientation, global or cosmopolitan perspectives, a degree of humility that recognizes the need to catch up by learning from foreign allies and customers, tolerance for ambiguity, and frugality) and home country cultural traits (such as emphasis on relationships, family control, and private equity capital). From these premises, we can conclude that EMMs could also be players in developing their innovative products and technologies to obtain competitive advantages against their established Western multinational counterparts.

Another case of an EMM accomplishment of innovation is Koc Holding's subsidiary Beko, in Turkey, the producer of "white goods—refrigerators, ovens, washing machines," which realized that it cannot continuously count on the licensing of Western technologies in building its products and continue to be competitive, so it developed its own R&D, but still in collaboration with Western allies, and introduced competitive products in Europe and North African markets in addition to its local Turkish market.

Google and a number of Western companies, for example, have recognized the capabilities of South Korean start-ups in software development, social networking, and mobile-game development. One such company is Classting, the producer of an educational social-media network app developed by a former high school teacher, which allows teachers to interact with students and their parents. Google has taken Classting representatives and others from South Korea to London and San Francisco to meet with venture capitalists. As a result, nine of those companies have collectively attracted $4 billion in outside investments. Although Google did not invest in these start-up companies, it stands to benefit from increased Internet usage more broadly (Cheng, 2013) , which will be driven by innovative start-ups. This example illustrates well how open ecosystems stimulate innovation.

Despite their reputation of being imitators in general, there are also innovative Chinese firms. For example, Tencent is well known for its creative Internet mobile services, exemplified by its very popular messenger systems, WeChat. Another Chinese firm, Xiaomi, a young company, has become a competitor to Apple and Samsung with its low-cost smartphones since its inception three years ago. Nonetheless, it is noted that innovation in China mostly tends to build up on existing technologies rather than developing radical innovations (Schuman, 2013).

Thus, we can conclude that although firms from developing economies may exhibit innovative behaviors sporadically, they are at a disadvantage to be innovative in comparison to Western firms because they lack the business ecosystems or interconnectedness of complementary players in the business market and platforms that Western firms enjoy. In fact, one of the major detriments to OI in developing economies is the lack of interfirm alliances to foster product or technology innovation, in particular, the nonexistence of financial networks to support start-up firms and the usually risk-averse behavior of large companies that seek quick returns for their investments.

5. Who are suitable partners for OI, and how can a firm create alliance portfolios?

In engaging in an OI project, a firm needs to identify suitable partners with complementary resources and capabilities. As a result, identifying potential partners and creating alliance portfolios are important processes (see chapters 3, 4, and 11) in adopting OI; thus we need to explicate the essential factors and means in pinpointing potential partners and building alliance portfolios so that firms can use their relational capital to undertake OI ventures successfully. For this purpose, relational drivers for OI need to be defined and assessed.

In choosing a potential partner with complementary and relational capabilities, a firm needs to consider the following qualities: the strategic intent of the candidate firm; the resource and competence portfolios, trustworthiness, and collaboration experience (OI experience, if any) of the firm; and the position of the firm in the value chain, referring to whether the candidate firm is a competitor (or potential competitor) or a complementor. Of course, this is a daunting task, but developing a portfolio of potential partners and adopting some guidelines for this process can help managers to make sound decisions. Chapter 3 suggests that focal firms choosing to engage in open R&D alliances could be more consistent in the development of breakthrough innovations when those projects are managed in the context of a firm's alliance portfolios and meta-organizations.

Screening the market for new ideas and developments in products, technologies, and business models gives some insights for potential partners. In doing so, the firm needs to take into account not only the developments in its own industry or usual partners, but also cross-industry developments from which it can pinpoint promising partners.

6. What is the role of trust in interfirm alliances?

Trust has been studied as a cornerstone of interfirm alliances; as a result, a number of scholars (Culpan, 2002; Das and Teng, 1998; Gulati, 1995; Currall and

Inkpen, 2002) have paid close attention to it in partner relationships. In both forming and managing alliances, a partner needs to trust its partner for a successful collaboration. Particularly, for joint R&D projects involving innovations in products/services or technologies, partners would like to be sure that their partners are trustworthy. In choosing such partners, previous relationships with the firms are important indicators, as we will elaborate on later. Gulati (1995) argues that familiarity with the partner breeds trust. Because of the importance of trust between partners, this issue is discussed separately in the conceptual framework below.

7. How can a company expect to cooperate while it competes with its potential partner at the same time?

One major dilemma with OI partnerships is "coopetition"—that is, how firms can cooperate while they compete (Brandenburger and Nalebuff, 1996). In their book, entitled *Co-opetition*, Brandenburger and Nalebuff (1996) recognized this duality and identified four groups of players: customers, suppliers, competitors, and complementors. Further, they argued that a player can be competitor as well as complementor. Moreover, in studying the impact of coopetition on a firm's innovation performance in the semiconductor industry, Park, Srivastava, and Gnyawali (2013) found that competition and cooperation intensities have non-monotonic positive relationships with a firm's coopetition-based innovation performance, and balanced competition (i.e., when competition is moderately high and cooperation is high) has a positive effect on innovation performance. So, it seems appropriate to conclude that coopetition could lead to high innovation performance if the alliance is chosen carefully and managed properly by balancing the cooperative and competitive intensities so that the joint sum of common and private benefits is maximized, as suggested by Park, Srivastava, and Gnyawali (2013).

8. Will there be new OI applications in the innovation ecosystems?

Traditionally, innovation is undertaken in internally centralized R&D departments concerned with new designs, technologies, materials, and products, aiming mostly at new designs and manufacturing processes; however, insightful studies that extend OI into unconventional and multidimensional innovation activities—like collaborations with different complementors, in addition to the partnerships in the upward and downward value chain activities (i.e., marketing, supply chain) (see chapter 6) and customer services—will stimulate novel ideas in those areas. As chapter 6 shows, open innovation activities need to be considered beyond manufacturing partnerships by encouraging supply chain partners, primarily customers and suppliers, as the source of knowledge flows into the focal firm. In this sense, Thomke and von Hippel (2002) suggest that customers could be potential innovators in creating value for the firm by offering novel ideas and suggestions.

The recent agreement between Amazon.com and the US Postal Service in making Sunday deliveries (i.e., a kind of incremental innovation) in selected cities in the United States represents an interesting partnership. By this collaboration, Amazon will enhance its customer service while the USPS will have an opportunity to use its idle resources and facilities on Sundays and will be able to generate additional revenues. By its Sunday shipping plan, Amazon's goal is to co-opt the shippers into its own shopping platform.

Conventionally, innovation is confined to a firm's R&D departments, which are seen as "cost centers," whereas, with the OI movement, new ideas and knowledge could spring up at various value-chain points by the contributions of partner portfolios and open ecosystems, including a variety of players, such as suppliers, subcontractors, and customers (see chapters 4 and 6). Of course, coordinating and integrating such a variety of players into an innovation game plan is not an easy task, while intrafirm collaboration for R&D projects still presents social and technical challenges (e.g., coordination of cross-functional teams and cross-departmental meetings). However, they can be overcome by leadership support, joint task forces, improved communications, and incentive systems. Later, we will provide some insights into meeting challenges in these new value chain activities in a typical OI process.

A dynamic innovation ecosystem is typically characterized by a continual realignment of synergistic relationships of people, knowledge, and other resources that promote the harmonious growth of the ecosystem in response to changing external forces; and the ability to cultivate good relationships in innovation ecosystems is a critical determinant of open innovation success. But, each company still needs to find its own approach to open innovation to match its objectives, capabilities, and resources (Lindegaard, 2011).

Moreover, Adner (2006) identifies three basic types of risk in innovation ecosystems: initiative risks (uncertainties of managing a project), interdependence risks (uncertainties of coordinating with complementary innovators), and integration risks (uncertainties presented by the adoption process across the value chain). The extent of these risks is intimately related to the target market in which the firm hopes to deploy its innovation. Firms that assess ecosystem risks systematically will be able to establish more realistic expectations, develop a more refined set of environmental contingencies, and arrive at a more robust innovation strategy. Collectively, these actions will lead to more effective implementation and more profitable innovation (Adner, 2006). Hence, in selecting partners in innovation endeavors, it is also important for a firm to assess these risks in matching its innovation strategy to its innovation ecosystems in alignment with the goals and objectives of the potential partner firms.

9. What is the relevance of firm size in engaging in OI?

The size of companies engaging in open innovation is another controversial question that deserves close examination. It would be interesting to inquire into the relevance of firm size in relation to its involvement in open innovation. It has become common to witness R&D collaborations between large established firms with good financial standing and start-up firms with creative ideas but in need of research funds and established business platforms to advance their research and to commercialize the end products or technologies. In particular, this trend can be observed in the CIS (both software and hardware), biotechnology, and pharmaceutical industries.

Chapter 10 shows that knowledge-intensive business start-ups (KIBS) engage in both market- and technology-based innovations and can resolve the ambidexterity question by tailoring their portfolio configurations in upstream and downstream domains.

Another form of these kinds of relationships is the partnerships between start-up companies and venture capital firms. Gruber and Henkel (2006) provide the examples of the formation of new ventures in the domain of open source software businesses. Moreover, as a result of a comparison of small- and medium-sized enterprises (SMEs) and large companies with respect to their engagements in OI, chapter 3 notes that there are some challenges for SMEs in partnering with large companies. It concludes that SMEs usually lack trust, fear mistreatment, and are overprotective of their knowledge, while large companies are more concerned about fitting the collaborative research into their strategic road maps and exposing their technologies to their competitors (see Table 3.1). In addition, based on the data drawn from Dutch companies, Van de Vrande, De Jong, and Vanhaverbeke (2009) show that OI concepts and practices have also been adopted by SMEs. They found that SMEs pursue open innovation primarily for market-related motives, such as meeting customer demands, or keeping up with competitors. Moreover, Verbano, Crema, and Venturini (2013) explain the profiles of Italian manufacturing SMEs that are involved in OI.

The above explanations suggest that OI is not restricted to only large companies, but even start-ups and SMEs can conveniently engage in OI when the resources and capabilities of partners match those criteria and/or factors as discussed earlier. In other words, firm size is less irrelevant, as long as there is complementary between the knowledge assets and competencies of the partnering firms. Along these lines, Lindegaard (2011) discusses the benefits of open innovation for both small and large business and specifically points out how open innovation fits for small business if they are natural innovators.

10. How have university-business collaborations changed with the emergence of OI?

Another important inquiry is how university-industry collaborations (chapter 9) have changed or will be changing their R&D activities with the emergence of OI. Although, as noted in chapter 9, university-industry R&D collaborations go back many years, OI has moved such relationships to new levels. We can make the following observations regarding university-industry R&D collaborations. First, increasing cross-industry technologies and knowledge developments have augmented the reliance of businesses on university R&D. Second, a number of universities have assumed more active roles in R&D endeavors by creating their own venture capital centers (i.e., an inside-out open innovation paradigm).

In general, after studying academia and business R&D relationships, Barnes, Pashby, and Gibbons (2002) developed a good practice model, which comprises the following guidelines: (a) the evaluation of new partners and building a collaborative environment, (b) the establishment of objectives, progress reporting, effective communication, and deployment of qualified project managers, (c) building a flexible management process to cope with changes, (d) the establishment of trust, commitment, and continuity, (e) the creation of measures for maintaining the interest and commitment of the partners, and (f) the maintenance of an appropriate balance between academic objectives and industrial priorities. All these suggestions are valid for university-industry R&D collaborations in the OI context as well, and we can also expand the triple-helix model (the involvement of three core players: university, business, and government) by considering multiple partnerships of unconventional parties, including suppliers, customers, angel investors, venture capitalists and even competitors in the value chain for creating new products and technologies from idea to market (see chapter 8 for details).

In the analysis of the role of OI in university-business R&D partnerships and a reassessment of these relationships between research centers and businesses for recent collaborative research, we have especially noticed that new materials and technologies (e.g., nanotechnology, biodiversity, biochemistry, and new energy sources) have emerged as significant areas.

Prospects for OI

To answer all of the critical questions raised above, we have developed a conceptual framework in which the drivers, managerial and organizational factors, and forms of open innovations can be analyzed and its dynamics can be understood. (See Figure 14.1.) Our framework assumes that the basic process of open innovation involves idea generation, which we call "value architecture," and that every innovation is initiated by a new idea and design reflecting a unique way of meeting unmet needs in the market. From this value architecture, value creation emerges, which is thought of as how a value can be created from the transformation of this new idea into a concrete result in the form of a product, technology, or business platform. Finally, the creators appropriate some of the value created out of all these accomplished endeavors. When this value is created through strategic alliances, alliance partners indeed expect to appropriate from the total value produced.

Furthermore, the framework consists of (a) the drivers of OI, including innovation ecosystems, merging industries and technologies, dispersion of knowledge, and the need for R&D collaborations; and (b) the management of open innovation, comprising managerial and strategic factors, including managerial mindsets, OI paradigms and strategic intent, and partner selection that will transform innovation paradigms and modes and lead to value creation and appropriation through strategic alliances. Let us explain each element of the model.

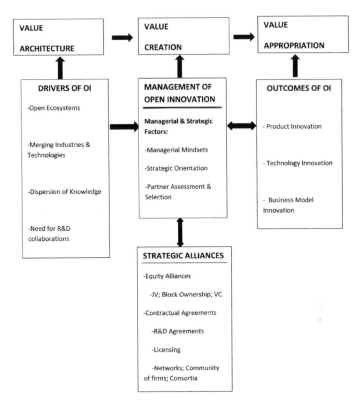

Figure 14.1 An Open Innovation Framework for Strategic Alliances (only selected strategic alliances are presented, but not all forms)

The Drivers of Open Innovation

Innovation or (Open) Ecosystems

According to a number of scholars (Adner and Kapoor, 2010; Chesbrough, 2006; West, 2003) open innovation occurs in a network of relationships among a number of actors involved in R&D activities, whether directly or indirectly or profoundly or marginally. A focal firm undertaking an innovation venture needs to interact with a web of other firms that contribute to the completion of the task. For example, Chesbrough (2006) recognizes the rise of "innovation intermediaries," which "either help innovators use external ideas more rapidly or help inventors find more markets where their own ideas can be used by others to mutual benefit" (139).

Moreover, Adner and Kapoor (2010) argue that "the success of an innovating firm often depends on the efforts of other innovators in its environment"(306). In the present market environment, there are interdependencies among an innovator (the focal firm) and other related firms in the upstream and downstream of the value chain. For example, in order to launch its innovative smartphones by translating its original designs into successful commercial products, Apple

Corporation needed to collaborate with a hardware maker, an advanced micro-chips maker, and other app developers.

After following the flow of inputs and outputs in the ecosystem to distinguish between upstream components that are bundled by the focal firm and downstream complements that are bundled by the firm's customers, Adner and Kapoor (2010) posit that the effects of external innovation challenges depend not only on their magnitude, but also on their location in the ecosystem relative to the focal firm. In addition, they "identify a key asymmetry that results from the location of challenges relative to a focal firm—greater upstream innovation challenges in components enhance the benefits that accrue to technology leaders, while greater downstream innovation challenges in complements erode these benefits" (1). Despite these challenges though, focal firms that understand the interdependencies in the ecosystem will be better equipped to undertake collaborative projects in upstream and downstream complements.

Converging Industries and Technologies
The lines across industries and technologies have been blurred, as seen in the health sciences, biochemistry, material sciences, and nanotechnologies. An automobile manufacturer today, for example, needs to incorporate electronics, computers, and alternative energy mechanisms into its final product to introduce an advanced and competitive vehicle. A number of industries, like natural gas and electricity, energy and communications, computer and telecommunication, and biology and chemistry, have been converging; and this trend poses both challenges and opportunities for the firms in such converging industries. The information and knowledge explosion, technological advances, and digital convergence are probably the main factors contributing to such convergences. It can be observed in the developments in fuel cells, smart homes and buildings, and energy and telecommunications (e.g., technological advances enabling using power lines for telecom), which represent some examples of converging industries. For example, smartphones, today, are the result of technological advances and digital convergence (i.e., a combination of phone, computer, camera, and a navigation system). Particularly, the advances in stem cells, biofuels, and biochemistry have been astonishing. All these convergences of industries and technologies often call for interfirm partnerships to launch innovative products and technologies.

Dispersion of Knowledge
Chesbrough (2006) claimed, "At its root, Open Innovation assumes that useful knowledge is widely distributed, and that even the most capable R&D organizations must identify, connect to, and leverage external knowledge sources as a core process in innovation" (9). This means that almost no single company possesses all the necessary knowledge resources to launch innovative products and processes. In this book, for example, with the cases of IBM, P&G, Philips, Shell, and Xerox, we have demonstrated that companies need to reach out to potential

partners to complement their resources and benefit from joint R&D endeavors. Also, as noted by the authors in previous chapters, many innovative ideas that were originally developed by start-up firms have resulted in innovative products and processes. In addition, universities and research institutions generate new knowledge that can be commercialized by collaborating with businesses. Basically, the sources of knowledge are not only vast and dispersed worldwide, but also conveniently accessible, thanks to the Internet and information technologies (e.g., open source software, search engines, big data, and databases).

Need for R&D Collaboration
Given the current trends in technology and knowledge developments, as discussed above, the basic premise of OI is that no firm has all the necessary resources or capabilities to undertake innovative R&D by itself (i.e., inbound OI) or that a firm often needs outside help to exploit its own untapped intellectual properties (i.e., outbound OI). Thus, OI inherently requires collaborations between firms, which may be large firms or SMEs. Also, potential partners may be companies anywhere in the value chain or open ecosystems as complementors. They range from suppliers to customers and even competitors at times. They can also be complementors from different industries.

Management of Open Innovation

Managerial and Organizational Factors

Managerial Mind-Sets
In the face of changing environments and market forces, managers must change their mind-sets about the traditional notion of closed innovation, and they must understand the importance of sharing ideas both inside and outside the organization, collecting collective intelligence, and utilizing the wisdom of strategic alliances in addition to other methods, such as crowdsourcing and accepting third-party apps, as mentioned in chapter 2. By building a culture that is open to the exchange of ideas within a larger network of emerging and evolving thinking, organizations will have a better chance for disruptive growth. Hence, managers should appreciate and exploit the knowledge resources of other firms in the upstream and downstream of the value chain and support and align with other complementors in open ecosystems to launch innovations in their organizations. They can accomplish this challenging task by communicating the value of OI to their employees, supporting and rewarding such initiatives, and reaching out to external sources to build collaborative R&D. As Pisano and Vergani (2008) state, "The new leaders in innovation will be those who can understand how to design collaboration networks and how to tap their potentials" (86). Moreover, those leaders should create and promote a corporate culture that supports OI so that other employees in the firm will not hesitate to undertake or get involved in collaborative ventures across firm boundaries. For example, overcoming the not-invented-here syndrome (Katz and Allen, 1982) could be a starting point.

Gassmann, Enkel, and Chesbrough (2010) also noted that creating a culture that values outside competence and know-how is crucial for open innovation practice.

Basically, adopting either inbound or outbound open innovation approaches leads to an engagement in interfirm collaboration. Traditionally, managers placed greater emphasis on internal R&D for launching new products and technologies, whereas today, given technological advances, the global dispersion of knowledge, and the blurring of lines across industries, almost no firm can afford to be a sole player in developing and launching innovations. Therefore, managers need to seek the contributions of other complementors, including start-ups and even firms in other industries, and competitors.

Strategic Re-orientation

As explained in chapter 2 in reference to the different OI paradigms or processes (Enkel et al., 2009), a firm can use three core paradigms for OI: outside-in process, inside-out process, and a coupled process, a combination of previous two processes. However, before engaging in any of these OI paradigms or processes, it needs to develop a strategic reorientation that emphasizes openness for collaborative innovation.

Related to the managerial mind-set for OI, organizational strategic reorientation should be developed to foster OI. Such a reorientation would reflect a strategic shift from relying only on in-house R&D to seeking out (inbound) external knowledge and sharing its own (outbound) knowledge with other organizations. As a result, new corporate strategy should spell out the objectives and means of achieving both inbound and outbound knowledge flows by allocating resources to search for potential entities (both start-ups and established ones), by creating teams that welcome working with outsiders, and by establishing a corporate culture that encourages collaborative work with foreigners. Such new innovation strategy will involve a formulation of clear R&D objectives and the allocation of necessary resources toward achieving such objectives in collaboration with complementor firms. Afuah (2009) contends that "innovation strategy is a game-changing innovation in products/services, business models, business processes, and/or positioning vis-à-vis competitors to improve performance" (4). In the context of strategic alliances, strategic innovation strategy is about an assessment of a firm's strengths and weakness and then linking with partners who can help to complement its resources and competencies and overcome its weaknesses.

Partner Assessment and Selection

The adoption of OI innovation strategy requires that a firm develops and manages a portfolio of potential partners with a variety of resources and capabilities, which complement its own capabilities. Therefore, the focal firm should continuously search for firms (both established large firms and start-up firms), auspicious fundamental complementary knowledge, and other resources to develop game-changing products, technologies, or business models. In this process, partner selection is the most important consideration, and it involves several components: the strategic intent of partner, the complementary resources and competencies of the potential partner, trust in the partner, the collaboration experience of the partner, and finally the position of the potential partner in the ecosystem. Let us examine these considerations closely.

(a) *Strategic Intent*: The strategic intent of a potential firm is critical, although identifying it can be challenging. Culpan (2002) states that "although at the outset, it is rather difficult to find out the strategic intent of the candidate firm, there are some signs such as strategic direction, resource repertoires, and leadership characteristics that give some clues about the intent of the candidate" (205). The current strategy and vision of the candidate firm reflect what direction it wishes to go and what innovative projects it is willing to undertake. The candidate firm's business platform, including product portfolio, technological moves, customer profiles, and market expansions, provides indications for its future directions. In particular, open innovation requires partners' openness, commitment, and willingness to share knowledge, which can be assessed by some concrete measures, such as copyrights, IP, and R&D spending.

(b) *Complementary Resources and Competencies of the Partner:* Deficiency in a firm's resources and competencies is the driving force for the firm's quest for a partner with complementary assets and skills to pursue an OI venture. However, there are different modes of complementing resources and competencies among firms in a collaborative venture. First, when both companies have symmetrical resources (e.g., rich cash position, talented design engineers, or technology platforms), combining them in a joint project can give them extra strengths to undertake demanding and risky R&D endeavors. For example, Pearson (2013) reports that Renault SA of France and Nissan Motor Corporation of Japan (two firms already in partnership) have added Mitsubishi Motors Corporation of Japan into a potentially far-reaching partnership to share factories and technology, as well as boost sales in North America and emerging markets partly through the joint development of electric vehicles. And, he adds that "the new partnership will involve more than the manufacturing of vehicles by one company for another. It seeks to build on the Nissan-Mitsubishi joint-venture in Japan called NMKV that is making a range of what are known as Kei cars—small vehicles that are generally limited to the Japanese market—for both brands. NMKV will be expanded under the new alliance to include the production of a new small vehicle, including a specific electric version, that would be sold globally" (B7).

Another scenario is that partnering firms may have asymmetrical assets or skill sets. For example, one partner may excel in product design while another one may have a unique business platform in reaching its customers. Under such circumstances, those complementary resources and competences of the partnering firms can invigorate the joint innovation process in developing new products or processes. The case in point is Blade.org, where there are three kinds of members: governing members (IBM and sixother founding companies that developed the blade platform), sponsoring members (distributors, developers of hardware and software, or service providers) and general members (end users). Each group of members brings their different resources and competencies to this collaborative community of firms in enhancing the blade platform. Likewise, the partnership between Amazon and the USPS for Sunday package deliveries illustrates how partners' complementary resources and competencies can be exploited.

Chapter 11 elucidates how focal firms may strategically utilize the partnership portfolios provided by a meta-organization for successful breakthrough innovations. It posits that by engaging in open R&D alliances, the focal firm can achieve the development of breakthrough innovations when such development projects are undertaken within an alliance portfolio where inbound and outbound knowledge flows are attained.

Since each partner's resources and competencies are extremely important for the success of an OI venture, firms need to pay close attention to identifying and choosing their partners accordingly. Such resources may include tangible, intangible, and human resources. Particularly, evaluating intangible and human resources requires careful review and examination to decide how they would be contributing to the accomplishment of the OI goals.

   (c) *Trust between Partners*: Trust between partners has been the center of attention in the alliance literature (Culpan, 2002; Das and Teng, 1998; Gulati, 1995; Inkpen and Currall, 1998) for many years. For example, after examining the notion of confidence in partner cooperation in alliances, Das and Teng (1998) suggest that it comes from two distinct sources: trust and control. And they argue that trust and control are parallel concepts and that their relationship is of a supplementary character in generating confidence. Additionally, Inkpen and Currall (1998) developed a framework of the antecedents and consequences of joint venture trust. And they considered the following factors as antecedents of trust in such a relationship: prior cooperative relationships, habitualization, individual attachment, organizational fit, and assessment of partner competence. They also proposed the consequences or outcomes of joint venture trust: forbearance, governance structures, relationship investments, increases in joint venture scope, and joint venture performance. From these explanations, one can conclude that trust in interfirm alliances is a complex but important aspect. Building and preserving trust between partners depends upon forbearance, governance structure (the extent of control), and nurturing partner communications and relationships, which, in turn, has an effect on the outcomes of the partnership.

More specifically, in reference to OI, Lindegaard (2011) discusses "what to consider before leaping into a partnership" by stating that "trust is an essential component of open innovation relationships and forging strong relationships takes time and personal commitment" (13). The consideration of how to build trust is fundamental to open innovation, in selecting a partner and in relation to the human side of innovation, in addition to its technical characteristics. We must note that trust is a two-way process: a firm should be concerned not only with the trustworthiness of other party, but also with how to build trust in itself. Forging open communication and strong relationships paves the way to establishing mutual trust between parties.

(d) *Collaboration Experience*: The collaboration experience of a potential partner (which is also related to trust in the partner) is another important component, and it is probably easier to identify in comparison to other qualities of the potential partner. The collaboration experience of the candidate firm can be a good gauge of its future behavior in cooperative ventures. Culpan (2002) acknowledges that the track record of the candidate in its previous collaborative ventures will probably tell a lot about its handling of present and future alliances. Also, Li and his colleagues (2008) suggest that firms use partner selection as a mechanism to protect valuable technological assets from appropriation in R&D alliances. A review of corporate history reflects a firm's collaborative experience and helps to determine how successfully it handled its prior collaborations. However, it must be noted that this particular aspect would not be used for the candidate firms without prior collaborations, such as new start-ups.

(e) *Position of the Partner Firm in the Innovation Ecosystem*: A firm's position in the innovation ecosystem is another critical characteristic to consider in OI ventures. A prospective partner may hold different positions in the value creation and appropriation process (e.g., supplier, distributor, customer, or competitor). For example, Gassmann et al. (2010) and West and Lakhani (2008) suggest that knowledge flow and sharing between a firm and its suppliers are important factors for open innovation. As mentioned in the case of Blade.org, sometimes customers can be contributors to technological innovation. Most complex collaborative relationships, however, will build partnerships with competitors, where there might be less trust between the partners. Nonetheless, as Hamel and Prahalad (1989) suggested and Pearson (2013) described (in reference to the recent Renault-Nissan-Mitsubishi partnership), competitors can be another potential source for new product or technology development. To build partnership with competitors, it is essential to make a close examination of their intent, organizational resources and capabilities, and track record of alliance performances. Moreover, it is important to determine what kinds of complementary assets and competencies a competitor brings to the table. Mistrust in a partner (particularly a competitor) appears to be a fundamental challenge in forming strategic alliances for open innovation. If the partner firms view a strategic alliance as a race to learn and to leave the partnership after achieving short-term gains, the partnership will not be sustainable or destined to failure. From the outset, the objectives of partners need to be clearly declared and communicated to build trust in and support for the alliance.

As recommended in chapter 4, in the partner selection, "firms may use indicators for alignment, such as the compatibility of project goals, partnership objectives, project expectations, commitment, and innovation and learning culture." Furthermore, firms are recommended to focus on both strategic and relational alignment in interfirm alliances. Moreover, chapter 4 suggests that firms need to invest in the alignment of expectations, commitment, and innovation culture.

Strategic Alliances

Dyer, Kale, and Singh (2001) contend that "strategic alliances—a fast and flexible way to access complementary resources and skills that reside in other companies—have become important tools for achieving sustainable competitive advantage" (37). They also suggest that developing dedicated alliance function is key to knowledge management and learning, which in turn create such values as greater alliance success rate from improved practices, greater abnormal returns, and the ability to form more alliances and to attract better partners. Since the fundamental premise of OI lies in the conception of collaboration between firms, it is important to understand various forms of interfirm collaborative arrangements that can lead to valuable innovation outcomes.

Firms wishing to exploit the benefits of OI through interfirm partnerships have several options to do so. Drawing on Figure 2.1 and Table 2.2 in chapter 2, we conclude that potential partners may engage in either equity-based alliances—comprising equity joint ventures (which we simply call "joint ventures") or block ownerships (one firm buying some equity in another one to build important ties) with respect to product and process innovations—or venture capital investments. Alternatively, partners may prefer contractual agreements (nonequity arrangements). As previous chapters indicated, building strategic ties through interfirm partnerships enables the partners to combine their resources and capabilities to undertake innovative projects. In comparing equity and contractual arrangements, equity investments are considered riskier and more difficult to govern than contractual agreements.

Joint ventures are formed by parent companies for a variety of reasons, but here we are interested in joint ventures created for innovation purposes. To this end, the principal objective of the joint venture is to share resources and competences for launching new products or processes (including new technologies or business models). In this sense, joint ventures are basically formed to gain new competencies, which translate into new products and processes from which the partners can eventually benefit. More specifically, such joint ventures are created between firms for either exploiting the symmetrical competencies of each other to leverage combined resources and competencies that will enhance the scale and scope economies of the venture or for deploying asymmetric competencies, where one partner's resource deficiencies are compensated by another's superior possessions (Culpan, 2002). In order for these kinds of joint ventures to work effectively, there must be diverse, but complementary, competencies provided by each partner. A majority of R&D joint ventures fall into this category.

Block ownership refers to equity participation by a firm in another firm so that they can build an organic tie to work on a R&D project. Sometimes, it could be a cross-holding of equity in each other by owning some percentage of equities of each other. It is believed that by such an investment, the partnering firms can have access to and control of R&D endeavors for joint purposes. In other words, such firms would have closer ties and collaborate comfortably in developing new products and technologies without worrying about dealing with a stranger. Renault's equity stake in Nissan, for example, paved the way to collaborate on new R&D projects together.

Venture capital investors generally support the innovative projects of SMEs by providing desperately needed capital, and, in return, they take some equity holding in the new venture. Such a collaboration represents a mutually beneficial arrangement by which innovative ideas can be capitalized and find their way toward commercialization.

Contractual agreements basically include bilateral R&D agreements; licensing, supplier, and customer agreements; network organizations; collaborative communities of firms; consortia; and university-business agreements for R&D. Companies can use contractual agreements in one form or another as effective means of achieving their innovation objectives. Although they involve some risks, they may be a fundamental necessity in undertaking certain innovative endeavors. Contractual agreements are more flexible in dealing with partners than equity partnerships, which are rather harder to break up. Another advantage of contractual agreements is that after a positive outcome, the parties can convert them into an equity partnership, having determined each other's capabilities and contributions and having built some trust.

The most common forms of R&D agreements include licensing and network organizations and university-business contracts, but we observe that there are an increasing number of collaborative communities of firms for the purpose of open innovation. Each particular form of contract presents its unique characteristics with respect to product or technology development.

OI Outcomes

Basically, we define primary OI outcomes as product/service innovation, technology innovation, and business model innovation. While product/service innovation means launching new products or services to meet the needs of customers and consumers, technology development refers to the means of creating the goods and services used by consumers in the market. In general, "technology is the making, modification, usage, and knowledge of tools, machines, techniques, crafts, systems, and methods of organization, in order to solve a problem, improve a pre-existing solution to a problem, achieve a goal, handle an applied input/output relation or perform a specific function. It can also refer to the collection of such tools, including machinery, modifications, arrangements and procedures" ("Technology," 2013). Technological innovation, therefore, can be defined as a novel combination of art, science, or craft employed to create the goods and service used by society (Quinn, Baruch, and Zien, 1997). Business model innovation refers to finding new business platforms in offering new or existing goods and services to the market. With the developments of new intellectual properties, "new kinds of business models are being forged in this new environment [emerging intellectual properties], with companies that play different by different rules than the established firm in their industries" (Chesbrough, 2006, 79). Through new business models, companies can enter into new, particular businesses or enhance their current business. An excellent example is eBay's online auction model, which provides auctioning services via the Internet with numerous participants who trade more efficiently on this platform than the traditional ways. Another most noted example of business model innovation is Google's web search engine, which it offers for free to the public while profiting from advertisements therein. Business model innovations have been common among information and communication technology (ICT) and social networking. By analyzing historical developments among the business domain, software domain, and the ICT platform domain, Aerts and his colleagues (2004) concluded that innovation in one domain may enable or drive developments in another.

Thus, we believe that sometimes the competitive advantage and profitability of a firm stem from launching a new business platform (e.g., electronic commerce, social networking), rather than new products or services. Toward this end, as Jelinek, Barr, Mugge, and Kouri in suggested chapter 9, managing big data collaboratively can enable firms to optimize the supply chain, developing closer relationships with customers and partners, predicting and reacting quickly to market shifts, or identifying areas for operational improvements and better accuracy of reporting.

Overall, the conceptual framework offered above explains the value architecture, creation, and appropriation in relation to the drivers and management and organization of OI in the context of various strategic alliances. It would be useful to analyze and understand the principal motives, processes, and dynamics of OI through interfirm partnerships and effectively deal with the challenges posed above in launching and managing OI.

Conclusion

In contrast to traditional practices based on the notion of a closed paradigm, companies have been increasingly using strategic alliances and collaborative partnerships to cultivate innovation and develop resources and competencies to compete in constantly changing global environments. As Pisano and Verganti (2008) suggested, collaborative approaches to innovation offer an array of choices and complex tradeoffs. They depend on a firm's strategic orientation, managerial mind-sets, resources, and capabilities in the context of interfirm partnerships. Developing a feasible approach to collaborative innovation starts with understanding the strategic position and overall road map to achieve competitive advantage and high rents. Toward this end, open innovation offers a viable strategy to sustain business growth and competitive advantage, as we have explained throughout this book.

We stress the need for strategic alliances between firms as a principal means to realize the benefits of open innovation. There is no denying that business is forever changing; so must innovation in order to grow business and keep pace with competition. As such, organizations must be agile, flexible, and adaptable to changes in the external context in adopting the open innovation paradigm through inter-firm partnerships. To this end, Kanter (1999), for example, asserts that "lean, agile, and post entrepreneurial companies can stretch in three ways. They can *pool* resources with others, ally to *exploit* an opportunity, or *link* systems in partnership. In short, they can become better 'PALS' with other organizations—from venture collaborators to suppliers, service contractors, customers, and even unions" (181). Specifically, companies must build the culture, human capital, values, and processes necessary to encourage entrepreneurial and open innovation thinking, as illustrated in chapters 1, 2, and 3. Moreover, there should be a balance between the structured, established processes of the organization and the flexibility that is necessary to support open innovation and disruptive growth.

The challenges defined and the conceptual framework offered in this chapter provide clear understanding and insights into the effective adoption and management of OI collaborative partnerships. From the strategic management perspective, the resource-based view, dynamic capabilities, and the knowledge-based view of the firm can provide more appropriate theoretical explanations and justifications for the need for open innovation. Despite some counterarguments that assert that "OI is just an old wine in a new bottle," (Trott and Hartman, 2009) the acceptance of OI has been overwhelming (Chesbrough and Brunswicher, 2014). Thus, we assert that OI will be used, along with closed innovation, at many organizations for the years to come. To supplement their knowledge bases, collaborative partnerships between firms in the forms of cross-industry innovation endeavors and widespread acceptance of open ecosystems will continue to grow.

Moreover, in the context of open ecosystems, OI applications will be seen not only in the upward and downward value chain, but also in multidimensional and multilevel scopes. In addition, we have observed that the notion of OI has been adopted by companies in a wide range of industries, beyond the industries of software development and biochemistry, and by many firms in emerging economies through strategic alliances or collaborative partnerships. As shown in our case examples above, many firms in China and Turkey are exploiting OI through collaborative arrangements, though at a smaller scale. This means that collaborating innovation partners may include a variety of complementors, such as different industry change agents and innovators (e.g., social networking firms, software developers, or biotech start-ups). As we pointed out previously, firm size seems less relevant in launching innovations; even SMEs can play a significant role in introducing new products or processes. Nonetheless, as business history attests, large companies have greater resources to engage in and support innovative products and disruptive technologies. Finally, university-business R&D collaborations have gained momentum with the popularity of OI in the forms of cross-industry R&D endeavors and the active roles of some universities as venture investors.

Our conceptual framework, based on the notion of value architecture and creation and appropriation processes, identifies the drivers of OI, organizational and managerial factors for managing OI, and principal strategic alliance forms. We have demonstrated that they are interrelated so that a particular form of strategic alliance, whether it is an equity investment or a contractual agreement, also affects the management of OI and the organizational design. Although OI through interfirm partnerships poses some challenges, it can be rewarding if the management of the focal firm is aware of those challenges and takes appropriate actions to deal with them in employing OI in this fashion.

In creating alliance portfolios, for example, we suggest that some critical factors, including the strategic intent of a candidate firm, the trust between partners, the resource and capability sets of parties, collaboration experience, and the position of the firm in the value chain or ecosystems, are important considerations. Further, we predict that current market conditions and interdependencies among firms will stimulate national and international firms to engage in OI through interfirm partnerships. In fact, as illustrated in previous chapters, interviews with managers experienced with OI applications indicate that OI through strategic alliances has been increasingly employed at large corporations (e.g., IBM, Proctor & Gamble, Shell, Phillips, and Xerox), as well as at SMEs (e.g., KIBS start-ups).

Another issue, "coopetition"—that is, cooperating while competing in an OI context—presents a major challenge in practice, as mentioned above (Brandenburger and Nalebuff, 1996). However, as the Mitsubishi example illustrates, even competitors may need each other's resources and competencies to create new technologies or products. Here the crucial task for the partner firms is to build mutual trust and design a collaborative mechanism that will yield strategic benefits for all the parties. When there are interdependencies between competitors, coopetition can work well. For example, if establishing a standard technology or format in a particular industry is essential for consumer acceptance, then coopetition can help to produce such a standard. Culpan (1993) suggests that firms can learn from each other and strengthen their knowledge and technologies while overcoming their weaknesses. So, through coopetition, partnering firms can enjoy value creation and value sharing.

Another pressing issue in OI applications is the quantitative measurement of the innovation performance of firms. This remains to be a critical problem because so far most of the research on the subject has been in the form of qualitative case studies praising the strategic value of such collaborative R&D ventures. However, we also need more quantitative models and methods that measure the innovation performance of partnering firms to draw reliable conclusions. For this purpose, researchers need to develop additional models and methodologies to fill this gap in literature.

Overall, in the face of increasing competition, blurring technology and industry boundaries, and the global dispersion of knowledge, firms need to explore new avenues to advance their products, technologies, and business platforms by aligning their innovation strategies with open ecosystems. Adner and Kapoor

(2010) aptly argue that an innovator firm's success hinges on the collaboration and efforts of other innovators in its environment, and the challenges faced by external innovators affect the focal firm's innovation performance.

As a result, even for those firms that have conventionally relied on closed innovation, now they need to take advantage of open innovation in creating value and capturing some of the value being created in the new era of e-business transformation and social media. Many forms of strategic alliances, consisting of both equity and contractual alliances, offer business platforms for value architecture, creation, and appropriation in the context of OI. Although the use of strategic alliances involves its own risks and complexities, it can be a rewarding paradigm in the end when handled properly as outlined above. Thus, in the future, OI is going to be a necessary innovation strategy rather than an option, as more external (e.g., innovation ecosystems) and internal (a firm's resource needs or unused assets) conditions dictate collaboration between firms for creative products, technologies, and business platforms. For this purpose, we hope that this book contributes to the understanding of OI concepts, research, and applications in the context of strategic alliances.

References

Adner, R. (2006). Match Your Innovation Strategy to Your Innovation Ecosystem. *Harvard Business Review*, 84(4), 98–105.

Adner, R., and Kapoor, R. (2010). "Value Creation in Innovation Ecosystems: How the Structure of Technological Interdependence Affects Firm Performance in New Technology Generations." *Strategic Management Journal* 31(3): 306–33. doi:10.1002/smj.821.

Aerts, A. T. M., Goossenaerts, J. B. M., Hammer, D. K., and Wortmann, J. C. (2004). "Architectures in Context: On the Evolution of Business, Application Software, and ICT Platform Architectures." *Information and Management* 41 (6): 781–94. doi:10.1016/j.im.2003.06.002.

Afuah, A. (2009). *Strategic Innovation*. New York: Routledge.

Almirall, E., and Casadesus-Masanell, R. (2010). "Open versus Closed Innovation: A Model of Discovery and Divergence." *Academy of Management Review* 35 (1): 27–47. doi:10.5465/AMR.2010.45577790.

Barnes, T., Pashby, I., and Gibbons, A. (2002). "Effective University—Industry Interaction: A Multi-case Evaluation of Collaborative R&D Projects." *European Management Journal* 20 (3): 272–85. doi:10.1016/S0263-2373(02)00044-0.

Barney, J. (1991). "Firm Resources and Sustained Competitive Advantage." *Journal of Management* 17 (1): 99–120. doi:10.1177/014920639101700108.

Brandenburger, A. M., and Nalebuff, B. J. (1996). *Co-Opetition*. New York: Currency Doubleday. (Please include a city of publication.)

Cheng, J. (2013). "Google Fosters South Korean Startups." *The Wall Street Journal*, November 18: 9.

Chesbrough, H., and Crowther, A. K. (2006). "Beyond High Tech: Early Adopters of Open Innovation in other Industries." *R&D Management* 36 (3): 229–36. doi:10.1111/j.1467-9310.2006.00428.x.

Chesbrough, H. W. (2003). *Open Innovation: The New Imperative for Creating and Profiting from Technology*. Boston: Harvard Business School Press.

Chesbrough, H. W. (2006). *Open Business Models: How to Thrive in the New Innovation Landscape*. Boston: Harvard Business School Press.

Chesbrough, H.W. and Brunswicker,S. (2014). "A Fad or Phenomenon?: The Adoption of Open Innovation Practices in Large Firms." *57*(2): 16-25.

Christensen, J. F., Olesen, M. H., and Kjær, J. S. (2005). "The Industrial Dynamics of Open Innovation—Evidence from the Transformation of Consumer Electronics." *Research Policy* 34 (10): 1533–49. doi:10.1016/j.respol.2005.07.002.

Collis, D., and Montgomery, C. (1995). "Competing on Resources: Strategy in 1990s." *Harvard Business Review 73* (4) (July–August): 119–28.

Contractor, F. J. (2013). "'Punching above Their Weight': The Sources of Competitive Advantage for Emerging Market Multinationals." *International Journal of Emerging Markets* 8 (4): 304–28. doi:10.1108/IJoEM-06-2013-0102.

Culpan, R. (1993). "Conceptual Foundations of Multinational Strategic Alliances." In R.Culpan (ed.), *Multinational Strategic Alliances*, 13–32. New York: International Business Press.

Culpan, R. (2002). *Global Business Alliances: Theory and Practice*. West Port, CT: Greenwood Publishing Group.(Please include a city.)

Currall, S. C., and Inkpen, A. C. (2002). "A Multilevel Approach to Trust in Joint Ventures." *Journal of International Business Studies* 33 (3): 479–95.

Das, T. K., and Teng, B.-S. (1998). "Between Trust and Control: Developing Confidence in Partner Cooperation in Alliances." *The Academy of Management Review* 23 (3): 491. doi:10.2307/259291.

Dyer, J. H., and Kale, P. (2007). "Relational Capabilities: Drivers and Implications." In C. E. Helfat, S. Finkelstain, W. Mitchell, M. A. Peteraf, H.Singh, D. J.Teece, and S. G.Winter., *Dynamic Capabilities: Understanding Strategic Change in Organizations*, 65–79. Malden, MA: Blackwell Publishing. (Please include all editors' names.)

Dyer, J. H., Kale, P., and Singh, H. (2001). "How to Make Strategic Alliance Work." *MIT Sloan Management Review 42* (4 Summer): 37–43.(Please include a volume number.)

Enkel, E., Gassmann, O., and Chesbrough, H. (2009). "Open R&D and Open Innovation: Exploring the Phenomenon." *R&D Management* 39 (4): 311–16. doi:10.1111/j.1467-9310.2009.00570.x.

Gassmann, O., and Enkel, E. (2010). "Creative Innovation: Exploring the Case of Cross-Industry Innovation." *R&D Management* 40 (3): 256–70.

Gassmann, O., Enkel, E., and Chesbrough, H. (2010). "The Future of Open Innovation." *R&D Management* 40 (3): 213–21. doi:10.1111/j.1467-9310.2010.00605.x.

Grant, R. M. (2008). *Contemporary Strategy Analysis*, sixth edition. Malden, MA: Blackwell Publishing. (Please include a city.)

Gruber, M., and Henkel, J. (2006). "New Ventures Based on Open Innovation—An Empirical Analysis of Start-Up Firms in Embedded Linux." *International Journal of Technology Management* 33 (4): 356–72.

Gulati, R. (1995). "Does Familiary Breed Trust? The Implications of Repeated Ties for Contractual Choice in Alliances." *Academy of Management Journal* 38 (1): 85–112. doi:10.2307/256729.

Hamel, G., and Prahalad, C. K. (1989). "Collaborate with Your Competitor and Win." *Harvard Business Review* 67:133–39.

Herzog, P. (2011). *Open and Closed Innovation: Different Cultures for Different Strategies*. New York: Springer. (Please include a city.)

Inkpen, A. C., and Currall, S. C. (1998). "The Nature, Antecedents, and Consequences of Joint Venture Trust." *Journal of International Management* 4 (1): 1–20. doi:10.1016/S1075-4253(98)00004-0.

Kanter, R. M. (1999). "Becoming PALs: Pooling, Allying, and Linking Across Companies." *The Academy of Management Executive* 3 (3): 183–93.

Katz, R., and Allen, T. J. (1982). "Investigating the Not Invented Here (NIH) Syndrome: A Look at the Performance, Tenure, and Communication Patterns of 50 R and D Project Groups." *R&D Management* 12 (1): 7–20. doi:10.1111/j.1467-9310.1982. tb00478.x.

Lindegaard, S. (2011). *Making Open Innovation Work*. North Charleston, SC: CreateSpace. (Please include a state.)

March, J. G. (1991). "Exploration and Exploitation in Organizational Learning." *Organization Science* 2 (1): 71–87.

Matzler, K., Füller, J., Koch, B., Hautz, J., and Hutter, K. (2014). "Open Strategy—A New Strategy Paradigm?" In K. Matzler, H. Pechlaner, and B. Renzl (eds.), *Strategie und Leadership*, 37–55. Wiesbaden: Springer Fachmedien. http://link.springer.com/ chapter/10.1007/978-3-658-04057-4_3 (Accessed March 30, 2014).(Please include an access date.)

Pal, N., and Lim, M. (2005). "Emergence of the Agile Enterprise." In *The Agile Enterprise*. New York: Springer, 11–32. http://link.springer.com/chapter/10.1007/0-387-25078-6_2 (Accessed March 12, 2014) (Please include a city and access date.)

Park, B.-J. (Robert), Srivastava, M. K., and Gnyawali, D. R. (2013). "Walking the Tight Rope of Coopetition: Impact of Competition and Cooperation Intensities and Balance on Firm Innovation Performance." *Industrial Marketing Management*. 43 (2): 210-221. doi:10.1016/j.indmarman.2013.11.003 (Please include volume, issue, and page numbers, as applicable.)

Pearson, D. (November 6, 2013). "Renault, Nissan Add Partner." *The Wall Street Journal*, B7.

Peteraf, M. A. (1993). "The Cornerstones of Competitive Advantage: A Resource-Based View." *Strategic Management Journal* 14 (3): 179–91. doi:10.1002/smj.4250140303.

Pisano, G. P., and Verganti, R. (2008). "Which Kind of Collaboration Is Right for You?" *Harvard Business Review* 86 (12): 78–86.

Prahalad, C. K., and Hamel, G. (1990). "The Core Competence of the Corporation." *Harvard Business Review* 68 (3):79–91. (Please include volume and issue numbers.)

Quinn, J. B., Baruch, J. J., and Zien, K. A. (1997). *Innovation Explosion: Using Intellect and Software to Revolutionize Growth Strategies*. New York: Simon & Schuster. (Please include a city.)

Schuman, M. (2013). "Why China Can't Create Anything." Time, November 18: 40.

Snow, C. C., and Culpan, R. (2011). "Open Innovation through a Collaborative Community of Firms: An Emerging Organizational Design." In T. K. Das (ed.), *Strategic Alliances for Value Creation*, 279–300. Charlotte, NC: Information Age Publishing.

Spender, J.-C. (1999). "Making Knowledge the Basis of a Dynamic Theory of the Firm." *Strategic Management Journal* 17 (Winter): 45–62. (Please include a volume number.)

Technology. (2013, December 24). Wikipedia. http://en.wikipedia.org/w/index.php?t itle=Technology&oldid=586617157 (Accessed 3/12/2014).(Please include an access date.)

Teece, D. J. (2009). *Dynamic Capabilities and Strategic Management: Organizing for Innovation and Growth: Organizing for Innovation and Growth*. Oxford: Oxford University Press.

Thomke, S. H., and von Hippel, E. (2002). "Customers as Innovators: A New Way to Create Value." *Harvard Business Review* 80 (4): 74–81.

Trott, P. and Hartman, D. (2009). "Why 'Open Innovation' is Old Wine in New Bottles." *International Journal of Innovation Management, 13* (4): 715–736.

Van de Vrande, V., de Jong, J. P. J., Vanhaverbeke, W., and de Rochemont, M. (2009). "Open Innovation in SMEs: Trends, Motives and Management Challenges." *Technovation* 29 (6–7): 423–37. doi:10.1016/j.technovation.2008.10.001.

Verbano, C., Crema, M., and Venturini, K. (2013). "The Identification and Characterization of Open Innovation Profiles in Italian Small and Medium-sized Enterprises." *Journal of Small Business Management,* Article first published online: 4 DEC 2013 DOI: 10.1111/jsbm.12091 (Please include a volume number.)

Von Hippel, E., and Krogh, G. (2003). "Open Source Software and the 'Private-Collective' Innovation Model: Issues for Organization Science." *Organization Science* 14 (2): 209–23.

Walker, J., and Loftus, P. (October 2, 2013). "Merck to Cut Staff 20% as Big Pharma Trims R&D." *The Wall Street Journal,* A1 and A2.

West, J. (2003). "How Open Is Open Enough? Melding Proprietary and Open Source Platform Strategies." *Research Policy* 32 (7): 1259–85. doi:10.1016/S0048-7333(03)00052-0.

West, J., and Gallagher, S. (2006). "Challenges of Open Innovation: The Paradox of Firm Investment in Open-Source Software." *R&D Management* 36 (3): 319–31. doi:10.1111/j.1467-9310.2006.00436.x.

West, J., and Lakhani, K. R. (2008). "Getting Clear About Communities in Open Innovation." *Industry and Innovation* 15 (2): 223–31. doi:10.1080/13662710802033734.

Index

Printed and bound in the United States of America